The Renaissance Reform of
Medieval Music Theory

Modern scholars have often portrayed hexachordal solmization –
the sight-singing method introduced by the eleventh-century monk
Guido of Arezzo – as the diatonic foundation of early music. Stefano
Mengozzi challenges this view by examining a representative sample
of the primary sources of solmization theory from Guido of Arezzo to
Gioseffo Zarlino. These texts show that six-syllable solmization was
only an option for sight-singing that never imposed its operational
"sixth-ness" onto the diatonic system, already grounded on the
seven pitch letters. It was primarily through the agency of several
"classicizing" theorists of the humanist era that the six syllables came
to be mistakenly conceived as a fundamental diatonic structure – a
"hexachord" built from the "tetrachord" of the ancient Greeks. The
book will be of particular interest to readers seeking to deepen their
knowledge of medieval and Renaissance musical thought with an eye
to major intellectual trends of the time.

STEFANO MENGOZZI is Associate Professor of Music at the
University of Michigan. His research focuses on musical theory in the
Middle Ages and Renaissance. This is his first book.

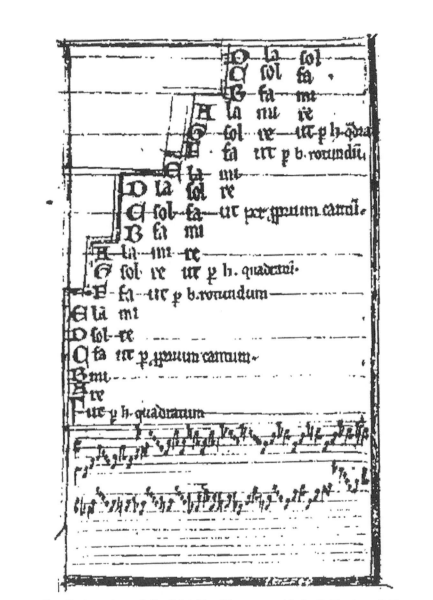

Frontispiece. An early English table of the gamut with the Guidonian syllables (from MS London, British Library, Harley 978, fol. 14r (thirteenth century)).

The Renaissance Reform of Medieval Music Theory

Guido of Arezzo between Myth and History

STEFANO MENGOZZI

CAMBRIDGE
UNIVERSITY PRESS

CAMBRIDGE
UNIVERSITY PRESS

University Printing House, Cambridge CB2 8BS, United Kingdom

Cambridge University Press is part of the University of Cambridge.

It furthers the University's mission by disseminating knowledge in the pursuit of education, learning and research at the highest international levels of excellence.

www.cambridge.org
Information on this title: www.cambridge.org/9781107442573

© Stefano Mengozzi 2010

First published 2010
First paperback edition 2014

A catalogue record for this publication is available from the British Library

ISBN 978-0-521-88415-0 Hardback
ISBN 978-1-107-44257-3 Paperback

Cambridge University Press has no responsibility for the persistence or accuracy of URLs for external or third-party internet websites referred to in this publication, and does not guarantee that any content on such websites is, or will remain, accurate or appropriate.

A mia madre e alla memoria di mio padre

Contents

Illustrations

Tables

Musical examples

Preface

This book virtually began in the early 1990s, during my graduate school years at the University of Chicago, when I first became aware of the increasing references to the hexachordal system in analytic studies of medieval and Renaissance music. In my initial phases of research, my concern was to evaluate the role of that system in medieval and Renaissance musical theory and practice as a way of assessing the merit of interpretive analyses that took that system as a point of departure. In due course I came to realize that hexachordal theory as we know it changed considerably during its long history, to the point that the version most frequently described today may be aptly described as a fifteenth-century creation. The overarching goal of this monograph is to present and discuss the documentary evidence that led me to formulate such a conclusion.

However, another theme runs between the lines of the pages that follow, namely the process by which particular images of early music come to guide our scholarly investigations – in other words, the ways in which we construct and reinforce the historical and cultural distance between modern listeners and pre-modern music; *us* and *them*. Inevitably, a reassessment of the role of the hexachordal system in medieval and Renaissance music amounts to reconsidering the demands that that system poses on modern listeners and scholars of early music, and to rethink the relationship between modern and pre-modern musical grammars. Last but not least, this is also a case study on the nature of music-theoretical texts from the pre-modern era, on their status of cultural artifacts that inevitably convey to us much more than the musical doctrines of their time. Indeed my interest is in showing how these texts transmit musical doctrines as much as fabricate them; how they can inform and explain, but also mislead and confuse.

What follows does not and cannot pretend to be a comprehensive history of hexachordal solmization, one that would require an examination of a far greater number of treatises and musical works. My goal, rather, is to chart the emergence and the consolidation of a particular strand of hexachordal theory that has been most frequently recognized in modern music historiography. I call it the "foundational strand" of hexachordal theory, which presents the six syllables of solmization (*ut, re, mi, fa, sol, la*), not just as an aid for sight singing, but rather as the expression of a configuration of musical space that was itself structured in overlapping segments of six notes. My narrative concentrates on those authors who contributed to the emergence of this view either by presenting hexachordal theory in those terms, or – paradoxically – by opposing the entire hexachordal method *tout court*. Thus, influential authors such as Marchetto of Padua, John Hothby, and Johannes Tinctoris who, to my mind, were uninterested in discussing hexachordal theory in foundational terms, make only cameo appearances in this study. Ultimately, what concerns me here is the history of the idea of the hexachord as a musical structure, which needs to be investigated not only as it took form in the texts of several influential authors, but also as intimately connected with new modes of intellectual inquiry, new means of textual transmission (the printing press), and changing cultural and religious values.

Having been a work in progress for almost two decades, this monograph has benefited immensely and in many ways from the responses of a great number of friends and colleagues, as well as from my prolonged exposure to related studies by scholars (and there are more than a few of them) with whom I disagree, sometimes passionately, more often only partially, and always (as I hope) respectfully. I am indebted to my mentors at Chicago, particularly Martha Feldman, Larry Zbikowski, Noel Swerdlow, and the late Howard Mayer Brown, for nurturing my interest in the history of music theory and for patiently teaching me how to interrogate and contextualize the sources; to Thomas Christensen for several thoughtful exchanges on this and other topics; and to Reinhard Strohm for his valuable comments on a 1993 seminar paper that has now become Chapter 6 of the present book.

My warmest thanks also go to all my colleagues in the Department of Musicology at the University of Michigan for their continuous encouragement and support, particularly to James Borders for many stimulating conversations and for his comments on early drafts of this book, but also to Christi-Anne Castro, Mark Clague, Jane Fulcher, Charles Garrett, Jason Geary, Joseph Lam, Louise Stein, Steven Whiting, and John Wiley, who continue to be for me a source of inspiration and a model of professionalism. I also wish to thank the School of Music, Theatre, and Dance of the University of Michigan for supporting this project in various ways since I joined the faculty in 2001.

I am grateful to many other friends and scholars with whom I have had fruitful exchanges of opinions on this topic through the years, particularly Loris Azzaroni, Margaret Bent, Bonnie Blackburn, Jeffrey Dean, Joseph

Dyer, Adam Gilbert, Leofranc Holford-Strevens, Mary Hunter, Dolores Pesce, Benito Rivera, Murray Steib, William Thomson, Peter Urquhart, Paul Walker, and Ronald Woodley, as well as several anonymous reviewers who have examined portions of this book and have offered insightful remarks. I feel particularly indebted to Bonnie Blackburn for kindly reading the entire manuscript and for helping me refine my argument in many ways. Needless to say, the theses expressed in the following pages are solely mine, as are any remaining inaccuracies and shortcomings in the text.

A post-doctoral fellowship awarded by the Whiting Foundation enabled me to conduct extensive research on this project in the most stimulating environment of the Franke Institute at the University of Chicago in 2003–4. My sincere thanks go to the Foundation, to director James Chandler and to the personnel of the Franke, as well as to the other post-doctoral fellows who resided at the Institute during that year, for several very special months of lively and fruitful discussions.

A small section of Chapter 7 is taken from my article "Virtual Segments: The Hexachordal System in the Late Middle Ages," which appeared in the *Journal of Musicology* 23 (2006), 426–67; an equally short section from Chapter 5 was originally part of my "The Ciconian Hexachord," in *Johannes Ciconia, musicien de la transition*, ed. P. Vendrix (Turnhout: Brepols, 2003), pp. 279–304. My thanks go to the publishers for allowing me to include those passages in this monograph.

The online databases of the *Thesaurus musicarum latinarum*, of the *Thesaurus musicarum italicarum*, and of the *Lexicon musicale Latinum medii aevi* have greatly facilitated my research; indeed this project may have taken another two decades to complete without the information made available by those resources.

Finally, I wish to thank most dearly my wife Karin and my son Arthur for patiently enduring the countless hours of reading and writing that this project has demanded from me. To the three of us, Angelo Beraroli's verse in praise of Guido's syllables – *Ut relevet miserum fatum solitosque labores* – easily applies to the publication of this book.

Abbreviations

AcM	*Acta musicologica*
AnnMusic	*Annales musicologiques*
AfM	*Archiv für Musikwissenschaft*
CS	*Scriptorum de musica medii aevi nova series a Gerbentina alfera.* Ed. E. de Coussemaker. 4 vols. Paris: Durand, 1864–76; repr. Hildesheim: Olms, 1989
CSM	*Corpus scriptorum de musica.* Rome: American Institute of Musicology, 1950–
EM	*Early Music*
EMH	*Early Music History*
GS	*Scriptores ecclesiastici de musica sacra potissimum.* Ed. M. Gerbert. 3 vols. St. Blasien, Typis S. Blasiensis, 1784; repr. Hildesheim: Olms, 1963
JAMS	*Journal of the American Musicological Society*
JM	*The Journal of Musicology*
JMT	*Journal of Music Theory*
LmL	*Lexicon musicale Latinum medii aevi.* Ed. M. Bernhard. Munich: Verlag der Bayerischen Akademie der Wissenschaften in Kommission bei der C. H. Beck'schen Verlagsbuchhandlung, 1992–www.lml.badw.de/
MD	*Musica disciplina*
ML	*Music and Letters*
MQ	*Music Quarterly*
MSD	*Musicological Studies and Documents.* Rome: American Institute of Musicology, 1951–
NG 2	*The New Grove Dictionary of Music and Musicians.* Rev. edition, ed. S. Sadie. 27 vols. London: McMillan, 2001
PesceGA	D. Pesce, *Guido d'Arezzo's* Regule rithmice, Prologus in Antiphonariium *and* Epistola ad michahelem: *A Critical Text and Translation with an Introduction, Annotations, Indices, and New Manuscript Inventories.* Ottawa: Institute of Mediaeval Music, 1999

RISM	*Rèpertoire international des sources musicales.* Series B III: The Theory of Music from the Carolingians to *c.* 1500. Munich: Henle, 1961–2003
SmitsE	Smits van Waesberghe, ed., *Expositiones in Micrologum Guidonis Aretini.* Amsterdam: North-Holland Publishing Company, 1957
SmitsG	Smits van Waesberghe, Joseph. *De musico-paedagogico Guidone Aretino eiusque vita et moribus.* Florence: Olschki, 1953
SmitsM	Smits van Waesberghe, Joseph. *Musikerziehung: Lehre und Theorie der Musik im Mittelalter.* Leipzig: VEB Deutscher Verlag für Musik, 1969
TMI	*Thesaurus musicarum italicarum,* http://euromusicology.cs.uu.nl/
TML	*Thesaurus musicarum latinarum,* www.chmtl.indiana.edu/tml/
VfM	*Vierteljahrsschrift für Musikwissenschaft*

∼ Introduction: Guido's hexachord: old facts and new questions

Was there a hexachordal season in the long history of Western music? Was there ever a period, perhaps five, seven, or eight centuries ago, during which the octave scale – that normative segment of musical space that we take so much for granted – did not possess the cognitive and normative weight that it undoubtedly has had since the Enlightenment? Could it be that the octave scale acquired its all-pervasive, dictatorial power through a slow and erratic historical process, and that an alternative scale of six notes was in fact the governing segment of musical practice and musical perception for much of the pre-modern era?

On the face of it, the hexachordal hypothesis seems eminently plausible. Around the year 1032, in his *Epistola ad Michahelem*, the Benedictine monk Guido of Arezzo (*c.* 995–1050) proposed a new method for sight singing based on the six syllables *ut, re, mi, fa, sol, la*, which corresponded to the first syllables of each verse of the Hymn of St. John "Ut queant laxis."[1] In the melody of the hymn, each of the first six lines began one diatonic step higher than the last one, the first line beginning on *C* and the last one on *a* (see Example I.1).

Thus, the *ut-la* syllables highlighted the major sixth C-a (later called "hexachord," i.e., "six strings"), an interval that features only one semitone, E-F (*mi-fa*), at its center (see Table I.1).

In Guido's intentions, the six syllables, often called *voces* by medieval theorists, were to help budding singers become familiar with the intervallic context surrounding each syllable, thus each pitch of the gamut. They learned, for instance, that *ut* always has a major third above, *mi* a major third below and a minor third above, and so on. When practicing a new melody, they would associate the notes on the page with the correct syllables, which in turn would trigger the memory of the correct intervals to be performed.

---

[1] The text of the hymn is by Paul the Deacon (end of the eighth century), whereas the melody is not documented prior to Guido's *Epistola* and may thus have been composed by Guido himself. See J. Chailley, "*Ut queant laxis* et les Origines de la Gamme," *AcM* 56 (1984), 48–69. For an excellent introduction to Guido's musical pedagogy, see D. Pesce, ed. and trans., *Guido d'Arezzo's Regule Rithmice, Prologus in Antiphonarium, and Epistola ad Michahelem, A Critical Text and Translation with an Introduction, Annotations, Indices, and New Manuscript Inventories* (Ottawa: The Institute of Mediaeval Music, 1999, hereafter *PesceGA*), pp. 1–38. See also "Guido of Arezzo," in *NG 2*, vol. 10, pp. 522–6.

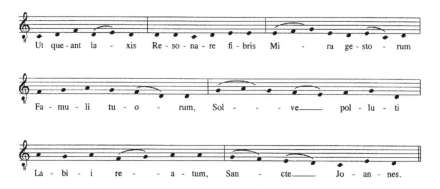

Example I.1. The hymn *Ut queant laxis*, possibly composed by Guido himself. My thanks to Murray Steib for assisting me with this example.

Table I.1. Correspondence between opening pitches and opening syllables for each of the six verses of the hymn *Ut queant laxis* (T = whole tone; S = semitone)

Ut queant laxis	**Ut = C**	
		T
Resonare fibris	**Re = D**	
		T
Mira gestorum	**Mi = E**	
		S
Famuli tuorum	**Fa = F**	
		T
Solve pollutum	**Sol = G**	
		T
Labii reatum	**La = a**	

In the fourteenth-century, Jacques de Liège referred to this technique as *solfatio*, after the syllables *sol-fa*; Renaissance theorists called it *solfisatio* or *solmisatio*, which led to the modern English term "solmization."[2]

There is evidence that by the end of the eleventh century the six syllables were being transposed on the segment G-e (with *mi-fa* on B-C), in addition to C-a. The placement of the six syllables on the major sixth F-d with B flat (with *mi-fa* on A-B flat) is already documented in Southern England/ Northern France around the year 1100 (more on this below). Thus, in a relatively short time medieval theorists extended the *ut-la* syllables to all the pitches of *musica recta* and positioned them on three possible locations within the gamut (see Table I.2 below): on C-a (the hexachordal segment

---

2 Jacques de Liège, *Speculum musicae*, ed. R. Bragard, *CSM* 3, 6 vols. (Rome: American Institute of Musicology, 1973), vol. 6, pp. 162–286 [*passim*].

Table I.2. The medieval diatonic system (Greater Perfect System), showing the series of pitch letters and the syllabic *deductiones*[3]

Γ	A	B	C	D	E	F	G	a	bb♭	bb♮	c	d	e	f	g	aa	bb♭	bb♮	cc	dd
														ut	re	mi	fa		sol	la
											ut	re	mi	fa		la		sol	la
													la	fa	sol	la	fa			
							ut	re		mi	fa	sol	la						
						ut	re	mi	fa		sol	la								
			ut	re	mi	fa	sol	la												
ut	re	mi	fa	sol	la															

³ Medieval pitch designations translate into the modern system as follows: Γ = G₁ (first line in Bass clef); A = A₁ (first space in Bass clef); a = a₂ (top line in Bass clef), and aa = a₃ (above middle C).

later called *proprietas per naturam* or *per proprium cantum*), on G-e (*proprietas per b quadratum* or *b durum*), and F-d with B♭ (*proprietas by b rotundum* or *b molle*). However, because the gamut features two C's, three G's – including the lowest pitch, marked with a Γ ("gamma") – and two F's, theorists from approximately the thirteenth century onward recognized seven *proprietates* ("properties") and as many *deductiones* ("deductions") where the former indicated a portion of the gamut spanning a major sixth, and the latter the unit of six syllables superimposed to it.[4]

Table I.2 is essentially a transcription of the frontispiece (from thirteenth-century England), one of the earliest illustrations of the gamut articulated into letters and syllables. One of the notable consequences of this arrangement was that some pitch letters, such as Γ *ut* or A *re*, belonged to only one *proprietas*; others (such as C *fa-ut* or E *la-mi*) to two of them; and others yet (such as c *sol-fa-ut* or d *la-sol-re*) to three of them. Pitch letters corresponding to two or three syllables could be used as points of "mutation" (*mutatio*) from one *proprietas* to the next. In order to solmize the octave from F to f, for instance, a singer would begin with the *proprietas per b molle*, with *ut* of F, and would switch to the *proprietas per naturam* on d, exchanging *la* for *re* and continuing on with *mi-fa* on e-f.[5] This basic menu of diatonic pitches, including letters and syllables, was called the system of *musica recta* or *musica vera* ("true or real music"). Any chromatic inflection of these basic pitches – i.e., notes indicated with a flat or a sharp – was considered part of *musica ficta* ("feigned music").[6]

Also, by the end of the eleventh century at the latest, musicians had introduced the practice of mapping the nineteen pitches of Guido's gamut (Γ-dd) onto the nineteen joints of the left hand in spiral order from the tip of the

[4] On the uses of the term *deductio* in medieval music theory, see the *LmL*, fasc. 6, cols. 783–6. I have discussed the subtle differences between *proprietas* and *deductio* in my "Virtual Segments: The Hexachordal System in the Late Middle Ages," *JM* 23 (2006), 440–58.

[5] Guido does not envision the technique of hexachordal mutation in his writings, although by the late-eleventh century theorists had recognized the possibility of transposing the *ut-la* syllables on the segment G-e, in addition to C-a. See *PesceGA*, pp. 27–8.

[6] For a general introduction to these concepts, see K. Berger, *Musica ficta: Theories of Accidental Inflections in Vocal Polyphony from Marchetto da Padova to Gioseffo Zarlino* (Cambridge University Press, 1987), pp. 2–11; and J. Herlinger, "Music Theory of the Fourteenth and Early Fifteenth Centuries," in R. Strohm and B. J. Blackburn, eds., *Music as Concept and Practice in the Late Middle Ages*, The New Oxford History of Music, vol. III, part 1 (Oxford University Press, 2001), pp. 246–9. The topic of *musica ficta* has been much debated for its direct relevance on issues of musical analysis and performance. See, for instance, M. Bent, "Diatonic *ficta*," *EMH* 4 (1984), 1–48; P. Urquhart, "Cross-Relations by Franco-Flemish Composers After Josquin," *Tijdschrift van de Vereniging voor Nederlandse Muziekgeschiedenis* 43 (1993), 3–41; and T. Brothers, *Chromatic Beauty in the Late Medieval Chanson: An Interpretation of Manuscript Accidentals* (Cambridge University Press, 1997).

thumb to the tip of the middle finger (at later time ee la, if recognized as a regular pitch, would be assigned to the nail of the middle finger, opposite to dd sol, or simply above the fingertip; see Fig. I.1).[7] Eventually, these nineteen positions on the Hand were called *loci* or *loca* ("places"). The Hand was a sort of musical "palm pilot" by which singers could quickly review the correct association of letters and syllables and the intervals between them. It was certainly used for collective musical instruction: as the master pointed to particular places on the Hand with his right index, his choirboys would mentally convert labels and places into sounds and sing the corresponding intervals. Versions of musical Hands appear to have existed in pre-Guidonian times.[8] However, in his writings Guido neither mentions, nor shows this mnemonic device, even though he undoubtedly contributed to its development.[9]

By all indications, then, Guido's method of sight singing with the *ut-la* syllables amounted to proposing a new articulation of the gamut based on the idea of a transposing "hexachord." While this is technically correct, it is important to understand that from the outset the hexachordal articulation of the gamut rubbed against an earlier principle of organization that was solidly grounded on the notion of octave duplication. To this pre-existing principle points the practice of indicating the diatonic pitches via the first seven letters of the alphabet, A-G.

An examination of the origins, the subsequent history, and the interrelationships between these two methods of pitch designation – the six syllables and the seven letters – soon reveals that they amounted to two quite different representations of musical space. If the sets of *ut-la* syllables pointed to a model of pitch organization set up into overlapping segments,

[7] For a more detailed description of the Hand, see K. Berger, "The Hand and the Art of Memory," *MD* 35 (1981), 87–120; K. Berger, *Musica ficta*, pp. 2–11; and A. M. Busse Berger, *Medieval Music and the Art of Memory* (Berkeley: University of California Press, 2005), pp. 85–94.

[8] For instance, as a way of visualizing the four tetrachords of the *enchiriadis* gamut (see below) and for memorizing chant formulae. See J. Smits van Waesberghe, *Musikerziehung: Lehre und Theorie der Musik im Mittelalter*, Musikgeschichte in Bildern, vol. III/3 (Leipzig: VEB Deutscher Verlag für Musik, 1969), pp. 122–3; and C. Meyer *Mensura monochordi: la division du monocorde (IXe-XVe siècles)*, (Paris: Klincksieck, 1996), pp. 241–4. Smits' study also features numerous reproductions of "Guidonian Hands" (pp. 123–43; I discuss this topic in more detail in Chapter 3). On the hand as a mnemonic aid for chant formulae, see T. A. Russell, "A Poetic Key to a pre-Guidonian Palm and the Echemata," *JAMS* 34 (1981), 109–18.

[9] On this point, see *PesceGA*, p. 20 (n. 68), and K. Berger, "The Hand and the Art of Memory," 115–18. It is unclear whether medieval musicians thought of Guido as the inventor of the Hand. The chronicler Siegebert of Gembloux, writing around 1100, appears to set a direct link between the Hand and Guido of Arezzo (Berger, "The Hand and Art of Memory," 116–18). Medieval music theorists, however, remain silent on this issue.

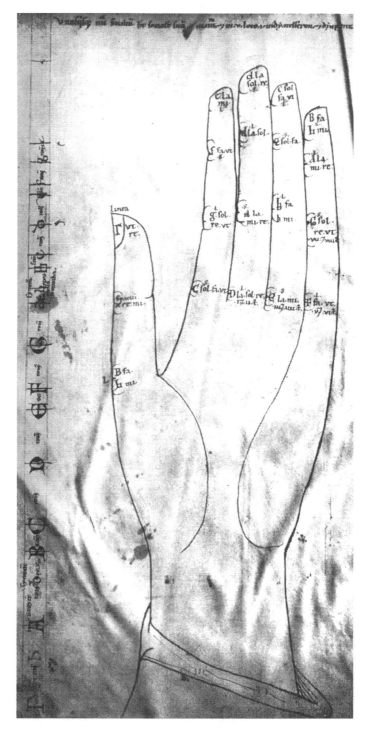

Fig. I.1. A Guidonian Hand (from Vienna Österreichische Nationalbibliothek, cpv 51, fol. 2v; twelfth century). This particular representation is relatively unusual in that it features a low Bb, with *re* on Γ and *mi* on A.

the series of pitch letters from A to G established a competing model that was continuous, linear, and cyclical, in the Middle Ages just as it is today. Until about the year 1000 theorists used other forms of alphabetic notation to indicate the diatonic pitches that did not reflect the principle of octave duplication.[10] Pseudo-Odo's *Dialogus de musica*, written near Milan around 1000, is the oldest extant treatise to use the seven letters A-G and to duplicate them to express the equivalence of pitches at the octave.[11] A few decades later, Guido adopted Pseudo-Odo's letter system without reservation, and called the pitches marked with the A-G letters (along with Γ) as *graves* (low), those marked with a-g as *acutae* (high), and those marked with aa-dd as *superacutae* (very high). Throughout his treatises, Guido designates the pitches consistently and exclusively by means of the seven letters.

The A-G letters were also known as *claves* ("keys"), because they were used as "clefs" positioned at the beginning of the musical staff to indicate unequivocally the notated pitches (thus they allowed the reader to "unlock" staff notation in the same way as a key opens a lock, as many medieval theorists pointed out). Occasionally, in a number of late authors, the term *clavis* refers to the combination of a letter and a syllable.[12] The fact that these letters represented points of division on the monochord has led some authors to limit their significance to the domain of speculative music. In fact, both the monochord and the seven letters had important practical applications. Alma Colk Santosuosso has listed about forty musical sources notated with letter notation (without syllables), from the eleventh to the fifteenth centuries.[13]

The long coexistence of these two different models of diatonic space – the cyclical one defined by the A-G letters and the segmental one projected by the *ut-la* syllables – poses a core set of questions that reverberate through the following chapters: Were these two models complementary, or rather alternative to each other? Were they equally important to the medieval understanding of musical space? Why did these two models exist at all?

---

[10] See, for instance, the notational system used in the late ninth century by Hucbald in his *De musica institutione*. See Y. Chartier, ed. and trans., *L'œuvre musicale d'Hucbald de Saint-Amand* (Saint-Laurent, Québec: Bellarmin, 1995), pp. 73–5.

[11] The *Dialogus* already documents the practice of using upper, lower, and double case to mark the same sound at different octaves (i.e., A, a, and aa).

[12] The vast semantic territory covered by the term *clavis* has been charted in F. Reckow, "Clavis," in *Handwörterbuch der musikalischen Terminologie*, ed. H. H. Eggebrecht (Stuttgart: F. Steiner, 1971), and more recently in M. Bernhard, ed., *Lexicon musicum Latinum medii aevi* (Munich: Bayerische Akademie der Wissenschaften, 1992), fasc. 5 (2001), cols. 525–44.

[13] See A. Colk Santosuosso, *Letter Notations in the Middle Ages* (Ottawa: The Institute of Mediaeval Music, 1989).

Most important, how did medieval authors understand the relationship between them, and which specific factors – musical, methodological, cultural – impinge upon such understanding through time? The answers to such questions transcend the limited domain of medieval music-theoretical thought and carry profound implications for our own reconstruction and interpretation of centuries of musical practice. Indeed, they concern the very nature of our relationship with the European musical past.

In recent times, the scholarly pendulum has swung in the direction of attributing a stronger structural significance to the *ut-la* syllables than to the A-G letters. The fact that the three-hexachord system was a central aspect of musical practice throughout the sixteenth century and beyond has led many scholars to conclude that it also provided a primary means of pitch organization and conceptualization during the Middle Ages and the Renaissance. According to this view, the enormous interest generated by Guido's introduction of the six syllables resulted not just in a new and accessorial method for sight singing, but ultimately in an entirely new way of articulating and conceptualizing the gamut – a new diatonic order grounded on the perceived primacy of the major sixth as a *de facto* musical scale. The "hexachordal season" of European music was indeed very real.

In line with such seemingly inescapable conclusions, many musicological studies from the last four decades have repeatedly reminded us that the musical space of the pre-modern era was radically different from the one we normally inhabit. Consider, for instance, the following statements:

In the later Middle Ages, the three-hexachord system, the overlapping of the "hard" (G-e, g-e'), "natural" (c-a, c'-a'), and "soft" hexachords (f-d', f'd"), was the presentation and the conceptual form of the tonal system.[14]

The composers [of the Renaissance] ... seem to have developed more abstruse ways of using the hexachord toward the end of the sixteenth century. As a means of expression it is sometimes more covert than overt: in either case, unless we have a knowledge of the gamut, we cannot hope to understand what the composer was attempting to communicate.[15]

In the opening of the motet [Johannes Lupi's "Ergone conticuit"] the altus and bass voices in the soft hexachord are placed against hard and natural hexachord passages in the superius and tenor.[16]

[14] C. Dahlhaus, *Studies on the Origin of Harmonic Tonality*, trans. R. Gjerdingen (Princeton University Press, 1990), p. 171.
[15] L. Pike, *Hexachords in Late-Renaissance Music* (Aldershot: Ashgate, 1998), p. 18.
[16] Urquhart, "Cross-Relations by Franco-Flemish Composers after Josquin," 20.

Example I.2. C. Monteverdi, "Cor mio mentre vi miro," (from *The Fourth Book of Madrigals*, 1603, bars 1–5).

The opening phrase [of Claudio Monteverdi's "Cor mio, mentre vi miro," from the *Quarto Libro di Madrigali*] purposively outlines the chordal spectrum of the one-flat hexachord. Beginning with a D-g dominant-tonic progression to g ("Cor mio"), the harmonies move mainly in a circle-of-fifths ordering to close within the phrygian cadence to A: in modern terms the sequence D, g, F^6, C, F^6, B^b, (d6/4), A … The soprano melody of these five bars moves downward from a' to e', the b^b serving as a catalyst to the descent. D-minor would appear to be the melodic and harmonic goal of the first phrase, as is confirmed at the beginning of the second … [see Example I.2].[17]

These excerpts, along with numerous others to be discussed in Chapter 1, embrace a foundational view of the Guidonian hexachord that is at odds with the model of musical space that is familiar to modern listeners. We are asked to understand – thus to *hear* – the vocal parts and the harmonic progressions of Renaissance polyphony as the product of a hexachord-based conceptualization of musical space, in the same way as classical harmony and phrasing imply the notions of pitch class and octave equivalence. Notice that such a thesis does acknowledge that the phenomenon of octave duplication had a role to play in medieval musical practice and theory; at the same time, however, it maintains that the hexachordal bonds uniting the diatonic sounds were both stronger and syntactically more significant in the domain of musical practice. In this perspective, the octave (*diapason*) possessed more of theoretical or speculative significance; to practical musicians of that age the octave span existed only as a composite segment, a "6 + 2" of sorts, which still did not have the paradigmatic value that it came to possess at later times.

The relative primacy of the hexachord over the octave is all that is needed to justify hexachordal modes of analysis. Still, this argument leaves modern

[17] E. T. Chafe, *Monteverdi's Tonal Language* (New York: Schirmer, 1992), pp. 59–60.

listeners in an impossible position: if the three-hexachord system was indeed the "conceptual form of the tonal system" in the Middle Ages, and if composers "communicated" to their listeners by assigning the musical notes to particular "hexachordal degrees", then the octave-based musical mindset of modern listeners can only be a crippling obstacle in appreciating the grammatical and syntactical well-formedness of early music. Such a conclusion precipitates a cognitive crisis of staggering dimensions, as it forces us to give up any legitimate expectation we may nurture of understanding the grammatical nuts-and-bolts of early music as we should, i.e., through our ears. At best, we can strive to painstakingly reconstruct that grammatical meaning on the musical score, through our eyes, charting the way in which alien minds once processed that shared musical meaning. Of course, we could still *enjoy* the music of medieval and Renaissance masters and respond emotionally to it. But we would have to give up any pretense or presumption that what *we* hear is even remotely close to what *they* heard no matter how hard we try – quite a paradoxical outcome indeed, considering that the theory of hexachord-based musical structure has been pursued in recent years as a legitimate attempt to better understand the musical space of the pre-modern era.

Consider, for instance, Eric Chafe's analysis of the beginning of Monteverdi's "Cor mio" quoted above (see Ex. I.2 above). The author observes that the opening six chords of the madrigal "outline the chordal spectrum of the one-flat hexachord" (F-G-A-Bb-C-D), as a medieval theorist would presumably have recognized it (much more on this in the following chapters).[18] At the same time, however, Chafe identifies the first two chords as a "D-g dominant-tonic progression to g," and D-minor as the apparent "melodic and harmonic goal of the first phrase."[19] The result is a sort of "harmonic schizophrenia," at least from the perspective of a modern listener: how can a chord function as a "dominant" and be part of a "hexachordal grouping" at the same time? Or how can we even trust our harmonic inferences (D as a melodic and harmonic goal) when the presumed

---

[18] In Chafe's harmonic system, each "hexachord" (harmonically reinterpreted) consists of six major or minor chords ordered along the circle of fifths. Thus the chords F-C-G-d/D-a/A-e/E are obtained by considering the six pitches of the "natural hexachord" (C-a) as chordal roots. See the chapter "Basic Issues in Seventeenth-Century Tonality" in Chafe's book, pp. 21–37.

[19] Chafe later qualifies this point by proposing that the piece "is not cast in the key of d as it is commonly understood today," but rather in a d mode in which [round b] and [square b] coexist while remaining conceptually separate by virtue of belonging to different "hexachordal groupings" (*Monteverdi's Tonal Language*, p. 66). Again, this is an analytic application of the basic tenet that the octave (d-mode) is in fact the result of constitutive and overlapping hexachords ("flat and natural areas").

hexachordal factors leading to such inferences are so foreign to our musical mindset? Finally, what is the status of the pitch E in Chafe's reading of this piece? If the first phrase of the madrigal outlines the one-flat hexachord, then E is an outsider and possibly a "dissonant" element of sorts. But then, E is also a regular member of the triads on C and A, which are considered part of the same hexachordal consortium that includes the D triad. Its full membership in that consortium, furthermore, becomes crystal clear the moment we are asked that first phrase of the madrigal (correctly, I think) as being directed to D. In short: which set of justifications might compel us to understand (and to *hear*) the pitch above the *finalis* – or, for that matter, any note above *la* or below *ut* – as belonging to a diatonic layer that is distinct from that of the *finalis* itself?

Again, there is great abundance of *prima facie* evidence for embracing the hexachordal approach to early music, as Chafe himself rightly points out. Most readers of this monograph are certainly aware that both Latin music theory and several musical works from the fifteenth and sixteenth centuries seem to offer strong corroboration to the foundational reading of the hexachordal system. In addition to being central to medieval and Renaissance musical training, the *ut-la* syllables appear to provide the structural backbone of motets and masses by the most accomplished Renaissance masters. Surely, when Josquin wrote his masses *La sol fa re mi* and *super voces musicales*, or when Sweelinck and Frescobaldi wrote keyboard pieces by the title *Ut re mi fa sol la*, they seemed to imply that what we take to be the "seventh note of the scale" was for them a member of a different diatonic order, and if we are ill-equipped to hear their music under those harmonic conditions, that is merely our problem, a telling sign of the reality of the drastic historical change that has occurred through time.

In short, a positive answer to the question of the "hexachordal season" of Western music, benign and plausible as it may seem at first, leaves all Western listeners and music scholars in a position of alienation vis-à-vis their own musical history, once we become aware of its real magnitude and implications. Yet a closer look at the documentary evidence and at the reception history of the hexachordal system points to a broad range of positions on the problem of medieval and Renaissance diatonicism. The "strong" interpretation of Guido's hexachord has not been unanimously endorsed in modern historiography, just as the six Guidonian syllables were not universally adopted as a pedagogical tool. To evaluate the merit of these alternative positions, *ergo* to explore the possibility of a "weaker" interpretation of the hexachord, seems a worthy goal that promises to solve the cognitive crisis I have just described. If it turns out that the structural significance of the "Guidonian hexachord" was relative rather than absolute, and circumscribed rather than boundless, then the historical and musical divide between *us* and *them* becomes suddenly more manageable.

For instance, some music scholars refer to the compositions cited above, and others of the same hexachordal family, as being not so much "based" on the hexachord as a rock-bottom structural foundation, but simply – or agnostically – as using "the solmization syllables in one way or another."[20] At the very least, this label has the advantage of being somewhat uncommitted, as it leaves open the possibility that a musical work may be "based on" the Guidonian syllables in the sense that its melodic material may have been *ordered* according to particular syllabic patterns, without thereby implying that the material *itself* is hexachordal in a strong sense, i.e., without necessarily affirming that the hexachord was "the conceptual form of the tonal system." To be sure, the implications of this "soft" interpretation of hexachordal theory have not been explored in musicological literature: to say that a composition is "based on" the syllables is tantamount to implying that it is "hexachordal" in a strong sense, as Blackburn herself suggests elsewhere in her Josquin chapter. As I will show in the following pages, however, such non-structural reading is in line with the great majority of theoretical sources from the Middle Ages, that is to say, roughly for the first half of the millennium-long history of the hexachordal system.

In an attempt to make the case for a "soft" understanding of Guido's hexachords, the present monograph pursues two closely intertwined objectives. Its goal is to provide a satisfactory answer to the question, now more urgent than ever, of whether medieval and Renaissance musicians indeed understood Guido's hexachord to be the primary diatonic "yardstick" of their musical space. After an initial survey of the scholarly understanding of the hexachordal system in the last century, my discussion takes a broad diachronic tour – though hardly an exhaustive one – of the early history of the six Guidonian syllables, which has remained largely unexplored to this day. For reasons that, as I hope, will become clear in the course of the book, such diachronic investigation is the necessary prerequisite for appreciating what humanist authors, much later, will have to say about Guido and his hexachords.

My argument runs entirely on my examination of primary sources, albeit from two slightly different angles. In the first part of my study I will

---

[20] See, for instance, B. Blackburn, "Masses Based on Popular Songs and Solmization Syllables," in R. Sherr, ed., *The Josquin Companion* (Oxford University Press, 2000), pp. 51–87.

approach my sources as "informants" on the basic questions of the nature and the function(s) of Guido's hexachord as understood in the Middle Ages. I intend to show that a substantial body of relevant historical sources from Guido to *c.* 1400 offers precious little to corroborate the "hexachord-as-diatonic-yardstick" theory. The Guidonian hexachord played a thoroughly marginal role in the musical pedagogies of Guido and Hermannus, in spite of these authors' reliance on the major sixth for particular practical purposes (Chapter 2). The set of six syllables *ut-la* was not even recognized as a diatonic unit until the thirteenth century, when a new breed of university-trained theorists turned Guido's guidelines for solmization into a fully fledged system, introducing along the way a new set of concepts and a new terminology (Chapters 3 and 4). On the whole, however, monastic music pedagogy remained relatively unaffected by such developments, perpetuating old pedagogical models that largely bypassed the *ut-la* syllables for basic practical purposes.

The second half of this study will address the historiographic side of the question, as it attempts to understand the historical circumstances that led to the emergence of the foundational view of the hexachordal system. In this section I will concentrate on a restricted number of texts from the fifteenth century that I consider have much contributed to the emergence of such a view. I will read these texts against a broader historical context, often comparing, second-guessing, and even refuting them. Here the topic of solmization appears in its interconnections with pressing issues of a much broader scope, such as religious and pedagogical reform, the authority of the church, and the search for new cultural models. In the opening years of the *quattrocento*, for instance, Johannes Ciconia favored a pedagogical *renovatio* that did away with Guido's hexachords altogether (though not with Guido's teaching) and resurrected a monochord-based method of instruction. The thrust of Ciconia's theses reveals important points of contact with the intellectual scene of the city of Padua, where the author conceived and compiled his treatise in the last decade of his life. The readoption of the monochord was also central to the teaching of Conrad of Zabern, the traveling *cantor* who taught music in the German reformed monasteries of the Bursfeld congregation in the 1460s and 1470s (Chapter 5). Around the same time, the Carthusian monk Johannes Gallicus mounted a devastating attack against the method of the six syllables, carefully inserting a wedge between Guido's teaching, as documented in his writings, and later hexachord-based musical pedagogy, arguing that a reform of musical pedagogy modeled on the techniques of the *antiqui padres* would contribute to religious and spiritual renewal (Chapter 6). Later, the Spanish Bartolomeo

Ramos de Pareja echoed parts of Gallicus' argument in his own critique of six-syllable solmization.

But there was also strong opposition to such calls for curricular reform, an opposition that gained steam at the end of the fifteenth century and in the same cultural area – Northern Italy – that earlier had served as a catalyst for the work of Ciconia and Gallicus. In his polemical reply to Ramos, for instance, Nicolaus Burtius defended Guido's method for sight singing as God-given and as the expression of the authority of the church. One of the preeminent theorists of his age, Franchino Gafori, subtly portrayed Guido as the musical heir of classical antiquity who had set church music on a new and solid basis by expanding the old *tetrachordum* of the Greeks into the *hexachordum* of the Christian age (Chapter 7).[21] Gafori's classicizing account of Guido's method in the printed version of his *Practica musicae* (1496) was more learned than accurate; yet it had a definite impact on subsequent generations of theorists into the eighteenth century. In Italy, for instance, Gioseffo Zarlino sought to link Gafori's notion of *hexachordum* to his reform of the modal system, itself part of an ambitious goal that aimed to recast the entire discipline of *musica theorica* on a solid scientific foundation by filtering it through the tight meshes of the deductive method (Chapter 8).

Thus the seemingly marginal and intermittent debate on the merit of six-syllables solmization that sputtered throughout the *quattrocento* is in fact all intertwined with the complex intellectual tensions and aspirations of the humanist era. At least some authors perceived the reform of sight singing as a local battle within the larger crusade for religious and spiritual renewal that characterized the entire age. By contrast, others saw the pressing calls for musical reform as a direct threat to the authority and infallibility of the church. But the dispute was also fought quite self-consciously at the rhetorical level, for its participants (or at least the shrewdest among them) understood perfectly well the need to deploy the most effective means of persuasion and to appeal to authority – antiquity, the church, or Guido – to one's own advantage, lest the battle be lost. Finally, it was indirectly a dispute over the *technological* means of persuasion. Sophisticated and compelling as it was, Gallicus' philological scrutiny of Guido's texts, confined to manuscript circulation, simply could not reach out to as many readers as did the multiple printed editions of Gafori's *Practica*, together with their

---

[21] In this book I adopt the spelling "Gafori" out of the several name forms in use for this author (Gaffurius, Gafurius, Gaffurio, Gafori). Likewise, all his primary taxts are listed under "Gafori" in the bibliography, regardless of the actural forms used in their original and/or modern edition.

elegant layout, their fanciful illuminations, and their thoroughly corrupt treatment of hexachordal theory.

Ultimately, this monograph aims to chart out the rich and convoluted history of the hexachordal system as a way of appreciating the cultural factors that transformed that system from a low-key method for sight singing into an all-around structural pillar of early music – in other words, from pragmatic tool to ideological symbol and music-historiographical category. What follows is in many ways the story of the manufacturing and successful "marketing" of a music theory, in the name of authority and tradition, through five hundred years of history. But my investigation is also meant to be an opportunity to see ourselves as active participants in that still ongoing story, and to reflect on the ever-ambiguous nature of our relationship with our musical past.

1 | Guido's musical syllables: conflicting views from modern historiography

Solmisation [war] vom 11. bis in das 17.,
ja 18. Jahrhundert herrschende Theorie der Melodik.

Hugo Riemann, *Handbuch der Musikgeschichte* (1923), p. 171

About a century after its publication, Hugo Riemann's sweeping portrayal of Guidonian solmization as the central diatonic yardstick of medieval and Renaissance "Melodik" has hardly lost currency among musicologists and music theorists. Some scholars might disagree on the fine print, but the general consensus is that the *ut-la* syllables of Guido of Arezzo eventually became so common that they *de facto* imposed a new conceptualization of diatonic space grounded on the segment of the major sixth. Crucial to this line of thought has been the argument that the practice of the musical Hand belonged to the sphere of day-to-day music making, rather than to the "abstract" constructions of the gamut of speculative theory, and that it *ergo* opened a privileged window into the inner workings of the medieval musical mind. Because all musicians were trained to solmize all semitones as *mi fa* (and similarly all other intervals), allegedly they came to understand their tonal space as featuring only one semitone, *pace* their different labels in the seven-letter system and the notion of octave duplication that they imply.

In the last four decades a number of scholars have attempted to come to grips with the hexachordal dimension of medieval musical space; at the same time they have explored the consequences of this particular configuration of musical space for the contrapuntal and harmonic language of numerous composers of the pre-common practice era – from Machaut to Josquin, and from Monteverdi to J. S. Bach. Two articles by Richard Crocker from around 1970 made the case that the Guidonian hexachord was the most important diatonic unit for practical musicians from the Carolingian era to the seventeenth century, when the role of primary space-definer was finally taken over by the octave for all intents and purposes.[1] Central to this argument was the thesis that the set of

---

[1] R. L. Crocker, "Perchè Zarlino diede una nuova numerazione ai modi?" *Rivista italiana di musicologia* 3 (1968): 48–58; "Hermann's Major Sixth," *JAMS* 25 (1972): 19–37. In the final page

six syllables was not just a pedagogical tool for sight singing, but rather the primary organizing agent of the ecclesiastical modal system from the eleventh century onwards.[2] Although Crocker's theses were by no means without precedents, they hit the scholarly scene at a time when the need to propose an adequate set of analytical tools for early music was especially urgent, and the idea of the hexachord as a central diatonic paradigm was appealing no doubt because it seemed to effectively discriminate between the sound universe of early music and the tonal grammar of later repertories.[3]

In subsequent years a number of musicologists active in American universities contributed towards clarifying the position of late-medieval theorists on this topic.[4] In particular, Margaret Bent and Karol Berger proposed the thesis that in medieval theory and practice the six syllables were understood as necessary to the seven letters for the precise definition of the intervallic distances between the steps of the gamut. In Bent's concise formulation, "it was *only when* yoked with hexachord syllables that the letters acquired unequivocal tone-semitone definition, even within the norms of *musica recta*."[5] This argument is part of Bent's "floating pitch" thesis, according to which polyphonic singers constantly renegotiated the actual pitch levels of the notes on the page on the ground of contrapuntal *and* hexachordal considerations.[6] In an earlier contribution, Bent had already proposed the

of the latter article, Crocker came to the conclusion that Guido's (and Hermannus') hexachord "remained the central concept for both chant and polyphony up through the sixteenth century."

[2] I will discuss at length these two key contributions respectively in Chapters 2 and 8.

[3] For a recent investigation of the history of analytical approaches to early music and its institutional and ideological underpinnings, see D. Leech-Wilkinson, *The Modern Invention of Medieval Music* (Cambridge University Press, 2002), chapter 4. See also my "Constructing Difference: The Guidonian Hand and the Musical Space of Historical Others," *Studies in Medievalism* 16 (2008), 98–121.

[4] See D. Pesce, *The Affinities and Medieval Transposition* (Bloomington, IN: Indiana University Press, 1987), esp. chapter III, "Hexachords: Seats of the Modes," 50–79, and K. Berger, *Musica ficta*.

[5] M. Bent, "Diatonic *ficta*," 10, emphases mine (but see the entire section titled "Staff, Hexachord, *clavis*," pp. 7–12).

[6] *Ibid.*, esp. 9–10. The author later offered a refinement of her position on this issue, taking distance from the theory (espoused by some scholars) that the solmization syllables were essential for resolving issue of *musica ficta* and counterpoint. See her "Diatonic *ficta* revisited, Josquin's *Ave Maria* in context," *Music Theory Online* 2.6 (1996), www.societymusictheory.org/mto/, also included in her *Counterpoint, Composition, and* Musica Ficta (New York: Routledge, 2002), pp. 208, which reinforces the point made in an earlier discussion (pp. 6–7). Yet Bent's position on this issue remains ambiguous. In the newly written "Introduction" to this volume, for instance, the author explains her understanding of a "step" as a "moveable point in the gamut of the staff, a movable rung of the ladder (*scala*), a letter that awaits hexachordal definition" (p. 22).

view of the gamut as hexachordally organized.[7] Although Karol Berger was not persuaded by the "floating pitch" thesis, he accepted the basic premise that the hexachordal syllables provided intervallic information that would not have been available to singers if they had considered the notated pitches only as letters. Thus, he read a passage from Johannes Tinctoris' *Expositio manus* to mean that hexachordal syllables were necessary for defining the intervals between the steps (*loci*) of the gamut.[8] Common to both Bent and K. Berger is the premise that the A-G letters conveyed the order of the *loci* within the Hand but not the actual intervallic distances between them, which could only be conveyed unequivocally by the six syllables of Guido.[9] Recent handbooks and textbooks on medieval and Renaissance music have generally endorsed this view.[10]

There is naturally a short distance between these interpretations of the hexachord as a "space-defining" and "position-finding" tool on the one hand, and Crocker's "hexachord-as-yardstick" thesis: all of these positions implicitly or explicitly assume that the diatonic steps of the medieval gamut were understood as rungs in the hexachordal ladder, or as "hexachordal scale degrees."

In the context of such formulations on the strictly music-theoretical front, another group of scholarly contributions has explored the music-analytic implications of the basic idea of the hexachordal structure of the gamut. A 1972 monograph by Gaston Allaire must be regarded as a ground-breaking publication, not only for its relatively early arrival on the scholarly

---

[7] "*Musica recta* and *musica ficta*," *MD* 26 (1972): 73–100; reprinted as chapter 1 of *Counterpoint, Composition, and* Musica Ficta, pp. 61–93.

[8] Tinctoris' text reads: "There are six universal syllables … which we may define one by one as follows: Ut is the first syllable, distant from the second by a whole tone," etc. ("Sex autem sunt voces universals … Ut est prima vox tono distans a secunda.") K. Berger observes that "The way Tinctoris introduces the syllables [in chapter 4 of his *Expositio manus*] shows clearly that their function was to define intervals" (*Musica ficta*, 190, fn. 8).

[9] K. Berger, *Musica ficta*, p. 4. Berger's position on this issue is related to his perception of the centrality of the musical Hand as a mnemonic tool in medieval music pedagogy (more on this in Chapter 4).

[10] See, for instance, A. Atlas, *Renaissance Music* (New York: W. W. Norton, 1999), pp. 34–6; L. Perkins, *Music in the Age of the Renaissance* (New York: W. W. Norton, 1999), p. 987; R. Wegman, "Musica ficta," in T. Knighton and D. Fallows, eds., *A Companion to Medieval and Renaissance Music* (Berkeley: University of California Press, 1997), pp. 265–74; D. Cohen, "Notes, scales, and modes in the earlier Middle Ages," in T. Christensen, ed., *The Cambridge History of Western Music Theory* (Cambridge University Press, 2002), p. 342; J. Herlinger, "Music Theory of the Fourteenth and Early Fifteenth Centuries," in R. Strohm and B. J. Blackburn, eds., *Music as Concept and Practice in the Late Middle Ages*, pp. 246–9; and S. Mead, "Renaissance Theory," in J. Kite-Powell, ed., *A Performer's Guide to Renaissance Music,* 2nd edn. (Bloomington, IN: Indiana University Press, 2007), pp. 343–51.

scene, but also for the scope of its inquiry.[11] The basic premise informing this study was that the daily use of solmization for sight singing had direct implications on the practice of composition; thus, to understand how a singer would have solmized a melodic part, following the notated clefs and accidentals, is tantamount to understanding the underlying structure of that piece:

The modern musicologist must analyze medieval and renaissance music in terms of *hexachords* and not in terms of *scales*, and he must regard the sharp and flat signs in that music as guides to solmization and not necessarily as symbols affecting the pitch of the notes they precede. The assumption that sharp and flat signs have had the same function and meaning throughout history is not tenable.[12]

Even in the advanced stages of professional music making, when singers no longer had to solmize their parts, the hexachordal principle embedded in the gamut continued to impact the perception of musical sound.[13] This means, for instance, that the shifts of hexachord (*mutationes*), by which singers mentally transposed the hexachord *ut-la* onto different portions of the gamut, carried a musical significance that was roughly analogous to the "modulations" and "tonicizations" of tonal music. Another key aspect of Allaire's theory was that the church modes also owed their *raison d'être* to the hexachordal system.[14] In the second half of the book, Allaire applied these basic principles to his analysis of musical works from the sixteenth century, often heavily editing their musical text in line with his solmization-based understanding of Renaissance diatonic space.

Christian Berger's study of fourteenth-century secular polyphony accepted Allaire's general interpretation of the notated accidentals (sharps and flats) as guides for solmization implying a hexachordal parsing of diatonic space.[15] Berger spent considerable time laying out the theoretical basis for his analytic project, partly in response to one of the main criticisms

[11] See G. Allaire, *The Theory of Hexachords, Solmization and the Modal System*, MSD 24 (N.p.: American Institute of Musicology, 1972).
[12] G. Allaire, *The Theory of Hexachords*, p. 4.
[13] G. Allaire, *The Theory of Hexachords*, p. 44.
[14] "... modes [were] understood as interlocking hexachords, rather than as scales in the modern sense. A mode is a static series of tones dependent upon the hexachords for structural definition, the mainspring of the system being the hexachord-order – that is, a set of interlocking hexachords" (G. Allaire, *The Theory of Hexachords*, p. 63).
[15] C. Berger, *Hexachord, Mensur, und Textstruktur: Studien zum französischen Lied des 14. Jahrhunderts*, Beihefte zum Archiv für Musikwissenschaft 35 (Stuttgart: Franz Steiner Verlag, 1992); another study that moved from the theoretical premises laid out by Allaire is J. Hirshberg, "Hexachordal and Modal Structure in Machaut's Polyphonic Chansons," in J. W. Hill, ed., *Studies in Musicology in Honor of Otto Albrecht* (Kassel: Bärenreiter, 1980), pp. 19–42.

directed at Allaire.[16] For instance, Berger embraced the view of the six *voces* as "space-definers" and of the octave as a derivative and merely nominal yardstick.[17] The hexachord as a diatonic unit ("die Einheit des Hexachords") acted as a sort of "glue" creating a functional context for the scattered dots in the diatonic landscape represented by the *litterae*. Particularly important to Berger's theory is the consideration of sharps and flats as the visible, notational markers of the hexachordal segments structuring actual melodies and detectible through musical analysis. Berger also shared Allaire's view of the hexachordal system as a telling sign of the "critical distance" separating the Middle Ages from us: to recuperate that counterintuitive model of pitch organization is to become aware of the historical limits of our modern expectations and categories of judgment about music, and to come closer to respecting the historical otherness of medieval musical culture.[18]

Long before C. Berger, hexachordal theory had played an important role in Carl Dahlhaus' theory of harmonic tonality.[19] Dahlhaus took the structural differences between the hexachordal articulation of musical space and the modern, octave-based one as a negative indicator of the presence of tonal thinking in early music: in other words, modern tonality could not have emerged as long as that model of diatonic space, in the form of the late-Renaissance "modal-hexachordal system," regulated the world of musical practice. At the end of his study, Dahlhaus offered numerous analyses of Renaissance polyphonic works by Josquin, Monteverdi, and others, moving from the premise of the hexachord as a basic principle of pitch organization. Dahlhaus' readings of Monteverdi's madrigals proposed a "harmonic" reinterpretation of the Guidonian hexachord, by which each note of the six-fold set functioned as the root of a chord. His goal was to come to terms with the tonal language of the early Baroque era, a sort of grey area between Renaissance modality and the harmonic tonality of

[16] See section 3 of Berger's study, "Die Darstellung des Tonsystems," pp. 85–143.

[17] "The octave module ... was during the Middle Ages a merely theoretical structure that did not have much significance for musical practice" ("Die Oktaveinteilung bleibt ... wärend des ganzen Mittelalters eine bloß theoretische Gliederung, die in der Praxis keine große Bedeutung hat," p. 97); "The hexachordal unit ... offered the singer the necessary information to securely navigate the steps and half steps of the scale. The hexachord was far more useful than the octave in musical practice, because chant melodies rarely featured intervals wider than the fourth" ("Die Einheit des Hexachords ... bot dem Sänger die notwendige Sicherheit im Umgang mit den Halb- und Ganztönen der Leiter. Weit mehr als die Oktave entsprach das Hexachord den Anforderungen der Praxis, da die Melodik des Chorals selten größere Intervalle als die Quarte aufwies" (*ibid.*; see also p. 98).

[18] See C. Berger, *Hexachord, Mensur, und Textstruktur*, pp. 18 and 85–7.

[19] C. Dahlhaus, *Untersuchungen über die Entstehung der harmonische Tonalität* (Kassel: Bärenreiter, 1968); for the English edition see R. Gjerdingen, trans., *Studies on the Origin of Harmonic Tonality* (Princeton University Press, 1991).

eighteenth- and nineteenth-century classical music. Dahlhaus' model has inspired Eric Chafe's own investigation of Monteverdi's music;[20] among other music-analytic contributions sharing such premises, most notable is Lionel Pike's recent analysis of Italian and English works from the late Renaissance.[21]

Some of the studies mentioned above were met with more than a dose of skepticism. Alejandro Planchart, for instance, questioned the "cavalier attitude" displayed by Allaire toward medieval theory, challenging in particular the notion that the concept of "hexachord order" was central to the Renaissance understanding of the diatonic space.[22] Along the same lines, Andrew Hughes pointed out problems in Allaire's understanding of the relationship between modes and hexachords, as well as in the analytical applications of the theory.[23] For her part, Sarah Fuller has also questioned the interpretations of the hexachordal system offered by Dolores Pesce and Christian Berger, observing that late-medieval theorists are on the whole less consistent in their reliance on the Guidonian syllables than suggested in the studies of these two authors.[24] In due course, other scholars have expressed discomfort with the dominant interpretation of hexachordal theory.[25] However, the strong view of the *ut-la* syllables as an organizing principle of the medieval gamut remains by all means a tenet in current studies of Renaissance music.

Earlier interpretations: Georg Lange, Jacques Handschin, and Walter Wiora

The widespread agreement of the last four decades on the structural significance of the hexachord in early music hides from view the many doubts and heated controversies that have permeated the scholarly contributions on the topic of Guido's syllables throughout the modern era. While it is true that

---

[20] Chafe, *Monteverdi's Tonal Language*.

[21] Pike, *Hexachords in Late-Renaissance Music*. See also, among others, the article by Jehoash Hirshberg on Guillaume de Machaut cited in the bibliography.

[22] See Planchart's review of *The Theory of Hexachords, Solmization and the Modal System: A Practical Application*, by G. Allaire, *JMT* 18 (1973), 213–23.

[23] A. Hughes, Review of *The Theory of Hexachords, Solmization and the Modal System: A Practical Application*, by G. Allaire, *JAMS* 27 (1974), 132–9.

[24] S. Fuller, Review of *The Affinities and Medieval Transposition* by D. Pesce, *JMT* 33 (1989), 439–48; "Modal Discourse and Fourteenth-Century French Song: A 'Medieval' Perspective Recovered?," *EMH* 17 (1998): 61–108 (a review-article of Christian Berger's monograph).

[25] Brothers, *Chromatic Beauty in the Late Medieval Chanson*, pp. 11–44, and Fuller, "Modal Discourse and Fourteenth-Century French Song," 78–9.

one encounters versions of the foundational reading of hexachordal theory throughout the long tradition of music historiography, musicologists on the whole hesitated to confer a clear structural weight to Guido's hexachords up until the first half of the twentieth century. At best, they were fairly evenly divided on this issue, and at any rate they did not develop the hypothesis of the hexachordally organized gamut into a music-analytic project.

A lengthy study by Georg Lange published in 1899, for instance, attempted to elucidate one of the central questions of the present monograph, namely the relationship between, on the one hand, the diatonic segment chosen as a tool for solmization (*Solmisationseinheit*) and, on the other, the core diatonic segment of the *Tonsystem* – understood as an ascending series of pitches indicated by pitch letters.[26] The article is still worth close reading, as it lays out a number of critical issues about the hexachord with unusual thoroughness and clarity.

On the whole, Lange oscillates between a "weak" and a "strong" conception of the Guidonian hexachord. At times, following the theses of his illustrious predecessor, August Wilhelm Ambros, he characterizes the hexachord as a "shadowy" segment (*hinter den Coulissen*) that could claim paradigmatic significance only for the purpose of solmization and that could not challenge, in any case, the centrality of the diatonic species of fourth, fifth, and octave.[27] In line with this view, Lange offers a lengthy discussion of the Guidonian principles of *affinitas* and *proprietas* of the seven pitch letters as constituting the conceptual background to the method of hexachordal solmization.[28] He observes that, when used for an extended period of time, such a method could in principle take on a cognitive-paradigmatic significance of its own in the mind of medieval singers, to the point of overshadowing the octave as the main diatonic unit of the musical system. Yet Lange also maintains that the underlying role of the octave as the regulative segment of the diatonic space was never put in jeopardy by the *Solmisationmasseinheit*, as demonstrated, for example, by the fact that Guido never meant to bypass or discard the seven pitch letters (*Tonbuchstaben*).[29]

---

[26] G. Lange, "Zur Geschichte der Solmisation," *Sammelbände der Internationalen Musikgesellschaft* 1 (1899–1900), 535–622 (see in particular section IV of the article, "Versuch einer neuen Erklärung des Hexachordensystems," 556–64). The article is now available at www.jstor.org.

[27] Lange, "Zur Geschichte," 557.

[28] Lange, "Zur Geschichte," 557–61. I will discuss Guido's theory in Chapter 2.

[29] Lange, "Zur Geschichte," 560. Or, as J. Handschin would put it several decades later, "the six tones [of the hexachord] presuppose the seventh" ("die sechs Töne setzen den siebenten voraus," *Der Toncharakter: eine Einführung in die Tonpsychologie* (Zurich: Atlantis, 1948; repr. Darmstadt: Wissenschaftliche Buchgesellschaft, 1995) p. 328). In an earlier passage, Lange had

In the final pages of the article, however, such "weak" characterization of the hexachord appears to give way to an alternative view that attributes a stronger cognitive and structural weight to that unit. Part of the problem here is Lange's systematic adoption of the term "hexachord," rather than of the historically more accurate *deductio*, in spite of his own observation that the former does not appear in medieval discussions of solmization.[30] Once Lange has operated this key terminological switch, it is a short step for him to present the medieval hexachord as a *de facto* diatonic *Masseinheit*, or a *Grundstock*, that originated as an expansion of the Greek tetrachord.[31] Lange also proposes the thought-provoking thesis that the hexachord achieved paradigmatic significance by virtue of controlling the *aural* dimension of notated pitches, with the seven *claves* regulating primarily (or even exclusively?) the *visual* aspect of notation conveyed by a combination of *claves* and *voces*:

> Solmisation bedeutet ganz allgemein die Lautierung der gesungenen Töne im Gegensatz zur Bezeichnung derselben. Diese wird bewerkstelligt durch die *claves* (Schlüssel), jede durch die *voces* (Stimmen); erstere stellen die Symbole der Töne für das Auge, letztere die für das Ohr dar. Durch das ganze Mittelalter hindurch wird dieser Unterschied streng festgehalten. Die Solmisation hat es also nur mir der hörbaren Tonsymbolik zu thun.[32]

Thus, with the advent of the hexachordal system, the aural identification of sounds (*Tonbenennung*) gained a conceptual edge over their visual representation (*Tonbezeichnung*).[33] In line with this view, Lange argues that the widespread use of the Guidonian *Durhexachord* throughout the Middle Ages and the Renaissance was a decisive step toward the final consolidation of Western "major-mode sensibility" (*Dur-Empfinden*), which had first appeared in the psalmodic practice of early Christian times in direct

---

portrayed the introduction of the six Guidonian syllables in music theory as strangely at odds with the recent practice of indicating octave equivalence by means of the seven letters A-G (Lange, "Zur Geschichte," 540–1).

[30] The key issue of the relationship between *hexachordum* and *deductio* is discussed in much detail in the following pages.

[31] Lange, "Zur Geschichte," 620.

[32] Lange, "Zur Geschichte," 535. Half a century later, Joseph Smits van Waesberghe argued along similar lines when he proposed that the hymn *Ut queant laxis* was crucial to shaping the musical hearing of young singers ("apud Guidonem hymnus est *adiutorium, ut auditus musicali modo efformetur*," in *Smits G*, emphasis in the original).

[33] Lange, "Zur Geschichte," 564. Georg Schünemann maintained the distinction in his "Ursprung und Bedeutung der Solmisation," in *Schulmusikalische Zeitdokumente. Vorträge der VII. Reichs-Schulmusikwoche in München* (Leipzig: Quelle & Meyer, 1929), pp. 41–52.

opposition to the Moll-Charakter of the Greek diatonic system, which consisted of a series of interlocked "Phrygian" tetrachords with the semitone at the bottom.[34]

Lange's observations on this point raise important questions about musical notation and aural memory; yet they rest on an overly rigid opposition between the visual and the aural, *Tonbezeichnung* and *Tonbenennung*. Lange's insight that hexachordal solmization functions as an "audible form of pitch representation" (*hörbares Tonsymbolik*) is on target, as long as it is recognized that the conceptualization and representation of musical pitch could, and very often did, bypass the syllables in medieval theory.[35] As Lange points out in his own review of the theory of the *proprietates tonorum*, the intervallic sequence suggested by the six Guidonian *voces* merely reflected the default distances that were pre-established within the letters (or *claves*) – an observation implying that the seven letters shaped the medieval recognition of musical sound independently of the syllables.[36] Conversely, the practice of juxtaposing the *voces* – the previously stored aural memories of sounds and intervals – onto notated pitches required the *visual* recognition of the intervallic distances between the notes.

Thus, it seems more appropriate to characterize solmization as the result of a coordination of visual information with aural memory, rather than as a purely aural act. That aural memory, in any case, can only have reinforced the perception of the heptachordal notion of the gamut, even when it traveled through the conduit of the six syllables. Guido himself called on singers to become familiar with the characteristic *proprietas* of each of the seven *claves* (and of the eight modal formulae), which may or may not be expressed by the six syllables.[37]

All this being said, Lange's distinction between the visual and the aural aspects of *voces* and *claves* provides a useful criterion for understanding

---

[34] Lange, "Zur Geschichte," 538. In a later passage, Lange further emphasizes the role of hexachordal theory in structuring the tonal system around one governing *Einheit*, as well as its significance in the history of Western tonality (563).

[35] I have explored this topic in my "*Si quis manus non habeat*: Charting Non-hexachordal Musical Practices in the Heyday of Solmization," *EMH* 26 (2007), 181–218.

[36] For this reason, it seems inaccurate to argue that "[das Hexachord-System] vermochte … den Halbtonschritt kenntlich zu machen, ein Vorzug, der der Tonbezeichnung mit den sogenannten Gregorianischen Buchstaben ganz abging" ("the hexachord system enabled [singers] to recognize the position of the semitone, an advantage that was lost by indicating pitch with the so-called 'Gregorian' pitch letters," Lange, "Zur Geschichte," 564), unless "kenntlich zu machen" is used in the "soft" sense of *darstellen* or *ausdrücken*, ("represent" or "express") and not with the stronger implication of *bestimmen* or *festlegen* ("determine" or "define").

[37] See, for instance, verses 349–62 of the *Epistola* (*PesceGA*, pp. 522–5).

conceptual dynamics of broad significance during the entire period considered in this study. It could indeed be argued that the Guidonian system, initially conceived as a practical tool for learning the intervallic properties of diatonic pitches (thus as *Tonbenennung*), had by the sixteenth century taken the semblance of an all-around principle of organization of the gamut (*Tonbezeichnung*). I wish to suggest that this gradual transformation affecting the music-theoretical literature was not the manifestation of some underlying change in the structural foundations of musical sound. Rather, it was a change in the "rhetoric" of the treatises due to a variety of causes, including the impact of the systematizing tendencies of the late-scholastic era, and the application of the solmization syllables to new pressing issues, such as the need to find a logical rationale for the use of accidentals. As a later chapter will show, solmization theory began acquiring a distinct "paradigmatic" weight in the thirteenth century, when several Northern-European theorists affiliated with the University of Paris began studying it from a systemic and even grammatical perspective, rather than from a strictly practical one.

Walter Wiora reached similar conclusions half a century ago, when he analyzed the "six-degree solmization system" in the context of the "seven-degree tonal system."[38] In line with the view expressed by Lange, Handschin, and Eberhard Preußner, Wiora characterized the Guidonian *voces* as providing "a better means of memorizing all the 'tone qualities' of the diatonic pitches than the abstract *litterae*." Yet he also went on to observe, citing Handschin, that "the aggregate of the diatonic qualities [*die Gesellschaft der Toncharaktere*] is seven-fold." If so, then the question becomes: "If the syllables are meant to represent the seven *Tonqualitäten* of the diatonic scale, then why are they six and not seven?"[39]

Following Handschin, Wiora observed that the six-syllable solmization system indeed did not contradict, but rather implied a heptachordal model of diatonic space.[40] The uneven match between syllables and letters was

---

[38] W. Wiora, "Zum Problem des Ursprung der mittelalterlichen Solmisation," *Die Musikforschung* 9 (1956), 263–74 (see in particular section 2 of the article, "Die sechsstufige Solmisation und das siebenstufige Tonsystem," 265–9).

[39] Wiora, "Zum Problem des Ursprung," 265.

[40] "Hexachordal solmization did not rest on an hexachordal tonal system [*Tonsystem*] and was not in opposition to an heptachordal one ... Not only is there a complete lack of evidence in support of such claims, but the exact opposite is clearly the case: the six-step method of solmization assumes a seven-step diatonic system" ("Andererseits aber beruht die hexachordische Solmisation nicht etwa auf einem hexachordischen Tonsystem und steht nicht etwa im Widerspruch zum siebenstufigen Tonsystem ... Dafüf fehlt nicht nur jeder Beleg, sondern umgekehrt ist es handgreiflich, daß die sechsstufige Solmisation das siebenstufige System voraussetzt," Wiora, "Zum Problem des Ursprung," 266).

calculated to offer a "guided misrepresentation" of the diatonic system that was advantageous to the singers, as much as it was imperfect:

> Because its structure differed from the basic scale [*die Grund Tonleiter*], solmization was able to fulfill the purpose for which it was designed, namely, to represent the diatonic system and its nature, but in a deliberately skewed fashion [*ja nur mangelhaft erfüllen*].[41]

And shortly thereafter:

> The medieval system neither mirrored the normative system of seven diatonic steps, nor ran contrary to it. If so, then the only remaining possibility is that it kept within the scope of that system, yet also highlighted an aspect of it that was not conveyed by the *A-G* letters, even though those letters matched perfectly the idea of seven scale degrees. The *voces* [i.e., the Guidonian syllables *ut-la*] do not convey the same as the *claves* [Latin in the original], but bring forth other sides of the musical system. They complement it by fulfilling different tasks.[42]

In the end, Wiora's understanding of the hexachordal system is based on a fundamental separation of roles between the octave, which regulated the basic structure of the diatonic system, and the particular needs of yet untrained singers in their early encounters with that structure. The hexachord took second seat to the octave in a *theoretical*, i.e., foundational sense, but had primary significance in a *pedagogical* one.[43]

As it is now clear, recent musical scholarship has followed along the footsteps of Riemann, Dahlhaus, Crocker, and Allaire, rather than Lange and Wiora. Yet, a revisitation of the "soft" understanding of hexachordal theory is in order. Accordingly, the following pages will present documentary evidence that contradicts rather clearly the structural reading of the hexachordal system, while supporting the pedagogical one. At the same time, however, this monograph also intends to cast light on the origins of the structural interpretation of the hexachord, which surprisingly stretch back in time to the end of the fifteenth century. The view of the hexachord as the "herrschende Theorie der Melodik" may be flawed, but it also has very deep roots in music historiography.

---

[41] *Ibid.*, 265 (emphasis mine).

[42] *Ibid.*, 267 (emphasis mine).

[43] "Die Reihe der einander überschneidenden Hexachorde ist als eine theoretisch sekundäre, doch pädagogisch primäre Ordnung über die Reihe der Oktaven gelegt," *ibid.*

Guido's doctrine of affinity

It is a striking paradox of music history that the pedagogical innovation responsible for Guido's quasi-saintly status in the modern era – the introduction of the *ut-la* syllables – plays a thoroughly negligible role in the four treatises securely attributable to the Aretino. The syllables are nowhere to be found in three of them (*Micrologus*, the *Prologus in antiphonarium*, and the *Regulae ritmicae*, according to a plausible chronological sequence), and are briefly introduced only in an early section of the *Epistola ad Michahelem* that makes for about twenty lines of Dolores Pesce's edition (excluding the musical notation of the melody *Ut queant laxis* that appears in most sources), out of a total of almost 400 lines.[1] Of course, such quantitative analysis is hardly a reliable sign of textual or doctrinal significance, and it utterly fails to explain the enormous interest generated by those syllables in later centuries. It does provide a *prima facie* indication, however, of the thoroughly marginal role of the syllables in Guido's pedagogy.

Elsewhere I have argued – with Walther Wiora and Jacques Handschin – that the greater part of the *Epistola* points to a heptachordal notion of the diatonic space, justified by monochordal divisions, rather than to a hexachordal one.[2] If so, what was Guido's rationale for selecting only *six* syllables as an aid for sight singing? The answer to this question, which was frequently debated in the Middle Ages, is to be found in the doctrine of *affinitas*, which Guido discusses at length in the early chapters of *Micrologus*. Using modern terminology, we may define *affinitas* as the similarity of diatonic position between any two sounds of the gamut.[3] Guido would speak of similarity of *modus vocis*, by which he meant the interval pattern adjacent to two pitches

---

[1] See *PesceGA*, lines 112–133, pp. 464–8. Pesce's introduction (pp. 1–38) provides an excellent overview of the salient issues concerning Guido's biography and his pedagogical writings.

[2] See my "Virtual Segments," 429–40.

[3] For a more detailed discussion of this key concept of Guidonian theory, see D. Cohen, "Notes, scales, and modes in the earlier Middle Ages," pp. 346–54; Pesce, *The Affinities and Medieval Transposition* and *PesceGA*, pp. 17–29, from which I adopt the translation of *modus vocum* as "interval pattern" (p. 23). The concept of *affinitas* might conceivably apply to any two pitches of the gamut. Guido, however, limits his discussion of this principle to pitches a fifth apart.

Table 2.1. Intervallic affinity at the fifth, highlighting the range TTSTT (*T* = whole tone; *S* = semitone)

b			
			f
T		*S*	
a			**e**
	T		
G			**d**
	T		
F			**c**
	S		
E			**b**
	T		
D			**a**
	T		
C			**G**
	S	*T*	
B			
			F

a fifth away from each other. Interestingly (in the light of the success of the term in later centuries), Guido also uses the term *proprietas* several times in his writings – particularly in the *Epistola* – as a virtual equivalent of *modus vocis*.[4] For instance, moving upwards from D within the diatonic scale one encounters a whole tone (E), a semitone (F), then three whole tones and another semitone (B-C; thus, T-S-T-T-T-S). The pitch A has a very similar *modus vocis* upwards (T-S-T-T), but not so similar downwards (T-T rather than T-S). Moving down, one finds a whole tone (C), a semitone, (B), etc. Likewise, the *modi vocum* of pitches F and C are very similar, in that they share an ascending major third (T-T) and a descending fourth (S-T-T). As the following scheme shows (see Table 2.1), the range of a major sixth

---

[4] In the *Regule rithmice*, for instance, he explains that the use of color lines in notation is to distinguish more clearly the "property of sounds" (*proprietas sonorum*) (line 231). In the *Epistola* the term occurs a handful of times. Shortly before introducing the *Ut queant laxis* melody, Guido stresses the importance of committing to memory "all descents and ascents and diverse properties of individual sounds" (lines 104–5; see *PesceGA*, pp. 376 and 462). Clearly, Guido thought of *proprietas* not as a transposable entity (as later theorists would do), but as the distinct intervallic context of each of the seven letters. The term occurs with this meaning in the *enchiriadis* treatises. See *PesceGA*, pp. 23–9.

(T-T-S-T-T) outlines the extent of the diatonic affinity between notes an ascending fifth (or a descending fourth) apart:

Table 2.1 shows that affinity between two notes a fifth apart is bound to break down on one particular point of the gamut, i.e., where the two parallel interval contexts involve the pitches B and F side by side. The reason for the existence of this interruption is clear: B and F are each other's opposite as far as their diatonic placement goes, that is to say, they have no *modus vocis* in common at all. So when they are encountered on the same "scale degrees," computed from two initial pitches a fourth or a fifth apart, there the range of affinity will break down. For instance, the B-F pair corresponds to the seventh degree starting from C and G, to the sixth from D and a, to the fifth from E and b, and so on (see the "header" and the "footer" of Table 2.1, separated by horizontal lines. The skewed position of B and F is to highlight their diatonic status as "affinity breakers").

Another way to understand the property of affinity is to think of it in terms of transposing fifth intervals, rather than in terms of a comparison of portions of diatonic space a fifth apart. That is to say: in the medieval (i.e., Guido's) gamut there are six "good," or perfect, fifths (C-G, D-a, E-b, F-c, G-d, and a-e) and only one "bad" or dissonant one – namely, the tritone b-f. Logically, by stacking up those six "good" fifths step by step, two *T-T-S-T-T*-series are generated that respectively connect all the notes at the bottom of the fifths (C-a) and those at the top (G-e). The periodic occurrence of the "bad" fifth B-F breaks the pattern.

Thus the concept of affinity, as developed by Guido, corroborates the opinion of those scholars who have described the medieval diatonic space as heptachordal, rather than hexachordal. In fact, the significance of the range of the major sixth within that space may be aptly described as *the result of the basic "heptachordality" of the system.* The range of affinity would have been different if the musical system had not been built around the principle of octave duplication and had not entailed the six "good" fifths and the single "bad" one. In fact, Guido implicitly admits to these conclusions when he proclaims that "affinity is perfect only at the octave" in the very title to chapter 9 of *Micrologus.*[5] In a technical sense, the observation is almost trivial: because the gamut is built on the principle of octave duplication from a chain of monochordal divisions, two pitches an octave apart will necessarily have identical *modi vocum.* With a historical perspective, however, it is highly significant that Guido chose to emphasize that point so clearly.

---

[5] "Also on the resemblance of notes, which is perfect only at the diapason," in W. Babb, trans., and C. Palisca, ed., *Hucbald, Guido, and John on Music: Three Medieval Treatises* (New Haven: Yale University Press, 1978), p. 65.

Thus, in the Guidonian gamut the affinity range of the major sixth high-lights the prominence of the *fifth*, rather than of the sixth itself.[6] This impor-tant observation becomes clear by reviewing the two main consequences of the doctrine of affinities. The first one has to do with modal theory. Guido saw a direct connection between the strong affinity at the fifth and the cus-tomary practice of transposing chant melodies to end on pitches located a fifth higher than the regular modal finals D, E, and F, respectively A, B, and C (thereby called *affinales*), because of the respective similarities of *modi vocum* between the two groups. The *finalis* of the Tetrardus mode G was granted no *affinalis*, because its *modus vocum* (T-T above and T-S below) is shared by no other pitch in the gamut.[7] Thus, it is the relationship of the fifth that has direct implications for musical grammar and musical percep-tion; the affinity range of a major sixth cannot even be considered the ulti-mate cause for the significance of the fifth, which is rather due to the very disposition of the pitches within the gamut.

The other practical application of affinities was the solmization system – or, rather, the possibility thereof: by yoking a set of six syllables *ut-la* to the common range of the major sixth, it became possible to indicate the same *classes* of intervals by the same name(s). For instance, all perfect fourth intervals of the kind T-T-S could be labeled *ut-fa*, whether they occurred as C-F, as G-c, or F-Bb; the minor third S-T could be labeled *mi-sol*, whether it was notated as E-G, as B-D, or as A-(Bb)-C. But the superimposition of the six syllables onto the letters did not produce – and was never supposed to produce – the effect of imposing a new, hexachordal order on the hep-tachordal gamut. Rather, it was to remind singers that the various diatonic intervals could be grouped together into *classes* and memorized as such. Its function was first and foremost pedagogical and mnemonic, rather than theoretical or foundational. Unlike the church modes, the hexachordal set was not designed to function as a background scale – precisely the reason why it could not serve as a classificatory tool. It is important to remember, at any rate, that neither Guido, nor later theorists made the explicit connec-tion between the concept of *affinitas* and the method of the six syllables. Guido may well have been aware of it, but again he had no interest in solmi-zation theory, just as he did not envision the use of the six syllables beyond a very rudimentary level of instruction. Furthermore, Guido's increasing

[6] Smits van Waesberghe recognized this point when he observed that "Guido may have elected six syllables because they could be transposed a fifth higher" ("animadvertimus Guidonem in eligendis his sex syllabis forte rationem habuisse transpositionis in quintam-sursum," in *Smits G*, p. 97).

[7] The pitch A also has a unique *modus vocum* (T-S above and T-T below), but it was not recognized as a *finalis* in the Middle Ages.

opposition to the use of Bb suggests that he would have resisted the inclusion of that pitch in the practice of solmization.[8]

Paraphrasing Walter Wiora, one might notice that the genius of Guidonian
solmization lies precisely in artificially assuming a simplified model of the
diatonic space for the purpose of "navigating" that space correctly – quite a
different goal from precisely mapping its internal articulation.[9] The fact that
Guidonian solmization taught medieval singers to think of all semitones as
mi-fa does not mean that those singers would have *perceived* their diatonic
space as featuring only one semitone. It was both a strength and a weakness of
the system that it concentrated on the size and the species of the intervals to
be performed, while disregarding their diatonic placement: *re-fa* could be both
D-F and A-C, even though the position of the two intervals within the D mode
was different, since D has a minor third, and A a major third below. Even the
practice of solmization acknowledged this difference in *proprietas* between the
two pitches by associating D with *sol*, and A with *la*, in addition to yoking both
of them to *re*. It was no doubt on account of this deliberately skewed view
of diatonic space that medieval authors, in line with Guido's *Epistola*, often
described solmization as a "first level" kind of musical training (*pro junioribus*)
that was presumably to be abandoned at a later stage of instruction.[10]

In turn, the direct link between the heptachordal nature of the diatonic
system and hexachordal affinities downplays the relationship between the
other operative agent of the gamut – the tetrachord – and Guido's hexachord.
The suggestion that Guido defined the major sixth as a new diatonic yardstick
by expanding the pre-existing tetrachord remains common in the scholarly
literature.[11] But it can be shown that such an interpretation more accurately
describes Hermannus' major sixth (to be examined shortly) than Guido's.

---

[8] See B. J. Blackburn, "The Lascivious Career of B flat" (forthcoming in a collection of essays
   by Oxford University Press). My thanks to Dr. Blackburn for sending me a copy of this article
   prior to publication.

[9] See the citation in Ch. 1, p. 40 above.

[10] See the beginning of *Micrologus*, ch. 7, where Guido explains that "since there are just seven
   notes – seeing that the others, as we have said, are repetitions – it suffices to explain the seven
   that are of different modes and different qualities" (Babb, trans., *Hucbald, Guido, and John*,
   p. 63; "Cum autem septem sint voces, quia aliae ut diximus, sunt eaedem, septenas sufficit
   explicare, quae diversorum modorum et diversarum sunt qualitatum," (Guido of Arezzo,
   Micrologus, ed. J. Smits van Waesberghe, *CSM* 4: American Institute of Musicology, 1955),
   p. 117).

[11] D. Cohen, for instance, has recently stated that the T-S-T tetrachord "is discernible as the
   nucleus of the Guidonian hexachord," and that "Guido's six note segment comprises, in effect,
   a T-S-T tetrachord plus the notes a whole tone above and below". See his "Notes, scales, and
   modes in the earlier Middle Ages," pp. 321 and 342. For a more detailed discussion of this
   point, see *Smits G*, p. 97.

Example 2.1. The *enchiriadis* tone-system, with Daseian notation (from the *Cambridge History of Western Music Theory*, 2002, p. 324).

The T-S-T tetrachord, such as D-G or A-D, is the building block of the unusual gamut featured in two widely distributed sources of the Carolingian era, the *Musica enchiriadis* and the *Scolica enchiriadis*. As the following graph shows, the author(s) of the two treatises conceived the gamut as a series of disjunct T-S-T tetrachords, wherever they may fall and thus without assigning structural priority to the principle of octave duplication. The result is a series of pitches ordered around the principle of *perfect* affinity of *modus vocis* at the fifth. In the graph, all notes marked with the same Roman numeral share identical intervallic context (see Example 2.1).

The particular significance of the T-S-T tetrachord is due to its embedding the four regular finals of the ecclesiastical modal system in exact order, D-E-F-G. *Musica enchiriadis* calls these four pitches "qualities," and identifies them in relation to their modal function: D is *protus* (i.e., the *finalis* of the *protus* mode), E is *deuterus*, etc.[12] Bower sees the centrality of the doctrine of the finals in *Musica enchiriadis* as a sign of the "congruence of the *enchiriadis* pitch collection with liturgical chant" (p. 156). He also posits a direct link between Guido's hexachord and the gamut of *Musica enchiriadis*, noticing that the six syllables for solmization expressed the diatonic qualities of his gamut:

In his theory of the hexachord, Guido creates a qualitative matrix with which he can navigate the multivalent functions reduced to a series of letters. At the heart of the Guidonian hexachord – the central four pitches – lies the qualitative tetrachord of the *enchiriadis* tradition.[13]

It is important to distinguish, however, between the common, "qualitative" function shared by Guido's syllables and by the tetrachord of *Musica enchiriadis* on the one side, and the different lengths of the qualitative segments being compared. Guido was no supporter of the gamut of *Musica enchiriadis* articulated into disjunct tetrachords. On the contrary, he criticized it for privileging

---

[12] C. Bower, "The Transmission of Ancient Music Theory into the Middle Ages," in T. Christensen, ed., *The Cambridge History of Western Music Theory*, pp. 153–8.

[13] Bower, "The Transmission of Ancient Music Theory," p. 163.

affinity at the fifth, rather than at the octave, and no doubt abhorred its implicit recognition of F# and C#. Guido also makes no references to the tetrachord either in his general discussion of affinity at the fifth, or in his treatment of the modal affinities between *finales* and *affinales*. But the important point is that a tetrachordal arrangement of the diatonic system, such as the one adopted by *Musica enchiriadis*, does not lead to the Guidonian model of affinity in and of itself, but only when it is subsumed under the overarching principle of octave duplication. It is not that Guido took the *enchiriadis* tetrachord and expanded it to a major sixth (whatever material adjustment that conceptual expansion may have entailed); rather, following the *Dialogus* he reintegrated that tetrachord in an octave-based diatonic context, and within that context he formulated his theory of affinity. In short, while the central four pitches of Guido's hexachord do correspond to the basic tetrachord of *Musica enchiriadis*, the significance of this correspondence may be *per se* negligible.

The last point to discuss here pertains to the significance of the hexachordal range in the context of contemporaneous musical practice. In his *De harmonica institutione*, Hucbald had listed the nine melodic intervals of chant in semitonal increments from the semitone to the major sixth (*diapente cum tono*), including the tritone. He also provided a six-line diagram with the notation of an antiphon, *Ecce vere Israelita*, whose range is limited to a major sixth. The diagram was meant to represent a six-string *cithara* that was tuned with the semitone in the central position (T-T-S-T-T), exactly like Guido's (and Hermannus') hexachord. It has been suggested that the prominence of the major sixth in these three authors points to the special status of the interval in the tenth and eleventh centuries.[14] Modern scholars have also suggested that the choice of a hexachordal unit for solmization was in line with the melodic style of Gregorian chant, which rarely exceeds the interval of a fifth.[15] Although there may be more than a grain of truth in that argument, medieval theorists were careful not to unduly conflate the major sixth as a melodic interval, occasionally found in chant melodies, with the span of a major sixth outlined by the six syllables (more on this in the Interlude).

---

[14] Cohen, "Notes, Scales, and Modes in the Earlier Middle Ages," p. 338; Crocker, "Hermann's Major Sixth," *Jams* 25 (1972), 27.

[15] So, for instance, Crocker, "From the Frankish point of view, the octave seemed too large a module"; "Hermann's Major Sixth," 29; C. Berger, "In vielen Fällen, or allem in Bereich des Chorals, wird dem Sänger der Umfang eines Hexachordes genügen," in *Hexachord, Mensur, Textstruktur*, p. 88; and M. Russo, " ... the arrangement of the solmization syllables into a unit of six notes, the hexachord, seemed well suited to a repertory which rarely presented intervals larger than a fourth or a fifth and virtually never used the octave," in "Hexachordal Theory in the Late-Thirteenth Century," (Ph.D. diss., Michigan State University, 1997), pp. 10–11.

The role of the major sixth in Hermannus Contractus' *Musica*

As Guido of Arezzo was composing his *Epistola ad Michahelem*, another Benedictine monk at the monastery of Reichenau, known as Hermannus Contractus (d. 1054), was attributing new significance to the major sixth in the context of modal theory and of the diatonic system as a whole. Hermannus' argument deserves a close scrutiny in the present monograph in that it has been taken, along with Guido's recent introduction of six-syllable solmization, as marking the beginning of the era of the major sixth in Western music.[16] The relevant passage reads as follows:

Ut vero coepimus ad huc unam de agnitione troporum regulam a maioribus qui-dem ut rudem massam effossam, sed non pleniter a rubigine excoctam videamus eamque ut diligentibus constare poterit lucidam et puram reddamus. Quae videlicet agnitio licet contracta sit brevitate, tamen lata et celebris est nobilitate; quia quod valde pulcrum in ea notatur, inter proprias et legitimas troporum sedes construitur. Est autem talis eius ratio.

Accipe tetrachordum quodcumque volueris, verbi gratia gravium, addito utrinque tono, habes terminos modorum qui fiunt sedes troporum. Sunt autem quatuor tropi, et totidem vocum modi. Primus modus vocum est qui tono deponitur et prima specie diapente intenditur; hic habet agnitionem in hac antiphona, *Prophetae praedicaverunt*, et *In tuo adventu*, et similibus quae sex chordas non excedunt. Hic modus in principalibus *proti* chordis, A, D, a, d, agnoscitur. Secundum modum ditono remissum et secunda specie diatesseron intensum in principalibus chordis *deuteri*, B, E, ♭, e, existentem, pandit haec antiphona, *Gloria haec est*, et similes seu autenticae seu subiugales, quae sex chordas non excedunt. Tercius modus tercia specie diatesseron remittitur et ditono intenditur, sicut *triti* principales chordae, C, F, c, f, declarant; huius indicium est in hac antiphona, *Modicum et non videbitis*, et similibus. Quartum modum vocum tono intensum et quarta specie diapente remissum *tetrardo* aptamus; quia ipsius principales chordae D, G, d, g illum conficiunt. Qui in his antiphonis, *Si vere fratres*, et *Multi venient* et similibus potest dinosci. Quae ergo dicta sunt in sex vocibus constructa tam senarii numeri quam maximi intervalli quod tot vocibus constat perfectionem demonstrant.

[To begin with, let us look at one rule for recognizing the modes which has hith-erto been dug out as a rough mass, so to speak, by previous writers, but not fully worked clear of dross, and let us state it in such a way that it may stand forth clear

---

[16] The article by Crocker, "Hermann's Major Sixth," 19–37, still offers the most thorough treatment of the role of the hexachord within Hermannus' theory. For partial responses to Crocker's article, see *PesceGA*, pp. 20–9, and Cohen, "Notes, scales, and modes in the early Middle Ages," pp. 351–4.

and pure for earnest students. This matter of recognition, to be sure, though it may be reduced to a brief statement, is nevertheless extensive and notable in character, since that which is very elegantly indicated in it finds a place among the proper and rightful foundations of the modes. Now such is its nature: take any tetrachord you wish – say, that of the *graves*; add a tone at both ends; you then have the limits of the tonal patterns which form the basis of the modes. There are four modes and as many tonal patterns [*vocum modi*]. The first tonal pattern is that which falls a tone and rises a first species Fifth; this is recognized in the Antiphon *Prophetae praedic-averunt*, in the *In tuo adventu*, and in similar ones which do not exceed six pitches in range. This pattern is recognizable on the principal pitches of *protus, A, D, a, d*. The second pattern, which falls two tones and rises a second species Fourth, and which is found on the principal pitches of *deuterus, B, E, [sqb], e*, is exemplified by the Antiphon *Gloria haec est*, and similar ones, whether authentic or plagal, which do not exceed six pitches in range. The third pattern falls a third species Fourth and rises two tones, as established on the principal pitches of *tritus, C, F, c, f*. An example of this occurs in the Antiphon *Modicum et non videbitis*, and the like. The fourth tonal pattern, which rises a tone and falls a fourth species Fifth, we assign to *tetrardus*, since the principal pitches of that mode, *D, G, d, g*, establish it, this can be recognized in the Antiphons *Si vere fratres* and *Multi venient*, and the like. These, then, which have been described as composed of six pitches, exhibit the perfection both of the number six and of the largest interval, which consists of that number of pitches.][17]

Hermannus' theory of the *sedes troporum* posits the major sixth as a portion of diatonic space that is shared by the eight modal categories and is thus sufficient for a *prima facie* recognition of those categories. Like all rules of thumb, the method is simple and easy to apply, yet it works better for some modal categories than for others. The normal range for Mode 2, for instance, is the minor sixth A-f, which does not easily map onto Hermannus' sixth. The same could be said for Mode 5, which often extends down to the *subfinalis* E. Mode 8 is equally problematic from the point of view of this method, as it frequently spans through a "Lydian" sixth (i.e., a third species of fourth G-c with one tone at both ends, F + G-c + d) rather than through Hermannus' major sixth C-a. On the one hand, the rule may effectively represent the melodic profile of mode 4, which often extends to a major third below the final E and a fourth above it. It also does not apply well to Mode 3, which very frequently reaches up to the *c* above the final, thus breaking the limit of Hermannus' sixth. In short, not always does the actual melodic *ambitus* of chant melodies fall squarely within the affinity range of

[17] Hermannus Contractus, *Musica*, ed. and trans. L. Ellinwood, (Rochester, NY: Eastman School of Music, University of Rochester, 1936), pp. 57–9.

the major sixth (as Crocker points out, "Hermann has to go to some trouble to pick out pieces that fall within the limits of a major sixth"[18]).

Perhaps for this reason Hermannus presents his rule only after a long discussion of the element of modal theory. In earlier chapters, he had already addressed the issue of the *agnitio troporum* at considerable length in reference to the constituent species of fourth, fifth, and octave, in line with his overarching goal of forming competent singers who can express competent judgments on "the science of composing melody" (p. 47). There is no question that to Hermannus the acquisition of such musical competence implies a deep familiarity with the building blocks of the modes:

Maxime tamen troporum tibi curae sit agnitio; propter quos fere omnis musicae laborat intentio. Ad quam rem multum proderit, siquis proprias cuiusque diapente et diatessaron species tam monochordi quam vivae vocis usu memoriae inculcaverit. Non enim quemvis audiens tropum quis sit indubitanter pronuntiare poterit; nisi iam dictis et deinceps dicendis diiu multumque exercitatatus fuerit. Sic ergo susum et iusum diatesseron species modulare.

[Let your chief concern be the recognition of the modes, for which every aim of music strives. To this end much will be gained if one will impress on the memory, by the use of both monochord and singing voice, the proper species of fifth and fourth belonging to each mode. For no one, on hearing any mode, will be able to state with certainty which one it is, unless he has long and often practiced the things I have already said and must again say. Inflect, therefore, the species of fourths up and down in this manner [Fig 2.1 (Fig 1.12 follows)].[19]

Hermannus' emphasis is unequivocally on the diatonic species and on the use of the monochord in musical instruction. But what is perhaps most remarkable in the long section of *Musica* dedicated to the modes is Hermannus' awareness that such a topic is of interest to a variety of different readers: future "composers" of new chant melodies, singers trying to orient themselves through the repertory, and general readers (call them "music lovers") who simply wish to deepen their knowledge of the laws of music. There is no need for Hermannus to tailor his handling of modal theory according to these different constituencies: rather, he advises all of them to identify modes *a posteriori* by recognizing the diatonic species.[20]

In his presentation of the rule, Hermannus identifies the final and the confinal of each mode as "the principal pitches" of the modal categories

[18] Crocker, "Hermann's Major Sixth," 20.
[19] Hermannus Contractus, *Musica*, ed. and trans. L. Ellinwood, p. 48.
[20] *Ibid.*, pp. 41–7.

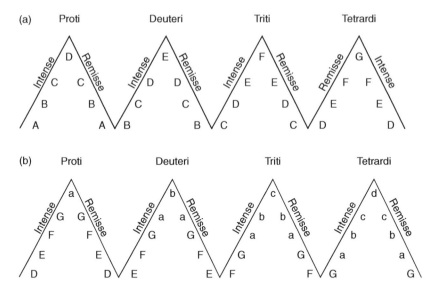

Fig. 2.1. The species of fourths and fifths as constitutive of the modes in Hermannus Contractus' *Musica*.

(i.e., *A, D, a, d* and *C, F, c, f*). The doctrine of the *sedes troporum* is effective for modal recognition to the extent that it highlights those principal pitches and defines the *ambitus* of the *modi vocum*. The first *modus vocum* (C-D + D-a) is typical of the *protus* mode because it contains the first species of fifth as a subset; the second one (C-E + E-a) features the second species of fourth and is thus proper to the *deuterus*; the third (C-F + F-a) includes the third species of fourth that is typical of the *tritus*, and the fourth *modus vocum* (G-d + d-e) contains the fourth species of fifth of the *tetrardus*. Although Hermannus derives the span of a major sixth from the tetrachord of the finals, the individual *modi vocum* for each mode implicitly downplay the structural significance of that tetrachord, pointing instead to the species of fourths and fifths as prime components of the modes (Fig. 2.1). Hermannus himself seems to allude to the derivative status of the major sixth when he introduces the rule of the major sixth with the wording: "… that which is very elegantly indicated in [the rule of the sixth] finds a place among the proper and rightful foundations of the modes."[21]

Having presented at great length the fundamentals of modal theory, toward the end of the treatise Hermannus introduces "the rule of the major sixth" that for understandable reasons has drawn considerable attention

[21] See p. 38 above.

from modern scholars. Notice, however, that from the outset Hermannus carefully qualifies his decision to bring this method to his readers' attention. Firstly, he calls it "*one* rule for recognizing the modes" (*unam de agnitione troporum regulam*). Secondly, he describes it through vivid metaphors as no more than an intuitive "rule of thumb" used by a majority of people ("… dug out as a rough mass … by previous writers, but not fully worked out clear of dross"). It is unlikely that a highly rational and systematic thinker like Hermannus would have described his hexachord-based method of modal recognition in such terms, if it was meant to carry the theoretical significance that is now attributed to it. Thirdly, Hermannus states that this rule is not in opposition with his previous account of the modes; to the contrary, the concise elegance and "heuristic value" of the rule are a direct consequence of its conformity to the general principles of modal theory ("… that which is very elegantly indicated in it *finds a place among the proper and rightful foundations of the modes*," emphasis mine). Such a wording suggests that Hermannus himself saw his rule of thumb as a synecdoche: the major sixth (i.e., the distinctive part) is useful only inasmuch as it faithfully represents the constituent combination of a fourth and a fifth (i.e., the modal whole). One may observe that just as the doctrine of hexachordal affinity observed by Guido was a function of the heptachordal nature of the gamut, in Hermannus the significance of the major sixth for modal recognition is a direct consequence of the structural role of the species: it is the *chordae principales* of the four modal *maneriae* (i.e., the four finals and their confinals within the double octave) that "establish" (*declarant, conficiunt*) each of the four distinct tonal patterns that may be neatly enclosed, *post facto*, within the major sixth.

Richard Crocker, however, proposed long ago a different interpretation of Hermannus' doctrine of the *sedes troporum*. Specifically, he sought to demonstrate that the function of the major sixth in Hermannus went beyond the immediate context of modal recognition to reflect the new organization of the diatonic system in the post-Guidonian era. He viewed the emerging interest in the major sixth in the first half of the eleventh century as part of an ongoing effort by post-Carolingian theorists toward reconciling practice and theory, that is to say, toward mapping the *modi vocum* of the four modal finals (D, E, F, and G) onto the gamut in a satisfactory way. By hinting at a hexachordal parsing of the gamut – Crocker argued – Hermannus provided a conceptualization of the diatonic space that facilitated the memorization of the *modi vocum* of the four finals and streamlined modal identification and classification. Crocker also implies in his article that Hermannus' hexachord could play the role of a paradigmatic "tonal pattern" in that it offered an effective mid-point between the tetrachord and the octave: while the former was not wide enough to account for the actual diatonic range that the four finals had in common, or at any rate for their habitual *modi vocum*, the latter was more an abstract acoustical principle than an effective regulator of musical practice. In the final analysis, Crocker argued that the major sixth of Guido and Hermannus proved to be a long-lasting diatonic paradigm in Western music because it comprised the "essential tone qualities" of the four finals.[22]

One easily agrees with Crocker's assessment of Hermannus' *sedes troporum* as a mnemonic aid. The problem of successfully relating the four finals to a background scale, however, had arguably been solved by Hucbald about two centuries before Hermannus, who indeed – like Guido himself – does not appear to have been concerned with this issue. Crocker read Hermannus' major sixth as the same *kind of* segment as the octave or the tetrachord. As we have seen, however, it would be more appropriate to regard Hermannus' major sixth as playing a diatonic function that runs parallel to those of the tetrachords and the octave, rather than in competition with them. Again, I wish to suggest that all these various diatonic ranges played a normative role within the medieval diatonic system and carried some paradigmatic significance for particular purposes, albeit with the octave serving as a general paradigm.

At the end of his article, Crocker suggested that the particular emphasis placed on the major sixth by Guido and Hermannus resulted in the elaborate system of hexachordal solmization centuries later.[23] But while Guido's contribution to later hexachordal theory is beyond doubt, the impact of Hermannus' treatise appears to have been relatively confined.[24]

Guido and Hermannus pointed to the major sixth for pragmatic reasons – sight singing and modal identification – that ultimately had little to do with each other, as confirmed by the vastly different and thoroughly separate reception histories of the two doctrines. In neither author did the range of the major sixth acquire a foundational significance. On the contrary, both Guido and Hermannus unequivocally proposed a limited use of the major sixth, confined to specific purposes and in the context of a diatonic system that had previously been set up in strictly heptachordal terms. Nor does the

[22] In Crocker's words, "the hexachord ... remained the central concept for both chant and polyphony up through the sixteenth century" ("Hermann's Major Sixth," 36–7).
[23] " ... the later hexachordal theory is nothing but the systematic application of the earlier concerns [by Hermannus and Guido] with the major sixth" (Crocker, "Hermann's Major Sixth," 36).
[24] H. S. Powers and F. Wiering, "Mode," § I-III, *NG 2*, vol. 16, p. 787.

pragmatic significance of the major sixth in these authors enhance its para-digmatic significance as an overall diatonic yardstick, as Crocker and others have often argued. In hindsight, however, Guido and Hermannus inadvert-ently planted the seeds of a potential confrontation between a hexachordal and a heptachordal model of musical space that will indeed occupy genera-tions of music theorists to come.

3 | Hands off! Singing without the syllables in the Middle Ages

Quiet beginnings

At first sight, Guido's guidelines for learning plainchant melodies with the help of the six syllables spread across Europe like wildfire. Already half a century or so after the composition of the *Epistola ad Michahelem*, John Cotto (also known as "of Afflighem") was able to claim that the six syllables *ut, re, mi, fa, sol, la* were used in England, France, and Germany, the Italians having adopted different pitch labels.[1] A couple of centuries later, the anonymous treatise *Summa musicae* reported that the six syllables were also popular among "the Hungarians, the Slavs, the Dane, and others on this side of the Alps." Drawing attention to these two passages, Christopher Page sees a parallel between the "Guidonization" of musical practice and the gradual embracing of Christianity in the religious and political institutions of Northern and Eastern Europe.[2]

---

[1] "Sex sunt syllabae, quas ad opus musicae assumimus, diversae quidem apud diversos. Verum Angli, Francigenae, Alemanni utuntur his: ut, re, mi, fa, sol, la. Itali autem alias habent, quas qui nosse desiderant, stipulentur ab ipsis. Eas vero, quibus nos utimur syllabas, ex hymno illo sumptas aiunt, cuius principium est: Ut queant laxis, [etc.]." ("There are six syllables that we adopt for use in music. They are different, among different people. The English, French, and Germans use these: ut, re, mi, fa, sol, and la. But the Italians have others, and those who wish to learn them may arrange to do so with these people. It is said that the syllables we use are taken from the hymn that begins *Ut queant laxis*"), from John Cotto, *De musica cum tonario*, ed. J. Smits van Waesberghe, *CSM* 1 ([Rome]: American Institute of Musicology, 1950), p. 49; English trans. W. Babb, ed. C. Palisca, *Hucbald, Guido, and John on Music* (New Haven: Yale University Press, 1978), pp. 103–4. John was partially correct in singling out Italy from the other European countries in this regard, as a handful of late-eleventh century Italian sources use the pitch labels *tri, pro, de, nos, te, ad* for the purpose of solmization, derived from the text *Trinum et unum*. However, the *ut-la* syllables are also well documented in Italy at that same time. On this point, see *PesceGA*, p. 548. On the name, the identity, and the whereabouts of John Cotto, see M. Huglo, "L'auteur du traité de musique dédié à Fulgence d'Affligem," *Revue belge de musicology* 31 (1977), 5–37; and J. Malcolm, "Epistola Johannis Cottonis ad Fulgentium Episcopum," *MD* 47 (1993), 159–69.

[2] C. Page, "Towards: Music in Medieval Europe," *The Musical Times* 136 (1995), 127–34. Although Page has dated the *Summa musice* to the early thirteenth century, later scholars have convincingly argued in favor of Gerbert's original dating to *c.* 1300. See C. Page, ed., *The Summa Musice: A Thirteenth-Century Manual for Singers* (Cambridge University Press, 1991), and the reviews by Joseph Dyer in *EMH* 12 (1993), 203–23, and Michael Bernhard ("La *Summa musice* du Ps.-Jean de Murs: Son auteur et sa datation," *Revue de Musicologie* 84 (1998) 19–25).

But what was involved in the process of dissemination of the solmization syllables? Was it comparable to a collective process of religious conversion, in which a new set of beliefs about God and mankind completely replaces an old one, suddenly perceived as meaningless or obsolete? Did Guido's introduction of a six-syllable method of solmization force a confrontation between two competing paradigms of music perception, based alternatively on the old tetrachord and on the new hexachord? If the advent of hexachordal solmization led to the emergence of a new and all-around diatonic yardstick, as many modern commentators would have it, then it would seem that such a cognitive battle would have to have taken place all around the active world of medieval musical practice, and that its traces would be clearly visible in the relevant documentary sources. To further credit this possibility, the history of music theory is punctuated with raging wars between the defenders of the old and the proponents of the new on issues such as modal theory, the division of the tone, notation, and tonality, to name only a few. Quite plausibly, the defenders of the tetrachordal articulation of the gamut would have voiced their opinions, if they had felt that Guido's proposal amounted to a new musical order.

However, exactly the opposite is true. Until the mid-thirteenth century, the music masters displayed no interest in developing a hexachordal terminology, much less in organizing the six syllables into a fully fledged system thought to be in competition with an earlier one. Instead, as the following pages will show, theorists simply "smuggled" the syllables into their graphs and tables surreptitiously, offering no explanation for their specific place and function within the diatonic system. The question of how to integrate the six syllables into the existing diatonic order was not a high priority for eleventh- and twelfth-century theorists; indeed it may not have been a question at all.

Even John Cotto's early endorsement of the syllables raises more questions than it answers. On the one hand, his testimony cited above on the remarkably quick transmission of Guido's method is at odds with the scant presence of the six syllables in music theoretical sources before the mid-thirteenth century (more on this later). On the other hand, there is a noticeable gap between John's comments on the usefulness of the syllables and his almost complete avoidance of them throughout his lengthy treatise. Shortly after the excerpt quoted above, John suggests that the Hand was an indispensable tool in musical pedagogy:

Per has itaque syllabas is, qui de musica scire affectat, cantiones aliquot cantare discat quousque ascensiones et descensiones multimodasque earum varietates plene ac lucide pernoscat. In manus etiam articulis modulari sedulus assuescat, ut ea postmodum quotiens voluerit pro monochordo potiatur et in ea cantum probet, corrigat et componat. Haec ubi aliquamdiu iuxta quod diximus frequentaverit et altae memoriae commendaverit, facilius procul dubio ad musicam iter habebit.

[So let him who strives for knowledge of music learn to sing a few songs with these syllables until he knows fully and clearly their ascents and descents and their many varieties of intervals. Also, let him diligently accustom himself to measuring off his melody on the joints of his hand, so that presently he can use his hand instead of the monochord whenever he likes, and by it test, correct, or compose a song. After he has repeated these things for some time, just as we have directed, and has thoroughly memorized them, he will have an easier, unperplexed road to music.][3]

In spite of such warm recommendation, however, John resorts to the syllables only on one occasion in the rest of the treatise when discussing the diatonic species (chapter 8), avoiding them altogether in the tonary and in the chapter on how to compose chants.[4] It seems reasonable to conclude that he still considered the seven letters as the primary means of pitch designation in the formation of church singers. One may also observe that in the citation above John does not point to the syllables as playing a leading role within the Hand; rather, he presents them as useful in memorizing the intervals in an early phase of musical instruction – exactly Guido's position. John also describes the Hand as preferable to the monochord not because of the new-fangled, hexachordally conceived gamut that it supposedly introduces, but rather because of an eminently practical reason, namely, its portability. In the end, he recommends that the "varieties of ascending and descending intervals" from the semitone to the *diapente* be committed to memory in the form of syllables, rather than through the letters, even though he undoubtedly understood the gamut to be structured heptachordally.

Whatever role John may have meant to assign to the six syllables, his explicit endorsement of them as a pedagogical aid turns out to be extremely unusual in the context of pre-thirteenth century music theory. Tables 3.1 and 3.2 chart the presence of the six syllables in the treatises compiled from 1050 to 1200 that are included in the *Thesaurus musicarum latinarum* (accessed on February 25, 2009).[5] Table 3.1 lists the sources that do not

---

[3] John Cotto, *De musica cum tonario,* ed. J. Smits van Waesberghe (American Institute of Musicology, 1950), p. 50; Babb, trans., *Hucbald, Guido, and John on Music,* p. 104.

[4] See Cotto, *De musica cum tonario,* ch. 8, pp. 67–71; Babb, trans., *Hucbald, Guido, and John,* pp. 110–12. The *Intervallehre* of chapter 8, from the unison to the major sixth, indicates the steps only by means of the Guidonian syllables (see *ibid.,* 112). It does not account for the variety of species that are available for most of those intervals.

[5] I am excluding from the count the copies of Guido's treatises from the eleventh and twelfth centuries, as well as other theoretical writings that do not deal with the rudiments of music.

Table 3.1. Treatises that do not mention the Guidonian syllables (*c.* 1050–1200)

N.	Date	Author	Title	TML	Content	Notes
1.	XI–XV	50 + sources	*Mensura cymbalorum*	ANOCYM	Tuning of bells	Smits v. Waesb., *Cymbala* (A.I.M., 1951)
2.	XI	Anon.	*Ad organum faciendum*	ADORFBA	*Organum* theory, intervals, conson.	Milan *organ.* treat. Eggebr./Zaminer ed.
3.	XI	Anon.	*De cantib. que supra mod.*	ANOCAN	Modal thr. pitch letters, Greek names	de La Fage Anon. 2, 87–89
4.	XI	Anon.	*De mod. formulis et tonar.*	ANODMF	Modal thr, *affinitas, modi vocum*	C. Brocket, CSM 37, 46–128
5.	*c.* 1075	Anon.	*De mus. et de transf. spec.*	ANODMT	Modal theory, B nat. vs. B flat.	MS Leipzig 1492, 94–98
6.	XI	Anon.	*Lectio Guidonis*	GUILEC	Intervals and consonances	Smits v. W. in *Note d'Archivio* 13, 1936
7.	XI	Anon.	*Libelllus tonarius*	ANOLIT	Large tonary	Sowa, *Quellen..* (1935): 81–154
8.	XI	Anon.	*[Spicilegium Rivipullense]*	ANOSPI	Modal theory. No pitch indications	K.-W. Gümpel in *AfM* 35 (1978): 57–61
9.	XI	Anon.	*Monocordi mensura*	ANOMONR	Monochord division	MS Leipzig 1493, fol. 52v (Riemann)
10.	XI	Anon.	*Quom. de arithm.*	ANOQUOM	Conson., modes, "septem sunt voces"	*GS II:* 55–61
11.	late XI	Anon.	*Tract. cuius. monachi*	WFANON1	Conson., modes, interval notation	J. Wolf, *VfM* 9 (1893): 194–226
12.	late XI	Anon.	*Comm. in Micrologum*	GUICOMS	Consonances, species, modal theory	*SmitsE*, 93–172. From Liège
13.	late XI	Anon.	*Liber specierum*	ANOSPEG	Species theory	*SmitsE*, 15–17, 31–58
14.	late XI	Anon.	*[Tractatuli XI, XIII–VI]*	ANOTRA17	Gamut and intervals; proportions	Ox. Bodl., Rawl. C 270 (ed. Smits 1979)
15.	pre-1048	Berno	*Musica seu prolog. in ton.*	BERNPRO	Modal theory, species	No influence by Guido on Berno's theory
16.	pre-1054	Hermannus	*Musica*	HERMUSE	Consonances, modal theory	
17.	pre-1054	Hermannus	*Versus ad discern. cantum*	HERVER	*Ter terni sunt modi*, interval notation	
18.	1068–78	Aribo.	*De musica*	ARIDEM	Species, modal theory (*Micrologus*)	Refers to Wilhelm of Hirsau, Guido
19.	*c.* 1080	Theogerus	*De musica*	THEMUS	Consonances, species, modal theory	Refers to Boethius and Guido
20.	pre-1091	Wilhelm H.	*De musica*	WILMUS	Consonances, species, modal theory	Mentions Boethius, Odo, and Guido
21.	pre-1083	Heinrich A.	*De musica*	HEIMUS	Consonan., *diapason* as "equisonans"	In dialogue form
22.	*c.* 1100	Frutolfus	*Tonarius Frutolfi*	FRUTON	Large tonary	Ed. C. Vivell 1919, 113–183
23.	*c.* 1100	Anon. II	*Tractatus de musica*	ANO2TDM	Conson, monoch. div, Greek labels	*GS I:* 338–342

mention the syllables at all, relying only on the seven letters in their discussion of modal theory, intervals, diatonic species, and monochord divisions. Table 3.2 lists the sources that do refer to the syllables and specifies the actual context in which those references occur within the treatises.

At a glance, Table 3.1 shows that the teaching and understanding of chant theory remained solidly grounded on the seven letters long after Guido's *Epistola*. Key topics such as the division of the monochord, the diatonic species and intervals, the consonances, modal theory, and discant were solidly grounded on a heptachordal notion of musical space that had resulted in the A-G notational system around the year 1000. As a matter of fact, the development and transmission of several kinds of letter notation coincided with the compilation of the treatises of Table 3.1.[6]

References to Boethius' *De institutione musica* and the Greater Perfect System, including to the Greek pitch terminology (hypate, lichanos, etc.), remain frequent even in this practical-oriented branch of music theory. There is no sense that the classical (and Carolingian) articulation of the gamut into tetrachords was being perceived as either outdated or somehow out of step with the medieval musical mindset or with new trends in musical practice. On the contrary, the tetrachordal units are still described as essential for an understanding of the octave, often described as representing the full diatonic variety of the gamut. Long before Renaissance humanism the medieval *magistri* – whether legitimately or not – saw their musical system as directly linked with that of classical antiquity.

The superimposition of different systems of pitch designation in the late Middle Ages – Greek names, A-G letters, and *ut-la* syllables – corroborates a well-known thesis, i.e., that the synthesis of speculative (Boethian) and practical music theory in the Carolingian era (primarily through Hucbald and the *Alia musica*) essentially guaranteed the perpetuation of the Greater Perfect System of the classical tradition at least until the sixteenth century. The double octave from *proslambanomenos* to *nete hyperbolaion* was of course extended to D-*sol* by Guido of Arezzo, and could not fully account for the intervallic variety of the vast body of chant melodies. Yet for centuries to come it remained the primary vehicle for understanding and visualizing the diatonic space, and served as the starting point for any discussion of the music fundamentals, such as intervals, modes, and consonances.[7]

---

[6] Colk Santosuosso, *Letter Notations in the Middle Ages*.

[7] See Bower, "The Transmission of Ancient Music Theory into the Middle Ages," pp. 136–67; and Cohen, "Notes, Scales, and Modes in the Earlier Middle Ages," pp. 307–8.

Furthermore, the persistence of the tetrachordal articulation of the gamut throughout the Middle Ages was no mere "theoretical inertia," or a mere appeal to the authority of the ancients. In what might be seen as a veiled reference to the fifth-generated scale of the *Enchiriadis* treatises, the anonymous *Quaestiones in musica* of c. 1100 explains that the tetrachord cycle, after the octave, is the one that best matches the series of tones and semitones of the gamut. The passage is ostensibly about the role of the tetrachord in the division of the monochord, but it can be read as an indirect statement on the primacy of the *septem discrimina vocum* within the musical system and of the tetrachord as a privileged subset of the octave. The reasoning by trial and error proposed by the author is of interest here in that it is thoroughly empirical, thus indicative, if only in a minimal sense, of a conceptualization of musical space that had practical and perceptual implications:

Quare magis dividatur monocordum per tetracorda quam per dicorda vel tricorda vel pentacorda. Divisum esse monocordum in tetracorda potius quam in dicorda vel tricorda vel pentacorda hec est ratio, quod nulla post diapason in nullo tanta est ut in tetracordis similitudo. Si enim in dicorda facta fuisset divisio, primum occurreret dissimilitudo, quia post tonum, qui est ab A in B, sequitur semitonium. Si autem in tricorda, itidem diversitas semitonia obsideret; nam post semiditonum, qui est ab A in C, sequeretur ditonus, qui est [a] C in E. At si divisio fuisset per pentacorda, eadem dissimilitudinis obviaret importunitas, quoniam quidem ab A in E est diapente, et ibi est semitonium faciens dissimilitudinem.

[Why is the monochord divided more often in tetrachords than in bichords, trichords, or pentachords? This is so because after the diapason the similarities of pitches at the fourth is the strongest among other intervals. For instance, if you divided the monochord in bichords, a break in the pattern would appear right away, because after the tone from A to B there is a semitone. If you divide it in trichords, the diversity of the semitone would emerge again, for after the minor third from A to C there is the ditone from C to E. And if you adopt a division into pentachords, the same break in similarity occurs because the fifth A-E would be followed by a semitone, which would be a non-matching interval [with the A-B tone of the earlier pentachord].][8]

Significantly, the possibility of a hexachordal articulation of the gamut does not even cross the author's mind.

The titles numbered 33–8 of Table 3.1 form an especially important subset, as they document the twelfth-century Cistercian reform of chant and

[8] R. Steglich, ed., *Die* Quaestiones in musica: *Ein Choraltraktat des zentralen Mittelalters und ihr mutmasslicher Verfasser Rudolf von St. Trond (1070–1138)* (Leipzig: Breitkopf und Härtel, 1911), p. 15, translation mine.

chant theory. It is striking that none of these sources appears to have any use for the six syllables, considering that they originated at a time when Guido's guidelines for sight singing were presumably gaining ground across the Continent.⁹ True, the historical significance of Guido of Cherlieu's text, with its detailed exposition of chant theory, is somewhat lessened by the fact that it is preserved in only one manuscript source dating to the early thirteenth century.¹⁰ All the key texts of the Cistercian musical reform, however, consistently adopt a "letters-only" approach to pitch denomination, suggesting that some long-standing institutions of music making, such as monasteries, cathedral schools, and musical chapels, may have routinely avoided the hexachordal system for a prolonged period of time. At the same time, there is evidence suggesting that the *ut-la* syllables in time did penetrate the Cistercian monasteries, to judge from the few Guidonian hands and other occasional references to the syllables found in sources connected with that order (see Table 3.6 below).¹¹

For instance, the chant treatise *Musica manualis*, probably from the fourteenth century, borrows lengthy excerpts from Guido Augensis, here called "Guido junior."¹² At the same time, the treatise not only provides a full account of the rudiments of solmization, but it also inserts routinely Guidonian syllables in place of Augensis' letters-only pitch designations.¹³

---

⁹ These sources include the preface to the reformed antiphonary beginning with the words *Cantus quem Cisterciensis*, which in the mid-twelfth century was distributed to the Cistercian houses with the antiphonary itself; the introductory letter by St. Bernard (*Inter cetera ques optime aemulati sunt*). For a modern edition, see F. J. Guentner, ed., *Epistola S. Bernardi De revisione cantus Cisterciensis, et Tractatus Cantum quem Cisterciensis*, CSM 24 (N.p.: American Institute of Musicology, 1974), and the far more substantial *Regule de arte musica*, attributed to Guy de Cherlieu (abbot Guido Augensis), now available in the edition of C. Maître, ed., *La réforme cistercienne du plain-chant. Étude d'un traité théorique* (Beernem, Belgium: Brecht, 1995).

¹⁰ Paris, St Geneviève, MS 2284, fol. 84–109v.

¹¹ A Guidonian Hand, for instance, was drawn on the last folio of an antiphonary for the monastery of Morimondo (West of Milan) more than a century after the original copying of the manuscript. See C. Maître, ed., *Un antiphonaire cistercien pour le temporal: XIIe siècle: Paris, Bibliothèque Nationale de France, Nouvelles acquisitions Latines 1411* (Poitiers: Maison des sciences de l'homme et de la société de Poitiers: Centre d'études supérieures de civilisation médiévale, 1998), fol. 202.

¹² The discussion that follows builds on my discussion of this topic in "*Si quis manus non habeat*: Charting Non-Hexachordal Musical Practices in the Age of Solmization," *EMH* 26 (2007), 181–210.

¹³ After quoting the verses of the hymn of St John, the anonymous author adds the following (and somewhat deceptive) sentence: "Quod traditum reor primitus a Guydone seniore, qui hunc versum ponit in musica sua, variis eum cantibus exempli causa nobilitans" (J. Wylde, *Musica manualis cum tonale*, ed. C. Sweeney, CSM 28 (Neuhausen-Stuttgart: American Institute of Musicology, 1982), p. 62).

The only known copy of the *Musica manualis* was entered in MS Lansdowne 763 by John Wylde, a lay priest and *praeceptor* of music at the Augustinian Waltham Abbey of the Holy Cross in the second quarter of the fifteenth century. It is significant that Wylde also copied the *Metrologus* – a thirteenth-century English commentary on Guido's *Micrologus* that favors the use of the syllables (more on this below) – in a later section of Lansdowne 763. Thus, there seems to be little doubt that Wylde regularly introduced his choir singers to the rudiments of solmization, even though the Cistercian chant reform was an important component of his teaching.[14] In short, the Augustinian *Musica manualis* documents the circulation of Cistercian music theory in non-Cistercian monastic communities, and of the relative flexibility that accompanied that transmission.[15] Along the same lines, one of the most influential Franciscan treatises of music, Egidius de Zamora's *Ars musicorum*, deals extensively with the six syllables, even though it is also rooted in Cistercian theory.[16]

Several patterns of transmission emerge from the sources listed in Table 3.2. Most prominent is the tendency to refer to the syllables only in passing and only once or twice in the entire treatise, typically in a graph, in musical examples, on the musical Hand, or on the page margins (see Table 3.2. n. 2–3 and 7–12). The fact that the syllables appear in these particular contexts points to them as a rule of thumb transmitted orally and rather casually from teacher to student. Although their use may have been broader and more pervasive than the list suggests, it is significant that the authors of this period do not seem concerned with providing a theoretical justification for resorting to them.

Table 3.2 also documents the custom of "retrofitting" the syllables to older pedagogical writings that originally had none. A case in point is the fifteenth-century copy of the *Dialogus de musica* that is preserved in Venice, Biblioteca Marciana, VIII 24 (Table 3.2, n. 1). In it, virtually all pitch

---

[14] For a discussion of the references to the three hexachordal properties in the *Musica manualis*, see B. J. Blackburn, "Properchant: English Theory at Home and Abroad, with an Excursus on Amerus/Aluredus and his Tradition," in D. B. Cannata, G. Ilnitchi Currie, R. C. Mueller, and J. L. Nádas, eds., *Quomodo cantabimus canticum? Studies in Honor of Edward H. Roesner*, Miscellanea 7 (Middleton, WI: American Institute of Musicology, 2008), pp. 81–98, esp. 82–3 and 86–7. My thanks to Dr. Blackburn for sending me a copy of her study prior to publication.

[15] A comparable freedom characterized the modeling of new tonaries onto pre-existing ones. See Michel Huglo's comments on the creation of the Dominican tonary from the Cistercian one in the thirteenth century (*Les Tonaires: inventaire, analyse, comparaison* (Paris: Société Française de Musicologie, 1971), p. 372).

[16] C. Meyer, "Die Tonartenlehre im Mittelalter," in T. Ertelt and F. Zaminer, eds., *Die Lehre von einstimmigen liturgischen Gesang, Gechichte der Musiktheorie* 4 (Darmstadt: Wissenschaftliche Buchgesellschaft, 2000), p. 183.

designations are expressed not with the seven letters, as in Pseudo-Odo's original text, but rather as *loci* (i.e., as *D la sol re* rather than simply as *D*). Berno's *Prologue* is included in this list (Table 3.2, n. 11) only because one of its fourteenth-century sources (Vatican Library, Reg. lat. 1146) intersperses with the text an image of the gamut with letters and syllables (reproduced in the *TML* site).[17]

There is evidence that the formula beginning "Primus cum sexto fa sol la semper habeto," designed for the recognition of the modes, was also appended to musical texts that were originally syllables-free (Table 3.2, n. 5–6). It appears, for instance, in a fifteenth-century Italian manuscript after a twelfth-century *Tractatus de musica* of Cistercian provenance.[18] When Adrien de La Fage included the *Tractatus* in his *Essais*, he added the modal formula, describing it as part of a longer appendix that he thought contemporaneous with the *Tractatus*.[19] Accordingly, the *TML* includes the formula in its twelfth-century filelist (as of February 25, 2009). These verses, however, are not documented in sources from that period, and most likely originated after *c.* 1250. The purpose of the formula was to remind church singers that the same melodic incipits belong to different modal categories:

Primus cum sexto fa sol la semper habeto
Tertius et octavus ut re fa atque secundus … [etc.].
[The first and the sixth modes will take fa sol la,
The second, the third and the eighth ut re fa …][20]

It is interesting that the St. Martiale treatise introduces these verses as a *rude documentum tonorum, sed valde utile … his qui intelligent* ("rudimentary

[17] The source is Vatican City, Reg. lat. 1146, fol. 17–21. My list does not include the *Ars musyce* (*TML*: WFANON2B), the *Ars musyce armonie* (*TML*: ANOARSMA), the *Ars et modus pulsandi organa* (*TML*: ANOAMPO) or the *Vatican Organum Treatise* (*TML*: ADORFAC), which date to the thirteenth or fourteenth centuries, even though the *TML* lists them in the twelfth-century filelist. The *Ars musyce* and *Ars musyce armonie* belong to the textual tradition of Ps. Thomas Aquinas and cannot have originated prior to ca. 1270. See M. Bernhard, *Die Thomas von Aquin zugeschriebenen Musiktraktate* (Munich: Bayerische Akademie der Wissenschaften, 2006), pp. 66–75.

[18] The source is Florence, Biblioteca Nazionale, II I 406, fols. 1–5. Jacques Handschin and Albert Seay placed the origin of this treatise in late-twelfth- or early-thirteenth-century St. Martial of Limoges; Sarah Fuller later recognized the distinctly Cistercian terminology and mode of exposition of the treatise. See A. Seay, "An Anonymous Treatise from St. Martial," *Annales musicologiques* 5 (1957): 13–42, and S. Fuller, "An Anonymous Treatise dictus de Sancto Martiale: a New Source for Cistercian Music Theory," *MD* 31 (1977): 5–30.

[19] The text of the complete appendix is now available in a transcription by Christian Meyer at www.lml.badw.de/info/i-fn406a.htm and www.lml.badw.de/info/i-fn406b.htm (a later section on discant).

[20] A. de la Fage, *Essais de diphthérographie musicale* (Paris: Legouix, 1864; repr. Amsterdam: Frits A. M. Knuf, 1964), p. 362, translation mine.

formula of the modes, yet useful to those who understand it"). Its useful-ness depends on the singer's familiarity with the entire psalm tones, as well as with as modal finals and ranges. Once again, the syllables serve as a pre-cious mnemonic clue that is, however, to be properly contextualized.

The "Primus cum sexto" modal formula also appears in the "Erfurt cento," a miscellany of excerpts originally from the eleventh and twelfth centuries and copied in the late thirteenth century, according to Adolf Becker.[21] The Erfurt cento may be taken as a symbol of the uneven penetration of the Guidonian syllables in the late Middle Ages; the source, however, is also problematic due to the incompetence and the sloppiness of its copyist. Most of its text avoids the Guidonian syllables altogether, except for the mnemonic formula "Primus cum sexto fa sol la semper habeto" (fol. 83v) and for the *Tetrachordenlehre* that follows (culled from Theogerus of Metz), which was updated according to the more common, thirteenth-century pitch denominations yoking *litterae* and *voces* (see Table 3.3).

Finally, Table 3.2 points to the significant role played by English theorists toward the development of the solmization system. The relevant sources here are not only the ones by Pseudo-Osbern of Canterbury (ca. 1100) and Theinred of Dover (ca. 1200), but also the above-mentioned *De musica* by John Cotto, who may have received his musical training in England, around 1080–1100, possibly before moving Afflighem, near Brussels, and eventually to Southern Germany, where he wrote his treatise.[22] In the post-Guidonian era, English authors appear to have had a special interest in the *ut-la* syl-lables, assigning them to new positions within the gamut. For instance, an early English compilation of music theory that Smits attributed to Osbern of Canterbury (Table 3.2, n. 5), may be one of the first to place the syllable *ut* not only on C and G, but also on F (see Fig. 3.1).[23] Typically, however, the Guidonian syllables appear throughout this manuscript only in the tables illustrating the consonances, never in the main text. Likewise, Theinred of

[21] See A. Becker: "Ein Erfurter Traktat über gregorianische Musik," *Archiv für Musikwissenschaft* 1 (1918–19), 145–65; A complete edition of the treatise is at 151–61. The cento is found in Erfurt, Wissenschaftliche Allgemeinbibliothek, Ampl. in 8° 94, fol. 80r-84r. Becker's original description of this text as a homogeneous "treatise" was later rejected. See the discussion of this point in Lochner, "Dietger (Theogerus) of Metz and his *Musica*," 297–303.

[22] That is now the generally accepted theory, first proposed by Huglo ("L'auteur", pp. 15–19) See also Babb, trans., *Hucbald, Guido, and John*, pp. 90–5.

[23] The source is Oxford, Bodleian Library, Rawlinson C 270, from ca. 1100. For its content, see J. Smits van Waesberghe, ed., *Codex Oxoniensis: Biblioteca Bodleiana, Rawlinson C 270*, Divitie Musicae Artis A. 10, 2 vols. (Buren: Frits Knuf, 1979), Pars A: Osbern of Canterbury (?), "'De vocum consonantiis' and 'De re musica'"; Pars B: "XVII tractatuli a quodam studioso peregrino ad annum MC collecti."

Table 3.3. Theogerus' *Musica* (chs. 10 and 11) compared with the relevant passage in the Erfurt cento

Theogerus, *Musica*, chs. 10–11 (ed. Lochner, p. 19).	Erfurt version ("Becker anonymous"), Becker, "Ein Erfurter," p. 161.
Ch. 10 De tetrachordis. […] Tetrachordum gravium ideo dicitur, quia graves voces ibi sonent. Tetrachordum finalium ideo dicitur, quia omnis regularis cantus ibi finitur. Tetrachordum superiorum ideo dicitur, quia superiores voces ibi sonent. Tetrachordum excellentium ideo dicitur, quia excellentiores voces ibi sonant. Ch. 11. Quomodo constent tetrachorda. Primum autem tetrachordum **constat ex tono, et semitonio et tono, et fit ab A. gravi usque in D. grave**. Secundum tetrachordum (similiter) **constat ex tono, et semitonio et tono, et fit a D. gravi usque in C. (G) grave**. Tertium tetrachordum **constat (item) ex tono, et semitonio et tono, et fit ab a. acuto usque in d. acutum**. Quartum tetrachordum (sicut et praecedentia) **constat ex tono, et semitonio et tono, et fit a d. acuto usque in g. acutum** […]	Tetrachordum gravium idcirco dicitur, quia graves voces ibi sonant, **et constat ex tono et semitonio et tono et fit ab A re gravi usque in D sol re grave**. Tetrachordum finalium idcirco dicitur, quia omnis regularis cantus ibi finitur **et constat ex tono et semitonio et tono, et sic a D sol re gravi usque in G sol re ut grave**. Tetrachordum superiorum dicitur, quia omnes voces superiores insonant **et constat ex tono et semitonio et tono et fit ab a la mi re acuto usque in d la sol re acutum**. Tetrachordum excellentium dicitur, quia excellentiores voces insonant, **et constat ex tono et semitonio et tono et fit a d la sol re acuto usque in g sol re ut acutum**.

Dover's *De legitimis ordinibus pentachordorum et tetrachordorum*, from the late twelfth century, surveys the distances between the pitches only through the seven letters in the main text, but adds the syllables on several accompanying graphs (Table 3.2, n. 12). Fig. 3.2 shows a reproduction of one of them from the only extant source of Theinred's treatise (Oxford, Bodleian Library, 842, late fourteenth century). One interesting feature of this graph is that the *ut-la* syllables are positioned only on the three basic pitches (G, C, and F) on the upper part of the table, whereas the placement of the syllables *tri, pro, de, nos, te, ad* and of the tone-semitone indications in the central part of the table implies the derivation of chromatic pitches. John Snyder has suggested that the solmization syllables in Theinred's tables may be later additions.[24]

---

[24] J. Snyder, "A Road Not Taken: Theinred of Dover's Theory of Species," *Journal of the Royal Musical Association* 115, (1990): 149; for an edition of Theinred's treatise, see Theinred of Dover, *De legitimis ordinibus pentachordorum et tetrachordorum: a critical text and translation,*

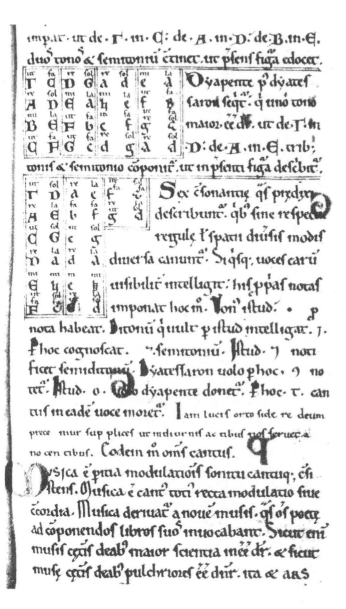

Fig. 3.1. Oxford, Bodleian Library, Rawlinson 270, fol. 3r.

Time and again, the music-theoretical sources from the eleventh and twelfth centuries confirm the impression that hexachordal solmization was not a major focus of liturgical musical training. Instead, the theorists of

with an introduction, annotations, and indices by J. Snyder (Ottawa: Institute of Mediaeval Music, 2006); see also J. Snyder, "Theinred of Dover on Consonance: A Chapter in the History of Harmony," *Music Theory Spectrum* 5 (1983): 110–20.

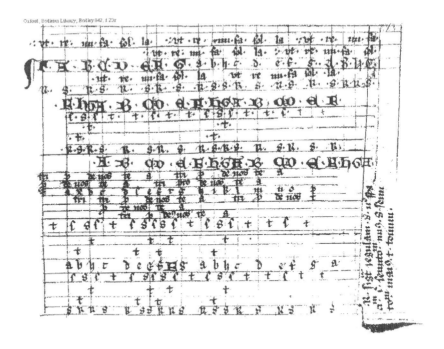

Fig. 3.2. Oxford, Bodleian Library, Bodley 842, fol. 23r.

the generations immediately after Guido were occupied by other pressing issues, such as developing pitch-specific types of notation that would facilitate the transmission and the teaching of liturgical chant, editing numerous chant melodies to realign them with the rules governing the church tones, and finally regulating the theory and practice of *organum* and improvised polyphony.[25]

Ironically, it was Guido himself who greatly contributed to the successful establishment of a notion of diatonic system that was based on the seven letters. In *Micrologus* – by far the most widely transmitted pedagogical treatise of the Middle Ages, preserved in around one hundred extant sources – Guido relies on the letters in virtually all topics of instruction, from the initial divisions of the monochord to the discussion of *affinitas, modi vocum,* and *organum* theory. In the *Prologus in antiphonarium,* the same letters function as clefs in musical notation. In his recent study on the transmission of *Micrologus,* Christian Meyer draws a direct relationship between the strong success of the treatise in the first two hundred years of its reception history and the contemporaneous Gregorian reform movement that

---

[25] For an overview of these issues, see Meyer, "Die Tonartenlehre im Mittelalter," pp. 135–215.

led to the general adoption of the musical staff and to a reform of the modal
system, among other changes in musical practice and pedagogy.[26]

But the reception history of *Micrologus* also highlights the marginal status of the six syllables within the entire written transmission of Guido's treatises and of Latin music theory as a whole. Elsewhere I have observed that
the overwhelming majority of medieval writers on music, from John Cotto
to the late fifteenth century, do not credit Guido with the invention of the
syllables, while they often mention him in connection with the expansion
of the gamut, the division of the monochord, and the invention of the staff.
Furthermore Guido's *Epistola*, which survives in more than fifty sources
from the eleventh to the fifteenth century, goes virtually unmentioned in
the corpus of Latin theory until a group of theorists active in Italy began
discussing the issue of the origins of solmization in the late *quattrocento*.[27]

Guido's *Micrologus* was both copied more frequently and cited more
often than the *Epistola*, yet its transmission history remained completely
syllables-free, as also did that of the *Prologus* and of the *Regule rithmice*. To
be sure, the text of the *Regule* in the Ottobeuren MS features the syllables
ut-la superimposed onto the pitch letters in the first presentation of the
gamut (v. 20).[28] Even this source, however, does not contradict the story
told by all the remaining ones, namely, that the six syllables entered medieval musical practice and theory from the side window rather than from the
front door, and – should any lingering doubts remain – without challenging
the pre-existing, letter-based diatonic order.

At the same time, however, the occasional wording in a treatise points
to the slow but steady rise of interest in the six syllables as an object of
theoretical investigation. One commentary of *Micrologus* that relies
extensively on the six syllables is the already mentioned thirteenth-century
English treatise called *Metrologus*.[29] The anonymous author of this treatise

---

[26] On the reception of Guido's *Micrologus* in the Middle Ages, see C. Meyer, "La tradition du
Micrologus de Guy d'Arezzo: une contribution a l'histoire de la reception du texte," *Revue
de Musicologie* 83 (1997): 5–31; M. T. Rosa Barezzani, "Guido d'Arezzo fra tradizione e
innovazione," in A. Rusconi, ed., *Guido d'Arezzo monaco pomposiano. Atti dei Convegni di
studio, Codigoro (Ferrara), Abbazia di Pomposa 3 ottobre 1997; Arezzo, Biblioteca Città di
Arezzo, 29–30 maggio 1998* (Florence: Olschki, 2000), pp. 133–49, and C. Ruini, "Eredità di
Guido nei teorici dei secoli XIII e XIV," in A. Rusconi, ed., *Guido d'Arezzo monaco pomposiano*,
pp. 171–7.

[27] On this topic see my "*Si quis manus non habeat*," 190–1.

[28] *PesceGA*, p. 324. Ironically, Gerbert took the Ottobeuren reading as the model for his
printed edition of the *Regule* (*GS* II, pp. 25–34). No doubt, this particular representation has
contributed to the widespread belief that Guido's entire musical pedagogy was grounded on a
hexachordal parsing of musical space. Significantly, Gaston Allaire refers precisely to that graph
in support of his hexachordal method of analysis. See his *The Theory of Hexachords*, p. 16.

[29] For an edition of this treatise, see *Smits E.* pp. 61–92.

approaches Guido's original text with a considerable degree of latitude. On the one hand, the sections on intervals and species are much expanded and recast in hexachordal terms, as shown in Table 3.4:

Table 3.4. Textual parallels between Guido's *Micrologus* (ch. 4, central comma) and *Metrologus* (significant divergences marked in bold)

MICROLOGUS, ch. 4	METROLOGUS
Diatessaron autem est, cum inter duas voces quocumque modo duo sunt toni et unum semitonium, **ut ab .A. ad .D. et a .B. in .E. et reliqua.** Diapente vero uno tono maior est, cum inter quaslibet voces tres sunt toni et unum semitonium, **ut ab .A. [-105-] in .E. et a .C. in .G. et reliqua.**	De diatessaron. Diatessaron est quaedam vox, quae habet in se duos plenos tonos et dimidium, id est semitonum, sicut **ut-fa, fa-ut, re-sol, sol-re, mi-la, la-mi,** tam in gravibus quam in acutis et superacutis. De diapente. Diapente est quaedam vox, quae habet in se tres plenos tonos et [-75-] dimidium, id est semitonum, sicut **ut-sol, sol-ut, re-la, la-re, mi-mi, mi-mi, fa-fa, fa-fa,** tam in gravibus quam in acutis et superacutis.[30]

On the other hand, the author of *Metrologus* completely omits Guido's meticulous presentation of the diatonic affinities (*Micrologus*, chapters 7–9), so that the six syllables operate in a sort of theoretical vacuum in spite of their textual prominence. And on one occasion the new wording adopted by *Metrologus* marks a significant departure from Guido's original text (see Table 3.5):

Table 3.5. Textual parallels between Guido's *Micrologus* (ch. 4, last comma) and *Metrologus* (significant divergences marked in bold)

MICROLOGUS	METROLOGUS
Habes itaque sex vocum consonantias, id est tonum, semitonium, ditonum, semiditonum, diatessaron et diapente. In nullo enim cantu aliis modis vox voci coniungitur, vel intendendo vel remittendo. Cumque tam paucis **clausulis** tota harmonia formetur, utillimum est altae eas memoriae commendare, et donec plene in canendo sentiantur et cognoscantur, ab exercitio numquam cessare, ut his velut clavibus habitis canendi possis peritiam sagaciter ideoque facilius possidere.	De notis vel syllabis **Sex sunt notae vel syllabae in quibus totus cantus disponitur, scilicet Ut Re Mi Fa Sol La.** Cumque tam paucis **notis vel syllabis** tota harmonia formetur, utillimum est altae eas memoriae commendare.[31]

---

[30] Guido of Arezzo, *Micrologus*, Smits E, p. 74.

[31] Guido of Arezzo, *Micrologus*, Smits E, pp. 105–6; *Smits E*, pp. 71–2.

Reporting a doctrine that was well established in his generation, Guido had spoken of six interval types (*sex vocum consonantias* or *clausulae*) as the building blocks of all melodies. To him, learning to recognize and perform these intervals at sight, or from memory, was the primary goal of musical training for church singers. A couple of hundred years later the author of *Metrologus* subtly but dramatically altered Guido's original passage by describing the six *notae vel syllabae, ut-la*, as "the basis of all harmony." This passage may be among the earliest ones to assign something of a foundational significance to the six syllables, inasmuch as it portrays them as necessary to harmony (*tota harmonia formetur*). In hindsight, this excerpt may be viewed as the initial fluttering of the butterfly that will lead to a powerful hurricane in a different place and time (see Chapters 6 and 7). Aside from such large-scale connections, however, it matters to observe that the conceptual weight and status of the syllables changes substantially the moment that they become the object of theoretical investigation. As long as they were simply "retrofitted" to pre-existing texts, pitches, and melodies (as they were in the sources of Table 3.2), they were no more than a practical tool for effectively navigating the gamut. But *Metrologus* documents an important change of perspective, a *mutatio* of sorts by which the syllables were portrayed no longer as a tool for singing unknown chants, but rather as musical "agents" in their own right capable of affecting "harmony."

A quick Hand count

To point out that the musical treatises until ca. 1250 tended to bypass the six syllables altogether obviously is not to argue that contemporaneous singers routinely avoided them. The casual references to the six syllables in eleventh- and twelfth-century sources, and the ease with which syllables could be added or omitted in the process of transmission of musical treatises, leaves open the possibility that hexachordal solmization was more common than suggested by the written evidence. Alternatively, a good portion of pedagogical treatises may have been lost – though it is difficult to imagine that these lost sources would significantly alter the current picture of the transmission of Guidonian theory. The method of Guido's syllables could have been transmitted orally for generations – passed on informally from one *cantor* to the next – before it was committed to paper. Nevertheless, it is significant that the composite picture emerging from the pedagogical treatises does not ascribe a prominent role to hexachordal solmization. It is certainly possible to imagine a scenario in which solmization did play a central role in medieval musical pedagogy and notational practices in its first two hundred years of existence.

Additional corroboration for these findings comes from a study of the written transmission of one the most popular devices at the center of the practice of solmization, namely the so-called Guidonian Hand, used by medieval and Renaissance singers as a visual tool for understanding the rudiments of musical space and for learning new melodies. The practice of the musical Hand was rooted in orality and memory; it was conceived as a "portable map" of musical space to which budding singers could turn to refresh their memory of pitches and intervals, particularly when a monochord was not available. Karol Berger has interpreted the practice of the musical Hand as one important chapter of the medieval art of memory, which was boosted in the late thirteenth century by the renewed interest in the rhetorical treatises by Cicero, the anonymous *Rhetorica ad Herennium* (then also thought to be by Cicero), and Quintilian.[32] When theorists such as Marchetto of Padua (*Lucidarium,* ca. 1318) and Johannes Tinctoris (*Expositio manus,* 1473) referred to the "places" of the notes on the Hand as *loca*, they were openly connecting them with the virtual *loca* of the mind by which the Ciceronian orator was able to commit to memory an entire speech.

Because it was an expression of oral culture, it is difficult to assess the precise ways in which medieval singers and musicians used the Hand. Yet, for the same reason the images of musical Hands that have come down to us in written form provide a *prima facie* indication not only on the actual popularity of this method – and by extension of Guidonian solmization in general – but also on the specific information conveyed by different types of Hands at different times. As it is always the case when dealing with past cultures, our only option is to interrogate the written testimonies on the scope and the magnitude of particular aspects of the oral traditions.

In his landmark study of music education in the Middle Ages and Renaissance, Joseph Smits van Waesberghe reproduced about two-dozen musical Hands from the eleventh to the sixteenth century.[33] Together, they display a considerable variety in the kind of information they provide. While some of them are "classical" Guidonian Hands, carrying letters and syllables on the nineteen finger joints of the hand, others display

---

[32] See K. Berger, "The Hand and the Art of Memory," 87–120.

[33] Smits van Waesberghe, *Musikerziehung. Lehre und Theorie der Musik im Mittelalter,* pp. 120–43, figs. 58–84.

only the pitches expressed in alphabetic letters. A few others refer to the rudiments of modal theory and to the diatonic intervals. Other more complex types also contain several lines of text and illustrate the division of the monochord (in one case) and the position of the notes on the staff. While it seems plausible to assume that all these subtypes may have played slightly different functions, there is still some uncertainty about precisely how and to what extent this mnemonic device was used, let alone by which categories of musicians and singers and in which specific circumstances.[34]

The following inventory of the Guidonian hands preserved in the extant manuscript sources of Latin theory is by all means preliminary, since many of those sources have not been readily available for first-hand inspection. Even so, it points to definite patterns of transmission that are central to our understanding of the history of the hexachordal system, and it provides indirect information on the extent to which singers used solmization in musical practice not only in the early phases of training, but also – through acquired habit – during their entire musical careers. The current list (see Tables 3.6, 3.7, and 3.8 below) results from collating the information from existing reference works on the sources of medieval and Renaissance music and other secondary sources, as well as on a partial first-hand survey of the primary sources. Most of the information has been culled from the recently completed *RISM* catalogue of music theory sources up to ca. 1500, as well as from the *TML,* the *LmL,* and other modern editions of medieval music theory.[35] In particular, the manuscript descriptions published in *RISM* provide a convenient starting point for a preliminary catalogue of musical Hands in Latin theory, as they consistently signal the occurrence of graphs, tables, and musical Hands in each manuscript.[36] The three tables that constitute the inventory represent three broad geographic areas of origin of the manuscripts, in accordance with *RISM* attributions: Table 3.6 lists sources

---

[34] For a recent overview of the use of the musical Hand, particularly in the early modern era, see S. Weiss, "The Singing Hand," in C. Richter Sherman and P. M. Lukehart, eds., *Writing on Hands: Memory and Knowledge in Early Modern Europe* (Carlisle, PA: Trout Gallery, Dickinson College, and Washington, D.C.: Folger Shakespeare Library, 2000), pp. 35–45 and Weiss, *"Diese manum tuam si vis bene discere Cantum*: Symbols of Learning Music in Early Modern Europe," *Music in Art* 30 (2005), 35–74.

[35] C. Meyer, Michel Huglo, *et al.*, eds., *RISM* B/III, 6 vols. (Munich: Henle Verlag, 1961–2003).

[36] In particular, the last and massive volume of the series integrates detailed information on manuscripts that had been described somewhat approximately during the early phases of the project (especially vols. 1–3).

Table 3.6. Guidonian Hands from Central Europe (*c.* 1050–1500)

N.	Source	Folio	Date	Origin	*RISM* B/III	Facsimiles – Notes
1.	Vienna 55	168v	End X	Germany	I, 36–7; VI, 62	*SmitsM*, fig. 70 Boethius, *enchiriadis*, Hermannus
2.	Munich 14965b	29v	c. 1100	St. Emmeram, Regensb.	III, 127–8; VI, 340	*SmitsM*, fig. 64. Letters, syllables, T-S indications
3.	Munich 7907	131	XII	Cistercian ab. (Germany)	III, 101–2; VI, 330	Cistercian antiphonary
4.	Graz 1584	48v	XII	Austria. Seckau?	VI, 16	Sequentiary
5.	Vienna 51	2v	XII	St. Emmeram – Cluny	I, 33–6; VI, 61	*SmitsM*, fig. 66. Guido, Herm., Cicero, geom., astron.
6.	Kassel Math. 1	45	XII	Southern Germany	III, 67–72; VI, 307	Guido, Hermann, Aribo, Frutolfus
7.	Rochester 92 1200	93v	XII	Austria or Bavaria	IV, 183–6; VI, 730	*SmitsM*, fig. 69. Hand is on the last *verso* of the MS
8.	Wolfenbüttel 334	4v	2nd hf XII	Augsb., St. Ulrich & Afra	III, 212–7; VI, 368	*SmitsG*, 113, fig. 13. Guido, Ps.-Odo, Herm., Udasc.
9.	Munich 9921	flyleaf	1160	Ottobeuren	III, 103–7; VI, 331	*SmitsG*, 129; *SmitsM*, fig. 65. Guido, Herm, Berno
10.	Vienna 787	46v	End XII	Baumgartenberg, Cisterc.	I, 37–9; VI, 66	*SmitsM*, fig. 73. Theogerus, Guido, Aribo
11.	Munich 18961	51v	End XII	Tegernsee	III, 142; VI, 345	Theogerus of Metz
12.	Heiligenkreutz 20	4	End XII	Heiligenkreutz? (Cist.)	VI, 16	Large cist. antiphonary, hymmary, canticles
13.	Graz 1010	70v	XIII	Neuberg (Cistercian)	VI, 15	Glossary of Osbern of Gloucester
14.	Rome lat. 3101	74v	XIII	Ilmmünster, Bavaria	II, 93–4; VI, 563	MS copied in 1077. See *SmitsM*, p. 134 and fig. 71
15.	Munich 9599	97r	XIII	Ab. Alderspach (Cisterc.)	NOT LISTED	*SmitsM*, fig. 67
16.	Munich 5539	1	End XIII	Regensburg	III, 91–4; VI, 328	See Göllner ed. of the MS (*MSD* 43) (hand not shown)
17.	Melk 109	1v	Early XIV	Regensburg?	VI, 28	Gradual
18.	Frankfurt a.M. VII 92	2v	1st hf XIV	Frankf., Dominican conv.	VI, 298	Source consists of two folios

No.	Manuscript	Folio	Date	Place	References	Description
19.	London 18347	27	XIV	Germany	IV, 43; VI, 388	*SmitsM*, fig. 75. Writings on canon law, sermons.
20.	Wilhering 28	front cover	XIV	Wilhering	I, 48; VI, 104	
21.	St. Florian XI.649	128r	XIV	St. Florian?	I, 32; VI, 52	
22.	Karlsruhe 29ª	1	XIV	SW Germany (Cisterc.)	III, 66–7; VI, 306	Theogerus, counterpoint treatise
23.	Erfurt 8° 93	1	hf 2nd XIV	Germ. (Coll Amplonian.?)	VI, 286	*SmitsM*, fig. 77; Guido, Cotto, Berno, Ps.-Odo, form
24.	Uppsala C 55	42v	End XIV	Prague?	VI, 694–5	Cntp, Ps.-Osbern, philos., Sacrob., *Distica Cathon.*
25.	Vienna 4702	87r	ca. 1400	UNKNOWN	I, 45; VI, 86	
26.	Prague V.H.21	137v	c. 1415	Czech	V, 13; VI, 144	Solm. treatise, grammar, rhetorique, *ars metrica*
27.	Frankfurt a.M. 170	129	1419	Constance or Reichenau?	III, 51; VI, 298	Tonary, chant treatise, *Legenda aurea*
28.	Munich 7614	87	c. 1420	Abbey of Indersdorf	III, 100; VI, 330	Solmization, modal theory, astronomical writings
29.	St. Gallen 937	694–5	1424	Southern Germany	VI, 718–9	*SmitsM*, fig. 78. Chant treatise
30.	Munich 6037	115v	1448	Ab. St. Sebast./Ebersberg	III, 98; VI, 329	Solm., *Intervallehre*, modal theory, Latin grammar
31.	Wroclaw I.Q.466	144v	1st hf. XV	UNKNOWN	V, 50; VI, 658	Solm. treat. by Nic. De Cosil; mel. of theol., poetry
32.	Erfurt 4° 375	61v	1st hf XV	Erf. Coll. Amplonianum	VI, 284	Solm. treat., computus, astronom. tables, grammar
33.	Munich 19818	272; 272v	1ˢᵗ hfXV	prov. Tegernsee	III, 149; VI, 347	Johannes de Muris
34.	Melk 1099	23; 37	Mid XV	Monastery of Melk	VI, 36–8	Large MS; chant theory, astronomy, *ars memorativa*
35.	Erlangen 613	319	1451	St. Jobst (Bayr?) Francisc.	III, 50–1, VI, 297	Last folio of MS (only folio dedicated to music)
36.	Munich 8093	168v	1456	Kelheim Franciscan Ab.	III, 102; VI, 330	Solmization, theological writings
37.	Munich 950	132v	1462	Monastery of Melk	NOT LISTED	
38.	Mainz 248	90v	1468	Southern Germany	III, 77; VI, 324	Chant theory, theology
39.	Graz 873	4	XV	Neuberg (Cistercian)	VI, 14	Compilation of theological writings, history

Table 3.6. (*cont.*)

N.	Source	Folio	Date	Origin	*RISM B/III*	Facsimiles – Notes
40.	Mainz 223	233v	XV	Mainz Karthäuser	III, 75–6; VI, 324	Psalm tones, solmization, canon law and theology
41.	Munich 4382	180	XV	German	III, 87–8; VI 327	Trad. Hollandr. V; chant theory, mathem., astronomy
42.	Munich 19694	9v	XV	Tegernsee	III, 148–9; VI, 347	Hugo Spechtshart, *Flores mus*; breviary, martirologue
43.	Munich 29770/4	fragm.	XV	UNKNOWN	III, 165; VI, 352	Link to digital image from *LmL* website
44.	Vienna 2390	7	XV	South German?	VI, 70	
45.	Vienna 3646	7v	XV	Mondsee	VI, 80–4	Rules for solmization, modal theory, coniuncta
46.	Vienna 3839	110v	XV	Mondsee	VI, 84–5	Solm., modal th., rule of St. Bened., prayers
47.	Vienna 15033	64v	XV	UNKNOWN	VI, 100–1	Rules for solm., Gospels, sermons
48.	Stuttg. (*olim* Don.) 880	7v	XV	Germany	III, 43; VI, 363	Chant treatise
49.	Munich 19693	4	2nd hfXV	Melk observance	III, 148; VI, 347	Chant theory
50.	Vienna 3571	228v	2nd hfXV	Mondsee	VI, 79–80	Mostly prayers and liturgical texts; musical diagrams
51.	Eichstätt 685	364v	2nd hfXV	Domin. Conv. (Eichstätt)	NOT IN RISM	Hand has letters only; syllables in main text
52.	Ebstorf V 3	200v	XV last 3rd	Benedict. Nunn. of Ebst.	VI, 280–1	K-W Gümpel in *Music in the Theater* (ed. Parisi, 55)
53.	Regensburg 103/1	3	Late XV	UNKNOWN	III, 191–3; VI, 360	Chant treatise, Cntp treatise, mensural theory
54.	Trier 44	319r-v	Late XV	Unknown /St. Matthias?	III, 196–7; VI, 365	Hands are part of Amerus' *Practica artis musice*
55.	Prague XI.F.2	4	Late XV	Clarisse Convent of Eger?	V, 15; VI, 145	Solmization treatise

No.	Shelfmark	Folio	Date	Origin	Reference	Description
56.	Vienna 12811	137		Marienthron, Carth., Aust.	VI, 99–100	Chant th., tonary, solm., modes; Astron. tables, calend.
57.	Wolfenbüttel 696	143v	Late XV	Brunswick church	III, 217–8; VI, 370	Chant treatise
58.	Basel A IX 2	286v	1481–86	Basel? Dominican	VI, 699–701	Chant th., rules for Domin. order, prayers
59.	Freiburg i.B. 22	19	1490	SW Germany	III, 51–2; VI, 298	Writings by Conrad of Zabern, chant treatise
60.	Freiburg i.B. 77	2v	1492–95	Germany	III, 52–3; VI, 299	Chant treatise
61.	Salzburg a.VI.44	32r; 62v	ca. 1490	Melker Observanz	I, 27–31; VI, 43–4	*Musica compendiosa.* Image: ANOMCOMP 01GF
62.	*olim* Strasb. B.II.15	144	aft. 1490	Franco/German?	VI, 243–6	Plainchant treatises, prayers
63.	Würzburg I.83	143v	1491–1501	Franciscan?	III, 222–4; VI, 371	Chant treatises, mensural theory
64.	Ottobeuren 54	52	1492–1511	South Germ. Ottobeuren?	VI, 358	Chant treatise
65.	Tübingen D e 4	222	End XV	Germany	III, 199; VI, 366	Chant treatises, Hugo Specthtshart, *Flores musicae*
66.	Munich 30058	1v	ca. 1500	Germany	III, 167–8; VI, 353	Chant theory
67.	Augsburg K 81	62v	1507	Augsburg	III, 4–5; VI,	Veit Bild, *Stella Musice*
68.	Munich 26770	43v	1500–7	Ab. Pruel? cop. D.Menger	III, 159; VI, 350	Chant theory
69.	Munich 30060	2	aft. 1509	Germany	III, 166; VI, 354	Simon De Quercu, *Opusculum musice*
70.	Munich 18932	10v	1516 (?)	Tegernsee	III, 137–9; VI, 345	Chant theory; writings on *ars metrica* and grammar
71.	Munich 6002	76	1529	Ab. St. Sebast./Ebersberg	III, 97; VI, 328	Chant theory; liturgical formulae in use at S. Sebast.
72.	Vienna 5160,	148	XVI	Mondsee	VI, 90–6	Solmiz., modal theory, coniuncta, astron., philosophy

Source: RISM, B/III.

Table 3.7. Guidonian Hands from Italy (c. 1050–1500)

N.	Source Folio	Date	Origin	RISM, B/III	Facsimiles – Notes
1.	Montecassino 318	291	Late XI	Ab. S. Maria di Albaneta	II, 64–69; VI, 527–36	*SmitsM*, fig. 61. Letters only on Hand. T-S ind.
2.	Rome Reg. lat. 1578	86r	XII	UNKNOWN	II, 118; VI, 587	*SmitsM*, fig. 63. Mostly letters only, a few syll.
3.	Paris 1412	202	XII	Morimondo. Cist. antiph.	VI, 235	13th-c. Hand in last fol. See C. Maître ed. (1999)
4.	Berlin 261	21v	1292	Lucca	III, 30–32; VI, 264	Treatise on *computus* and music
5.	Rome Vall. C 105	155v	XIV–XV	Italian (Benedictine)	II, 91–92; VI, 602	*LmL*: Anon La Fage. II
6.	Barcelona 883	67	c. 1400	Italy	V, 72–78	
7.	Bologna BU 2931	33, 33v	Early XV	Italian. Bologna?	VI, 445–48	Provenance: Conv. San Salvatore (Bologna)
8.	Siena L.V.36	1v	1st hf XV	Italy	VI, 605–608	
9.	Lucca 359	49v; 55v	1st hf XV	Northern Italy	VI, 509–512	Both Hands in Prosdocimo, *Plana musica*
10.	Bologna A56	115; 121	1st hf XV	Sabbioncello (de Obizis)	VI, 450–52	Facs.: Prosd., *Plana musica* (ed. Herlinger, 254)
11.	Catania U.R. D39	130	1453–73	Southern Italy (Sicily?)	VI, 466–71	From Aragonese musical chapel of Npls/Sicily?
12.	Berlin 1520	7v (?)	1463	Italian	VI, 272–73	"Manus haec quam vides in se plura continet"
13.	Venice VIII.85	83r	1464	Italian	II, 128–29; VI, 622	
14.	Sevilla 5–1–43	a2v	1470–90	Naples or Florence	V, 109–110; VI, 688	Chansonnier (Plamenac); "S. Nicola doce me …"
15.	Washington J6	80v; 100v	c. 1470	Cop. J.F.Preottonus in VE	IV, 191–96; VI, 731–32	Copied in Monastery of St. Giorgio in Venice
16.	Rome 5129	160v	c. 1470	Italian	II, 96–97; VI, 568	"Sancte Nicola doce me cantare"
17.	London 22315	50r	1473	Cop. N. Burtius in Parma	III, 47–48; VI, 389	*SmitsM*, fig. 84. Only 1 syllable per pitch letter.
18.	Berlin 576	187v, 188	1475–1500	Italian	VI, 261	2 folios on chant theory after sect. on *computus*
19.	Bologna Univ. 2573	4v	1475?	Naples	VI, 443–45	Hand in J. Tinctoris, *Expositio manus*, ch. 2.
20.	Stuttg. (*olim* Donau.) 250	95v	1476	Italy	III, 42–43; VI, 362	Musical section in a compil. of theolog. writings
21.	Napoli VIII.D.12	52r	XV	Italian	II, 70–72; VI, 538	"Manus Boecii." Contains three fifteenth century Hands.

No.	Manuscript	Folio	Date	Place/Language	Reference	Notes
22.	Florence Ashb. 1119	26r	XV	Italian	II, 47–49; VI, 481	A. Seay in *Certaldo* 1962, 118–40 (Paolo da F.)
23.	Venice VIII.35	first verso	XV	Italian	VI, 616–20	*olim* 3046; Huglo, *Tonaires* 415–16
24.	Berlin Mus. 1599	1v	XV	Italian	III, 36; VI, 275	*SmitsM*, fig. 80. Hand with banner "Pythagoras"
25.	Pesaro Oliver. 1336	32v	XV	Bologna (Sinib. da Volt.)	VI, 557–62	MS from 13th c., Hand added in the 15th c.
26.	Vipiteno, Arch. Com.	6	XV	South Tirol (Vipiteno)	VI, 633–34	End of musical section of the MS
27.	London 34296	1v	XV	Italy (written in Italian)	IV, 56–57; VI, 390	
28.	Berkeley 1087	single *folio*	XV–XVI	Italy	IV, 144–45; VI, 724	Hand similar to Ghent 70 (71) (Table 3.8, 1. 17)
29.	Venice VIII.64	27v	XV–XVI	Italy (Veneto?)	VI, 620–21	MS owned by Giovanni del Lago
30.	Parma 1158	55v	2nd hf XV	Lodi (owned by Gafori)	VI, 546–48	"Sancte bassiane doce paulum grecum cantare"
31.	Rome Corsin. 2067	15	2nd hf XV	Northern Italy	VI, 597–601	"… sicut patet in hac manu" (no Hand featured)
32.	Brussels, II 4147	1v	1477–1490	Naples-Giov. d'Aragona?	VI, 125–27	Woodley (2007), www.stoa.org/tinctoris/
33.	Oxford, Can. Lit. 216	168r	1475–1500	Mantua	UNLISTED IN RISM	*New Grove2* 23: 645, s.v. "Solmization," § 1, 2
34.	Rio de Janeiro 18	610v	1480–1490	Pavia, Rome (Garl. *Intr.*)	VI, 135–36	*Musica plana* J. de Garl. (ed. Meyer, 1998), 142
35.	Valencia 835	3v	1483–1485	Naples-Ferd. I d'Aragon	V, 131–34; VI, 690	Hand in J. Tinctoris, *Expositio manus*, ch. 2.
36.	Bergamo MAB 21	53	1487	Bergamo, S. Maria Magg.	VI, 434–43	Fols. 1–19 contain first draft of Gafori's *Practica*
37.	Bruxelles 16.857	37	c. 1490	Italian	VI, 112–13	Comp. of treatises on astron. and math. 2
38.	Florence II.XI.18	195v	late XV	Venice or Central Italy?	VI, 491–93	Hand on last *verso* of the MS
39.	Bologna A 48	33v	late XV	Northern Italy	VI, 449	
40.	Milan Trivulz. 2146	31	late XV	Florence for Asc. Sforza?	VI, 519–24	
41.	Pesaro Oliver. 83	13	c. 1503	Pesaro/Modrus (Croatia)	VI, 553–57	
42.	Perugia Comun. 1013	3v	1509	Venice	VI, 551–53	

Source: RISM B/III.

Table 3.8. Guidonian Hands from France, Burgundy, and England (c. 1050–1500)

N.	Source	Folio	Date	Origin	RISM B/III	Facsimiles – Notes
1.	Rome Reg. lat. 577	100r	c. 1045	Sens, St. Pierre le Vif	II, 111–12; VI, 581	SmitsM, fig. 62. Odorannus of Sens Letters only
2.	Paris 7203	5v	XII	Loire Vall. (Fleury?)	I, 99–100; VI, 187–81	SmitsM, fig. 68, letters and Greek names only
3.	Leiden 194	1r	XII	Liège, St. Jacques?	136–7; VI, 643	See Santosuosso's facs. of MS (Ottawa, 191). Letters only
4.	Paris 7211	132r	XII	Luxeuil (Burgundy)	I, 101–5; VI, 191–3	SmitsM, fig. 59; for memorizing the eight tones
5.	Paris 7211	149v	XII	Luxeuil (Burgundy)	I, 101–5; VI, 191–3	J.-B. Thibaut, Monuments … latine. (1912), 72
6.	St. Petersburg 62	11v	Late XII	Wherwell (England)	VI, 669	MS contains works on computus (Herm. Cont.) and geom.
7.	Paris, 16201	1v	End XII	Central France	I, 123; VI, 225	On last verso of the manuscript
8.	El Escorial S.III.5	141v	c. 1200	France	V, 87–8; VI, 685	SmitsM, fig. 72. From E. Salomon; Scient. artis musicae
9.	Milan Amb., D 75 inf.	6r	1274	France (Périgord?)	II, 55; VI, 514	SmitsM, fig. 74
10.	London Royal 12.C.VI	52	c. 1275	Bury St. Edmund?	IV, 93–4; VI, 399	Ieronimus of Moravia. TML: IERTDMI 02GF, not a facs.
11.	Paris 16663	16; 188v	bef. 1306	Paris, St. Jacques?	I, 124; VI, 226–7	SmitsM, fig. 76. Meyer, J. de Garl. (1998). "Rep. 3a", 49
12.	Rome Reg. Lat. 1146	63r	XIV	England	II, 112–16; VI, 582–3	End of MS containing works by J. Gerson
13.	Paris 17487	23r	1447	Paris. Coll. Navarre?	VI, 230–1	
14.	Wroclaw I.Q.466	144v	1st hf XV	Unknown	V, 50; VI, 658	SmitsM, p. 132. Hand added in MS (n. 2)
15.	Paris 7203	5r	XV	See n. 2	I, 99–100; VI, 187–8	Two Hands in one of two small fols added to original MS
16.	Cambr. Tr.,R.14.52	256a r	Late XV	England	IV, 15; VI, 380	SmitsM, fig. 81 (5v); fig. 82 (108v); K. Berger 1987
17.	Gent 70 (71)	5v; 108v	1503–4	Gent, Abb. of St. Bavo	I, 65–9	SmitsM, f. 60. Interv., props., no sylls. MS dates to XIVc.
18.	London Harley 281	3r	XVI	France?	IV, 74–8; VI, 394	

Source: RISM

from Central European areas; Table 3.7 lists sources from Italy, and Table 3.8 from France and England.

The inventory is necessarily selective. It includes only representations of the musical gamut on hand-shaped "tables," omitting the more abstract representations of the gamut or various other kinds of "solmization tables" in which the musical notes are simply mapped in spatial or scalar order from low to high. Although it could be legitimately argued that there is in fact no substantial difference – regarding the type of information conveyed to the user – between a typical Guidonian Hand and a solmization table, the two visual aids are functionally quite different from each other. Whereas solmization tables provided a synoptic view of the diatonic system that was meant to assist singers to understand its structure, the Hand is thought to have been the conduit by which that diatonic structure was imprinted in the singers' memory and later recalled at will.

Likewise, I have excluded from the inventory those frequent references to a "manus musicalis" that go as far as to locate the pitches of the gamut on the finger joints, but without showing the actual figure. Examples of this practice include the Vatican Organum Treatise and the Seay anonymous discussed above (twelfth century); the anonymous *Summa musice* and *De plana musica breve compendium* from the tradition of Pseudo-Lambertus (thirteenth century); Johannes Boen's *Musica* and the first Berkeley treatise by Goscalcus (fourteenth century). It is also important to realize that the term *manus* is occasionally used as a synonym for *gamut*, as shown by several fifteenth-century references to the "manus Boethii". (Johannes Wylde; MS Naples, Biblioteca Nazionale, VIII D 12, f. 52r), or even for "monochord" (Adam of Fulda).

Several conclusions may be drawn from this preliminary inventory. First, the aggregate number of about 140 extant Hands is comparatively low when judged in the context of the ca. 1,300 manuscript sources itemized in RISM.[37] Even after excluding from the count the numerous sources that are speculative or generic in purpose – such as those containing Boethius' *De institutione musica*, or Bartholomeo Anglicus' *De proprietatibus rerum* – the proportion between extant Hands and extant manuscripts indicates that these visual aids were on the whole rather peripheral to medieval musical training.

[37] See Christian Meyer's "General Preface" to *RISM* B/III, vol. 6, "Addenda, Corrigenda" (Munich: Henle, 2003), p. 17.

Table 3.9. Select pre-1400 Italian sources without Guidonian Hands

Source	Date	Origin	Facsimiles – Notes
Florence, Conv. Soppr. F III 565	end of 11th century	Centr. Italy	Guido's treatises, *Dialogus*, Aurelian, Hucbald, Hucbald, *ench.*
Krakow, Jagellonska 1965	ca. 1100	North. Italy	*ench.*, Hucbald, Berno, monochord division, modes
London, Add. 10335	ca. 1100	North. Italy	Guido's treatises
Vallicelliana B 81	11th/12th century	Centr. Italy	Guido's treatises, *Dialogus*, Berno, Cassiodoro
London, Add. 10335	end 11th/early 12th c.	North. Italy	Guido's treatises, *Dialogus*, tonary, gamut
Oxford, Digby 25	end of 12th century	Cen. Italy	Tonary, gamut
Piacenza 65	1142	Piacenza	Tonaries, Trad. Guido, modal theory
Berlin 265	12th century	Italy	*Comm, sup. tonos*, Guido (*Micr. and Reg.*), *Dialogus*
Geneva, Bodmer 77	12th century	Tuscany	Guido's treatises, tonary, Regino, *ench.*, *Dialogus*
Paris 7461	late 12th century	Centr. Italy	Guido's treatises, *Dialogus*
Piacenza 54	13th century	Piacenza	Modal theory, tonary
Verona, Capitolare CCLXIV	13th century	Italy	*Micrologus*, other Guidonian excerpts, Berno
Venice, Marciana VIII.20 (3574)	13th century	Italy	Berno, Hermann, tonary, modal theory
Pesaro Oliveriana, 1336	end of 13th century	Bologna	Guido's treatises, Anon. Cisterc., Isidor, gamut
Naples VIIID 12	12th, 14th, and 15th	Italy	Anon. Pannain, Capuanus, Muris, ctpt., mensuration
Milano, Ambrosiana D 5	ca. 1325–50	Italy	Guido's treatises, *ench.*, Marchetto, Franco
Paris 652	14th century	unknown	*Alia musica*, Guido (excerpts), Aurelianus, Isidor
St-Dié 42 (Italian or Flemish)	end of 14th century	Italy / Fland.	Marchetto, Franco, Trad. Garlandia, Muris, monoch. Divis.
Brussels 4144	end of 14th century	Italy	Marchetto, *Lucidarium*, Muris
Chicago 54.1	end of 14th century	Italy	Marchetto, *Lucidarium*, Muris, ctpt, mensuration
Oxford, Can. Misc. 212	ca. 1400	Bologna?	Pseudo-Odo, *Dial.* Ench., Hucb.
Sevilla, Colombina 5-2-25	late 14th/early 15th	North. Italy	Marchetto, *Lucid.*, interv. and ctpt, modes, Muris., Murino
Barberini 307/St. Paul 135	late 14th/early 15th	North. Italy	Vetulus de An, Trad. Garl., Vitry, Isidor, Aurelian
Florence, Redi 71	mid-14th; early 15th	Florence?	Gamut, ctpt, mensuration
Barcellona, Catalunya 883	14th/15th century	Italy	Numerous tracts on ctpt, mensur., Anon. Cisterc., Garland

Source: RISM, B/III.

Second, the inventory suggests that the method of the Guidonian Hand was far from uniformly adopted across Europe throughout the Middle Ages. Rather, its fortune waxed and waned at different times and in different regions. About half of the extant Hands (ca. 74 out of 140) come from German-speaking areas, particularly from monastic establishments in Bavaria and in the neighboring Alpine regions. On the opposite side of the spectrum, there are no extant Hands from the Iberian Peninsula, Scandinavia, or Eastern Europe, in spite of the fact that those areas (particularly Spain) were quite active on the front of both musical practice and music theory. More striking still is the realization that fewer than twenty extant Hands in total originated in France, the Low Countries, and England, considering that the network of cathedral schools in these regions trained scores of future professional singers and composers during the period under consideration.

Third, the chronological profile of the extant Hands is as skewed as the geographic one. About 70 per cent of them (96 out of 140) were drawn in the fifteenth century, with only 44 originating in the previous 350 years. Such an uneven distribution is partly to be expected, since the sheer volume of extant music theory manuscripts from after 1400 is considerably larger than that from the pre-1400 era. Yet the dearth of such illustrations in early pedagogical treatises is consistent with the marginal presence of six-syllable solmization in music theory before ca. 1250. It gives pause for thought, for instance, to realize that only about half a dozen Hands survive from pre-1400 Italy, considering that approximately sixty Italian sources from that period have survived – a ratio of one Hand to every ten sources. In comparison, the ca. 175 Italian sources dating to the fifteenth century contain about 40 Hands, more than twice the ratio of the earlier period, but still amounting to less than a massive presence. Curiously, the French scenario is exactly the opposite, with as many as ten out of twelve extant Hands originating between the eleventh and the fourteenth centuries, and only one Hand from after 1400. Central European areas present a more balanced distribution across time, with two-dozen Hands originating in the pre-1400 period and about fifty from after 1400 (including six of uncertain origin), over a total of ca. 440 sources (see Table 3.6).

One or more Guidonian Hands would have been perfectly at home in many French and Italian pedagogical compilations from before 1400. Table 3.9 lists some of the most representative of these sources, which transmit the core pedagogical writings of the entire Middle Ages (i.e., the *Enchiriadis* treatises, Hucbald, Pseudo-Odo's *Dialogus*, Guido of Arezzo's four treatises, Marchetto's *Lucidarium*, and other tracts on modal theory, counterpoint, and mensuration). While it is true that many Guidonian Hands may have circulated as flyleaves, which are by nature highly perishable items, there is a distinct possibility that many medieval *musici* and *cantores* on the whole did not view the Hand as a privileged mode of representation of musical space, or even as a primary tool for sight singing.

For instance, of the seventy sources of Guido's *Regule, Prologus,* and *Epistola* that served as the basis of Pesce's recent edition of those writings, only twelve contain musical Hands: Rochester 12 9200, Erfurt 8° 93, Ghent 70 (71), Kassel, Math. 1, London 281, Munich 9921, Munich 5539, Montecassino 318, Paris 7211, Vienna 51, Wolfenbüttel 334, and Washington J6.[38] At least three of these Hands (London 281 and the two Hands in Paris 7211), are not "Guidonian" in a proper sense, since they do not feature solmization syllables (see Fig. 3.3).[39] In virtually all these sources many folios separate the Guidonian Hands from Guido's own writings, a layout suggesting that those Hands were not meant specifically to illustrate Guido's pedagogy. Likewise, among the fifteen extant sources of Marchetto's *Lucidarium,* only Rome, Reg. lat. 1146 (from fourteenth-century England), Venice, Marciana VIII.85 (from fifteenth-century Italy), and Washington J6 (from the 1460s) feature musical Hands, again not intended as visual aids to Marchetto's treatise.[40]

The transmission of other treatises confirms what one might label a "hit-or-miss" pattern: for instance, both Amerus' *Practica artis musicae* (1271) and Johannes de Garlandia's *Introductio musice plane* (ca. 1270) feature Hands only in one source out of several extant ones.[41] Exceptionally, all three extant sources of Johannes Tinctoris' *Expositio manus* (from ca. 1473) feature a Hand at the end of chapter 2, appropriately introduced by the text

---

[38] See the description of these sources in *PesceGA*, pp. 39–222.

[39] A facsimile edition of the entire manuscript is available. See A. Colk Santosuosso, *Paris, Bibliothèque nationale, Fonds latin 7211: analysis, inventory, and text* (Ottawa: Institute of Mediaeval Music, 1991).

[40] For a description of these sources, see J. Herlinger, ed. and trans., *The Lucidarium of Marchetto of Padua* (Chicago University Press, 1985), pp. 21–63.

[41] A complete text of Amerus' *Practica* is found in MS Trier, Seminar-Bibliothek 44, fols. 318–36 (from late-fifteenth-century Burgundy). According to *RISM* B/III, vol. 3, two Guidonian Hands appear at fols. 319 *recto* and *verso* of this manuscript. The other two sources of this treatise are Oxford, Bodleian Library, Bodley 77, fols. 138v-139 (a partial source of English origin from the fifteenth century), and Bamberg, Staatsbibliothek Lit. 115, fols. 65–79 (from fourteenth-century Eastern France, tonary not included). The only source of Garlandia's *Introductio* containing a Guidonian Hand as part of the treatise is an Italian manuscript now in Rio de Janeiro, Biblioteca Nacional, Cofre 18, fols. 610r-617r (the Hand, showing only the five fingers but not the palm, is at fol. 610v; it is reproduced in C. Meyer, ed., *Musica plana Johannis de Garlandia*, Collection d'études musicologiques 91 (Baden-Baden and Bouxwiller: V. Koerner, 1998), p. 142). The other sources are Barcelona, Biblioteca de Catalunya, M 883, fol.s

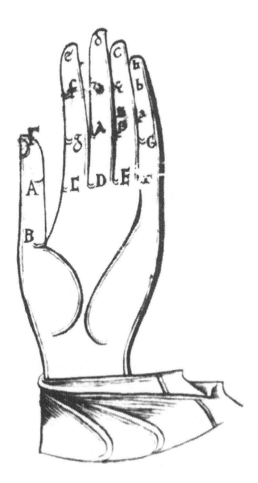

Fig. 3.3. Paris, Bibliothèque nationale, lat. 7211, fol. 132r.

(*ut patet sequenti figura*).[42] One wonders if these hands were ever used in actual musical instruction, however, since the three sources carrying the *Expositio* did not have a practical function, but rather were conceived as anthologies of Tinctoris' writings.

71v–78r; Saint-Dié, Bibliotheque Municipale 42, fols. 68r-83r (edition in *CS* 2: pp. 157–75), and Washington, D.C., Library of Congress, Music Division ML171 J6 Case, fols. 56r–70r (ca. 1465–89).

[42] The sources are Bologna, Biblioteca Universitaria 2573, fol. 3–17v (from Naples, ca. 1475); Brussels, Bibliothèque Royale II 4147, fol. 1–9v (from France or Flanders, late fifteenth century), and Valencia, Biblioteca General i Històrica de la Universitat, MS 835, fol. 2–14v (copied in Naples for King Ferdinand I of Aragon in 1485–8). Both the original text and a new English translation of the *Expositio manus* are now also available at R. Woodley, ed., *The Theoretical Works of Johannes Tinctoris: A New Online Edition* (in progress). URL: www.stoa.org/tinctoris/.

Other sources confirm that musical Hands circulated as self-standing one-page tracts – i.e., as "handouts" in the true sense of the word. Not infrequently they were penned on manuscript flyleaves sometimes long after the compilation of the codex in which they appear.[43] Large-sized Hands were regularly posted on the wall for the benefit of entire groups of monks or choirboys. All such formats confirm Michel Huglo's characterization of the Hand as an "echo of the oral teaching of music in the schools since the twelfth century."[44] Nevertheless, the evidence of the written sources, indirect as it may be, again suggests that the actual impact of such practices on late medieval music education may need to be reconsidered.

To the category of "flying Hands" may also belong MS St. Petersburg, Public Library, Q. v. I. N. 62, a liturgical calendar for the use of the Benedictine nunnery of Wherwell (from Hampshire, Southern England). Only the last two pages (fols. 11 and 12) of this twelfth-century fragment contain musical material, namely a musical Hand, a table with the pitches of the gamut (with captions in Anglo-Norman) and a Latin commentary. The Hand of fol. 11v (see Fig. 3.4), featuring letters and only some Guidonian syllables, may be a copy of an older model. On the other hand, the table of the gamut is especially interesting: each of the basic nineteen pitches is inscribed into a roundel that indicates the pitch letter, the solmization syllable(s), the position of the note on the staff ("en reule," "en space"), and the relevant hexachordal properties, which musicians had to know in order to execute correctly the mutations across hexachords.[45] The Hand of fol.

[43] Musical Hands on single sheets are preserved in Washington, D.C., Library of Congress, Music Division, ML 171 G 85 Case (dating to 1469, of possible English origin), and in Berkeley (USA), University of California, Music Library, MS 1087 (end-fifteenth or early-sixteenth century, Italian origin). See *RISM* B/III, vol. IV, pp. 144–5 and 190–2. Examples of Guidonian Hands added at a later time are found in Paris 1412 (Table 3.7, n. 4), Pesaro 1336 (Table 3.7, n. 18), and London 281 (Table 3.8, n. 18).

[44] See M. Huglo, "La place du *Tractatus de Musica* dans l'histoire de la théorie musicale du XIIIᵉ siècle: Etude codicologique," in C. Meyer, ed., *Jérôme de Moravie: un théoricien de la musique dans le milieu intellectuel parisien du XIIIe siècle*, Actes du Colloque de Royaumont, 1989 (Paris: Créaphis, 1992), pp. 37–9. Huglo observes that a musical Hand appears indeed on a wall in the music room of the Franciscan mission of San Antonio de Padua in California (p. 37). This was no doubt a practice imported from Europe. Klaus Niemöller mentions a 1482 document from Braunschweig, according to which a local school hired a painter "eine Hand in die Schule zu malen" (K. Niemöller, *Untersuchungen zu Musikpflege und Musikunterricht an den deutschen Lateinschulen vom ausgehenden Mittelalter bis um 1600* (Regensburg: Bosse, 1969), p. 610).

[45] The musical portion of this manuscript is discussed in J.-B. Thibaut, *Monuments de la Notation Ekphonétique et Neumatique de l'Eglise Latine* (St. Petersburg, 1912; reprint Hildesheim: Georg

Fig. 3.4. St. Petersburg, Public Library, Q.v.1 n. 62, fol. 11v.

11v, which may be older than the pattern of roundels, features letters and some Guidonian syllables. The roundels, however, are historically more sig-nificant in that they document the existence of mutation theory as early as the late twelfth century. They are quite similar to the medallions found in Magister Lambertus' *Tractatus de musica*, but the two sets are not directly related, as Lambertus' medallions include the pitch *e*-la and adopt slightly different letters for some of the other pitches (compare Fig.3.5 and Fig. 3.6). There is another quite intriguing connection with Continental theory: the Wherwell text makes a clear distinction between the "regular" mutations

Olms, 1984), pp. 71–2. Perhaps in order to be able to arrange all the roundels in three rows of six, the author has allocated the first two pitches of the gamut, Γ and A, to the same roundel.

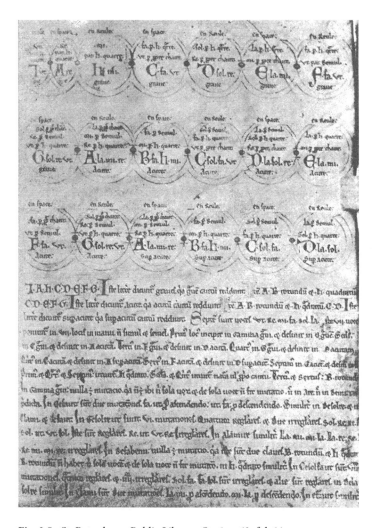

Fig. 3.5. St. Petersburg, Public Library, Q.v.1 n. 62, fol. 11r.

(to and from the property "by nature") and the "irregular" ones (from *durus* to *mollis* and vice versa), one that is later found in books 2 and 6 of Jacques de Liège's *Speculum musicae*, (ca. 1330).[46] In more than one way, the Wherwell source is an extraordinary document that appears to anticipate later developments in terminology and mode of representation of solmization theory.[47]

---

[46] Jacques de Lièges, *Speculum musicae*, ed. R. Bragard, vol. VI, pp. 179–85.

[47] For a new transcription and a brief discussion of the theoretical treatise from Wherwell Abbey, see now A. B. Yardley, *Performing Piety: Musical Culture in Medieval English Nunneries* (New

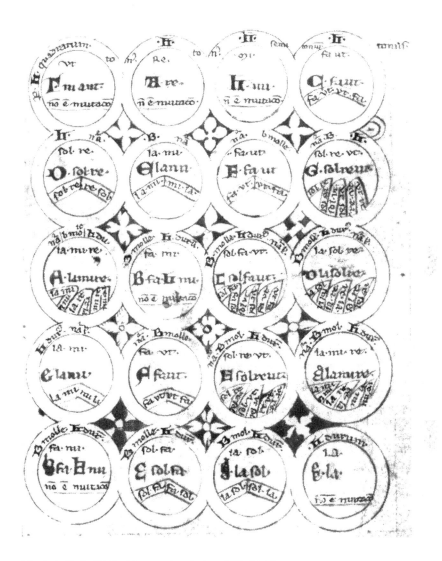

Fig. 3.6. Paris, Bibliothèque nationale, lat. 6755, fol. 74v.

Finally, the uneven concentration of musical Hands in different regions may reflect different chapters in the long history of music education within

York: Palgrave MacMillan, 2006), pp. 60–4 and 239–42. According to Bonnie Blackburn, the Wherwell roundels document the earliest known use of the term *properchant* to indicate the "natural" property C-a: see her "Properchant: English Theory at Home and Abroad," p. 92. My thanks to Dr. Blackburn for independently confirming the dating of this source to ca. 1200, and for drawing my attention to Yardley's study.

the church. There is probably a direct relationship between some of the "let-ters-only" musical Hands originating from twelfth- and thirteenth-century France and England and the adoption of various forms of alphabetic musi-cal notation in those same areas, as part of the program of reforms of the Benedictine order initiated by William of Volpiano shortly after the year 1000.[48] One particular folio in Rome, Vatican Library, reg. lat. 577 – the eleventh-century manuscript of Odorannus of Sens – shows the derivation of alphabetic notation from the division of the monochord.[49] It is prob-ably not a coincidence that several of these "letters-only" musical Hands originated from the same monastic institutions in North-West Europe – St. Pierre le Vif, Fleury, and St. Pierre de Luxeuil in France – that also produced a significant number of tonaries and antiphonaries in alphabetic notation.

Similar considerations cannot be applied to the Italian sources, because their exact origin and provenance is too often uncertain. The Central European Hands, however, originated in monastic environments to an overwhelming degree (see Table 3.6). Two particular waves of monastic reform appear to be linked to the relatively large number of Hands from this area. The first one is the Cistercian musical reform of the twelfth cen-tury, which boosted the teaching of music within the order and revised the existing chant melodies. The Guidonian Hands from several Cistercian monasteries in Germany and Austria (Baumgartenberg, Heiligenkreutz, Alderspach, and Neuberg) confirm that local institutions did not always follow the rigorously "letters-only" musical doctrine promoted in the offi-cial texts by St. Bernard and Guido Augensis. The other wave of reform that appears to have strongly affected the practice of the Hand is the Melk/ Benedictine one, which took hold in Southern Germany and Austria in the wake of the Italian reform movement of the Congregation of S. Giustina/ Cassinensis. The massive number of fifteenth-century musical treatises of German and Austrian origin (counting only the manuscripts) confirms the high premium placed on education by those who joined this monastic reform movement. Thus, the many Guidonian Hands from that time and place do not reflect a generalized use of the solmization system across musi-cal establishments, but rather the pedagogical methods used for the train-ing of a specialized audience, namely, young monks and nuns with little or no previous musical experience.

---

[48] On this topic, see Colk Santosuosso, *Letter Notations*, pp. 83–92. For additional images of musical Hands featuring only the letters, see *Smits M*, pp. 129 (fig. 62), 133 (fig. 68), and 135 (fig. 70).

[49] See Colk Santosuosso, *Letter Notations*, p. 124.

We should not be surprised to find evidence of a more limited use of the Hand than it is generally believed, just as we should not expect that a general uniformity in the repertory of liturgical chant should necessarily produce a uniform method of musical training. Whereas all medieval singers had to memorize the repertory and acquire intimate familiarity with the rudiments of music (such as intervals, modes, and discantus techniques), that familiarity could no doubt be acquired by different means that may or may not have involved the use of the six syllables and their placement on the Hand. After all, Guido offered a complete method for training singers that relied far more on the letters than on the syllables, and that made no provisions for mapping pitches on the Hand. Indeed, the availability of alternative methods for singing, and the need to choose the better ones among them, was the root cause of heated arguments in the fifteenth century, as the second part of this monograph will show. In order to appreciate those debates, however, it is necessary to examine in some detail the hexachordal method that was bequeathed to the fifteenth century.

4 | The making of a system: medieval music semiotics in transition

By *c.* 1300, at the latest, the hexachordal system had acquired the form and the conceptual apparatus that were bequeathed to the Renaissance and the modern era. It was by all means a complex, meticulously constructed edifice. Theorists charted in detail the yoking of each letter with one, two, or three syllables, explaining at length the reason for this combinatorial variety. They also defined three specific pitch ranges within the gamut on which the six syllables *ut-la* could be positioned: C-a (*proprietas naturalis* or *proprium cantum*), G-e (*proprietas per b-quadratum*, or *durum*), and F-d with b flat (*proprietas per b-rotundum*, or *molle*) (Fig. Front1, frontispiece verso).[1] Theorists also began charting all the possible "mutations," that could be performed on each and every pitch of the gamut.[2] To mutate is to change "hexachord" or, more precisely, *deductio/proprietas*. A singer solmizing G as *sol,* for instance, would re-label that pitch as *ut* or *re* if higher notes followed, so that the entire melody could be solmized. Mutation was the crowning principle of the entire system, by which a singer could apply the six syllables to any melody irrespective of its range.

The main purpose of this chapter is to highlight the role of the late-medieval university "mind-set" – by which I mean the mix of educational models, philosophical interests, and rhetorical practices that traditionally go under the label of "scholasticism" – in driving the notable developments that affected hexachordal theory in the second half of the thirteenth century.[3] My claim is that the spur for transforming Guido's sparse guidelines for solmization into a fully fledged system came not from the

---

[1] The label *proprium cantum*, or *properchant*, for the *proprietas* on C is a distinctly English practice. On this topic see Blackburn, "Properchant: English Theory at Home and Abroad," pp. 81–98.

[2] Both the mechanism of mutation and the term "mutatio" were already known by the late-twelfth or early-thirteenth century, as documented by the manuscript from Wherwell Abbey in the Russian National Library of St. Petersburg (see Chapter 3, pp. 76–9).

[3] Dorit Tanay has pursued this approach in her monograph on the role of Aristotelian philosophy, mathematics, and grammar in the development of rhythmic notation in the late Middle Ages. See her *Noting Music, Making Culture: The Intellectual Context of Rhythmic Notation, 1250–1400* (Holzgerlingen: American Institute of Musicology, 1999).

world of musical practice – which seems to have been quite contented with the letters-based method of sight singing recommended by Guido – but rather from a new, systematizing approach to *musica practica* proposed by university-trained minds. The object of my investigation consists of a number of mostly French musical treatises written in the second half of the thirteenth century and in the early fourteenth century.

Most of the authors discussed below appear to have had some exposure to university education; others taught or may have taught at the University of Paris. In the former group one may include the Dominican monk Hyeronimus de Moravia, for instance, whose encyclopedic *Tractatus de musica* (from ca. 1275) cites Thomas Aquinas' commentary on Aristotle's *De caelo et mundo*. In 1304, the only extant copy of the treatise was bequeathed to the library of the College of the Sorbonne by its owner, Pierre of Limoges, and chained with many other frequently used books in the chapel of St. Ursula.[4] Aristotelian concepts, along with numerous references to Boethius and Isidor, also figure in the *De musica* by the Benedictine monk Engelbert of Admont, who studied at Prague and Padua and became abbot of St. Peter's in Salzburg. Very little is known of the English cleric Amerus/Aluredus, who came to Italy at the service of Cardinal Ottoboni Fieschi and penned a *Practica musice artis* in 1271 during an Italian sojourn, and of the French canon Hélie Salomon who wrote a *Scientia artis musice* in 1274. Both treatises are markedly scholastic in content and language; the treatise by Amerus was known at the University of Oxford in the mid fourteenth century, since Johannes Hollandrinus quoted from it in the treatise (now lost) that he wrote in the 1350s or 1360s while a student in that town.[5]

One writer who likely was a *magister* at the University of Paris is Johannes de Garlandia (fl. ca. 1270–1320), the author of a treatise on *musica plana* that is much concerned with systematizing Guido's six syllables, and of a second landmark treatise on rhythmic notation (*De mensurabili musica*).[6] Garlandia was a contemporary of Lambertus (Pseudo-Aristotle), who either authored or compiled a comprehensive *Tractatus de musica* that has been

---

[4] See Huglo, "La place du *Tractatus de Musica*," pp. 33–42, at p. 35.

[5] Hollandrinus' treatise was widely influential in the fourteenth and fifteenth centuries. On the textual relationships between Amerus and Hollandrinus, see the introduction to A. Rausch, ed., *Opusculum de musica ex traditione Iohannis Hollandrini: a Commentary, Critical Edition, and Translation* (Ottawa: The Institute of Mediaeval Music, 1997), pp. 23–4, and Blackburn, "Properchant: English Theory at Home and Abroad," pp. 89–92.

[6] For a recent account of Garlandia's life and career, see R. Baltzer, "Johannes de Garlandia," *NG 2*, vol. 13, pp. 139–42.

tentatively dated to ca. 1265–75.[7] There is evidence that Lambertus' treatise circulated at the University of Paris;[8] Jeremy Yudkin has plausibly identified him as a *magister* at that university and as the dean of the abbey of St. Vincent in Soignies in the region of Hainaut.[9]

My attempt to highlight the role of scholasticism in the shaping of the hexachordal system has no direct bearings on the current debate on the presence of music in the curriculum of the University of Paris in the late thirteenth century.[10] While there is circumstantial evidence that music lectures did take place in thirteenth-century Paris, as we have seen, other indicators (such as the decrease in the number of copies of Boethius' *De institutione musica* from that period, and the general vagueness of university statutes and regulations on this matter) point to different conclusions, as Dyer forcefully argues in his article. More importantly for this discussion, even if music lectures took place at the University of Paris (and elsewhere) in the thirteenth century, they are not likely to have involved topics such as chant and mensural theory.[11] The treatises by Garlandia and Lambertus, then, may reflect unofficial forms of musical instruction that were not part of the regular academic curriculum at Paris, even though they may have taken place in intellectual circles with strong connections with the university. Peripheral as it may have been to the academic curriculum, however, thirteenth-century music theory was a discipline in rapid transformation, due in large measure to its assimilation of scholastic modes of argumentation and terminology.

[7] Pamela Whitcomb has proposed the identification of Johannes de Garlandia with a bookseller active at the University of Paris in the first two decades of the fourteenth century. See her "Teachers, Booksellers and Taxes: Reinvestigating the Life and Activities of Johannes de Garlandia," *Plainsong and Medieval Music* 8 (1999), 1–13. On Lambertus, see R. Baltzer, "Magister Lambertus," in *NG 2*, vol. 14, pp. 169–70.

[8] See M. Everist, "Music and Theory in Late Thirteenth-Century Paris: The Manuscript Paris, Bibliothéque Nationale, *Fonds lat.* 11266," *The Royal Musical Association Research Chronicle* 17 (1981), 52–64.

[9] The so-called Anonymous of St. Emmeram, himself a student and/or a teacher at the University of Paris with Notre-Dame connections, refers to Lambertus as a *magister*. See J. Yudkin, "The Anonymous Music Treatise of 1279: Why St. Emmeram?," in *Music and Letters* 72 (1991), 181–3.

[10] For the latest contribution to this topic, see the study of J. Dyer, "Speculative 'Musica' and the Medieval University of Paris," *Music and Letters* 90 (2009), 177–204, which discusses the documentary evidence at length and provides ample citations of the relevant secondary literature. My thanks to Prof. Dyer for sending me a copy of his article prior to publication.

[11] Dyer, "Speculative 'Musica'," p. 186, and O. Weijer, "La place de la musique à la Faculté des arts de Paris," in L. Mauro, ed., *La musica nel pensiero medievale* (Ravenna: Longo, 1999), pp. 171–2.

The six syllables and late-thirteenth-century scholasticism: *proprietates*, *mutationes*, and *phantasmata*

Consider, for instance, Johannes de Garlandia's treatise on *Musica plana*.[12] Its prose is characteristically philosophical and rigorous even in its own verbosity; it proceeds methodically from definitions to learned explanations and analyses of subtle relationships derived by logical necessity. Garlandia is most sensitive to issues of language and rhetoric, as when, in the introduction, he inserts a short paragraph on the very meaning and etymology of "introduction."[13] The bulk of the treatise directly evokes the scholastic rhetoric of the *questio* – for instance, in the practice of beginning a new paragraph with the formula *Si queratur quid sit* (p. 65, 71), which typically leads to an articulate and exhaustive answer. The text also offers pointed comparisons between grammar and music (as it speaks of "subiectum et predicatum musice"), a topic I will explore later in some detail. As Meyer has pointed out, the content of the treatise is more practice-oriented than the earlier *reportationes* of the *Musica plana*; yet it offers a practical teaching clothed in scholastic rhetoric, which tends to become mired in speculative subtleties. At times the subject matter seems to be no more than an opportunity for logical speculations, as in the following passage:

Et ideo prima vox *ut* non ad alias voces, scilicet *re, mi, fa, sol, la,* reducitur, sed alie voces, scilicet *re mi fa sol la* ad ipsam primam vocem, scilicet *ut,* causa dignitatis referentur, quia a digniori inchoandum est, ut dicit philosophus, quia in omnibus rebus naturalibus tam integralibus quam etiam subjectivis constituitur fundamentum ad

---

[12] One clarification on the issue of the authorship of Garlandia's chant treatise is in order. In its most recent version, the text is transmitted, with minor variants, in four Italian sources dating from the late fourteenth to the late fifteenth century, three of which carry the words *Introductio musicae planae ... secundum magistrum Johannem de Galandia [sic]* in the *incipit* (see Meyer, ed., *Musica plana Johannis de Garlandia*, p. 63). Several extant versions of a *musica plana* treatise that belong to the textual tradition of the *Introductio* originated in France and England in the second half of the thirteenth century (the earliest source, Paris, Bibliothèque Nationale, lat. 18514, has been dated to the late-thirteenth/early-fourteenth century). Garlandia relied on one (or more) of these versions to compile his own text, which is now lost. The *Introductio* represents a later, anonymous version that according to Meyer may have originated around Venice or Padua in the first half of the fourteenth century, after Garlandia's death. The high textual consistency among the four sources of the *Introductio* suggests that they are reliable witnesses of Garlandia's teaching. Christian Meyer's recent edition of the treatise (see Meyer, ed., *Musica plana Johannis de Garlandia*, p. 123). contains both the text attributed to Garlandia, and four different versions of it, which Meyer considers *reportationes* of "students" of sorts dating to the end of the thirteenth century.

[13] *Ibid.*, p. 63.

quod omnia referuntur et propter hoc dicimus quod ad semetipsum descendit et non ad alias, sed alie ad ipsum sicut dictum est.

[Therefore the first syllable *ut* is not reduced to the remaining ones – *re, mi, fa, sol, la* – but rather *re mi fa sol la* are referred back to the first syllable by virtue of its special status. This is so because, as the philosopher says, all things of nature, both in the subjective and in the integral parts, have a foundation to which everything reverts, and for this reason it is said that everything is reduced to it and not to other parts, but rather those other parts to it, as I have said before.][14]

One senses here that Garlandia may be less interested in discussing the syllables as an aid for sight singing than in working out their abstract and functional relationships with the help of Aristotelian logic. Similarly, the concept of *proprietas* adopted in the *Introductio* is essentially an abstract-logical entity that imposes a new order on the gamut. Garlandia observes that, "In every melody there are three properties [C-a, G-e, and F-d with Bb], since it can be demonstrated that they suffice to all songs." These segments are called *proprietates* "because they provide us, naturally and properly (*proprie*), with the information on how to correctly sing tones and semitones" (*Ratio quare proprietates dicuntur, talis est; quia natural-iter proprie in notitiam vere canendi tonos et semitonos agendi legitime nos introducunt*).[15]

By Garlandia's generation, the term *proprietas* was firmly rooted in the music-theoretical vocabulary. Its meaning, however, was rapidly changing. Recall that to Guido of Arezzo and his predecessors, the concept of *proprietas* was not tied to the transposable segment of a major sixth; rather, those earlier *magistri* had tied that concept to the specific diatonic context surrounding each of the *seven* diatonic letters. Singers were advised to memorize those diatonic contexts, so that they could quickly recall them while sight singing without the aid of the six syllables. But whereas the Carolingian and Guidonian notion of *proprietas* implicitly confirmed the basic "heptachordality" of the musical system, by Garlandia's generation it had raised the major sixth to the status of a diatonic yardstick. The concept was no longer presented as a mnemonic device, but rather as a principle of musical organization embedded in the gamut.

Indeed, Garlandia shows precious little concern with the actual inter-vallic distances between letters and syllables. Even after yoking the two together into *loci*, he still does not relay that crucial piece of information to his reader. He does take care of pointing out the type of *proprietas* to which

---

[14] *Ibid.*, p. 70. The language and the argument of this passage is fully thomistic in character, even though it is ultimately grounded in Aristotelian philosophy ("ut philosophus dicit").
[15] *Ibid.*, p. 69.

each syllable-*cum*-letter belongs. But such information has no more than an abstract or combinatorial value. All a singer really needs to know is that any note solmized *re*, for instance, is both preceded and followed by a whole tone, and so forth for the other syllables.[16]

Complicating the late-medieval status of *proprietas* (and its syllabic counterpart, *deductio*) is the fact that some writers omit that concept altogether, thus implicitly denying its relevance for the parsing of musical space. The French cleric Elias Salomon had argued that the modes unequivocally rule over the Guidonian *proprietates*.[17] In his *Scientia artis musicae* he writes:

Contra, quod toni non regant omnem cantum. Nam in doctrina Gallicorum de huius arte conti[n]etur, quod pars quaedam alicuius antiphonae, responsorii, vel alterius cantus, quodammodo cum pluribus punctis regitur per naturam, hoc est dictum, per ut, re, mi, fa, sol, la. Nec ita bene explanavit. Quaedam pars eiusdem cantus regitur per .b. quadratum, quaedam pars regitur per .b. molle, et plura similia phantasmata, quae dicunt contra huius regimen litterarum, cantuum et punctorum de palma, super quibus male et ultra dimidium iusti pretii sunt edocti.

[There is an opposing view that the tones do not rule all chant. French teaching about this art holds that a certain part of a given antiphon, responsory or other chant is ruled naturally (*per naturam*) through several notes, i.e., by *ut, re, mi, fa, sol, la*. But this is not a very good explanation. [They say that] one part of a given chant is ruled by square B, another by soft B and many similar fantasies, which they claim to be against the rule of the letters, chants and notes of the Hand, about which are less than badly and more than half the fair price informed.] [18]

Even though the passage is not altogether clear, it seems that Salomon's term *phantasmata* indicate the *proprietates*.[19] According to Aristotle, the *phantasmata* (literally, "mental images," or the products of *phantasia*) are central to the faculties of memory, dreaming, and perception, Such images reproduce the *form* of the external objects perceived through the senses, yet without

[16] I have discussed Garlandia's solmization theory more in detail in my "Virtual Segments," esp. pp. 447–50.

[17] For a general discussion of Salomon's treatise, with particular emphasis on issues of performance practice, see J. Dyer, "A Thirteenth-Century Choirmaster: The 'Scientia Artis Musicae' of Elias Salomon," *MQ* 66 (1980), 83–111.

[18] *GS* III, p. 41. The English translation is by Joseph Dyer, who is preparing a new edition of Salomon's treatise.

[19] This is also the interpretation proposed by Henderson ("Solmization Syllables in Music Theory, 1100–1600," Ph.D. diss., Columbia University, 1969, p. 78). On the other hand, Mariamichela Russo has suggested that Salomon is here objecting to the view that a song may be classified only according to the status of the B key ("Hexachordal Theory," p. 140). Although these two views are in the end similar, the fact that Salomon mentions specifically the categories "per naturam," "per B quadratum," and "per B molle" suggests that he is indeed referring to the theory of the *proprietates* by authors such as Garlandia and Lambertus.

their *matter*. The disparaging tone of Salomon's reference to the *phantasmata* may indicate that he regarded the three hexachordal groupings of the letters to be irrelevant to the pitch organization of any melody.[20] No doubt for this reason, the famous Hand accompanying Salomon's treatise orders the nineteen *loci* of the gamut (here called *puncti*) without assigning them to the *proprietates*, thus in a sense continuing the twelfth-century tradition of considering the syllables (*voces*) only as individual units (see Fig. 4.1).

It seems of course contradictory to dismiss the *proprietates* as a figment of the imagination while at the same time assigning a controlling power (*regimen*) to the "syllables of the Hand." Perhaps the difficulties with this passage vanish when we consider that Salomon in his text uses the term *punctus* to indicate both a notated sound and the Guidonian syllable by which that sound is articulated or pronounced.[21] By opposing the concept of *proprietas*, Salomon may be saying that the hexachordal patterns do not apply to the *puncti* as notes, but only to the *puncti* as solmization syllables that serve to articulate those notes. Earlier sections of the *Scientia* appear to corroborate this distinction.

The *Practica artis musice* by the English clerk Amerus, probably written in August 1271 in Viterbo, closely recalls Garlaudia's mode of argumentation.[22] After a lengthy introduction, replete with learned citations from the Bible, St. Jerome, Isidor of Seville, and Boethius, he raises a series of *quaestiones*, to which he offers his response. Why is the lowest pitch marked with a gamma (Γ)? Why is gamut mapped onto the left hand, rather than onto the right one? How many *cunae* (literally "cradle," Amerus' term for *proprietas*) are found in the musical Hand? Why is one *cuna* incomplete? And so on. The next chapter is titled "If you know this Hand, you know all the mutations and all that is necessary to the gamut" (*Si quis scit istam manum, scit omnes mutaciones et quicquid est necesse ad gamma*). The image of the Hand that follows shows all the complexity of late-thirteenth-century hexachordal theory and of the mental operations required for navigating it.[23] Each joint

---

[20] On the term *phantasmata* in connection with Aristotle's theory of memory, see R. Sorabji, *Aristotle on Memory*, 2nd edn. (London: Duckworth, 2004), and J. Sisko, "Space, Time, and Phantasms in Aristotle, De Memoria 2, 452B-7–25," *The Classical Quarterly* 47 (1997), 167.

[21] The relevant passages bearing out this distinction are in *GS* III, 19 ("Caput IV. Rubrica de numero et natura punctorum et litterarum"), and 20 ("De natura cuiuslibet puncti per se"), and in Russo, "Hexachordal Theory," p. 149.

[22] The little information we have on this author comes from the prologue to the treatise. See Amerus, *Practica artis musicae*, ed. C. Ruini, ([N.p.]: American Institute of Musicology, 1977), pp. 14–7.

[23] For a facsimile and a modern transcription of this Hand, see Amerus, *Practica artis musicae*, pp. 24–5 (the transcription is also available in the *TML: AMEPRA01GF*).

Fig. 4.1. Milano, Biblioteca Ambrosiana, D 75 inf., fol. 6r. From Elias Salomon, *Scientia artis musice* (1273).

features not only the pitch letter and the corresponding syllables, but also the *cunae* underlying those syllables (*proper cantum, per b*, and *per ♮*). The diagrams in the lower part of the palm clarify the information provided on the joints. They indicate what the "root pitches" (*radices*) are for the three *cunae*: in ascending order, the syllable *ut* may be placed on G in the *cuna* for "♮," on C for "proprium cantum," and on F for "b"; the syllable *la* will fall on *e, a,* and *d* respectively. The numbers on the right indicate the total count for each *cuna*: as Amerus explains in the text, there are three of them beginning on G, and two each beginning on C and F. With all this, Amerus' Hand – and many others like it – again makes no mention of the intervallic distances between adjacent *loci*, which become clear only in the next diagram. Whether knowledge of those distances was assumed or not, this circumstance further suggests that authors such as Amerus and Garlandia were interested in the combinatorial aspects of solmization, rather than in its practical ones.

Nevertheless, Amerus clearly thinks of the musical Hand as a musical fundamental. The student who knows his Hand will *know* "*all* the mutations and everything that is *necessary to* the gamut," particularly where the "roots" of the *cunae* are. Together, the foundational flavor of these terms (*necesse, radices, scire,* and *proprietates*) easily leads to the conclusion that the entire mechanism of overlapping segments mapped on the Hand is in fact a *sine qua non* for singing and even a basic mode of organization of the gamut.

In short, the generation of Garlandia, Salomon, and Amerus found themselves navigating a hypertrophied terminological and conceptual universe that may have been intellectually and systemically rewarding to late-medieval minds, but at the cost of complicating the basic relationship between *sounds*, rungs in the ladder, and their designating *labels*, that had been the great achievement of Carolingian and Guidonian times. Amerus himself feels the need to tease out letters, discreet sounds, syllables, and notes from one another:

Notandum … quod viginti tres littere et totidem voces, idest note, possunt dici in gamma propter duplicem clavem et duplicem vocem in utroque b-fa-♮-mi. Nota quod non debet dici C-fa-ut habet duas voces, quoniam falsum est, quia in notis suis semper est univox et non due voces, sive dicatur fa-ut sive ut-fa, sed dicitur C-fa-ut habet duo diversa vocabula vocum, vel duas notas, idest signa sive nomina vocum, et eodem modo dico de omnibus clavibus plures notas habentibus.

[Note that twenty-three letters and as many discreet sounds, i.e. notes, may be counted in the gamut by including the two different pitches and the two discreet sounds found in b-fa-♮-mi. Note that it is false to say that C-fa-ut has two discreet sounds, because for every note there is always one sound only and not two, whether one says fa-ut or ut-fa; rather, one should say that C-fa-ut has two different Guidonian syllables, or two notes, that is to say, two signs or names of notes, and the same is true for all other pitches (*vocabula vocum*) with multiple notes.][24]

---

[24] Amerus, *Practica artis musicae*, ed. Ruini, p. 22, translation mine.

Amerus is aware of the basic difference between sounds and labels, but seems trapped in his own confusion of *res* and *verba*. It is clear that he wishes to use *vox* to indicate a "discreet sound" marked by a *littera* or *clavis*. A Guidonian syllable, in this context, is a *vocabulum* or *nomen vocis* for designating that *vox*. But Amerus' use of *nota* is ambiguous: in the first phrase the term seems to be a synonym for *vox*, and in the last one for *vocabulum vocis*. Perhaps Amerus is being led astray by the then recent practice – which may be originally English – of indicating on the Guidonian Hand not just the *loci* marked by letters and syllables, but also the position of each pitch on the musical staff using square notation (see Fig. 4.2). Typically, the Hands belonging to this group did not indicate one square note per pitch, as would seem logical, but as many square notes (perhaps what Amerus calls *notae* or *signa*) as the number of syllables corresponding to that *locus*. This solution may seem coherent to the eye, yet it is logically redundant and it further obscures the already complicated relationship between *vox*, *vocabulum vocis*, *signum*, and *nota*. Thus, I suggest that in the citation above *nota* is best understood as "Guidonian syllables" (*vocabulum vocis*).

Late-medieval pitch nomenclature was evidently a thorny affair for Scholastic authors, thus all the more so for modern translators. The important consideration here is that Amerus' hexachordal system was centered around the *notae* understood as *vocabula vocum* (i.e., the pitch labels, also known as *voces*), rather than around the pitches themselves (i.e., the *litterae* or *claves*).

It is with such distinctions in mind that we may approach the great interest in the doctrine of mutation during Amerus' time. The backbone of the list of mutations that follows is the same continuous series of diatonic pitches – from Γ to dd – that had been recognized by Guido and Pseudo-Odo centuries earlier. But the emphasis is now no longer on the musical *res*, but rather on the musical *verba* superimposed to them in overlapping layers, and on the (virtual) shifts between them:

Gamma-ut habet unam notam, nullam mutacionem. A-re unam notam, nullam mutacionem. B-mi unam notam, nullam mutacionem. C-fa-ut habet duas notas et duas mutaciones: fa-ut ascendendo, ut-fa descendendo, fa-ut de ♮ quadrato in cantum proprium, ut-fa de proprio cantu in ♮ quadrato. D-sol-re habet duas notas et duas mutaciones: sol-re ascendendo de ♮ quadrato in proprium cantum, re-sol descendendo in ♮ quadratum. E-la-mi habet duas notas et duas mutaciones: la-mi ascendendo de ♮ quadrato in proprium cantum, mi-la descendendo de proprio cantu in ♮ quadratum. F-fa-ut habet duas notas et duas mutaciones: fa-ut ascendendo de proprio cantu in b molle, ut-fa descendendo de b molle in proprium cantum. G-sol-re-ut habet tres notas et sex mutaciones: sol-re ascendendo de proprio cantu in b molle,

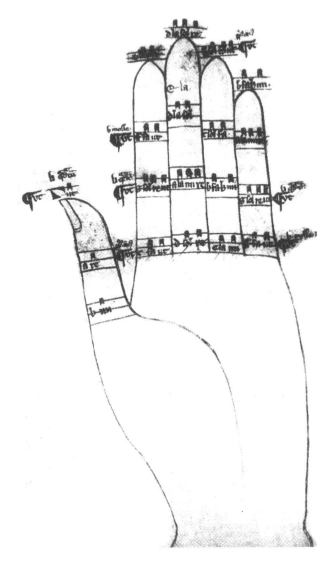

Fig. 4.2. London, Royal C VI, fol. 52v.

re-sol descendendo de b molle in proprium cantum, sol-ut ascendendo de proprio cantu in ♮ quadratum, ut-sol descendendo ♮de ♮ quadrato in proprium cantum, re-ut ascendendo de b molle in ♮ quadratum, ut-re ascendendo de ♮ quadrato in b molle. A-la-mi-re habet tres notas et sex mutaciones: la-mi ascendendo de proprio cantu in b molle, mi-la descendendo de b molle in proprium cantum, la-re ascendendo de proprio cantu in ♮ quadratum, re-la descendendo de ♮ quadrato in proprium cantum, mi-re ascendendo de b molle in ♮ quadratum, re-mi ascendendo de ♮ quadrato in b molle. B-fa-♮-mi habet duas claves et duas notas: fa in semitonio et mi in pleno tono, et ideo non habet mutacionem quia oportet quod omnis mutacio sit in eadem voce. C-sol-fa-ut habet tres notas et sex mutaciones: sol-fa descendendo de b molle in ♮ quadratum, fa-sol descendendo de ♮ quadrato in b molle, sol-ut ascendendo de b molle in proprium cantum, ut-sol descendendo de proprio cantu in b molle, fa-ut ascendendo de ♮ quadrato in proprium cantum, ut-fa descendendo de proprio cantu in ♮ quadratum. D-la-sol-re habet tres notas et sex mutaciones: la-sol ascendendo de b molle in ♮ quadratum, sol-la descendendo de ♮ quadrato in b molle, la-re ascendendo de b molle in proprium cantum, re-la descendendo de proprio cantu in b molle, sol-re ascendendo de ♮ quadrato in proprium cantum, re-sol descendendo de proprio cantu in ♮ quadratum. E-la-mi ut supra. F-fa-ut ut supra. G-sol-re-ut ut supra. A-la-mi-re ut supra. B-fa-♮-mi omnes iste claves quantum ad mutaciones ut supra. C-sol-fa habet duas notas et duas mutaciones: sol-fa ascendendo de b molle in ♮ quadratum, fa-sol descendendo de ♮ quadrato in b molle. D-la-sol habet duas notas et duas mutaciones: la-sol ascendendo de b molle in ♮ quadratum, sol-la descendendo de ♮ [-32-] quadrato in b molle. Quocienscumque ut incipitur super g, totus cantus eius est per ♮ quadratum; quociens incipitur ut super f, est per b molle; quociens ut incipitur super c, est per proprium cantum.[25]

Such painstaking laundry lists of letters and syllables, the triumph and pleasure of mechanistic *ratio* for its own sake, will become the norm in four-teenth- and fifteenth-century music theory, down to Tinctoris' *Expositio manus* (1473) and Gafori's *Practica musica* (1496). But once budding sing-ers had memorized these instructions (as they certainly were compelled to do), would they have been able to sight sing effectively? And did profes-sional singers rely on such guidelines in their daily activities? We will prob-ably never know, but excerpts like this no doubt made Guido turn in his grave; eventually, they would trigger the wrath of Johannes Gallicus, who in the mid-fifteenth century lambasted the technique of mutation as nothing but "empty verbosity" (see Chapter 6). By then, Gallicus was trying hard to bring back the teaching methods of post-Carolingian times, and with them an approach to *musica practica* that privileged pragmatism over systematic-ity. But that was far into the future. In the late thirteenth century, treatises such as Amerus' *Practica* seemed more intent on contemplating each and every combinatorial possibility embedded in the hexachordal machinery than to provide a manageable method for sight singing.

In sum, Parisian theory after 1250 took the decisive step of parsing the gamut in major-sixth segments according to the anchoring of the *ut-la* syl-lables on G, C, and F, so that the syllables in the end appeared to be in the driver's seat of musical theory and practice. In the musical writings of the thirteenth-century Parisian school, the syllables indeed bring much action and depth to musical space: the overlapping of the *proprietates*, their

---

[25] Amerus, *Practica artis musicae*, pp. 30–2.

tripartite distinction into *natura*, *b mollis* and *b quadrus*, and the mechanism of hexachordal changes (*mutationes*) all demand quick thinking and good memory from the singers. There is now a fully fledged system to be negotiated by theorists in their scriptoria and by singers in their chapels. Post-1250 visual representations of the gamut also seem to confirm the new prominence of the syllables over the venerable letters: such representations now take the form of true bi-dimensional tables that contrast with the linear graphs of the Carolingian and post-Carolingian era, which had limited themselves to showing the sequence of letters and (at most) the *maneriae* expressed in Roman numerals I-IV and the corresponding *daseian* signs. The difference between the two types of representation rests all in the syllables: completely absent in the old, linear type, they greatly dominate the new one numerically and even geometrically, by virtue of their intriguing layout and varying degrees of overlap (see Frontispiece). By contrast, the letters are literally marginalized and overpowered in their predictable order from low to high. It would be counterintuitive, for both medieval and modern readers alike, to look at such tables and interpret them as "letter-centered."

Yet the seven letters, and the principle of octave duplication that they expressed, did not lose their paradigmatic significance with the coming of age of the hexachordal system in the thirteenth century. Rather, the new emphasis on the syllables found in the treatises was the natural outcome of the ongoing expansion of Guido's method into a system, and no doubt also of the increased adoption of solmization in more and more European churches and monasteries. As theorists and the *magistri* of the Scholastic era concentrated on how to articulate musical space in hexachords for the purpose of sight singing, they adopted a conceptual apparatus and a terminology suggesting that such articulations were *objectively there*, as a default organization of that space that even trumped the space-defining role of the seven letters. Once the all-encompassing system was erected, it provided a framework for seeing and interpreting all aspects of pitch organization. The task for the historian is to place that system in historical perspective, keeping in mind the circumstances in which it was created. Such a perspective no doubt should take into account the persistence of letters-only music pedagogy and chant notation throughout the Middle Ages.

The virtual character of *mutatio* and the *coniunctae*

A study of the medieval understanding of hexachordal mutation strengthens the thesis that the six Guidonian syllables were perceived as accessorial even by the same authors who at times portray them as the structural pillars of the diatonic edifice. Medieval theorists leave no doubt that mutations were artificially *made* by solmizing singers, rather than objectively *located* or *embedded* in the notated part, as they consistently speak of "fieri mutatio," "sumitur mutatio," and the like, when describing the act of performing a hexachordal shift.[26] Garlandia himself, in his discussion of this topic, writes that "mutations were invented by necessity" and that should always be *made* by the singers only when forced to do so.[27] Mutations (unlike modal changes or tonal modulations) were not meaningful musical events, but rather mere operational shifts that took place in the singer's mind, as confirmed by the fact that there is almost always more than one note that can serve as a "launching pad" to the next *deductio*, and often more than one correct way to solmize a sequence of notes.

By the same token, the late medieval theory of *coniunctae* that appears in treatises such as the Parisian Anonymous (later attributed to a "Goscalcus francigenus," ca. 1375), Anonymous XI (late fifteenth century), and other sixteenth-century authors may be interpreted as an ingenious way of providing a diatonic justification for the chromatic notes of the gamut (otherwise known as *musica ficta*), rather than as a way of deriving them. Thus, modern musicological literature frequently discusses the topic of *musica ficta* in connection with the notion of "ficta hexachords" by which the

---

[26] See, for instance, Hieronymus of Moravia, *Tractatus de musica*, chapter XII, ed. S. M. Cserba, Freiburger Studien zur Musikwissenschaft, 2 (Regensburg: Pustet, 1935), pp. 49–55; Meyer, ed., *Musica plana Johannis de Garlandia*, pp. 72–7; W. Odington, *De speculatione musice*, ed. F. Hammond, *CSM* 14 ([Rome]: American Institute of Musicology, 1970), p. 99; Ps.-Aristoteles, *Tractatus de musica*, in *CS* I, p. 256; Jan Herlinger, ed. and trans., *The Lucidarium of Marchetto of Padua* (University of Chicago Press, 1985), pp. 280–98; Anonymous XI, *Tractatus de musica plana et mensurabili*, in R. J. Wingell, "Anonymous XI (CS III): An Edition, Translation, and Commentary," 3 vols. (Ph.D. diss., University of Southern California, 1973), vol. 1, p. 12; A. Ornithoparchus, *Musice active micrologus*, book 1, chapters 6 and 10 (G. Reese and S. Ledbetter, eds., *A Compendium of Musical Practice: Musice active micrologus, by Andreas Ornithoparcus; Andreas Ornithoparcus, his Micrologus, or introduction, containing the art of singing by John Dowland* (New York: Dover, 1973), pp. 21–3 and 31). Predictably, the corresponding Italian idiom is "fare le mutationi" (for instance, P. Cerone, *Le regole più necessarie per l'introduttione del canto fermo*, ed. B. Baroffio (Pisa: Libreria Musicale Italiana Editrice, 1989), pp. 12–14). French theorists, in turn, typically use the expression "faire muances." See, for instance, the *Instruction méthodique fort facile pour apprendre la musique pratique* by the Dutch-born Corneille Blockland de Montfort (first published in 1573), chapter 3, p. 17; and Jean Yssandon's *Traité de la musique pratique* (1582), p. 8 (both treatises now bound in one volume by Minkoff Reprints [Genève: 1972]).

[27] "Et sciendum est quod quantumcumque possumus operari cantum per has voces universales ad omnem musicam, scilicet *ut re mi fa sol la*, debemus mutationes vitare et eas precavere nisi quia totaliter possint evitari vel precaveri. Se dum venerit necessitas mutationem agendi, tunc debet fieri et non aliter, quia causa necessitatis inventa fuit mutatio" (Meyer, ed., *Musica plana Johannis de Garlandia*, p. 72).

syllable *ut* was placed on letters other than G, C, and F.[28] The term *coniuncta* is the Latin equivalent of the Greek "synemmenon" ("conjunct"). Just as in the Greater Perfect System the conjunct tetrachord established *trite synemmenon* one half step above *mese* (or *b flat* above *a*) so theorists in the fourteenth century began to transpose the six Guidonian syllables on letters other than the regular C, F, or G for the purpose of locating a number of flattened or sharpened notes. A *coniuncta* placing *ut* on A, for example, would include C# as a regular step by associating it with the default syllable *mi*; a coniuncta with *ut* on B flat would generate E flat as *fa*, and so on.

But in which sense (if at all) were the *coniuncta* "hexachords" necessary to the conceptualization, or the location, of those accidentals? Interestingly, the first treatise of the Parisian anonymous (the earliest known source to present this particular theory) points to a *coniuncta* as a virtual operation performed by the singer, when it describes it as "the *mental transposition* of any property or hexachord from its own location to another location above or below," (emphasis mine).[29] The treatise also uses the passive verbs "accipitur" or "incipitur," thus suggesting that it is either the theorist or the singer that creates a *coniuncta* for the purpose of "introducing," or singing, a chromatic step, just like an orator will fabricate mental images, or *phantasmata*, to memorize his speech. In his discussion of this topic, Oliver Ellsworth also points out the virtual nature of the *coniunctae* when he states that "a coniuncta is ... not a concrete entity – a hexachord on a 'foreign' pitch. It is rather the operation or the process that creates such a hexachord."[30] One may add that the "hexachord" so created is not a concrete entity either, but rather it is only an *ad hoc*, mental parsing of the gamut for the purpose of solmization. The mechanism becomes clearer if we understand it not in terms of "transposing hexachords" (a Renaissance idea, as we will see), but rather in terms of the key medieval distinction between *proprietas* and *deductio*: whereas the transposition of the *deductio* is real (in the sense that a *coniuncta* effects a repositioning of the six syllables on different notes of the gamut), the act of framing the accidental step within a new *proprietas* is purely the result of an *intellectualis transposicio* for the sake of convenience

---

[28] For a recent example, see Mead, "Renaissance Theory," 2nd edn., (Bloomington, IN: Indiana University Press, 2007), pp. 343–51.

[29] "Coniuncta est alicuius proprietatis seu deduccionis de loco proprio ad alienum locum secundum sub vel supra intellectualis transposicio" (from O. B. Ellsworth, ed. and trans., *The Berkeley Manuscript* (Lincoln: University of Nebraska Press, 1984), pp. 52–3). This definition could be extended to cover the three main *deductiones* of *musica recta* as well. The *deductiones* of *musica recta* were no less *mental* and no more *real* than those of *musica ficta*. Only the starting points differed.

[30] O. B. Ellsworth, "The Origin of the Coniuncta: A Reappraisal," *JMT* 17 (1973), 91.

(in other words, a *proprietas* is *there* only as the "virtual" bedrock of the transposed *deductio*, which in turn exists only as pitch labels, not real sounds).[31] A singer considers the accidental note as the third or fourth step of an imagined *proprietas*, so that he can correctly sing it as either *mi* or *fa* of the corresponding *deductio* (depending, of course, on whether it is a sharp or a flat).

The relatively widespread transmission of *coniuncta* theory as a way of justifying the accidental steps should not lead us to conclude that the chromatic expansion of the gamut would not have been possible without it.[32] To be sure, Karol Berger has convincingly shown that "the logic of the solmization syllables" was perhaps the most important factor in setting the outer limits of "the universe of musica ficta."[33] Late-medieval theorists recognized *fa* notes that could only be sharpened (such as C and F) and *mi* notes that could only be lowered (such as A and E).

Once again, however, the fact that the Guidonian syllables provided a sort of conceptual scheme for understanding, or regulating, the use of accidentals does not imply that solmization was essential to the accidentals' *raison d'être*. Berger points out that the mid-fourteenth-century treatise by Johannes Boen set the limits of *musica ficta* following the logic of staff notation, as opposed to that of solmization, by maintaining that any note could be preceded by a flat or a sharp regardless of its position within the Guidonian system.[34] Boen might certainly represent a minority view, yet what is significant here is the fact that a non-hexachordal understanding of the accidentals *is* documented. A few decades later, in the first quarter of the fifteenth century, Prosdocimo de' Beldemandis showed how *all* accidentals – not just the eight or ten that were typically obtained via the *coniunctae* – could be derived through targeted divisions of the monochord.[35]

---

[31] On the subtle, but key differences between *hexachordum, deductio*, and *proprietas* see my "Virtual Segments," pp. 440–7 and Chapter 7 below, pp. 187–99.

[32] Ellsworth also argues against drawing such an inference when he observes that: "The primary consideration [in *coniuncta* theory] is the location of the semitone and the accidental that indicates its presence. The hexachord involved, on the other hand, is a theoretical foundation for the new accidental and is of secondary importance" ("The Origin of Coniuncta," 92).

[33] K. Berger, "The Expanding Universe of *Musica Ficta* in Theory from 1300 to 1550," *JM* 4 (1986), 415.

[34] K. Berger, "The Expanding Universe," 414–5. In his recent study of the *tabula monochordi* of Magister Nicolaus de Luduno (copied around 1400 in an Italian source), Peter Lefferts downplays the significance of hexachordal considerations for generating the notes of the chromatic genus. See P. Lefferts, "A Riddle and a Song: Playing with Signs in a Fourteenth-century Ballade, *EMH* 26 (2007), 121–79.

[35] In his *Parvus tractatulus de modo dividendi monacordum* (1413, revised between 1425 and 1428) Prosdocimo locates on the monochord first the seven diatonic notes of *musica recta*

Several decades earlier, however, the English tract *Sequitur de sinemenis* had generated the chromatic notes of the gamut by performing a chain of ascending perfect fifths from B natural to A sharp, and a chain of descending perfect fifths from B flat to G flat. In short, monochordal computations of the accidental notes may well have been historically older than *coniuncta* theory.[36]

Why six syllables?

As late-thirteenth century theorists began to take a closer look at the Guidonian syllables and to explore their combinatorial possibilities, they inevitably came to raise new questions about the basic tools at their disposal, as we saw, for instance, in Amerus. One *quaestio* became especially urgent: given the fact that the syllables and the letters are intended to map onto each other for the purposes of pitch denomination and sight singing, what is the reason for establishing two *uneven* sets of six and seven units? The answers that the *magistri* provided to this query are especially interesting to our discussion, in that they cast light on the key issue of how medieval theorists and musicians understood the relationship between musical syllables and letters.

In his own discussion of this point, Magister Lambertus argues along similar lines when he affirms the necessity of having no fewer than seven letters to define the musical *voces*. He writes:

Sed queritur quare plures sint littere quam voces, cum tamen voces per has litteras exprimantur. Videtur enim quod iste due littere, scilicet F et G sint superflue, cum per sex precedentes sex voces lucidissime declarentur. Solummodo sicut tantum sex voces, ita et sex litteras tantum ad exprimendum illas sex voces hoc modo dicimus adinventas, scilicet: gamma ut, A re, B mi, C fa ut, D sol re, E la mi. Sed quia

(which he calls *musica vera*), then the five flats, and finally the five sharps, to generate a seventeen-note octave. For the two chromatic divisions, see, J. W. Herlinger, ed. and trans., *Prosdocimus de Beldemandis: 'Brevis summula proportionum quantum ad musicam pertinet' and 'Parvus tractatulus de modo monacordum dividendi,'* (Lincoln: University of Nebraska Press, 1987), pp. 90–3 and 100–5. See also K. Berger's discussion of Prosdocimo's treatise in "The Expanding Universe," 415–8. For an overview of chromatic divisions of the monochord, see C. Meyer, *Mensura monochordi: la division du monocorde (IXe–XVe siècles)*, pp. xxxiv–xxxvii and xlviii–liii.

[36] This short treatise was first published by Coussemaker (*CS* 1, 364–5), and is now available in the new edition and English translation by Jan Herlinger as "Appendix B" to Prosdocimo's *Little Treatise* (pp. 123–35). The earliest extant source of *Sequitur de sinemenis* is a section of London, British Library, MS Royal 12 C. VI, which has been variously dated to ca. 1275 (Herlinger), to the end of the thirteenth century (*LmI*), and to the fourteenth century (Meyer).

consideravimus quod tam vocum immobilitas, quam litterarum paucitas omnium proportiones cantuum non sufficeret propagare, G latinum in octava clavi locavimus, et eidem tres voces concessimus, scilicet: sol et re et ut, quatinus per ipsas ascensum et descensum competenter ostenderet, et ad [gamma] grecum G latinum diapason consonaret.

[One may wonder why there are more letters (*litterae*) than syllables *(voces)*, given that the latter are expressed by the former. It may seem indeed that these two letters, F and G, are superfluous, after the other ones have been articulated through the six syllables. For just as there are only six voces, so we can say that only six letters have been introduced to express those six voces, as follows: *gamma ut, A re, B mi, C fa ut, D sol re, E la mi.* But because we have realized that both the fixed order of the *voces* and the paucity of the letters is not sufficient to outline all the consonances of chant, we have placed the Latin letter G on the eighth key and we have attributed three syllables to it, namely *sol, re,* and *ut,* so that through them the melodic ascent and descent may be properly shown, and so that the Latin G may form a consonance of the octave with Greek T (gamma).][37]

Although Lambertus does not justify the inclusion of letter F, he seems to imply that it is included by default within the range of the octave that calls for letter G. But the crux of the matter here is that Lambertus is caught – not uncommonly – in a terminological trap. Generations of earlier theorists (including, of course, Guido of Arezzo), had used the term *vox* to mean a "pitch" or a "musical sound" that could be effectively indicated by a *littera,* a Guidonian syllable, or a combination of the two. When *vox* itself is understood as "Guidonian syllable" – as it happened increasingly in the thirteenth century – the implication is that the *voces* are part of a six-fold unit, and the old plain notion of pitch letters or syllables designating *voces* becomes nonsensical.

Along the same line of argument, Jacques de Liège also raises the question of why the standard number of *littere* is higher than that of the *voces* ("Quare autem plures sint littere quam voces queri potest"), a frequent topic of discussion among medieval theorists:[38]

Cur enim sex tacte voces in sex primis contineantur litteris, id est in [gamma]ut, Are, Bmi, Cfa, Dsol, Ela, videntur cetere due scilicet F et G superflue.

---

[37] Ps.-Aristotle, *Tractatus de musica,* p. 254, translation mine.
[38] See among others: E. Salomon, *Scientia artis musicae,* ("Quaero, quare non sunt septem puncti vel plures, sicut sunt septem litterae?" in *GS* III, p. 19); Engelbert of Admont in *De musica* ("Capitulum XIV. Quare in manu sint VI. notae et VII. litterae musicales, et non plures," in *GS* II, pp. 295–6); [Ps.]-Wylde ("Cur non nisi sex note nominibus designetur, cum sint septem vocum discrimina," in J. Wylde, *Musica manualis cum tonale,* p. 63).

Table 4.1. The major sixth as the aggregate
of the three species of fourth

3rd species of fourth:	C	D	E	F		
1st species of fourth:		D	E	F	G	
2nd species of fourth:			E	F	G	a
	C-a hexachord					

[Since the six syllables mentioned above are contained in the first six letters, that is, [gamma]-*ut*, A-*re*-, B-*mi*-, C-*fa*-, D-*sol*, E-*la,* are the remaining two letters, F and G, considered superfluous?][39]

The author's own answer is that six letters only could not generate all consonances ("… quia litterarum illarum paucitas ad omnem consonantiarum expressionem non sufficit"), and that seven letters are necessary to indicate the seven distinct sounds of the monochord, as Guido himself would have put it ("Quare scilicet septem tantum sunt monocordi vocum discrimina, que septem tactis distinguuntur litteris").[40] On the other hand, the justification for the choice of six syllables, according to Jacques, lies in their ability to embrace all three species of fourth, with the semitone at the top (C-F), in the middle (D-G) and at the bottom (E-a) (Table 4.1).

Such an explanation will remain common among later theorists – Nicolaus Burtius and Franchino Gafori, to name only two – who likewise strived to make sense of Guido's original choice of six syllables. It is hard, however, to see what the particular advantage of the "all-tetrachord" property might be for practical purposes. The *ambitus* of most chant melodies was determined by the conventions of modal theory, which emphasized combinations of fourths and fifths, not of the three species of fourth. But the point is not that Jacques' answer was speculative or inadequate, but rather that it was not at all immediate. Vice versa, the question about the number of pitch letters did not arise, as it was simply a matter of course. It was the syllables that had to justify their existence, and such justification invariably ended up confirming – if at times a bit circuitously – the primary role of the seven letters as the true building blocks of musical space.

For instance, in his chapter dedicated to the question "Why six syllables?" Engelbert of Admont can offer only a specious explanation, namely, that six syllables are in use because some *loci* carry only one of them, some carry two, and some as many as three:

---

[39] Jacques de Liège, *Speculum musicae*, ed. R. Bragard, vol. 6, p. 166, translation mine.
[40] *Ibid.*

Cum igitur infimis gravibus adscribatur singulis una nota tantum, supremis vero acutissimarum duae notae, mediis vero tres notae, ratione praedictae necessitatis, exceptis E. la. mi. et F. fa. ut. et B. fa. ♮. mi, quibus ubique propter semitonium, quod semper ibi occurrit ascendendo et descendendo, non adscribuntur nisi duae notae solae. Una vero nota et duae aliae diversae ab illa, et tres diversae ab illis tribus faciunt VI. numero: patet ergo, quod non erant necesse aliae notae nisi sex numero, cuius rationem et causam etiam superius promisimus reddere in hoc loco.

[For the reason explained above, to the lowest notes of the gamut correspond only one syllable, to the highest ones two syllables, and three to the median ones. The only exceptions are E la mi, F fa ut and B fa ♮ mi, to which only two syllables are ascribed because they involve the ascending or descending semitone. Thus, we have one syllable, plus two, plus three, for a total of six: therefore, no more than six syllables will be necessary, as we wished to demonstrate.][41]

On the other hand, Engelbert's account of the seven musical letters is no exercise in mirror-climbing, even though it proposes a questionable reading of Virgil's famous line from the Aeneid on the number of note qualities:

Sunt etiam VII. litterae tantum, quibus voces designantur, quia primarum et simplicium consonantiarum musicalium sunt VII. differentiae tantum, secundum illud Virgilii: Septem discrimina vocum et caetera videlicet semitonium, tonus, semiditonus, ditonus, diatessaron, diapente, ac diapason: quae tamen non est consonantia differentialis secundum Guidonem, quia non facit aliam speciem vocis, sed eandem in acutis, quae erat in gravibus, et sub eodem tenore variato solum per acutum et grave […]Ad septem vero praedictas simplices et primas musicas consonantias variandas et denotandas in libris et instrumentis musicis sufficiebant VII. litterae supradictae. Vel potius ideo sufficiunt VII. litterae designantes VII. voces: quia in VII. vocibus usque ad octavam perficitur diapason, in qua omnis cantus musicus sufficienter cantatur: et quidquid ultra cantatur, est idem tenor diversificatus solummodo per acutissimum et gravissimum.

[There are only seven letters by which we designate the musical sounds, because there are only seven different types of primary and simple consonances, in accordance with Virgil's "seven distinctions of tones," etc. These are the semitone, the tone, the minor third, the major third, the fourth, the fifth, and the octave which, however, is not a consonance of different pitches (*consonantia differentialis*), as Guido observes, because it does not lead to a new sound, but to the same sound in the high and low range. The seven above-mentioned letters are sufficient to indicate those seven musical consonances in musical books and instruments. Furthermore, the seven letters suffice to designate the seven musical sounds because those sounds fill out the octave, which provides a sufficient span for every musical song: whatever

---

[41] Engelbert of Admont, *De musica, tractatus primus*, ch. 14, p. 296.

is sung beyond the octave is nothing but the same note placed only in a higher or lower range.][42]

Virgil's *septem discrimina vocum* referred to musical pitches, not to intervals.[43] Nevertheless, Engelbert's account of the seven *litterae* is noteworthy for its unequivocal appeal to octave duplication as a fundamental axiom of musical space.

That the issue of the reciprocal functional relationship between letters and syllables was a thorny one in the late Middle Ages is confirmed by an anonymous fifteenth-century author who added his commentary to an earlier text belonging to the tradition of Johannes Hollandrinus (or Valendrinus), who had been active in the mid-fourteenth century in Oxford and Prague. The text of the commentary is particularly interesting because the anonymous author quotes abundant excerpts from the original text, which he then follows with his own discussion of it, usually preceded by the formula *Circa litteram notandum*, or "It should be observed about that paragraph that …".

Early on in his treatise, for instance, the author cites the following passage, presumably from Hollandrinus himself, which appears to assign a structural priority to the syllables over the letters:

Et in qualibet earum [i.e., organica, harmonica, rigmica, etc.] sonus sextupliciter variatur ad voluntatem primorum instituentium et communem assensum omnium subsequentium his sex silbis Ut re mi fa sol la. Primum namque sonans vox, flatus aut pulsus, Ut sic dicto vocabulo nominatur, qui ulterius per unum tonum sine intervallo [recte: sive intervallum?] ascendens re dicitur. Deinde per tonum elevatus mi vocatur, super quam per semitonium ascendens fa, ut placuit, appellatur, deinde sol et ultro la. Et hae voces seu sillabae sex litteris capitalibus propter sui dignitatem prioratus hoc modo designantur: T A B C D E. Nam prima, quae Ut nominatur, per gamma sive per G graecum designatur. … A re B mi C fa D sol E vero la repraesentat.

[In all of its varieties [i.e., generated by wind or string instruments or by voices alone], musical sound comes in a six-fold arrangement through the six syllables, Ut re mi fa sol la, according to the will of the early musicians and by common consent of their followers. The first tone, played on either wind or keyed instruments

[42] *Ibid.*

[43] The expression, widely quoted throughout the Middle Ages, comes from Virgil's description of Orpheus in *Aeneid*, VI: 645–7: "Nec non Threïcius longa cum veste sacerdos/Obloquitur numeris septem discrimina vocum; Jamque fidem digitis, jam pectine pulsat eburno," ed. J. B. Greenough, *Perseus Digital Library*, Tufts University. URL: www.perseus.tufts.edu/hopper/; ("There, too, the Thracian priest, the long-robed Orpheus, plays, accompanying with seven tones; and now his fingers strike the strings, and now his quill of ivory"), A. Mandelbaum, ed. and trans., *The Aeneid of Virgil* (Berkeley: University of California Press, 1971), p. 154.

[described in a previous section], is called Ut, which then ascends by one tone or interval called re. Another ascending whole tone leads to mi, then by half step to fa, as the early musicians agreed to call it, and finally to sol and la. And these *voces* or syllables were assigned by choice to the six capital letters Γ A B C D E. Indeed the first syllable Ut was assigned to gamma, or Greek G; likewise, A represents re A, B mi, C fa, D sol, and A mi.][44]

Perhaps as a result of the prominence of the six *voces* in the musical practice of his time, Valendrinus is led to regard those *voces* as the primary source of tone variety in the gamut, so much so that he is willing to consider the set of six letters (Γ-E) as derived from the syllables *ut-la*. According to this logic, the letters represent the syllables, not vice versa (*hae voces seu sillabae sex litteris capitalibus … designantur*). Such reasoning, as should by now be clear, simply turns eleventh- and twelfth-century music theory on its head. The anonymous commentator, however, feels the need to insert the following corrective:

Unde per hoc non est putandum, quod solum sex essent litterae seu claves musicales. Quia huiusmodi septem sunt, ut clarius infra patebit, et post septimam litteram reiteratur prima et consequenter aliae sequentes. Quicunque enim diapason tangit et [-163-] ultra diapason vadit, reiteratio potest dici, ut ait magister Johannes de Muris in musica sua theoretica.

[However, one should not conclude from this that there are only six musical letters or keys. There are indeed seven of them, as it soon will become clear, and after the seventh the first one is repeated, then all others in turn. Indeed, whoever strikes the diapason and goes beyond it obtains a repetition of sounds, as magister Johannes de Muris says.][45]

With no exception – to my knowledge at least – the late Scholastic theorists who attempted to justify the choice of six syllables for solmization missed the point entirely. With hundreds of exemplars of Guido's *Micrologus* and the *Epistola* in circulation, not one of them appears to have connected that original choice with the doctrine of diatonic affinity at the fifth, which those treatises had discussed so clearly and extensively. This observation inevitably raises questions on the reading habits and on the use of sources of Scholastic theorists, who indeed – as other details confirm – do not seem to have had a first-hand knowledge of earlier music treatises, including those by Guido. As we will see, the general lack of familiarity of late-medieval

---

[44] Anonymous, *Opusculum monacordale*, in F. Feldmann, *Musik und Musikpflege im mittelalterlichen Schlesien*, Darstellungen und Quellen zur schlesischen Geschichte, vol. 37 (Breslau: Trewendt und Granier, 1938), p. 162.

[45] *Ibid.*, pp. 162–3.

theorists with eleventh- and twelfth-century chant theory will persist well into the humanist era (and beyond).

A semiotic approach to the hexachordal system

As the present analysis has demonstrated, the creation – or at the very least the codification – of a fully fledged hexachordal system in mid-thirteenth century Paris went hand in hand with a renewed inquiry into the classification and the organization of musical sound. The theorists of that generation brought a distinctly philosophical and grammatical framework to the study of the rudiments and of the organizing principles of music. In the process, the relationship between musical *res* and *verba* became increasingly fragmented and complicated. The basic musical "hardware" – the gamut, the intervallic distances between the pitches, pitch sets and subsets – had not changed significantly from the Carolingian and post-Carolingian era (the only notable exception being the addition of chromatic pitches to the gamut). On the other hand, however, new labels and concepts designed to navigate and rationalize that hardware were rapidly added to the old ones, making increasingly difficult the task of effectively relating all components of the system to one another, as demonstrated by the excerpts cited above from the commentary on Valendrinus. The subtle functional differences between *deductio* and *proprietas* (perhaps even *hexachordum*) or between *vox, claves, nota, signum,* and *locus* posed no fewer difficulties to them than they do to us.

This new music-theoretical environment changed the scope of the relationship between music and grammar that had been in place for centuries. The issue was no longer one of exploring the superficial similarities between the components of speech (letters, syllables, words, and entire texts) and the parts of music (pitches, intervals, phrases, entire songs), along the footsteps of – for instance – the ninth-century *Musica enchiriadis*.[46] Rather, it was one of establishing effective links between the musical system on the one hand, and the plethora of operative principles and designating labels brought in by the ever expanding solmization theory on the other. In this sense, one may speak of a new semiotic awareness in the theoretical approach to Guido's syllables that developed at the end of

---

[46] The widely transmitted *Musica enchiriadis* (ninth century), for instance, opens precisely with such an analogy. See R. Erickson, ed. and trans., *Musica Enchiriadis and Scholica Enchiriadis* (New Haven: Yale University Press, 1995), pp. xxxvi–xxxvii; 1.

the thirteenth century.[47] It was no longer a matter of simply attaching the Guidonian syllables to pitch letters and intervals; now the syllables were understood as playing an active role in the complex chain of signification that linked the notes on the page with the sounds of the gamut and with the mnemonic traces of the basic intervals in the singer's mind.

Consider, for instance, how Johannes de Garlandia introduces his reader to the topic of the *proprietates*:

Sunt autem in omni cantu tres proprietates, cum iste tres ad demonstracionem et evidentiam totius cantus sufficiant, scilicet ♮ quadrum, natura vel proprius cantus quod idem est, et b molle. Ratio quare proprietates dicuntur talis est, quia regulariter proprie in notitiam vere canendi tonos et semitonos agendi legitime nos introducunt.

[There are three properties to all songs, because three are sufficient to demonstrate and articulate all songs, namely, by ♮, by nature or properchant, and by ♭. The reason why they are called properties is that they deliver to us, rightfully and truthfully, the proper information for singing tones and semitones.][48]

In a characteristically verbose fashion – notice the redundant use of modifiers, such as "vere," "regulariter," "proprie," and "legitime" – the passage affirms rather strongly the three properties as both the controlling agent embedded in "all songs," and the means by which the distances between the letters is established ("sunt autem in omni cantu tres proprietates … in notitiam vere canendi … nos introducunt"). The three properties, in this account, are no longer just a tool for sight singing, but rather an essential musical signifier: implicit in Garlandia's definition is that, without them, the singer would not have access to "the proper information for singing tones and semitones." More, the *notitia canendi* is brought to the singers rightfully and truthfully by the properties, and verbalized by the six syllables, because the "raw musical matter itself," i.e., the series of tones and semitones of the gamut, unfolds in accordance with the *modus operandi* of the properties to begin with. This may be the reason why, several paragraphs later, Garlandia

---

[47] Among earlier contributions on the philosophical and intellectual background to medieval music theory (particularly mensural notation), see J. Yudkin, "The *Copula* According to Johannes de Garlandia," *MD* 34 (1980), 67–84, and D. Tanay, *Noting Music, Marking Culture* (see n. 3 above). On the relationship between music and grammar in the earlier part of the Middle Ages (up to the twelfth century), see M. Bielitz, *Musik und Grammatik* (Munich: Katzbichler, 1977). For an analysis of the signifying strategies of early chant notation in the West, see L. Treitler, "The Early History of Music Writing in the West," *JAMS* 35 (1982), 237–79.

[48] Meyer, ed., *Musica plana Johannis de Garlandia*, p. 67.

states very clearly that "each property contains and encompasses six letters *and* six syllables."[49]

Likewise, Hélie Salomon's roughly contemporary definition of the musical Hand portrays it also as an essential element in the music-semiotic chain between sound and mind:

Quid est palma in hac scientia? Palma est clavis, figura, sive instrumentum continens omnimodam notitiam artis musicae, seu omnium, quae recte cantari possunt, manifestationem, sine cuius notitia scientia nulla; nec alias cantor, sed ioculator seu iauglator [sic] reputatur.

[What is the Hand in this science? It is the key, the figure, and the medium containing all the knowledge [necessary to] the art of music, i.e., the explanation of everything that can be sung correctly. Without this knowledge, the science of music is nil, and a singer is not reputed as such, but a joker and a wailer.][50]

One may also mention the anonymous *Summa musice*, which describes the six syllables as sufficient "for signifying each and every song" ("ad significationem cantus uniuscuiusque").[51]

It was arguably by inaugurating the "semiotic" approach to the Guidonian syllables that thirteenth-century music theorists profoundly departed from the pre-existing tradition of solmization. True, one may observe that the introduction of the doctrines of hexachordal properties and mutations had already marked a significant departure from Guido's intended use of the syllables.[52] Those innovations, however, still remained within the boundaries of a pedagogical conception of the syllables, conceived as a "soft" and dispensable tool for sight singing. They simply expanded the range of what a singer could do with Guido's method, without going as far as to consider those operations as being in any way structurally significant. But the moment that texts such as *Metrologus* and Garlandia's *Introductio* began to describe the function of the syllables as being central to the creation and the notation of musical sound, they crossed the Rubicon between music pedagogy and music theory, *ars* and *scientia*. By that transition the syllables relinquished their earlier status of mnemonic markers, and became *de facto* musical signs able to confer actual meaning to musical pitches and intervals. The conceptual transformation was

---

[49] "Et sic quaelibet proprietas sex litteras et sex voces continet et comprehendit," Meyer, ed., *Musica plana Johannis de Garlandia*, p. 70.

[50] Salomon, *Scientia artis musicae*, p. 23.

[51] See Page, ed. *Summa musice*, p. 157.

[52] Maria Teresa Rosa Barezzani makes this point in her "Guido d'Arezzo fra tradizione e innovazione," in A. Rusconi, ed., *Guido d'Arezzo Monaco pomposiano*, pp. 133–51.

subtle, slow, and not without resistance, yet it has continued to unfold down to the present time.

Future research may provide additional evidence of the pervasiveness of the "semiotic turn" in thirteenth-century solmization theory. But the visible traces of that turn stretch all the way to the Renaissance, as demonstrated by the *Margarita philosophica* by the Carthusian prior Gregor Reisch. The volume, which enjoyed great success in the sixteenth century after its original publication in Freiburg in Brisgau in 1503, is an introduction to the liberal arts in the form of a dialogue between a *discipulus* and a *magister*. Predictably, the first petal of Reisch's philosophical daisy deals with grammar, the unavoidable entry point to the other disciplines;[53] and when the author comes to discussing the elements of musical practice, in book V, treatise 2, he uses a terminology that is clearly mediated from grammar.[54] Reisch speaks, for instance, of the seven *claves* as the yoking of the basic discreet sounds of the monochord and the first seven *litterae grammaticae* as the "keys" to unlocking the secrets of music. The discussion then turns to the syllables, "by which every melody progresses" (*per quas sepius repetitas omnis cantus progreditur*). Singers do not specifically pronounce those syllables when they sing, Reisch explains; rather, they utter "the sounds that are signified by the syllables" (*sed sonos potius per illas significatos*).[55]

But in which way, asks the *discipulus*, do the seven original "keys" express the Guidonian syllables, as they unlock the notation? (*Sed quomodo dicte claues has voces reserando manifestant?*). The magister answers by reviewing the semiotic link between notes and syllables:

Eo. Nam cum singulis clauibus singule ponuntur voces vna vel plures: vti patuit supra in monochordi descriptione. vnum posita claui cum nota in linea vel spacio: ipsam non vocem quamlibet, sed eam tantum que cum tali iungitur significare necesse est.

[In this way: one or more syllables are superimposed onto the individual keys, as demonstrated in the description of the monochord above. One key also corresponds

[53] T. Heath, "Logical Grammar, Grammatical Logic, and Humanism in Three German Universities," *Studies in the Renaissance* 18 (1971), 33–4.

[54] For the musical portion of Reisch's text, see G. Reisch, *Margarita Philosophica cum additionibus novis: ab auctore suo studiosissima revisione quarto super additis, Liber V: De principiis musicae* (Basilee: Michael Futerius, 1517), f.mvijr-oiiijr; reprint, Düsseldorf: Stern-Verlag Janssen & Co., [1973], pp. 175–203).

[55] *Ibid.*, fol. nvv. The musical example that follows this passage shows six notes on the staff in ascending and descending order and without clef, as C-a or G-e. Presumably, these are to be interpreted as *signa vocum*, not as *claves*.

with one note on the staff; it is not, however, yoked to any syllable whatsoever, but only with that syllable that is necessary for the key to signify.][56]

Notice the emphasis on the necessity of correctly constituting the note/syllable pair for music signification to occur.

The role of the syllables in Reisch's semiotics of musical notation is fairly clear, in spite of some ambiguities in his prose: the *litterae grammaticae* are yoked to the discreet sounds of the monochord to yield the *claves*; these, in turn, denote the syllables, which signify the notes on the page. Quite possibly, this is among the clearest textual evidence to be found in late-medieval theory in support of the solmization system as a *sine qua non* of musical grammar, though thirteenth-century theorists clearly paved the way for such a position. Indeed, when Reisch observes that singers do not pronounce the syllables, but only the sounds "signified by them," (*sed sonos potius per illas significatos*), he implies that the syllables fulfill their basic music-semiotic function whether they are actually pronounced or not. By some kind of osmotic process, the hexachordal grouping of the *proprietates* has filtered down to the very structure of the diatonic system.

The excerpts cited here, along with the ones from Lambertus' *Tractatus* and the anonymous *Metrologus* discussed above, qualify the syllables as an indispensable element of medieval music semiosis; more importantly for my argument, they point to a grammatical-ontological model of the tonal system in which the pitch relationships conventionally constructed by the six syllables are perceived as real. Together, these excerpts constitute a new branch of solmization theory that will run alongside the older, "pedagogical" branch into the early modern era, and will eventually lead to the foundational view of Guido's six syllables that has persisted until the present time.

It is not clear whether the heightened semiotic function ascribed to the syllables by thirteenth-century theorists originated as a result of speculative interests, or rather from the daily practice of solmization. We do not know whether Garlandia, Lambertus, and Amerus were active as music practitioners, in addition to serving as musical *magistri* of sorts on or outside the premises of the University of Paris. They may have described solmization as key to the "signification" of music after observing how the six syllables had become "second nature" to the singers of their generations and perhaps to themselves. Alternatively – though this possibility is less likely – the distinct

---

[56] *Ibid.*, fol. nvv., translation mine.

foundational tone of those accounts might be considered as no more than a rhetorical strategy designed to emphasize the usefulness of the method in the early stages of instruction. But the important point is that the understanding of solmization theory they proposed was the product of speculative and scholastic interests that were quite remote from, and even at odds with, Guido's intended purposes and motivations. About a century later, in a markedly different intellectual environment, other authors will indeed begin to open a chasm between the doctrines of the "followers of Guido" and those of Guido himself.

∾   Interlude: All hexachords are "soft"

The "hexachords" in the title above refer to the major sixth of Guido and Hermannus and their transpositions, that is to say, to the portion of the gamut singled out by those two authors in connection with their doctrines of *affinitas* and *sedes troporum* (see Chapter 2 above). These are the hexachords of solmization commonly discussed in musicological literature. Terminological precision, however, is here more important than ever, lest we lose sight of key differences between diatonic segments of the same length, yet of a different nature.

To review my argument thus far, medieval writers consistently refrained from calling the Guidonian set of six syllables a "hexachord"; instead, they used the terms *deductio* to designate the six syllables, and *proprietas* the hexachordal portions of the gamut upon which the set of six syllables could be positioned, beginning on G, C, and F.[1] Beginning at least with Theinred of Dover in the twelfth century, *hexachordum* was one possible label for indicating the interval of a sixth, recognized to exist in two different sizes, major and minor. The *hexachordum major* (such as the "Guidonian" C-a, but also the "non-Guidonian" types of F-d with ♮ and D-♮) was more often called *tonus cum diapente* (or *diapente cum tono*), whereas *hexachordum minor* was identical with *semitonum cum diapente* or vice versa. In short, the consistently enforced medieval distinction between *hexachordum* and *deductio/proprietas* reflected the different natures of these formally identical diatonic segments: *hexachordum* designated the sixth in the "hard" sense of real-sounding *intervals*; contrariwise, the conceptual dyad of *deductio/proprietas* was "soft," as it had to do with either pitch *labels* (the *deductio ut-la*) or with a purely mental and *ad hoc* segmentation of the gamut by which the syllables were to be correctly matched with the letters. Even though the *proprietates* were expressed by pitch letters – thus "hard" musical sounds – their "sixth-ness" existed only as virtual or operative segments with no musical significance *per se*. The virtual and *ad hoc* nature of the dyad *deductio/proprietas* made it a useful, yet also dispensable tool for sight singing throughout the Middle Ages – as the first part of this monograph has shown – quite

[1] See my "Virtual Segments," 440–6.

in spite of the occasional wording to the contrary that one encounters in the music-theoretical literature from that time. That virtual nature is also the primary reason why the English term "hexachord" is a poor translation for the medieval terms *deductio* and *proprietas*. Most troublesome is its failure to preserve the key conceptual distinction between the "virtual segment" *ut-la* and the actual melodic or contrapuntal intervals (C-a and G-e, but also A-f and E-c) featured in actual musical works.

In sum, a contextual reading of the relevant music-theoretical literature confirms that the hexachordal system was understood in the Middle Ages as a "soft" superstructure overlaid on a "hard" heptachordal layer that had long been in place as the foundation of the diatonic system. Thus, the answer to the question that has inspired this monograph – was there ever a time when the hexachord served as a "central diatonic set" in Western music, in practice if not in theory – can only be unequivocally negative, unless one is careful to limit the range of application of that diatonic set to the specific task of solmization. The "hexachords" commonly used by medieval and Renaissance musicians for pitch designation and sight singing were by definition "soft" even when they were technically of the *durus* type – ever *verba*, never *res*.

At least some recent scholarship on this issue has hinted at the structural dependency of the syllables from the letters within the medieval gamut – although, as we saw in Chapter 1, the most common view has been that of an equal partnership between the two, with the letters establishing the order of the pitches and the syllables defining the actual distances. For instance, in his wittily titled article "*Mi chiamano Mimi* … but my Name is *Quarti toni*," Ross Duffin has argued that the name of Ockeghem's *Missa My my* refers not to the opening interval of a descending fifth (E-A) in the Bass, but rather to the overall diatonic imprint of the Mass, which falls squarely within the category of the fourth mode, or more precisely within the plagal *deuterus maneria* with final on E.[2] As Duffin explains, the constituent diatonic species of this modal category (in ascending order) were the second species of fourth B-E (solmized *mi-mi*) in the lower position, and the second species of fifth E-b (solmized again *mi-mi*) in the upper position.[3] Thus, even though Duffin embraces the view of "solmization practice as a way of thinking about music from [the Renaissance] era," he implicitly drives a wedge between a convenient label for a modal category ("Mi *chiamano*

[2] R. W. Duffin, "*Mi chiamano Mimi*… but my Name is *Quarti toni*: Solmization and Ockeghem's Famous Mass," *EM* 29, (2001), 164–85.
[3] As we know, in practice the notes A and C carried far more weight than B in deuterus works; nevertheless, B was the nominal confinal.

Mimi …") and a real modal category that reflects some identifiable features of the piece ("… but my name *is quarti toni,*"). Or, to put it another way, Duffin implicitly recognizes here that the *"durus* hexachord" from which the Mass takes its name (*Mi-mi* on E-b), is structurally *soft* when compared with the constitutive species of the *quartus tonus* (E-b, b-e) that is responsible for the "tonal flavor" of the Mass.

Similar considerations apply to other musical works, mostly from the fifteenth and sixteenth centuries, that make explicit or implicit reference to the six solmization syllables, whether in the title, in the actual text set to music, or through other techniques such as the *soggetto cavato* or the *inganni* of early Baroque instrumental music. While it is technically true that such works are "based on" the solmization syllables, as it is sometimes argued, it would be misleading to suggest by such wording that those references to the Guidonian syllables were the direct result of a hexachordally conceived notion of musical space. The very survival of the solmization syllables in eighteenth-century musical practice provides a powerful argument to the contrary. For instance, Johann Joseph Fux in Vienna and Johann Christopher Pepusch in London still recommended the use of six syllables in fugal writing in the first quarter of the century, that is to say, at a time when the adoption of the modern system of major/minor keys in compositional practice was a fait accompli. None other than Haydn and Beethoven solmized their "tonal" scales with the *ut-la* syllables in their early training, so that the same keynote in different octaves would correspond to different syllables.[4] Guidonian solmization did not interfere with "common practice" tonality in the eighteenth century, just as it did not affect Renaissance "modality."

What remains to be addressed is the historiographic side of our topic. In other words: if it is possible to ascertain with relative ease that the hexachord never played the role of normative diatonic yardstick in Western music, then why has musical scholarship so often argued otherwise, at least since the days of Charles Burney and John Hawkins? In order to begin addressing such a question, the second half of the present monograph concentrates on the growing debate on the merits and shortcomings of solmization that occupied several generations of *magistri* during the Italian *quattrocento*. In the first half of the century, prominent authors such as Johannes Ciconia and Johannes Carthusiensis advocated a letters-only approach to pitch conceptualization and musical training that entailed the complete abandonment

---

[4] On this point, see J. Lester, *Compositional Theory in the Eighteenth Century* (Cambridge, MA: Harvard University Press, 1992), pp. 171–2.

of the Guidonian syllables. This proposed pedagogical reform, however, appears to have attracted few followers. Far more successful was the counterargument that several late-fifteenth-century theorists mounted in defense of the hexachordal system. Its centerpiece was the thesis that with his syllables Guido had not only provided a most useful pedagogical tool for sight singing, but had in fact changed the very structure of the diatonic system by substituting the old *tetrachordum* of the Greeks with his new *hexachordum*. One may interpret these two diametrically opposed positions as alternative solutions to the relatively unstable "double-layer" model of syllables and letters that the Parisian *magistri* had developed into a fully fledged system. To Ciconia and John the Carthusian, musicians could safely disregard the "upper" layer of the syllables and concentrate on the "lower" one, i.e., on the letters "of Gregory." Against this view, their opponents argued that the "lower" layer of the letters was itself hexachordally patterned at the very moment that the syllables were superimposed onto them. The scope of the debate, however, far exceeded the limited boundaries of music pedagogy.

PART II

Reforming the music curriculum in the age of humanism

5 | Back to the monochord: church reform and music theory in the fifteenth century

Johannes Ciconia and the Paduan reform movement (ca. 1400–1410)

Composer and *magister* Johannes Ciconia of Liège (ca. 1370–1412) settled in the Northern Italian city of Padua in the mid-to-late 1390s after spending several years in other Italian centers. Ciconia was a member of the household of Philippe d'Alençon, a French cardinal of Roman obedience who was nominated abbot *in commenda* at S. Giustina in the mid-1390s. Through d'Alençon Ciconia was introduced to the Paduan intellectual and religious elite, particularly to Francesco Zabarella, who was to be Ciconia's main patron for the remainder of his life.[1]

It was through the patronage of Zabarella that Ciconia became first *mansionarius* and *custos*, then most likely *cantor* at the Cathedral of Padua, a benefice that involved the training of young singers, among other duties.[2] Possibly to fulfill this particular responsibility, toward the end of his short life Ciconia wrote an ambitious and highly original treatise called *Nova musica* in which he unfavorably compared the hexachordal system with the monochord-based model of music education of the Carolingian era. Aside

---

[1] For a recent monograph of the life and career of this composer, see A. Kreutziger-Herr, *Johannes Ciconia (ca. 1370–1412): komponieren in einer Kultur des Wortes* (Hamburg: K. D. Wagner, 1991). The volume by P. Vendrix, ed., *Johannes Ciconia, musicien de la transition* (Turnhout: Brepols, 2003) focuses primarily on Ciconia's secular works. On Ciconia's relationship with d'Alençon and Zabarella, see in particular G. Di Bacco and J. Nádas, "Verso uno 'stile internazionale' della musica nelle cappelle papali e cardinalizie durante il Grande Scisma (1378–1417): il caso di Johannes Ciconia da Liège," in A. Roth, ed., *Collettanea I: Capellae Sixtinaeque Collectanea Acta Monumenta* 3 (Vatican City: Biblioteca Apostolica Vaticana, 1994), pp. 7–74, and A. Hallmark, "*Protector, imo verus pater*: Francesco Zabarella's Patronage of Johannes Ciconia," in J. A. Owens and A. M. Cummings, eds., *Music in Renaissance Cities and Courts: Studies in Honor of Lewis Lockwood* (Warren, MI: Harmonie Park Press, 1997), pp. 153–68.

[2] On Ciconia's activities at the Cathedral of Padua, see in particular A. Hallmark, "Gratiosus, Ciconia, and Other Musicians at Padua Cathedral: Some Footnotes to Present Knowledge," in *Certaldo IV* (Certaldo, 1986), pp. 69–84; B. Haggh, "Ciconia's *Nova musica*: A Work for Singers in Renaissance Padua," paper presented at the Conference on Renaissance Music in Lisbon and Évora, May 2003 (forthcoming; the article is currently available online at www.music.umd.edu/Faculty/haggh-huglo/barbeleven.html.

from the nature and the merit of Ciconia's views on solmization *per se*, my goal here is to revisit the issue of the intellectual allegiances of the *Nova musica* in the context of the Paduan culture of its time. As I hope to demonstrate, the bold rejection of solmization proposed by Ciconia is but one aspect of a broader musical reform that, in turn, is attuned to contemporaneous ideological and cultural trends in the Veneto.

In the decades around 1400 the Northern Italian city of Padua was a vibrant cultural center engaged in a thorough reassessment of the educational and religious practices of the time. The main protagonists of this debate were high-ranked intellectuals and public officials active in the civic and religious institutions of the city, i.e., pedagogues, canonists, university professors, prelates, and abbots, who on the whole shared a general commitment to providing new models for the culture of their time. Several factors contributed to the emergence of a Paduan humanist movement in those years. Firstly, in his long Paduan sojourn, Francis Petrarch had initiated a debate on the goals of education, emphasizing the merit of the *studia humanitatis* (moral philosophy, poetry, history, and rhetoric) and of the study of the classics over the traditional medieval curriculum based on grammar and dialectics. Secondly, Padua was the seat of a flourishing university that attracted the leading scholars of the time and was open to the new scientific and intellectual trends that developed in peer institutions, such as Paris, Oxford, and Bologna. Thirdly, the defeat of the Carrara family, who had ruled Padua for most of the fourteenth century, by the hands of the Venetians in late 1405 had resulted in a scholarly and intellectual environment that was less directly controlled by the center of political power (the *signore*) than ever before. Indeed, the prestige of the University of Padua only increased after the defeat of the Carrara, as it became the premier educational institution across the territory of the Venetian Republic. In addition to the university, the cathedral and the Benedictine monastery of S. Giustina were important centers of learning at the forefront of the movement for the reform of the church, as well as vibrant centers of music making. Padua's religious leaders provided the spur for sweeping reforms in contemporaneous monastic life, and were at the center of a complex network of diplomatic activities and legal strategies directed at resolving the problem of the Great Schism in the Catholic church.

During the age of the Great Schism (1378–1417) the advocates of church reform across Europe increasingly turned to the words and the acts of the church fathers as a source of wisdom in their quest to reform the church in head and members. These were often the same figures that were also proposing sweeping changes in the school curricula. A case in point is Pierpaolo Vergerio the Elder (1370–1444/5), who during his Paduan residency (until 1405) taught logic at the University of Padua, maintained close contact with Ciconia's patron Francesco Zabarella, and was a leading figure at the Council of Constance. During that time he also wrote *De ingenuis moribus,* known as one of the first humanist statements of a philosophy on education that emphasized the role of the liberal arts, and particularly moral philosophy, history, and rhetoric, in shaping the character of the learner.[3] Vergerio's extraordinary career provides the best example of a Paduan humanist who strived to place the moral wisdom of the classics at the service of church and civic reform – an intellectual program in which the teaching of Cicero and Seneca was as valuable as that by Jerome and Augustine. John McManamon observes that Vergerio was instrumental in moving beyond the fourteenth-century image of Jerome as a hermit devoted to a life of poverty, instead celebrating the church father for his civic activism, his knowledge of letters, and his philological acumen, essentially transforming him into "humanism's patron saint".[4] If Vergerio had a special admiration for Jerome, Camaldulensian monk Ambrogio Traversari (1386–1439) practically invented the discipline of patristic scholarship, translating Greek and even Hebrew texts into Latin, searching libraries for ancient manuscripts, and restoring patristic texts to their original form. It was primarily because of Traversari's stature as a scholar that leading humanists such as Guarino da Verona and Vittorino da Feltre included the study of the church fathers in the curriculum of their schools.[5]

Among the prominent intellectuals who were active in Padua in the first years of the *quattrocento,* humanist pedagogue Vittorino de' Rambaldoni da Feltre (1378–1446) deserves special mention here by virtue of his marked interests in Boethius' *De institutione musica,* to which he later introduced his

---

[3] On Vergerio's treatise, see J. McManamon, *Pierpaolo Vergerio the Elder: The Humanist as Orator* (Tempe, AZ: Medieval and Renaissance Texts and Studies, 1996), pp. 89–103. For an overview of the early humanist views of education, with particular emphasis on Paduan intellectuals, see B. Kohl, "Humanism and Education," in A. Rabil, Jr., ed., *Renaissance Humanism: Foundations, Forms, and Legacy,* 3 vols. (Philadelphia: University of Pennsylvania Press, 1988), vol. III, "Humanism and the Disciplines," pp. 5–22.

[4] McManamon, *Pierpaolo Vergerio the Elder,* pp. 123–35. For an overview of the humanist appropriation and idealization of Jerome in the Renaissance, see H. M. Pabel, "Reading Jerome in the Renaissance: Erasmus; Reception of the 'Adversus Jovinianum,'" *Renaissance Quarterly* 55 (2002), 470–97.

[5] The classic study on this topic is C. Stinger, *Humanism and the Church Fathers: Ambrogio Traversari (1386–1439) and Christian Antiquity in the Italian Renaissance* (Albany: State University of New York Press, 1977).

student Johannes Gallicus.[6] Vittorino may have first been exposed to musical scholarship while living in the house of private mathematician Biagio Pelacani, who has been proposed as the author of several musical tracts on *musica speculativa* preserved in Paris, Bibliothèque nationale, lat. 7372.[7] However, Vittorino did not approach music simply as a quadrivial science. To the contrary, he was fully aware of music's communicative power, thus of its ability to contribute to the development of moral character. Although there are no documents that place Vittorino and Ciconia side by side, it is quite likely that the two would have exchanged views on the current status of music, on musical scholarship, and on music pedagogy. Both the content and the reformist thrust of Ciconia's *Nova musica* would have been well suited to Vittorino's scholarly interests and background.[8]

To humanists such as Vergerio, Vittorino, and Traversari, the church fathers were first and foremost models of virtue that could inspire moral renewal in the present time, just as the early church as an institution was an example to imitate for its unswerving dedication to fulfilling the apostolic mission that Christ himself had mandated. Two of the most prominent canonists of the age, Jean Gerson and Zabarella, appealed to the structure and decision-making process of the *ecclesia primitiva* – i.e., the church in its first four hundred years of existence – to make the case that the authority of the council of bishops and cardinals superseded even the authority of the Pope in ecclesiastical affairs.[9] Besides Christ's apostles, the four evangelists, and the apostle Paul, the four main Latin fathers (St. Ambrose, St. Augustine, St. Jerome, and St. Gregory the Great) embodied the purity of faith and the theological wisdom of the *ecclesia primitiva*. Furthermore, because the early church was thought to have received the divine law directly from Christ, its statutes had authority over those of later centuries.[10]

However, the most astute fifteenth-century reformers did not look at the condition of the primitive church in a dogmatic fashion, or as the only

---

[6] See C. Vasoli, "Vittorino da Feltre e la formazione umanistica dell'uomo," in N. Giannetto, ed., *Vittorino da Feltre e la sua scuola: umanesimo, pedagogia, arti* (Florence: Olschki, 1981), pp. 13–33, and C. Gallico, "Musica nella Ca' Giocosa," in N. Giannetto, ed., *Vittorino da Feltre e la sua scuola*, pp. 189–98.

[7] On this subject, see C. Panti, "Una fonte della 'Declaratio musicae disciplinae' di Ugolino da Orvieto: Quattro Anonime 'Questiones' della Tarda Scolastica," *Rivista Italiana di Musicologia* 24 (1989), 3–47.

[8] On this point, see Gallico, "Musica nella Ca' Giocosa," p. 190.

[9] Thus, the council could be summoned even without papal authorization (as it was the case with the Councils of Pisa in 1409 and of Constance in 1414), and could even ask for the resignation of the pontiff (or pontiffs) in particular circumstances, as it happened at Constance. On the particular authority conferred by Gerson to the *ecclesia primitiva*, see L. B. Pascoe, S. J., "Jean Gerson: The 'Ecclesia primitiva' and Reform," *Traditio* 30 (1974), 379–409.

[10] L. B. Pascoe, S. J., "Jean Gerson," 381.

acceptable historical model for the modern church. Gerson, for instance, viewed the Christian church as an ever-evolving structure that could not, and should not, be brought back to its original form. Education historian W. H. Woodward has detected a similar attitude in the teaching of Latin scholar Gasparino Barzizza in Padua during the years 1407–21.[11]

A "non-classicizing" attitude pervades Ciconia's *Nova musica* as well, inasmuch as the treatise aims not only at restoring the musical wisdom of pre-Guidonian times, but also at integrating into the study of music the positive insights that have accumulated since then (as well as, of course, at ridding the discipline of the corruptive elements that have also accrued through time). At the beginning of his treatise, Ciconia also stresses the interconnections between music and the other liberal arts, a theme that was dear to the philosophy of education embraced by early Paduan humanists such as Vergerio and Barzizza.[12]

Ciconia did not have the intellectual vision, much less the rhetorical skills, of a Traversari or a Vergerio. His idea of musical *renovatio* was shallower that that of some of his fellow Paduans, and in any case is carried out in *Nova musica* in a rather crude and tentative fashion. However, Ciconia's enthusiasm for the musical doctrines of the Carolingian era, his sensitivity for musical sound and affect, and his taking distance from the corrupt ways of the *guidonistae* of his time recall too closely the anti-scholastic agenda of the early humanists (and specifically of monastic humanism) for those similarities to be merely coincidental, especially considering that Ciconia conceived and wrote *Nova musica* in the very cradle of humanism.[13]

Ciconia's *antiqui auctores*

The historical categories of "humanism" (let alone its "early" variety), and "church reform" are complex, with highly porous boundaries. Musicologists

---

[11] W. H. Woodward, *Vittorino da Feltre and Other Humanist Educators* (Cambridge University Press, 1897; reprint edn., Toronto and Buffalo: The University of Toronto Press in association with the Renaissance Society of America, 1996), pp. 10–1.

[12] See the citation from *Nova musica* below, pp. 126. On this point, see R. G. G. Mercer, *The Teaching of Gasparino Barzizza with Special Reference to his Place in Paduan Humanism* (London: The Modern Humanities Research Association, 1979), p. 121.

[13] On the trend toward "affective theology" in the early fifteenth century, see J. Leclercq, O.S.B., "Monastic and Scholastic Theology in the Reformers of the Fourteenth to Sixteenth Century," in E. Rozanne Elder, ed., *From Cloister to Classroom: Monastic and Scholastic Approaches to Truth* (Kalamazoo, MI: Cistercian Publications, 1986), pp. 178–201, and D. Martin, "The Via Moderna, Humanism, and the Hermeneutics of Late Medieval Monastic Life," *Journal of the History of Ideas* 51 (1990), 179–97.

have long regarded the Italian humanist movement as generally hostile to polyphony and in favor of the quasi-improvised, monophonic settings of Latin poetry. This theory has recently been challenged by scholars such as Reinhard Strohm and Margaret Bent, who have produced compelling examples of manuscript sources and specific polyphonic works promoted by patrons with marked humanist orientations.[14] At the same time, students at the University of Padua attended the lectures on Ciceronian rhetoric and grammar by Gasparino Barzizza, but also those on dialectics by Vergerio and Paolo Veneto.

Likewise, Ciconia's *Nova musica* cannot be squarely aligned with one or the other camp or disciplinary orientation. The treatise synthesizes a scholastic mode of argumentation with a humanistically inclined call for *renovatio*, as well as a combination of speculative and practical topics.[15] The first three books of *Nova musica* amount to a traditional presentation of the elements of music (intervals, species, consonances, modes, and proportions). The fourth book, "De accidentibus," illustrates Ciconia's original contribution to the discipline. The point of this section is to show that all the rudiments discussed in the first three treatises are nothing more than music's grammatical inflections, since the "accidental" occurrences of certain pitches, intervals, and consonances in actual compositions give music its meaning (*accidentia ... in quibus per varias significationes omnis cantus declinatur*). To study musical accidents, then, is to engage in a music-analytic activity that leads to appreciate the peculiarities of a musical work. Aside from its content and organization, the treatise is cast in a learned and even "pretentious" style that seems designed to address an already well-educated audience.

Scholars have provided diametrically opposed views of Ciconia's treatise. Most commentators – such as Annette Kreutziger-Herr, Oliver Ellsworth, Margaret Bent, Philippe Vendrix, and Marc André – have placed *Nova musica* in the tradition of *musica speculativa*, mostly on the ground of the section of the treatise dedicated to the musical proportions.[16] André, in

---

[14] R. Strohm, *The Rise of European Music, 1380–1500* (Cambridge University Press, 1993), pp. 540–50; M. Bent, "Music and the Early Veneto Humanists," *Proceedings of the British Academy* 101 (1998), 101–30.

[15] As Leofranc Holford-Strevens has aptly put it, "Although Ciconia's Latin has some stylistic pretension, it could no more have passed for humanistic than the motet-texts that speak in his name," in "Humanism and the Language of Music Treatises," *Renaissance Studies* 15 (2001), 423; Susan Fast has also noticed the influence of modal logic in Ciconia's language (see her review of *Ars cantus mensurabilis per modos iuris*, by M. Balensuela, ed., and *Johannes Ciconia: 'Nova musica' and 'De proportionibus'* by O. Ellsworth, ed., *Plainsong and Medieval Music* 4 (1995), 214–5).

[16] See Kreutziger-Herr, *Johannes Ciconia*, pp. 117–28; M. André, "L'œuvre théorique de Johannes Ciconia," *Revue de la société liégeoise de musicology* 4 (1996), 23–40; P. Vendrix, "Johannes Ciconia,

particular, sees the book on proportions as engaging primarily the issue of musical temporality from a scholastic perspective.

Other scholars, however, have proposed a different view of the treatise since a landmark 1955 article by Suzanne Clercx, in which the author emphasized Ciconia's paramount concern with the "material means" of music: intervals, species of consonances, diatonic modes, etc. According to Clercx, the speculative aspects of the treatise do not outweigh the role of "musical experience" in Ciconia's exposition.[17] Recently, Barbara Haggh has supported Clercx's hypothesis by arguing that both the content of the treatise and its forty-five references to chant pieces make it most likely that it was destined for his young singers at the Cathedral, even though only fewer than half of those chant melodies appear to be Paduan.[18] Haggh has also cast precious light on the sources that Ciconia consulted while compiling his treatise, showing that he may have visited Bologna in order to access rare texts.[19] Such an attitude suggests that Ciconia viewed *Nova musica* not only as a textbook for the use of cathedral schools, but also as the expression of deep-seated beliefs on the status of music education in his time, and as a manifesto for a reform of the music curriculum that he evidently felt was much needed.[20]

cantor et *musicus*," in Vendrix, ed., *Johannes Ciconia*), pp. 30–5; M. Bent, "Ciconia, Prosdocimus, and the Workings of Musical Grammar," in Vendrix, ed., *Johannes Ciconia*, pp. 68–70.

[17] S. Clercx, "Johannes Ciconia théoreticien," *Ann Music* 3 (1955), 57–62.

[18] See Haggh, "Ciconia's *Nova musica*," near footnote references 13 and 65 (no page numbers). Haggh also observes (near footnote reference 14), that the examples of two- and three-part polyphony in *Nova musica* are in parallel motion, whereas contrary motion was the standard practice at the cathedral.

[19] See Haggh, "Ciconia's Citations in *Nova musica*: New Sources as Biography," in S. Clark and E. E. Leach, eds., *Citation and Authority in Medieval and Renaissance Musical Culture: Learning from the Learned* (Woodbridge, UK: Boydell, 2005), pp. 45–56.

[20] One might even point to the monks of St. Giustina as the intended readers of the treatise. The *antiqua musica* that Ciconia wishes to restore is essentially the theoretical tradition from Hucbald to Guido that for centuries had constituted the core basis of monastic music education. The new approach to musical studies adopted in the treatise would have been perfectly attuned to the program of reforms that began at S. Giustina in 1409. Moreover, S. Giustina had an active musical life and was an important center of production of music manuscripts during and after Ciconia's Paduan sojourn through the agency of one of its monks, Rolando da Casale, who was an acquaintance of Ciconia and a student of Zabarella. Yet it is unlikely that a reform of music education would have been a high priority for abbot Ludovico Barbo, who appears not to have fostered the *studia litterarum* at the monastery (see G. M. Picasso, "Gli studi nella riforma di Ludovico Barbo," in *Los monjes y los estudios. IV semana de estudios monasticos*, Poblet 1961 (Abadia de Poblet, 1963), pp. 295–324). On music at S. Giustina, see G. Cattin, "Ricerche sulla musica a S. Giustina in Padova all'inizio del primo *quattrocento*. Il copista Rolando da Casale. Nuovi frammenti musicali nell'archivio di stato," *Annales musicologiques* 7 (1964), 17–41; and Cattin, "Tradizione e tendenze innovatrici nella normative e nella pratica liturgico-musicale della Congregazione di S. Giustina," *Benedictina. Fascicoli di studi benedettini*, 17 (1970), 254–99.

The issue of the intellectual orientation of *Nova musica* needs to be analyzed carefully, as the significance of Ciconia's critique of solmization depends on it.[21] Whatever may have led Ciconia to write the treatise, its frequent characterization as "speculative" does not do justice to its purpose, its general organization, and quite possibly its destination. It is not just that practical issues having to do with singing, performance, and the classification of melodies are freely interspersed with more abstract presentations of diatonic species and proportions; more importantly, Ciconia often connects those more abstract segments of the treatise with aspects of *musica practica*: his discussion of intervals and species is accompanied by short musical examples showing how those intervals "are sung" (*canitur sic*);[22] the monochord is presented in the treatise as an instrument that both demonstrates numerical ratios and facilitates sight singing;[23] and in the revised version of the book he wishes to connect the proportions with the conventions of mensuration.[24] As I have discussed elsewhere, Ciconia also cites abundantly – and without acknowledging the source – from Marchetto of Padua's *Lucidarium* (ca. 1318), an unquestionably "practical" manual.

Ciconia's treatise does open with a speculative tone, with a lengthy section on celestial harmony, the definition of music, and particularly on the nine Muses. The overall purpose of this introduction, however, is not speculative *per se*; rather, it strives to emphasize the moral and spiritual potential of music and music making. To Ciconia, for example, celestial harmony is not coterminous with the music of the spheres. Instead, it is the song of angels that the faithful seek, as it strives for a spiritual union with God. Likewise, the topic of the Muses is no mere homage to the Platonic ideal of *musica mundana*, as it will be later in Gafori's *Practica musicae* and *De harmonia* (see Chapter 7). Rather, in Ciconia this passage is to emphasize the moral dignity and the nobility of music as a science of sound. The myth of the Muses was important to those early humanists who wished to defend the arts and to stress the historical continuity between pagan and Christian times. The interpolation – in the Florence manuscript of *Nova musica* – of a chapter on the nine modes of mystical teaching and knowledge granted by the Muses, is mediated from Fulgentius' *Mythologiarum* (I.15).[25] The passage is

[21] If the treatise is indeed speculative, then the attack against the *guidonistae* can be dismissed as a bit of an anomaly; on the other hand, if it is viewed as concerned with musical practice and training, as I think is the case, then that critique is of considerable import.

[22] See O. Ellsworth, ed. and trans. *Johannes Ciconia: 'Nova musica' and 'De proportionibus'*, (Lincoln: University of Nebraska Press, 1993), pp. 126 and 144.

[23] *Ibid.*, pp. 86–96 and 302–5.

[24] *Ibid.*, pp. 440–3.

[25] F. P. Fulgentius, *Opera*, ed. R. Helm (Leipzig: B. G. Teubner, 1898), pp. 26–7.

central to the argument in defense of poetry proposed by Coluccio Salutati in his *De laboribus herculis*, a work that Ciconia may have known. Thus, the rather cryptic references to the Muses in *Nova musica* may be read as part of Ciconia's declared intent of refurbishing musical studies.

Recent studies have emphasized the particular blend of speculative and practical approaches to music as typical of the Paduan intellectual milieu of the *trecento*. In the first decade of the fourteenth century, Paduan philosopher Pietro d'Abano was instrumental in developing and promoting a perceptual notion of musical sound in his famous commentary to Aristotle's *Problems* that he completed in Padua.[26] Central to Aristotle's (and Pietro's) discussion is musical experience and the sensorial pleasure (*delectatio*) that it generates in the listener. Abano's Neo-Aristotelian perspective, then, values music as a rhetorical and practical activity; indeed, the Paduan philosopher makes a reference to the contemporaneous technique of *bordonizare* in his discussion of musical pleasure.[27] Lovato finds traces of this Aristotelian musical philosophy in the sections that the treatises by Marchetto, Prosdocimo, and Ciconia himself dedicate to the topics of consonance and the division of the tone.[28]

In short, Ciconia's *Nova musica* is only partly related to the tradition of *musica speculativa*. More interesting, and more prominent in the treatise, are rather the fingerprints of the Paduan music scholarship of the *trecento*, as well as of the proto-humanist and reformist movement of ca. 1400. Consider, for instance, the author's announcement of the intellectual program of *Nova musica*:

Musicam antiquam antiquorum voto editam, quam ipsi explicare nequiverunt ad plenam scientiam, novo stilo renovere cupimus, et que non erant apta relinquere, et que minus habebat perficere, et inaudita imponere. Quis enim auctorum ad exemplum grammatice artis declinationes musice que sunt in cantibus invenit? Aut quis dudum audivit? Quis putaret hanc habere accidentia et declinationes sicut grammatica, genera et species sicut dialectica, et numeros et proportiones sicut arithmetica?

---

[26] On this topic, see L. Mauro, "La musica nei commenti ai 'Problemi': Pietro d'Abano e Évrart de Conty," in L. Mauro, ed., *La musica nel pensiero medievale* (Ravenna: Longo, 1999), pp. 31–69; A. Lovato, "Dottrine musicali nel Trecento padovano," in O. Longo, ed., *Padova carrarese* (Padova: Il Poligrafo, 2005), pp. 215–25.

[27] Mauro, "La musica nei commenti ai 'Problemi,'" p. 45, n. 53.

[28] Lovato, "Dottrine musicali nel trecento padovano," pp. 216–24. Not surprisingly, a renewed interest in music as heard can also be traced in thirteenth-century French theorists. See J. Haines and P. DeWitt, "Johannes de Grocheio and Aristotelian Natural Philosophy," *EMH* 27 (2008), 47–98, and the section on Johannes de Garlandia and Anonymous IV in G. Gross, *Chanter en polyphonie à Notre-Dame de Paris aux 12e et 13e siècles* (Turnhout: Brepols, 2007), pp. 107–34.

[The ancient music, produced by the will of the ancients, which they themselves were unable to expand into a complete doctrine, we wish to revive in a new style, to leave out those things that were not appropriate, to perfect those that were inadequate, and to add those of which they were unaware. Who among the authors, in imitation of the art of grammar, has discovered the declensions of music that are in songs? Or who before has heard these? Who would have believed it to have accidents and declensions like grammar, genera and species like dialectic, and numbers and proportions like arithmetic?][29]

In this new disciplinary vision, which seems directly inspired by Vergerio, music has become akin to a language, thus a legitimate member of the trivium. At the same time, Ciconia does not wish to disown music's quadrivial grounding in the laws of numerical proportions.

Neither does Ciconia fail to pay homage to the contribution of the "ancients," not as much – however – the music writers of classical Greece, who will attract the interest of later music scholars, but rather those of Christian antiquity and particularly of the Carolingian era.[30] More importantly, Ciconia freely cites "music theorists" (such as Boethius, Hucbald, the *Enchiriadis* treatises, and Guido of Arezzo) and ecclesiastical authors (such as Augustine, the Venerable Bede, Gregory the Great, Amalarius of Metz, and Remigius of Auxerre), indeed with a remarkable emphasis on the latter, rather than on the former. One also wonders whether Ciconia deliberately misattributed some of his sources to well-known church fathers in order to increase their authoritativeness in the eyes of the clerical readers for whom the treatise was most likely conceived (more on this later). If Marchetto had referred to Berno of Reichenau as Bernardus, Ciconia seems to have gone a step further by also attributing his citations from the *Liber glossarum* to "Hieronymus," those from Aurelianus Reomensis to the Venerable Bede, and those from Regino of Prüm to Remigius of Auxerre, author of a well-known commentary on Martianus Capella's *De nuptiis*. It seems likely that unaware readers of Ciconia's generation would have immediately thought of St. Bernard of Clairvaux and of St. Jerome when encountering the names of "Bernardus" and "Hieronymus" – without further specifications – in a treatise that intentionally pursued a wholesale *renovatio* of the *antiqui auctores*.

In spite of such misattributions, the pursuit of disciplinary renewal led Ciconia to peruse musical and non-musical sources that were not customarily

---

[29]   *Ellsworth, ed. and trans, Johannes Ciconia*, pp. 52–3.

[30]   Ciconia does refer to the *musici* of classical antiquity several times in the treatise – for instance in his discussion of various types of monochords in book 1, ch. 20 – but only in a generic and necessarily second-hand fashion, since he had no Greek.

in use in his time, and to mention rare chant melodies. Barbara Haggh has recently discovered that several definitions of musical terms found in Ciconia's treatise come from the *Liber glossarum*, a general dictionary that had never been cited by Italian theorists in previous times. The short tract *Quid est cantus*, most of which is quoted in *Nova musica*, also enjoyed very little circulation; Haggh suggests that Ciconia may have encountered the only extant copy in the Vatican Library, from the eleventh century, during his sojourn in Rome.[31] Highly unusual in the early 1400s were also Ciconia's extensive references to the *enchiriadis* treatises, which had progressively fallen out of fashion in the previous two centuries, and to Aurelianus' *Musica disciplina*.[32] Other sources used by Ciconia have not yet been identified.

One of the most intriguing appearances in *Nova musica* is that by Amalarius of Metz (ca. 775–850), the author of a *Liber officialis* that created much controversy in its author's lifetime and beyond for proposing a dramatized view of the Christian liturgy. Apparently, Ciconia found in this source a suitable description of the role of church singers:

Amalarius: Cantores sunt laudatores Dei, quorum cantus ad eius laudes, ceteros excitat. Cantor enim est quasi bubulcus, qui iubilat bubum, ut hylarius trahant aratrum. Trahentibus bubum aratrum scinditur terra, quando cantores intimos anhelitus commoventes trahunt dulces sonos.

[Amalarius: Singers are praisers of God, and their song arouses others to His praises. A singer is like the plowman who shouts to his oxen so that they may pull the plow more cheerfully. When the oxen pull the plow, the earth is split; when singers stir their innermost breaths, they pull along sweet sounds.][33]

We may interpret this passage in the light of an earlier chapter from book 1 in which Ciconia spurs the reader to actively seek God's celestial harmony.[34] Such an advice is in line with the proposition that church singers are "praisers of God" who in turn *arouse* others to spiritual devotion, presumably by bringing the faithful a bit closer to that celestial harmony. It is an idealized portrait of music making in the church that marks a definite departure from the traditional medieval perception of church singers as (at best) poorly educated.[35] More importantly, Ciconia's definition implies a

---

[31] See Haggh, "Ciconia's Citations in *Nova musica*," pp. 45–7 and 54.

[32] Most *enchiriadis* sources were indeed copied between the tenth and the eleventh centuries. On the rich reception history of this pair of treatises, see Erickson, ed. and trans., *Musica Enchiriadis and Scholica Enchiriadis*, pp. xlvi–liv.

[33] Ellsworth, ed. and trans. *Johannes Cifconia,*, pp. 308–9.

[34] *Ibid.*, pp. 54–5.

[35] An example of such characterization that Ciconia certainly knew is found in Book 11 of Marchetto's *Lucidarium*, in which the author equates the "cantor" to an "incompetent musicus"

vision of sacred music as an essential part of the liturgy playing a distinctly "affective" role. Implicit in Ciconia's words is a recognition of music as a rhetorical, communicative art.

It is significant that Ciconia would resort to embrace a definition of church singers as unusual as that by Amalarius, indeed that he would even feel the need to emphasize the spiritual and devotional function fulfilled by church singers. Perhaps it is not too far-fetched to read these portions of *Nova musica* as an index of the author's sympathies for the movement of the *devotio moderna* that was gaining momentum in the early fifteenth century and that directly inspired the monastic reform introduced by Ludovico Barbo at S. Giustina beginning in 1409.[36] Indeed, the only polyphonic style that Ciconia describes in one chapter of *Nova musica* is note-against-note counterpoint for two voices – i.e., the same type of *organum simplex* that was advocated by late-medieval church reformers, such as Thomas à Kempis, John Wycliffe, and Denis the Carthusian.[37] By the same token, one may wonder whether Ciconia's apparent disinterest in polyphonic mensuration is to be connected with his vision of a *nova musica* within the church. While it is tempting to embrace this hypothesis, in the end Ciconia's short account of *organum simplex* lacks any reference to religion or spirituality, thus in this case complicating the task of locating *Nova musica* in its proper historical context, rather than facilitating it.

Of good and bad music teachers

In his treatise, Ciconia repeatedly expresses his discomfort with Guidonian solmization; in the process, he also strives to separate the teaching of Guido from that of Guido's followers.[38] Firstly, when discussing the foundations of musical sound, Ciconia emphatically downplays the significance

---

who is unable to correctly judge the mode of a composition ("… dicimus, quod tales iudicantes cantus de tonis solum propter ascensum et descensum non musici, sed caeci erratores, quam cantores potius dici possunt," Herlinger, ed. *The Lucidarium of Marchetto of Padua*, pp. 392–4). Needless to say, the Boethian portrayal of the singer as a "beast who does not know what it does" was still alive in the early fifteenth century – which makes Ciconia's heightened view of the singer all the more significant.

[36] See R. Pitigliani, *Il Ven. Ludovico Barbo e la diffusione dell'*Imitazione di Cristo *per opera della Congregazione di S. Giustina* (Padova: Badia S. Giustina, 1943).

[37] On the resistance to the use of polyphony in sacred music in the late Middle Ages, see the recent monograph by Rob C. Wegman, *The Crisis of Music in Early Modern Europe: 1470–1530* (New York: Routledge, 2005), esp. chapter 2, pp. 17–48.

[38] For a more detailed discussion of Ciconia's critique of solmization, see my "The Ciconian Hexachord," in Vendrix, ed., *Johannes Ciconia: musicien de la transition*, pp, 279–304.

of Guidonian theory both as a musical science and as an aid for training singers by insisting that musical pitch finds its ultimate justification (*defensionem*) in the division of the monochord, rather than on the Guidonian Hand. Secondly, in accordance with such a view, throughout his treatise Ciconia indicates musical pitch by relying exclusively on the seven letters from A to G and on the Greek letter names. Such a choice, relatively unusual in late-medieval writings on music, reflects Ciconia's intention to provide an alternative to the doctrines of the *guidonistae*, particularly to their practice of using the *ut-la* syllables to designate pitches. On the other hand, Ciconia quotes a number of excerpts from *Micrologus*.

In the chapter entitled "On learning to sing" ("De addiscendo cantu") at the end of book 2, Ciconia unfavorably compares the technique of Guidonian solmization with the monochord:

Si quis cantum musice scire cupit, primum quidem investigare opportet in mono-cordo et in cantu positionem ordinem et figuras septem litterarum gravium, acu-tarum, et superacutarum, que sunt in lineis et in superlineis cum ordinatis coloribus suis. Deinde coniunctiones vocum. Post hec unum e duobus eligat. Aut computum, ut Guidoniste, aut monocordum, qui numquam [-304-] fallit, ut bonus magister. Ad hoc etiam cantus consonantiarum et specierum maximum prestant intellectum. Igitur, prudens lector, post agnitionem litterarum et vocum coniunctiones modo in computum, modo in monocordum, modo in cantus consonantiarum et specierum operam det, ita ut ab exercitio numquam cesset, donec ignotos cantus ut notos suaviter cantet, ut Guido refert.

[If one wishes to know a song of music, it is necessary to find – on the mono-chord and in the song – the position, arrangement, and symbols of the seven graves, acutae, and superacutae letters that are on and above the line, with their prescribed colors; then, the conjunctions of pitches [*coniunctiones vocum*]. After this, one should select one of two things: either the hand [*computum*], like the Guidonists, or the monochord, which, like a good teacher, never misleads. An understanding of the consonances and species will also be most important for this song. Therefore, prudent reader, after the recognition of the letters and the conjunctions of pitches – whether on the hand, the monochord, or the consonances and species of sounds – one should work so that he never ceases to practice until he may pleasantly sing unknown songs like known ones, as Guido reports.][39]

Ciconia's endorsement of the monochord as a "good teacher" (*bonus magister … qui numquam fallit*) is reminiscent of the Pseudo-Odonian *Dialogus de musica*, a key pre-Guidonian source that will also inspire the pedagogical methods of later authors such as Conrad of Zabern (see below). Ciconia

---

[39] Ellsworth, ed. and trans. *Johannes Ciconia*, pp. 304–5, slightly changed.

may have had some familiarity with this text, considering that it often circulated in close proximity with Guido's writings.[40] By contrast, the musical Hand (*computus*) can mislead singers, and is therefore an unreliable tool for sight singing. Unfortunately Ciconia does not elaborate on his poor opinion of the musical Hand. His use of the term *computus* in this context, however, may hint at the nature of his criticism. The reference is to the technique of "computing" the date of Easter on the fingertips of one hand that was required fare for medieval clerics. The mechanism of the computus was closely reminiscent of the practice of the musical Hand favored by the *guidonistae*.[41] By linking the two, Ciconia may be referring to the cumbersome system of cross-labels and mutations that was central to the practice of solmization.

It is noteworthy that one of the most talented and learned musicians of his generation would express himself so passionately and unequivocally against Guidonian solmization and in favor of recuperating the practice of the monochord in musical instruction. No doubt, the choice of avoiding any reference to the syllables in a musical treatise from around 1410 must have startled contemporaneous readers and singers. In hindsight, Ciconia's *Nova musica* may have initiated a debate on the merit of solmization that occupied music theorists for generations to come, as the remainder of this monograph will show. In the end, however, the historical significance of Ciconia's treatise lies not in its content per se, but in its unequivocal ties with the vibrant reformist movement of one of the cultural capitals of the age.

Liturgical chant as an instrument of devotion: a perspective from Conrad of Zabern

To speak of a fifteenth-century *renovatio monochordi* seems counterintuitive in light of the increased presence of solmization in pedagogical treatises from that period. After all, as we have seen in Chapter 3, the great majority of extant musical Hands originated in fifteenth-century Italy and Germany. However, the two trends are not necessarily mutually exclusive: the high number of post-1400 music-pedagogical treatises points to a renewed emphasis on musical training in general, particularly

---

[40] M. Huglo, "Der Prolog des Odo zugeschriebenen 'Dialogus de Musica,'" *Archiv für Musikwissenschaft* 28 (1971), 135–7.

[41] For a general description of the computus, see K. Berger, "The Hand and the Art of Memory," 105–11.

in monastic houses. In this context, it is only natural that different teachers at different times and places would adopt a variety of pedagogical approaches, leading to a confrontation on the merits and shortcomings of those methods. Within this larger picture, it is difficult to quantify the impact of a hypothetical *renovatio monochordi* in fifteenth-century musical life; clearly, much more research on this issue is necessary before meaningful conclusions can be drawn, keeping in mind that the documentary evidence on this issue may remain, at any rate, inconclusive. To name only one complicating factor: the term "monochord" in the late Middle Ages was a short-hand label for a number of instruments that could be and often were used for learning new melodies, such as the hurdy-gurdy, the trumpet marine, and – most important of all – the clavichord, also known as "monochord" in fifteenth-century Europe.

Specific information on the means and methods of musical training at that time are notoriously vague.[42] But for the purpose of the present monograph it is significant that a few prominent *cantores* and *musici* from that period favored the use of the monochord in musical instruction, vis-à-vis the Hand – if not as a practical aid physically present in the music lesson, at least as a way of conceptualizing and explaining the diatonic space to budding musicians in the pages of musical treatises.[43] From the perspective of a history of musical thought, it is also significant that those who auspicated a return to the monochord as a privileged teaching aid were also guided by a renewed interest in the approaches to musical training proposed by tenth- and eleventh-century authors. Thus, the small revival of Carolingian and Guidonian sources in the fifteenth century, already traced by Christian Meyer as it pertains to Guido's *Micrologus*, may be part of the same pedagogical trend that aimed either at founding ways to simplify the method of solmization, or at overhauling it altogether.

We encounter a sign of this trend in the mid-fifteenth-century writings by the *magister* Conrad of Zabern, which reveal important thematic links with Ciconia's treatise. After graduating from the University of Heidelberg early in his life, Conrad – a priest from the diocese of Speyer, as well as a

---

[42] See E. M. Ripin, *et al.*, "Clavichord," *NG 2*, vol. 6, pp. 4–18.

[43] Ugolino of Orvieto explains that the operations of the monochord involve two mental faculties, namely, the sense, by which we obtain a visual comprehension of the intervals, and the intellect, by which the proportions (underlying those intervals) are rationally demonstrated ("In monochordi namque compositione duplex intervenit operatio, sensus, scilicet, quo figuraliter comprehendimus spatia, et intellectus qua [*recte*: "quo"] ipsorum proportiones ratione monstrantur"), from *Tractatus monochordi*, in Ugolino of Orvieto, *Declaratio musicae disciplinae*, ed. A. Seay, 3 vols., *CSM* 7 (Rome: American Institute of Musicology, 1959–62), vol. III, p. 227.

theologian and a celebrated preacher – is documented as having taught music in three universities of the Rhine valley (Freiburg, Heidelberg, and possibly Basel), and in Ingolstadt. In addition, he visited monasteries and cathedral schools in many other German towns – including Strasbourg, Speyer, Worms, Mainz, and Würzburg – where he presented his monochord-based method of training church singers.[44] Conrad appears to have been especially close to the Benedictine monasteries of the Bursfeld Congregation, which had promoted in Germany a monastic reform modeled after S. Giustina (indeed, one of the main protagonists of the Bursfeld reform and Abbot of the Bursfeld monastery, Johannes Dederoth, had sojourned at S. Giustina during his travels in Italy). Conrad's musical pedagogy is worthy of close consideration in the context of the present study in that it suggests that a key trend in Northern Italian music theory – a renewed interest in the musical doctrines of the remote past at the expense of the post-Guidonian tradition – was also gaining currency north of the Alps.

A marked reformist agenda pervades Conrad's extant writings on music and places him in the same group with previous *renovatio* theorists, such as Johannes Ciconia and Johannes Gallicus. Like Ciconia, Conrad pursued a program of pedagogical reform that harked back to the musical teaching of the pre-Guidonian era. It is possible to recognize two distinct steps in such a program. On the one hand, Conrad advocated the readoption of the monochord as an essential aid for inexperienced singers when learning new melodies. The treatises *Novellus musicae artis tractatus* and *Opusculum de monochordo* – largely an expansion of the section on the monochord in *Novellus tractatus* – illustrate in detail the author's position on this point. On the other hand, Conrad also left unusually precise guidelines on the attitudes and behaviors that are appropriate to church singers, as well as on the place and liturgical function of choral singing. These guidelines constitute the treatise *De modo bene cantandi* of 1474, which was copied in a number of musical and non-musical manuscripts from the late fifteenth century, both in Latin and in the vernacular.[45]

It is this last treatise that provides a full picture of Conrad's music – pedogical goals and his strong commitment to reforming musical practice

---

[44] This account of Conrad's activities is based on K.-W. Gümpel, ed., "Die Musiktraktate Conrads von Zabern," *Akademie der Wissenschapten und der Literatur Mainz* (Wiesbaden: Steiner, 1956), pp. 149–58. On the renewed role of the monochord in Conrad's Pedagogy. See Gümpel, "Das Tastenmonochord Conrads von Zabern," *AFM* 12 (1955): 143–56, which includes a photograph of a modern reproduction of Conrad's "keyed monochord".

[45] For a modern edition of Conrad's three treatises, see K.-W. Gümpel, "Novellus musicae artis tractatus," pp. 184–244; "Opusculum de monochordo," pp. 245–59; and "De modo bene cantandi," pp. 260–82.

within the church. The text lists six main "requirements" (*requisita*) that the author thinks indispensable for the attainment of a proper level of *decorum* by church singers. These are: "singing as one voice and one spirit" (*concorditer cantare*), "respecting the exact duration of the notes," (*mensuraliter cantare*), "choosing a medium range," (*mediocriter cantare*), "adjusting the style of singing to the liturgical occasion" (*differentialiter cantare*), "singing with devotion," (*devotionaliter cantare*), and "singing with elegance and decorum," (*satis urbaniter cantare*). In these precepts, Conrad invites singers to choose carefully their tempo and vocal range, to avoid embellishments and *rusticitates* (unrefined uses of the voice), and to ban secular tunes from the divine service.[46] Thus the treatise, which had no historical precedents in Latin music theory, takes as its point of departure an affective view of music and singing that had also transpired in Ciconia's *Nova musica* (mediated, as we have seen, from Amalarius of Metz), as well as in Johannes Gallicus' *Ritus canendi*, to be examined below. This position is directly connected with Conrad's celebration of the "devout holy fathers" (*devoti sancti patres*) as models of piety and devotion. Indeed the singers' carefully prescribed behaviors during the ritual are an important part of a larger program of spiritual *renovatio* that aims at staving off the corrupted musical practices of the *moderni*. Conrad provides the basic guidelines for that behavior in the fifth requirement for good singing, *devotionaliter cantare*:

Devotionaliter cantare, quod est quintum, est sic cantare, quod quilibet simul cantantium in forma maneat in eis notis, quae a devotis patribus nobis sunt traditae, ita quod nullus illas in plures frangat vel ab eis quomodolibet recedat in quintam supra vel in quartam infra aut in aliam concordantem saliendo vel ad modum discantus divagando et ab eis declinando. Omnes enim tales recessus a sanctorum patrum devota melodia plus in auditoribus impediunt quam generent devotionem, nec in cantantibus devotionis signa, sed potius reprehensibilis levitatis indicia esse videntur. Et quod amplius est, sunt choro non parum praeiudiciales, quia saepe sunt vel fiunt occasio confusionum et errorum in cantando, quia ceteri in vera nota sive melodia praescripta manere curantes non solum per huiusmodi quorundam extra veram notam divagationem impediuntur in suo proposito, sed etiam eorundem sic divagantium auxilio fraudantur, qui, si cum eis in vera nota manerent eosque fideliter iuvarent, melius se mutuo a confusionibus praeservarent, prout nemini venit in dubium. Item etiam sic est devotionaliter cantandum, ut ab omnibus simul cantantibus sub ipso cantu, ubi et quando oportet aut consuetum est fieri, reverenter capita detegantur eademve inclinentur nec non genua flectantur, et sic de aliis

[46] For a more detailed analysis of this treatise, see J. Dyer, "Singing with Proper Refinement from *De Modo Bene Cantandi* (1474)," *EM* 6 (1978), 207–27, which features the text and the English translation of the last of Conrad's precepts, *satis urbaniter cantare*.

devotionis indiciis, quae omnia cooperantur ad devotionem, quam cantus ecclesi-
asticus tam in cantantibus quam in aliis fidelibus ipsum audientibus generare debet
ex institutione. Item etiam sic est cantandum devotionaliter, ut nulla melodia, quae
a devotis sanctis patribus nobis non est tradita, sed a diaboli ministris introducta,
ut infra dicetur, inter divinae laudis carmina umquam cantetur; huiusmodi enim
melodiae adulterinae penitus sunt reiciendae a divino officio. Et tamen heu in pler-
isque ecclesiis quasi cotidie sunt in usu. Exemplariter loquar, ut intelligar: Nonnulli
scolarium rectores placere nescio cui cupientes, sed haud dubium diabolo per hoc
servientes, etiamsi nescii, quorundam mundialium carminum melodias sumpse-
runt et illas super his, quae de potioribus sunt inter divinae laudis carmina, hoc
est super hymnum angelicum Gloria in excelsis et super Symbolum Nicaenum ac
super Sanctus et Agnus Dei, ut poterant, aptarunt haec sub eisdem mundialibus
melodiis cantando dimissis devotis sanctorum patrum melodiis nobis praescriptis.
Quae mundialium carminum melodiae dum cantantur in officio missae, non solum
plurimos christifideles, ut sciens scio, scandalisant, sed etiam multos praesertim
iuvenes vel carnales homines plus de domo choreae quam de regno caelorum cogi-
tare faciunt in devotionis impedimentum non modicum, nimirum quia huiusmodi
melodias vel eis similes in domo choreae saepe audierunt.

[To sing devotionally (my fifth precept) is to sing in such a way as to remain
close to those notes which have been given to us by our devout fathers, so that no
singer breaks those notes or departs from them a fourth or a fifth higher in the way
of discant. All these departures from the devout melodies of our holy fathers are a
hindrance to devotion in the listeners, rather than an aid to it and are not signs of
devotion in the singers themselves, but rather are taken to be signs of a reprehen-
sible lightness. What is more, there are in choirs not a few badly intentioned ones
who are or become an opportunity for confusion and mistakes, because the remaining singers, striving to follow the prescribed note or melody, are not only prevented
from doing so by the melodic wanderings of the first group, but are also deprived of
the help of those "wanderers" who, if they adhered to the notated parts with them
and helped them consistently, they would preserve themselves much better from
confusion, as no one would doubt. Furthermore, it is necessary to sing in a devout
way, meaning that all singers, whenever it is appropriate or customary during the
performance of a chant, should raise or bow their heads, genuflect, and perform
other similar gestures of devotion all at the same time. All of these acts contribute
to a general mood of devotion, which liturgical chant is expected to foster both in
the singers and in the congregation. Furthermore, to sing devotionally is to always
avoid singing any melody that has not been transmitted to us by our devout holy
fathers, and that the ministers of the devil have introduced among the songs of
divine praise; likewise, lascivious melodies are to be completely rejected from the
divine office; yet, today they are used almost on a daily basis in most churches. For
instance, some school rectors – trying to please I don't know whom, but no doubt
unknowingly serving the devil in the process – took a number of secular melodies
and adapted them as best as they could to the most sacred [*de potioribus*?] texts

of the divine praises, that is to say, to the angelic hymn *Gloria in excelsis*, to the *Symbolum Nicaenum* [i.e., the *Credo*], the *Sanctus* and the *Agnus Dei*, singing these texts with those secular melodies and rejecting the devout songs that the holy fathers have prescribed for us. When these secular melodies are sung during the mass, they not only scandalize many among the faithful, as I can say with confidence; they also induce many young and sensuous people to think of a dance hall, rather than of the kingdom of heaven. Thus they are not a small impediment to devotion, certainly because they have often heard similar melodies in dance halls.][47]

As Joseph Dyer has pointed out, Conrad has much in common with other fifteenth-century music reformers – namely, a general antipathy against polyphony; a strong concern that the actual performance of chant (i.e., the choices regarding tempo and pronunciation, but also the overall "chemistry" of the singers) be integrated into the liturgy as much as possible; and a consideration of singers as self-conscious promoters of a spiritual attitude among the congregation.[48] To these traits one might add the deliberate pursuit of a program of *renovatio antiquitatis* that closely recalls the attitude about the past of contemporary Italian theorists.

Conrad's *Magistri*: Pseudo-Odo, Guido, and John

The historical models of Conrad's musical reform were, predictably enough, some of the most prominent and widely read authors of the monastic tradition of music theory from the ninth to the eleventh centuries: Pseudo-Odo's *Dialogus*, Guido's *Micrologus*, and John of Afflighem's *De musica*. What Conrad found in the writings of these authors was in essence analogous to what had attracted Ciconia – and, as we will see in the next chapter, Johannes Gallicus several decades earlier, namely, a monochord-based method of training singers that could provide a viable alternative to the Hand of the *guidonistae*. To frame Conrad's musical pedagogy in these terms might well seem disingenuous, for the German *magister* did not openly criticize the method of solmization and may even have used it in his own music lessons. A comprehensive assessment of his position on this point, however, leads to

---

[47] Gümpel, ed. "Die Musiktraktate Conrads von Zabern," pp. 270–1, translation mine.

[48] Dyer, "Singing with Proper Refinement," 211–12. On this aspect of fifteenth-century musical thought, see now Wegman, *The Crisis of Music*. Some distinctions are in order, however. Conrad was no Wycliffe, Erasmus, or Savonarola, and would certainly dislike seeing himself counted among those who contributed to bringing music into a state of "crisis." The real problem that he sought to address with his musical pedagogy lay in the generally poor conditions of German musical chapels of his time.

the conclusion that Conrad saw the monochord as a far more reliable tool for singing than the Hand.

Having established that the monochord and the seven *claves* are organized according to the same principle, Conrad cites a passage from Guido's *Micrologus*, chapter 5, in which the author draws a parallel between the seven letters and the seven days of the week and points out that singing at the octave makes "the same melody resound in the *graves*, acutae, and *superacute*, as if a single thing."[49] In support of the notion of equivalence of the sounds at the octave, Conrad then adds a second quotation from the *Dialogus de musica*.

[L]oquitur dominus Odo in suo Dialogo quaerenti discipulo, cur per monochordum eaedem litterae fiant in prima et secunda eius partibus, respondens in haec verba: Hoc ita fit, ut unaquaeque littera correspondeat suae consimili litterae in octavo scilicet loco positae cum tonis et semitoniis, videlicet ut ubi in prima parte sit tonus vel semitonium, sit et in secunda parte. Similiter de ditonis et semiditonis, ut sic omnis cantus simul cantari possit in prima parte monochordi et etiam in secunda.

[To a query of his student, who wonders why the same letters are found in both sections [i.e., octaves] of the monochord, *magister* Odo answers in the following fashion: it is as you say, so that any two letters at the distance of an octave, the two share the same intervallic sequence – that is to say, whatever sequence of tones and semitones you find in the first part you will also find in the second. The same can be said for major and minor third and for all other intervals, so that any song can be sung at the same time in both parts of the monochord.][50]

Conrad also takes from the *Dialogus* the observation that "an instrument teaches (the practice of singing) better than a teacher (*Dialogus*, ch. 1), as well as another excerpt in which the monochord is praised as a most patient and marvelous instrument that teaches its own maker things that it itself does not know. (*Dialogus*, ch. 4):

D. Nunc autem qualiter cantum notare possim, ut ego illum absque magistro comprehendam, primum audire exspecto, ut cum exempla regularum dederis, eum melius recognoscam, et si penitus quidquam mente excesserit, ad tales notas indubitanter recurram. M. Litteras monochordi, sicut per eas cantilena discurrit, ante oculos pone; ut si nondum vim ipsarum litterarum plene cognoscis, secundum easdem litteras chordam percutiens ab ignorante magistro mirifice audias et addiscas. D. Vere, inquam, magistrum mirabilem mihi dedisti, qui a me factus me doceat, meque docens ipse nihil sapiat. Imo propter patientiam et obedientiam sui eum

[49] Babb, trans., *Hucbald, Guido, and John*, p. 62.
[50] Gümpel, ed., "Die Musiktraktate Conrads von Zabern," p. 194, translation mine. The original passage in Pseudo-Odo's *Dialogus* can be found in *GS* I, pp. 254–5.

maxime amplector; cantabit enim mihi quando voluero, et nunquam de mei sensus tarditate commotus verberibus vel injuriis cruciabit. M. Bonus magister est, sed diligentem auditorem requirit.

[Discipulus: Now I would like to hear how I can notate a song so that I can comprehend it without a teacher, and so that I can interpret it correctly through the rules that you have given me. And if something exceeds my capacity, I can rely securely on these notes. Magister: Place in front of your eyes the letters of the monochord, by which the melody unfolds. And if you do not yet fully know the properties of those letters, you will hear and learn them perfectly from an ignorant master by plucking the string in accordance to those letters. Discipulus: You have truly given me a wonderful master that will instruct me even though I made it, and who will be able to teach me even though it knows nothing. Because of its patience and reliability I have the utmost trust in him. It will indeed sing to me according to my need, and it will never subject me to physical or verbal abuse after becoming frustrated with my mental tardiness. Magister: It is a good master, but it requires a diligent listener.][51]

By the same token, Conrad's references to Guido may be understood as part of his overall goal of moving away from solmization and in favor of a letter-based model of musical instruction. Following countless others before him, Conrad only cites passages from Guido's *Micrologus*, not from the *Epistola*. Furthermore, throughout his treatise he explicitly connects Guido with the divisions of the monochord, with the three main consonances or *symphoniae*, and with modal theory, but only once with the six syllables. On the whole, although Conrad retains Guido's syllables in his musical pedagogy (at least in *Novellus tractatus*), he remains lukewarm about them.

From the Hand to the monochord

Conrad is a rare author to offer an unusually detailed account of the precise functional relationship between letters and syllables. In the *Novellus tractatus*, he explains that the seven letters or *claves* were pre-positioned to the syllables for the purpose of eliminating the *inconvenientiae* of six-syllable solmization. Indeed, the identity of the letters at the octave matches the equivalence of sounds at the *diapason* that is fundamental to the logic of the monochord:

Cum igitur experti musici decrevissent septem cantus iuxta praedictum modum coincidentiae et intersectionis simul in monochordo collocare, ita ut per hoc in uno loco diversorum cantuum diversae saepe concurrerent voces, iam duae iam

[51] Gümpel, ed., "Die Musiktraktate Conrads von Zabern," p. 194, translation mine.

tres, decreverunt pariter pro clariori distinctione et intelligentia totius monochordi ac manus musicae litteras quasdam alphabeti, quae claves dicuntur, ipsis
vocibus praeponere [...] Quemadmodum ergo in monochordo octava clavis
cum prima est eadem, etsi non omnino, quod propter diversam earum figu-
rationem addo, ita nimirum vox octava cum sua prima in soni concordia est
eadem, sed tamen non omnino, quia sonus ille gravis, scilicet primae, ille acutus,
scilicet octavae.

[After the most learned musicians had instituted seven *cantus*, overlapping and
intersecting as described above, so that two or three syllables often corresponded
to one place on the monochord, they decided at the same time to pre-position the
letters of the alphabet, called *claves*, to those syllables, in order to clarify better the
functioning of the monochord and of the musical Hand. [...] Just as on the monochord, then, the eighth *clavis* is the same as the first one (albeit not completely, so
as shown by the use of different case letters so the eighth syllable is the same as the
first one in the concord of sound, yet not completely so because the sound of the
first syllable is low, whereas that of the octave syllable is high.][52]

Conrad's position on Guidonian solmization, however, is considerably
more ambiguous, and perhaps flexible, than Ciconia's. In the early portions
of *Novellus tractatus*, he even presents it as a *sine qua non* for the singers and
musicians of his time, going as far as to claim, for instance, that the seven
letters or *claves* and the six syllables constitute the basis of the "science" of
singing.[53] In line with this view, he advises beginning singers to learn by
heart all the positions of the notes within the Hand. Conrad's exposition,
however, remains distinctly pragmatic. He avoids the teaching of *proprietates* and *deductiones* that by his time had become a staple of Guidonian
theory, preferring instead the more practical term *cantus* (see the beginning
of the last citation).

More importantly, Conrad points out that the mapping of the diatonic
space via the seven *deductiones* (or *cantus*) has several *inconvenientia* that
originate from the overlapping of those segments. In the first place he mentions the unfortunate problem of "retrogradation" (*inepta nimis retrograda-
tio*), which arises in the practice of solmization when the first syllable *ut* is
taken above *la* in ascending melodies and the last syllable *la* is taken below
ut in descending melodies. Conrad writes that such labeling "is evidently
absurd" (*quod omnino absurdum videtur*), thus questioning the counterintuitive use of lower syllables for higher sounds. Secondly, Conrad decries the
complete abandonment of the technique of mutation on the part of singers,

[52] *Ibid.*, p. 194, translation mine.
[53] *Ibid.*, p. 188.

in spite of the fact that mutation is essential to the method of solmization (*omnium mutationum musicalium totalis evacuatio*) – a point that may be interpreted as a veiled criticism of a casual or *ad libitum* use of the syllables that is documented in other fifteenth-century sources. Lastly (and most disturbingly, in Conrad's view), the practice of solmization may produce notable and multiple distortions of the musical intervals and concordances, and ultimately in the entire art of music:

Tertio, quod longe detestabilius foret, multarum proportionum et modorum musicalium variarumque concordantiarum notabilis et multiplex vitiatio, ipsius monochordi falsificatio, et per consequens totius musicae artis pertur- batio. Multa enim diatesssaron, diapente, ac diapason sic caruissent suis semi- toniis, quae tamen … omni modo habere debent et sine quibus rite concordare nequivissent.

[Third, and most regrettable of all, is the notable and continuous alteration of the musical proportions, of the modes, and of the various concordances, the falsifica- tion of the monochord, and consequently the distortion of the entire art of music. Many species of, diatessaron, diapente, and diapason would thus be deprived of their semitones, which however … they must have, for without them the singing could not be concordant.][54]

The keyed monochord is a far better option than the Hand for sight sing- ing, as Conrad points out, for instance, in the following passage from the *Opusculum de monochordo*:

Primum tamen, si alicui opus fuerit, ascensus et descensus illos, qui in sex notis sine mutatione decurrentes communiter ipsis incipientibus primo proponi solent, per monochordum addiscat. Similiter et proportiones illas, quae in uno simplici cantu sunt reperibiles, imitatione chordae saepe frequentando perfecte per omnia apprehendat se in eis sufficientissime habituando, ita ut sine monochordo eas iam infallibiliter cantare sciat.

[First, however, if anyone needs it, let him learn on the monochord those ascend- ing and descending series of notes that beginners are commonly taught in groups of six notes without mutation. Likewise, let him learn perfectly those intervals that are found within one simple *cantus* by imitating the sound of the string and by becoming used to them, so as to learn how to sing them eventually even without the monochord.][55]

The bulk of the *Opusculum* consists of a detailed review of the eight advantages that derive from using the monochord in music instruction. These may be summarized as follows:

---

[54] *Ibid.*, p. 192, translation mine.
[55] *Ibid.*, p. 251, translation mine.

1. The monochord facilitates the communication between teachers and students by offering a visual representation of the gamut (*probatio ad oculum*).
2. It offers a reliable basis for practicing the correct notes of any melody.
3. While sight singing, the monochord helps to verify the accuracy of the intervals performed and to correct the mistakes.

The overall content of the *Opusculum* marks a decisive turning point from the positions of the *Novellus tractatus*. Recall that the teaching of the earlier treatise had relied on Guido's syllables (if in a somewhat simplified fashion), to the point that it taught the reader how to locate the seven *cantus* on the monochord. The *Opusculum*, however, appears to move away from that syllables-based pedagogy, as it quotes Pseudo-Odo's advice of singing *per litteras*.[56] Indeed, the last quote suggests that Conrad now considers the syllables as alternative to the monochord rather than complementary to it.

In the end, which method(s) of musical instruction were adopted in German fifteenth-century monasteries? The answer to this key question involves an examination of the numerous music theory manuscripts now preserved at the Bavarian State Library in Munich and in other centers in the region. It may turn out that most monastic institutions indeed used the Guidonian syllables in the beginning stages of musical training, as attested for instance in the short musical tract from the Ebstorf nunnery (Lower Saxony) recently studied by Karl-Werner Gümpel.[57] But if Conrad's treatises are any indication of actual musical practice, it is likely that in certain areas the use of the monochord would have supplanted that of the Hand by the middle of the fifteenth century.

---

[56] *Ibid.*, p. 250.
[57] My brief remarks on this source rely on K.-W. Gümpel, "A Didactic Musical Treatise from the Late Middle Ages: Ebstorf, Klosterarchiv, MS V,3," in S. Parisi, ed., *Music in the Theater, Church, and Villa: Essays in Honor of Robert Lamar Weaver and Norma Wright Weaver* (Warren, MI: Harmonie Park Press, 2000), pp. 50–64.

6 | Normalizing the humanist: Johannes Gallicus as a "follower of Guido"

An informed reader of Nicolaus Burtius' *Musices opusculum* (Bologna, 1487) might well have raised his eyebrows upon leafing through the early pages of the treatise. Several years earlier, a Spanish theorist active in Bologna by the name of Bartolomeo Ramos de Pareja had given to the press an iconoclastic treatise called *Musica practica* (1482) in which he had proposed radical reforms of both the Guidonian hexachordal system and Pythagorean tuning. In presenting his case, Ramos had been harshly critical of the pedagogical tradition of his time, famously mocking Guido himself as being "perhaps a better monk than a *musicus*." The only author who had appeared in a positive light in Ramos' treatise was one Carthusian monk named Johannes Gallicus (alias "Legiense," i.e., "from Liège"), who in turn had had plenty to say about Guidonian solmization in his *Ritus canendi vetustissimus et novus*, written in the early 1460s.

Burtius, as is well known, conceived his *Opusculum* as a direct reply to Ramos' radical views, in particular defending Guido's method from the attacks of the Spanish *prevaricator*. But there is an intriguing twist in the story, namely Burtius' passionate claim, restated at crucial junctions in his treatise, that his views on solmization were in fact one and the same with Gallicus, whom he presented unhesitatingly as a follower of Guido. Ramos, in Burtius' view, had appropriated Gallicus' positions for himself:

Praeterea nedum insectatur Guidonem, sed etiam quoscumque noverit illius sequaces objurgat, lacerat et quodam canino latratu stimulat. Laudat nonnumquam Johannem Carthusiae monachum, qui maximis praeconiis opere suo extollit Guidonem: ecce contrarietas.

[Not only does [Ramos] attack Guido, but he also scolds, abuses, and torments all those he knows to be followers of Guido with a certain dog-like barking. At times he praises the Carthusian monk Johannes, who extols Guido with the strongest praises in his work. What a contradiction!][1]

---

[1] N. Burtius, *Florum libellus*, ed. G. Massera (Florence: Olschki, 1975), p. 54; C. A. Miller, trans., *Nicolaus Burtius: Musices opusculum*, MSD 37, American Institute of Musicology, 1983), p. 26.

So our Renaissance reader might have wondered: how could two authors who held such radically different views on solmization as Ramos and Burtius both appeal to Gallicus in support of their positions? What did Gallicus have to say on this issue, and why were his views so consequential? Unfortunately, our reader would have been unable to answer his question securely, as the one text that would have solved the dilemma – Gallicus' treatise – was in all likelihood not readily available to him, since it was never given to the press.[2] As the following discussion will show, Gallicus' *Ritus* casts precious light on the confrontation between Ramos and other Northern Italian theorists of his generation. It also emerges as a key chapter not only in the long history of solmization, but also in the wider battle for musical reform in the humanist era, fought under the banner of *renovatio antiquitatis*.

In the introduction to the *Ritus canendi* (book I, chapter 2) Gallicus offers precious information on his educational background, calling himself a *grammaticus* and *musicus* and "an eager inquirer and follower of antiquity on every issue" ("… solicitum proponendae vetustatis in omnibus sectatorem et inquisitorem"). He also claims to have become a Carthusian monk in Mantua, where he attended for some time the school of Vittorino da Feltre, whom he describes as "a man thoroughly imbued with both Greek and Latin letters" (*viro tam litteris Greacis quam Latinis affatim imbuto*). Probably around the time of compilation of the *Ritus canendi*, Gallicus became acquainted with the English Carmelitan monk John Hothby, a prolific theorist who may have contributed to shaping the Carthusian's views on music. At the final period of his life Gallicus settled in Parma, where he apparently had Burtius as a student, and where he died in 1474.

The *Ritus canendi* fully honors Gallicus' self-ascribed labels of *grammaticus*, *musicus*, and "follower of antiquity." The choice of those three attributes may be indicative of the kind of training that he received from Vittorino, known for his strong interest in quadrivial sciences and for his paramount concern for the moral education of his students. At his school, called "Ca'

---

[2] The *Ritus canendi* has survived in only two manuscript copies from the late-fifteenth century: London, British Library, Add. 22315, fol. 1r-60r (copied by Burtius himself around the time of Gallicus' death in 1474), and the presumably more recent London, British Library, Harley 6525, fol. 1r-76r. There are two modern editions available of Gallicus' writings, both based on the Harley MS: *CS* IV, pp. 298–396, and J. Gallicus, *Ritus canendi*, ed. A. Seay, (Colorado Springs: Colorado College Music Press, 1981, 2 vols. Coussemaker's edition includes two additional treatises from the final folios of the Harley MS that he wrongly considered part of *Ritus canendi* and that may or may not be by Gallicus (see the description of the sources in Gallicus, *Ritus canendi*, vol. 1, pp. v-vii). All citations below are taken from the Seay edition, while the graphs and the tables are reproduced from Burtius' copy of the treatise.

Giocosa," Vittorino played the lyre and lectured on the *De institutione musica* by Boethius, which provided the material for much of the survey of the fundamentals of music in book 1 of Gallicus' *Ritus canendi*.[3]

There is no solid ground, however, for the claim that "Gallicus' ideas on the division of the tone and solmization are directly attributable to Feltre," as one author has claimed.[4] The wide temporal gap between Gallicus' training at Vittorino's school (1443–1446, the year of the teacher's death) and the compilation of the *Ritus canendi* (1458–1464) militates against the hypothesis of a direct influence between the two, even though Vittorino may have been instrumental in exposing Gallicus to Ciconia's negative views on the Hand and the *guidonistae*. Clearer signs of a Vittorino influence on Gallicus' treatise, however, may be found in the unusual rhetoric and mode or argumentation of the *Ritus canendi*, as the following discussion will attempt to show. If Gallicus knew of Ciconia's critique of Guidonian solmization, it is also possible that the English Carmelite and music theorist John Hothby may have served as a *trait d'union* between the two. As Oliver Ellsworth has observed, Hothby may have owned one of the two extant copies of Ciconia's treatise at some point in time, since his name is penned in the cover of the manuscript.[5] The inscription, however, is in a later hand and may thus not be reliable.[6]

Whatever the case may be, Gallicus' passionate plea for readopting the pedagogical methods of Guido's time is in line with the general humanist reform of education and learning that Vittorino actively promoted at his school. What remains to be debated is the answer to the dilemma posed by Burtius' treatise: in which sense was Johannes the Carthusian a "follower of Guido?"

Gallicus' program of disciplinary *renovatio*

In the narrowest sense, the overarching goal of Gallicus' *Ritus canendi* was an eminently practical one: to provide a simple and efficient way to introduce uneducated monks to the rudiments of singing. Gallicus felt very strongly

---

[3] For a discussion of the relationships between Gallicus' music theory and Vittorino's pedagogical program, see especially Gallico, "Musica nella Ca' Giocosa," pp. 189–98.

[4] See C. Adkins, s.v. "Gallicus," in *NG 2*, vol. 9, p. 474. On Gallicus' new interpretation of the Greek *tonoi*, see C. Palisca, *Humanism in Italian Renaissance Musical Thought* (New Haven: Yale University Press, 1985), pp. 280–3.

[5] The manuscript is Rome, Biblioteca Apostolica Vaticana, MS lat. 5320 (copied in Italy in 1476). See Ellsworth, ed. and trans. *Johannes Ciconia*, pp. 4; 35–6.

[6] See B. J. Blackburn, E. E. Lowinsky, and C. A. Miller, eds., *A Correspondence of Renaissance Musicians* (Oxford: Clarendon Press 1991), p. 26, n. 10.

the need to reform the teaching of chant in the monastic and church schools of his time. Even a passing glance at his treatise shows that his position on this issue was on the whole aligned with Ramos', inasmuch as he saw the method of six-syllable solmization as part of the problem, rather than of the solution. In Gallicus' view, the method of singing via the six syllables – then at a peak in popularity – was to be replaced by the alternative method of the seven letters that had been used by the early fathers and that was grounded on the "true and unchanging" foundations of music described by Boethius.[7] Thus the *ritus vetustissimus* for singing would become *novus* again.

But Gallicus' program of musical *renovatio* goes deeper and further than the confined boundaries of musical pedagogy, as it addresses the broader issue of the function of music in the Christian ritual as a conveyer of "affectus," thus of chant as an instrument of piety and devotion. Particularly impressive for its time is the author's assessment of the origin and purpose of solmization in the context of Guido's pedagogical *œuvre*. In short, Gallicus combines his spiritual ideals with excellent philological skills and a clear view for the future of music and music education within the church. Such ingredients, combined with the author's knowledge of the material and his engaging writing style, combine to produce what is undoubtedly one of the most provocative musical treatises of the Italian *quattrocento*.

The very first sentence of *Ritus canendi* best illustrates the basic axiom that underlies the whole of Gallicus' argument in his treatise:

Omnium quidem artium, etsi varia sit introductio, ducit tamen ad unum, haud secus quam si per varias semitas in eundem plures convenerint locum. Gallus etenim fari docet uno ritu Latinum, et alio Romanus aut Italicus, qui tandem in unam concurrunt, Latinae linguae scientiam quam prisci profecto Romani vocarunt, imitati Graecos, grammaticam.

[Although there are different ways to gain access to the arts, nevertheless they all lead to the same result, just as many different people may arrive at the same place through various paths.[8] Likewise, the French teach Latin one way, the Romans and the Italians another, all of which, however, are subsumed into one science of the Latin language that the ancient Romans, imitating the Greeks, called "grammar."][9]

---

[7] In Massera's words, Gallicus' goal is not to propose "una nuova 'practica', ma una saggia riforma dell'insegnamento della musica per riportare alle sue origini la 'vecchia' pratica. E per 'pratica' si deve intendere, secondo l'accezione per allora adottata dagli scrittori di musica, la stessa scienza nell'attualità della sua comunicazione, nel momento più squisitamente metodologico," in Burtius, *Florum libellus*, p. 16.

[8] Gallicus, *Ritus canendi*, vol. 1, Praefatio, p. 1. Throughout the chapter all translations are mine except where otherwise indicated.

[9] *Ibid.*

This common core that ties together all musical traditions is nothing more than the sequence of tones and semitones of the gamut, perceived as "the common measures of all melodies without which nobody sings and has ever sung."[10] In the fifteenth century, such a view was no doubt widespread, the direct result of the Boethian-Pythagorean musical philosophy that had dominated "Western" culture since classical antiquity. Such a universalist stance is based on the author's belief that the seven basic *constitutiones* of the diapason and bisdiapason, which provide the foundation for the diatonic modes, are common to all types of music.[11] Even if members of one musical culture may not be able to comprehend and appreciate the specific modes and melodic tropes of another, they will still be able to describe them in terms of the intervallic sequence of the fourth, the fifth, and the octave. This is so on the basis of the fact that "whereas the tones or modes are the result of choice [*ad beneplacitum*], the series of pitches and the diatonic species are common to all languages."[12]

But while Gallicus acknowledges that different musical cultures (as we might call them) are free to choose distinct diatonic configurations or "modalities," he also maintains that not *all* methods for teaching the rudiments of music are created equal. Quite to the contrary, the overarching goal of his treatise is to demonstrate that the method of singing used by the early church fathers (the *ritus canendi vetustissimus*) was manifestly easier and more effective than the one commonly used in Gallicus' time. It is that method that should be reintroduced in the church, Gallicus argues, if music is again to inspire the faithful to devotion:

... non dico novam introducere volens, sed magis in Ecclesia Dei sub Domino Papa Pio Secundo renovare nitens, veram antiquorum patrum atque brevem et facilem de sonis ac vocibus practicam. Oportuit primum eis qui quos nostris temporibus canere docent in ecclesiis, tanta rei prolixitate fatigant totque verborum ambagibus antequam veniantur ad rem afficiunt, ut obruti saepe tedio mox a coepto discendi proposito recedant. Opportuit, inquam, illis primum ostendere quam multifarie potest quis ad huius artis pervenire notitiam, dein quis sit introducendi modus facilior atque praestantior viris potissimum ecclesiasticis demonstrare.

[10] "... tonum et semitonium, quae communes omnium melodiarum mensurae sunt, ac per consequens huius artis origo, medium et finis," Gallicus, *Ritus canendi*, vol. 2, p. 50; "... tonos et semitonia, sine quibus nemo canet aut cecinit umquam" (*Ibid.*, p. 55).

[11] "Ex quo quidem colligimus nil esse vel umquam fuisse tropos tam Graecos quam Latinos, tamque seculares quam ecclesiasticos nisi constituiones illas nilque rursum aliud constitutio quam consonantiarum iuxta Boetii diffinitionem coniunctio," Gallicus, *Ritus canendi*, vol. 1, p. 71.

[12] "... tropi, toni, vel modi fuerit ad bene placitum, soni vero species et constitutiones omnium sunt communes linguarum," (*Ibid.*, p. 72).

[I do not wish to introduce a novelty, but rather to bring back in God's church, under the tenure of Pope Pius II, the true, concise, and easy practice of the musical sounds and notes developed by our ancient fathers. It is necessary first of all to those who currently teach the rudiments of singing in our churches. These singers struggle with such laborious methods and are negatively affected by so much useless verbosity, that they soon abandon the entire endeavor before they reach their goal, overcome by tedium. It is fitting to show them that there are many ways to be initiated into this art, and finally to demonstrate an easier and better method of singing, particularly for church singers.][13]

The two main parts of the treatise, clearly outlined in the rest of the introduction, correspond to the two stages of Gallicus' program of *renovatio*. In Part I, largely based on Boethius, the author will lay out the foundations of the diatonic system, including the derivation of the diatonic steps from the division of the monochord and a detailed discussion of the consonances and their species. All this is a lengthy preparation for Part II, in which the author shows that the method of singing via the seven letters is both older than, and by far preferable to, hexachordal solmization. It is interesting that the image of the monochord attached to one of the two extant sources of the *Ritus canendi* is a "keyed monochord" very similar to the one described by Conrad of Zabern (see Fig. 6.1 below). This detail would seem to suggest that Gallicus used the monochord in musical instruction; in his text, however, he makes no reference to such practical use of the instrument.[14]

At first sight, Gallicus' program is strikingly similar to that of later humanists such as Heinrich Glarean, who tried to present his twelve-mode system as a "proper renewal of antiquity" (*proba antiquitatis instauratio*).[15] Gallicus' "antiquity," however, is relatively recent, as it includes the "fathers" (*antiqui* or *nostri patri*) of the Carolingian and post-Carolingian era, that is to say, roughly from the *enchiriadis* treatises to Guido. His pedagogical models, which he labels the *brevem et facilem practicam*, were firmly anchored in monastic life and primarily concerned with the education of church singers. By contrast, Glareanus' antiquity – and also that which inspired Gafori, Zarlino, Vicentino, and the members of the Camerata de' Bardi among others – was primarily the Greco-Roman antiquity of classical humanism, to which sixteenth-century

---

[13] *Ibid.*, p. 1.

[14] The manuscript with the image of the monochord is Add. 22315, fol. 15r. Seay observes that this sheet is in a different hand and was likely imported from another source. A similar image was to appear in Harley 6525 (fol. 19v), but the dedicated sheet is blank. For additional details on this image of the monochord, see Gallicus, *Ritus canendi*, vol. 1, p. 45.

[15] H. Glarean, *Dodecachordon* (Basel, 1547), fol. a2v; C. Miller, ed. and trans., *Henricus Glareanus: Dodecachordon*, MSD 6, 2 vols. ([N.p.]: American Institute of Musicology, 1965), vol. I, p. 38.

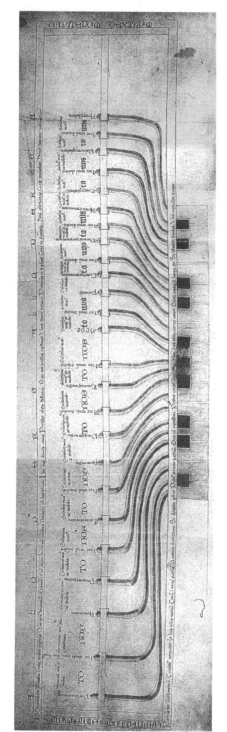

Fig. 6.1. Gallicus' monochord (from London, British Library, Add. 22315, fol. 15r-15v).

authors turned less for practical reasons (the adequate training of church singers), than in response to intellectual and aesthetic interests such as the renewal of musical style, the reform of the modal system, or the rediscovery of the chromatic and enharmonic genera.[16] Perhaps one may speak of an early wave of musical humanism – thus far largely unexplored by Renaissance scholars – that passed through the treatises of authors such as Ciconia and Gallicus and had very little in common with the second, classicizing wave of the Gaffurios and the Zarlinos of later decades.

Philology meets music theory: Guido historicized

To music theorists before Gallicus, Guido was an *auctoritas*, a source of wisdom on musical matters, a quasi-oracular figure whose teachings had absolute validity regardless of contingencies of time and place, like those by Pythagoras, Boethius, or Aristotle ("the Philosopher"), or any other *auctoritas*. The particular circumstances and motivations that had led Guido to formulate his musical pedagogy were irrelevant to medieval authors between John of Afflighem and Johannes Ciconia and to the textual tradition of glosses and commentaries to which they belonged. Guido's writings were quoted, often misquoted (especially after 1200), at times criticized, but rarely, if at all, contextualized. Moreover, because of their authoritative status, those writings were taken at face value and cited inasmuch as they corroborated the opinions of the writer or the established orthodoxy. What is distinctly missing in medieval music theory is a rigorous textual exegesis that would highlight possible contradictions and limitations in the text of any *auctoritas*.

Time and again, medieval authors are eager to support their argument by appealing to the Aretine monk: *testante Guidone* and *secundum Guidonem* are frequent incidental phrases in Latin music theory. Beginning in the thirteenth century, Guido already occupies a particular place in the history of plainchant. To Johannes de Garlandia, he corrected and reorganized the body of chant first brought to light by Gregory the Great[17]; Jerome of

---

[16] As Sarah Fuller has pointed out, however, Glarean still considered his modal reform as part of a larger program of Catholic renewal (see S. Fuller, "Defending the Dodecachordon: Ideological Currents in Glarean's Modal Theory," *JAMS* 49 (1996), 193–4). In this general sense at least, he was still voicing the ideals and the aspirations of fifteenth-century musical reformers such as Ciconia and Gallicus who, like Glarean, saw the renewal of musical learning as central to the educational and spiritual missions of the church.

[17] "Musica plana est illa que … a beato Gregorio primo fuit edita, et postea a Guidone monaco fuit correcta, composita et ordinata," Meyer, ed., *Musica plana Johannis de Garlandia*, p. 64.

Moravia portrayed him as the most notable musical genius since Boethius[18]; Franco of Cologne as a member of the Boethius-Pope-Gregory-Guido triumvirate.[19] Predictably, Guido is also featured in the miniature music-history-at-your-fingertips (*metra de inventione musicae*) reported by the anonymous commentator of Johannes Valendrinus (or Hollandrinus) that the *Lml* identifies as 'Traditio Hollandrini I':

Pitagoras reperit, transfert Boetius ipse.
Investigat Guido Tubalque registrat.
Jubal epilogat, normasque ponit Johannes.
Ordinat ac supplet Gregorius Ambrosiusque.

[Pythagoras found it, Boethius transmitted it, Guido studied it, and Tubal recorded it. Jubal summarized it, and Johannes [of Afflighem] laid down its rules. Gregory and Ambrose organized and completed it.][20]

Later authors, such as Matthaeus Herbenus, Johannes Tinctoris, Adam of Fulda, and others, would include Guido in their long genealogies of *musici* from antiquity to their present time.[21] But with all the frequent citations from *Micrologus* and the open praises to Guido *doctor peritissimus*, a critical and contextual appreciation of Guido's contribution to musical pedagogy lay beyond the intellectual pursuit of medieval authors.

The few and feeble attempts to engage Guido's writings in a more critical and historical fashion are very few and far between. Jacques de Liège briefly connects Guido's pedagogy to the poor status of music education in his time, while John of Tewkesbury, the author of the *Quatuor principalia* (ca. 1350), wondered whether Gregory the Great or Guido invented

---

[18] "Guido autem, quem post Boetium plurimum in hac arte valuisse fatemur," Cserba, ed., *Hieronymus de Moravia: Tractatus de musica*, p. 46.

[19] "Cum de plana musica quidam philosophi sufficienter tractaverint, ipsamque nobis tam theorice quam practice efficaciter illucidaverint, theorice praecipue Boetius, practice vero Guido monachus, et maxime de tropis ecclesiasticis beatus Gregorius ..." in Franco of Cologne, *Ars cantus mensurabilis*, ed. G. Reaney and A. Gilles, *CSM* 18 ([Rome]: American Institute of Musicology, 1974), p. 23.

[20] Anonymous, *Opusculum monacordale*, in Feldmann, *Musik und Musikpflege im mittelalterlichen Schlesien*, p. 159. The stanza evidently circulated in Northern Europe, as it appears also in the *Musica* by Johannes de Szydlow. See W. Gieburowski, *Die 'Musica Magistri Szydlovite': ein polnischer Choraltraktat des XV. Jahr. und seine Stellung in der Choraltheorie des Mittelalters, mit Berücksichtigung der Choraltheorie und -Praxis des XV. Jahrhundert in Polen, sowie der nachtridentinischen Choralreform* (Posen: St. Adalbert, 1915), p. 11.

[21] See Herbenus Traiectensis, *De natura cantus et miraculis vocis*, ed. J. Smits van Waesberghe, Beiträge zur rheinischen Musikgeschichte 22 (Köln: Arno Volk, 1957), p. 17; J. Tinctoris, *Proportionale musices*, in A. Seay, ed., *Johannis Tinctoris Opera theoretica*, 3 vols., *CSM* 22 ([Rome]: American Institute of Musicology, 1975–8), vol. 2a, p. 10; A. von Fulda, *Musica*, in *GS* III, p. 337.

the six syllables.[22] But Guido is also mentioned in two medieval chronicles that enjoyed a wide distribution in the Middle Ages, namely Sigebert of Gembloux's *Chronicon ab anno 381 ad 1113* and Vincent of Beauvais' *Speculum historiale* (a thirteenth-century compilation largely modeled on Sigebert's text). As we will later see, the brief account of Guido's contribution in these two chronicles was very important to Gallicus.

Perhaps Vittorino da Feltre's fingerprints are found in the *Ritus canendi* not as much in the specifics of Gallicus' thesis, but rather in the strategy of argumentation adopted in the treatise and in its expository tone, which often has the flavor of an oral presentation by a *magister* speaking to his pupils in engaging and colorful language. Whatever the case may be, Gallicus had a key interest in placing Guido himself at the center of his discussion, not just this or that chapter of chant theory. It was vitally important to Gallicus to evaluate Guido's exact words on solmization in the context of his entire music pedagogy, and as a particular solution to the pressing problem of finding effective methods for sight singing. Equally important to him was an assessment of Guido's method of the six syllables against earlier ones, and to measure the advantages and shortcomings of each of them. In short, Gallicus posed new interpretive questions about Guido that required the adoption of a rather novel, historical-philological approach to music writings (though it may well be the other way around: Gallicus' philological background, together with his obvious dissatisfaction with current methods of sight singing, led him to pose those new questions about Guido).

The second book of Part II of the *Ritus* goes to the very heart of the matter. After lambasting the ignorance of those modern singers who waste their time trying to master the six syllables and the complexities of polyphony, Gallicus begins his lengthy analysis of the role of solmization within Guido's own writings. Significantly, his point of departure is Vincent of Beauvais' paragraph on Guido, which appropriately sets the tone for his own historical analysis:

Ex historiali speculo, libro vigesimo sexto, quis ut, re, mi, fa, sol, la primus adinvenerit, quove tempore totum in manu sinistra locaverit. Conradus ad imperium

---

[22] "I believe Guido, the monk, to have been an expert in both the theory and the practice of music. However, he dedicated himself to the practice of music because few, in his generation, knew how to sing correctly and with confidence," in Jacques de Liège, *Speculum musicae*, ed. R. Bragard, vol. II, p. 12, translation mine; "Dicunt autem quidam beatum Gregorium praedictas sex voces invenisse, cum illum hymnum composuisset, videlicet: Ut queant laxis etc., tamen Guido, qui compositor erat grammatis, pueris suis edocendis in principio praedictum hymnum tradidit, qui sex diversas habet particulas, et a sex diversis incipit vocibus videlicet, ut, re, mi, fa, sol, la. Verumtamen sive beatus Gregorius inventor illorum vocum extiterat, sive Guido, non est ex humano ingenio, sed divina erat inspiratio (J. of Tewkesbury, *Quatuor principalia*, in *CS* 4, p. 220).

anno Domini millesimo vigesimo quinto mundi, scilicet, MLXXVIIII [recte: MXXIV] sublimatus, imperavit annis quindecim. Claruit eo tempore in Italia Guido Aretinus multi inter musicos nominis. In hoc etiam philosophis praeferendus, quod ignotos cantus etiam pueri facilius discant per eius regulam, quam per vocem magistri aut per usum alicuius instrumenti, dum sex litteris aut syllabis modulatim appositis ad sex voces, quas solas regulariter musica recepit, hisque vocibus per flexuras levae manus distinctis, per integrum diapason se oculis et auribus ingerunt intentae et remissae elevationes vel depositiones earundem sex vocum.

[From [Vincent of Beauvais'] *Speculum historiale*, ch. 26: Who first introduced the syllables ut, re, mi, fa, sol, la, and when were they located on the left hand. Emperor Conradus, who ascended to the throne in the year 1025, ruled for fifteen years. At that time the name of Guido of Arezzo was famous among Italian musicians. He was preferred to the philosophers in that he introduced a rule by which even young singers were able to learn unknown chants more easily than through the teacher's voice or an instrument. He paired six musical sounds to six pitch letters or musical syllables, which he accepted as regular. With these six letters or syllables, positioned on the joints of the left hand, singers perform all the ascending and descending intervals between those six musical sounds through the octave.][23]

Gallicus is quick to point out, however, that the syllables were no more than a "small novelty" (*parva novitas*) with a limited role in Guido's pedagogical writings. Far more significant, he argues, was the invention of the staff and the introduction of the seven letters, which Guido substituted to the *daseian* notation of the *enchiriadis* treatises.[24] It was primarily through these innovations, rather than through the six syllables, that Guido sought to reform the musical pedagogy of the church.[25] To prove his point, Gallicus cites the following three verses from Guido's *Regulae ritmice* (he recalls them a total of four times throughout his treatise, a sure sign of the significance he attributed to them):

Solis notare litteris Optimum probavimus,
Quibus ad discendum cantum Nihil est facilius
Si frequentetur fortiter, Saltem tribus mensibus.

[We have proven that it is best to notate only in letters.
Nothing is easier than these for the purposes of learning song,
If they are used frequently for only three months.] [26]

[23] Gallicus, *Ritus canendi*, vol. 2, p. 47. Conrad II was crowned King of the Germans in 1024 and Holy Roman Emperor in 1027. He died in 1039.

[24] *Ibid.*, p. 47–8.

[25] Guido was not the first author to use the seven letters, of course, but medieval theorists did recognize him for introducing the staff and for expanding the gamut beyond aa (or *nete hyperboleon*).

[26] Gallicus, *Ritus canendi*, vol. 2, pp. 1, 4, 48 and 58. I have used the translation found in W. Kreyszig, ed. and trans., *Franchino Gaffurio: The Theory of Music* (New Haven: Yale University

To Gallicus, then Guido was fully convinced that the method of singing via the seven letters was the most efficient and expedite. The main evidence supporting this conclusion came from Guido's *Epistola*[27] in which the author explains to Brother Michael that he resorts to the syllables when training the *pueri*.[28] Gallicus seems to imply here that Guido never envisioned the use of solmization beyond the early stages of training, and that he would have certainly opposed the kind of mental computations that were required of advanced users of the system. In short, Gallicus' argument is closely reminiscent of Ciconia's strategy of separating Guido from the *guidonistae* of his time: he strives to present his proposed musical reform as perfectly in line with the core principles of Guido's teaching, while resolutely rejecting the method of hexachordal solmization not just as counterproductive for sight singing, but also as thoroughly marginal to Guido's own pedagogy.

> … aliquid novi fabricare nolo, sed veram huiusce rei doctrinam brevem ac per-facilem, qua nos piius ille Dei servus canere docet per litteras, innovare contendo ….vobis ostendere volo … quod per illam solam attendendo tonos ac semitonia discere modulari Deo valeatis breviter ac faciliter, absque tot verborum ambagibus totve nihili, quae vos ita fatigare solent illis litterarum [*recte*: syllabarum?] et non vocum mutationibus.
>
> [I do not intend to fabricate anything new, but rather to bring back the true, concise, and simple method of this discipline by which that pious servant of God [i.e., Guido of Arezzo] teaches us how to sing via the seven letters … I wish to demonstrate to you … that you will be able to learn how to modulate your voice to God by attending to tones and semitones, and without all those useless verbosities of solmization and those mutations of pitch labels, but not of sounds.][29]

Such a sophisticated argument was possible at all only to an author unusually well versed (compared to the average *magistri* of his time) in the art of textual exegesis.

Gallicus' contextual reading of Guidonian theory informs other parts of the *Ritus*. In the early pages of Part II of his treatise, for instance, he observes that the high significance that Guido had placed on pitch letters

---

Press, 1993), p. 172. For the original text, see *PesceGA*, lines 215–17, pp. 372–4. It is interesting to observe that the reading "frequentetur fortiter" in Gallicus' text is undocumented in the sources of the *Regule*, which consistently have "assidue utantur" instead. Gallicus may have quoted these verses by memory.

27   " … propter infantulos fabricare syllabas, quibus nempe tonos magis faciliter aut elevarent aut deponerent ac semitonia …" Gallicus, *Ritus canendi*, vol. 2, p. 48.

28   "Nam et ad eundem Pomposiae monachum et in eadem epistola sic sit Guido: Sit, inquit, haec symphonia, qua ego docendis pueris in primis atque ultimis utor," *Ibid.*, pp. 48–9). The citation is from the *Epistola ad Michahelem*, verses 118–20 (*PesceGA*, pp. 464–7).

29   Gallicus, *Ritus canendi*, vol. 2, p. 4.

and intervals in *Micrologus*, chapter 4, is a sure sign of the marginal role of the syllables in his musical pedagogy.[30] Any attempt to argue otherwise contradicts the available textual evidence:

Ex quo patet illum non sex illas excogitasse syllabas pro rei veritatis quae tonus est cum reliquis abolitione, sed pro parva puerorum ac rudium velut quodam baculo sustentanda capacitate. Cum praesertim, ut audis, tonos ita commendet ac semitonia nihilque penitus scribat de tot illis mutationibus et verborum ambagibus, ubi fatetur in certis suis epistolis se reperisse quidem, ut re mi fa sol la.

[Guido's list of intervals makes clear that he did not invent the six syllables in order to abolish the truth of the matter of tones and the other intervals, but rather to support 'as with a walking stick' (*quodam baculo*) the still limited skills of young and uneducated singers. As you can see, he endorses the sequence of tones and semitones, and does not mention at all those mutations and redundancies of words even in his *Epistola*, where some credit him with having found the syllables ut, re, mi, fa, sol, la.][31]

Gallicus feels so confident about his control of the sources that he challenges his readers to reach conclusions different to his own, with a sense of prowess that borders on cockiness. In his chapter titled, very explicitly, *Omne quidem in ut, re, mi, fa, sol, la superfluum, quod non sit aut in allegata illa Guidonis epistola aut in hac symphonia* [i.e., Ut queant laxis] *saltem expressum*, he writes:

Cernis, lector, vario ritu cecinnisse veteres et ad ultimum modernos ut, re, mi, fa, sol, la, non ea quidem puritate, qua confectum est usque nunc exercuisse. *Quaere, queso, praefatam Guidonis epistolam in quo se nobis illas fabricasse sex syllabas insinuat, et si tot ibi fa ut, ut fa, sol ut, ut sol, aut huiuscemodi simile, cum naturis illis, b mollibus et [bequadris] duris nimia verbositate quidem egentibus inveneris, volo me per omnia fuisse mentitum.* Quae proculdubio tanto debent estimari superflua, quanto verum obfuscando sensus discentium taedio nimis opprimunt. Quot, quaeso, viri tonsurati Deum alacriter in ecclesiis laudarent ardentique desiderio cantum illum eis, qui Dei sunt suavissimum, neque tamen lascivum quem nobis tradidere Sancti, patienter addiscerent, nisi tot ambages verborum, tot varii naturarum, [be] quadrorum et [b] mollium ordiens, totus non iam vocum, sed syllabarum superfluae mutationes rudium animos ac ingenia fatigando debilitarent? Quidam rem attentare conantes fabulas illas memoriae mandant, sed antequam ad id pervenerint, quod discere cupiunt, tanta garrulitate verborum attediati, iam expensis aliquando pecuniis totum in medio relinquunt. Alii vero phylacteria illa, ut vulgo loquar, non parvo labore crebri discunt. Sed nil praeter fa ut, ut fa, sol ut, ut sol, et his similia

---

[30] *Ibid.*, p. 6. Gallicus cites the relevant passage from *Micrologus* at this point.
[31] *Ibid.*, p. 6.

totis diebus in ore volventes, affecti quoque taedio tandem a docente cantore discedunt, sicut ante nescii. Aliqui tamen et illam mentetenus habent superfluam sex syllabarum verbositatem et elevandi vocem atque deprimendi per illas non parvam practicam, verum ultra procedere volentes, dum verba sacra cum illis syllabis, in quo totus fructus est accordare volunt, parum aut nihil in tota vita sua proficiunt. Quare? Quum absque dubio tonum et semitonium, quae communes omnium melodiarum mensurae sunt, ac per consequens huius artis origo, medium et finis, funditus ignorant.

[You see, reader, that the ancients sang in various ways and finally the moderns down to our own day practised ut re mi fa sol la, but not with the same purity with which the scheme was devised. *Search, I beg you, in that letter by Guido in which he is alleged to have concocted those six syllables for us, and if you find there all those fa ut, ut fa, sol ut, ut sol and the like, with those excessively verbose properties by nature, hard, and soft for the uneducated, then consider me wrong about everything else I have said.* Without a doubt, the six syllables must be considered all the more superfluous, as they oppress the minds of the learners with confusion and tedium. How many clerics, I wonder, would fervently praise God in the churches and would patiently learn for God's faithful, with genuine passion, that most suave yet not lascivious song that our early fathers bequeathed to us, if all these intricacies of words, all the various orders by nature, [bequadro] and [round b], and all these superfluous mutations not just of voices, but of syllables, did not greatly debilitate the talent and the will of the singers? There are some who, doing their best at trying this method, learn these trifles by heart, but before they have mastered what they wish to learn, they give up in the middle of the enterprise, bogged down by its sheer verbosity and having already spent quite a bit of money. Others learn those absurdities, to call them plainly, after not a small effort. But filling their mouths every day with nothing but fa ut, ut fa, sol ut, ut sol, and the like, and seized by tedium, they leave in the end their singing master, as ignorant as before they had started. Others, however, who keep in mind that verbosity of the six syllables and the not small practice of raising and lowering the voice through them, wishing to move on to the next step, where they yoke the all-meaningful holy words to those syllables, progress little or nothing in their entire lives. Why? No doubt because they are all but ignorant of the tones and semitones that are the shared principle of all melodies, thus also their origin, their means, and their ultimate goal.][32]

This extraordinary passage conveys all the core ideas shaping Gallicus' treatise. First, he boldly challenges his reader to prove him wrong on the issue of the role of the syllables in Guido's pedagogy. Then he compiles a

---

[32] *Ibid.*, pp. 49–50, italics mine. For the opening sentence of this excerpt I have adopted the reading "non ea quidem puritate" from Coussemaker's edition of Gallicus' text, based on Harley 6525, fol. 58v (see *CS* IV, p. 374). The variant "non ea quidem pravitate" elected by Seay (after Add. 22315, fol. 47r) is likely a corrupt reading. My thanks to Leofranc Holford-Strevens for helping me interpret this passage.

list of the bad effects of poor teaching: young singers are giving up music in droves in spite of their best intentions, demoralized by the difficulty posed by solmization. Others never go past the early stages of training. Many lose considerable sums of money in the process. Ultimately, this state of affairs has caused the decay of chant singing in churches and monasteries, which in turn results in a less inspiring liturgical and spiritual experience for the faithful. Here we encounter the broader dimension of Gallicus' musical reform, namely, his understanding of liturgical music as a unique vehicle of piety and devotion. Thus, his seemingly marginal campaign for reforming the musical pedagogy of his time has tremendous religious implications: at stake is nothing less than the spiritual growth and well-being of his own monastic community and of Christianity at large (more on this in the next section).

The image of the gamut that accompanies Gallicus' discussion of Guido's *Micrologus* (see Fig. 6.2) shows multiple ways of labeling and notating the diatonic pitches: Greek pitch terminology, the A-G letters, plus *daseian* and square notations. It also indicates the distances between the pitches (*tonus, semitonus*). Significantly, the graph avoids the syllables, and all around the frame it features the three verses of Guido's *Regule* (*Solis notare litteris ...* etc.), which Gallicus sees as the golden rule for sight singing.

Gallicus observes that the gamut may be mapped on the left hand to facilitate memorization ('causa brevitatis et memoriae labilis'), keeping in mind that Hands are not necessary for singing ('Nam si quis manus non habeat, ergo cantum discere non potest? Id credere stultum est'). But even those who want to resort to the musical Hand need not yoke the letters to the syllables, as Gallicus makes clear when he directs the reader to locate "Γ" (not Γ *ut*) on the tip of the left thumb, "A" (not A *re*) on the first joint, etc. (though more on this later).

The last part of book 2 of Part II deserves a detailed discussion. This section, titled "A true, easy, and short way of singing via ut, re, mi, fa, sol, la," is written as an imaginary teaching lesson between a *magister* and a *discipulus* (Gallicus may have used the *Enchiriadis* treatises as a model).[33] Gallicus does have some use for the Guidonian syllables, after all, although not the traditional use. First, the *magister*, true mouthpiece of Gallicus' views that he is, invites the *discipulus* to sight sing by identifying the notated sounds only as pitch letters. The *discipulus*, however, is not convinced. "Why are you not teaching me the correct use of the six syllables" – he wonders – "when the

---

[33] "Modus canendi per ut, re, mi, fa, sol, la facilis, verus atque brevissimus," Gallicus, *Ritus canendi*, vol. 2, book 2, sec. 3, pp. 53–63.

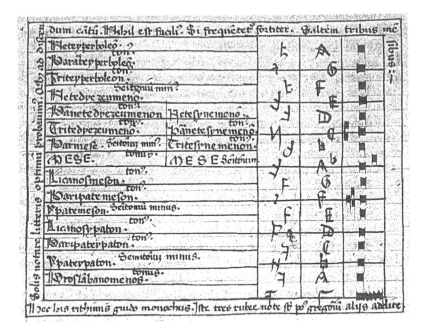

Fig. 6.2. Gallicus' gamut (from London, British Library, Add. 22315, fol. 30r).

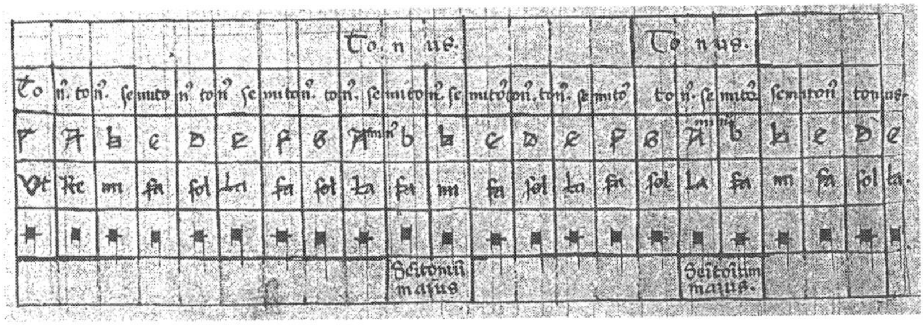

Fig. 6.3. Gallicus' simplified gamut (from London, British Library, Add. 22315, fol. 49r).

entire world is using them?'[34] The *magister* fulfills his student's request by presenting a simplified gamut that contains neither the Greek pitch names, nor the *Daseian* signs, and that features only *one* syllable for every pitch letter (see Fig. 6.3). This one-to-one correspondence of syllables and letters makes for a radical departure from tradition, considering that in the standard medieval gamut most letters corresponded to two or three syllables.

---

[34] "Sed et illud me non parum sollicitat, quod totus mundus, ut ita loquar, sex illis syllabis utitur ad cantandum," *Ibid.*, p. 55.

The advantage of this arrangement, according to the *magister*, is the complete elimination of the "hexachordal" mutations, indeed of "hexachords" altogether. The *magister* describes his proposal by formulating what one might call the "*fa* rule": he explains that it is really unnecessary for the pitches that lie above the semitone (C and F) to carry multiple syllables, such as *ut, fa,* or *sol.* The syllable *fa* by itself expresses their diatonic position. Likewise, all notes on the lower side of the semitone will be *mi* (as recognized also by traditional hexachordal theory), and the two whole tones above *fa* will be *sol* and *la.* Beyond *la,* in the diatonic system, there can only be either *mi* or *fa,* and the cycle continues. Thus Gallicus formulates his "*fa* rule": Find your *fa* and find everything else. There are indeed seven *fa*'s on the Guidonian Hand."[35]

It is of course possible to disagree with Gallicus that the position of one *fa* will automatically clarify that of the other *fa*'s in a particular diatonic context. The position of the semitones is ultimately dependent on the letters in conjunction with the *clavis* (clef) at the beginning of the staff and on the notated accidentals (leaving aside here the issue of *musica ficta*). Yet this observation only strengthens Gallicus' own strong preference for a letters-only method of singing, and he is certainly not assigning any prescriptive role to the syllables. Incidentally, Gallicus' reform of the Hand, which essentially uses the syllables *ut* and *re* only for low gamma and low A, turns out to be quite close to the *Fasola* system widely adopted in England and North America in later centuries and known as the "English," "Lancashire," or "four-note" *sol-fa.*[36] In line with the earlier illustration of the gamut, the Guidonian Hand that follows (London, Add. 22315, fol. 50r) shows only one syllable per letter (Fig. 6.4).

Yet even here Gallicus does not miss the opportunity to provide to his reader a basic abstract of Guidonian pedagogy. The large body of text in the center of the palm reads:

Inventor huius regulae Guido fuit Aretinus, illo Romano principe Conrado, sicut legimus, regnante Christe post annos mille cum viginti quinque, non tamen id instituit tot cum verbositatibus. Hic Benedicti monachus mirifice decoravit totum antiphonarium his lineis et spaciis et canendum litteras magis laudat quam syllabas quae sunt Ut, re, mi, fa, sol la, sic dicens illis in rhythmis: Solis notare litteris Optimum probavimus, [etc.]

---

[35] Habe fa et totum habes; sunt autem in manu Guidonis septem fa, quam hic tibi depingam (*Ibid.*, p. 57).

[36] See B. Rainbow, "Fasola," *NG 2*, vol. 8, pp. 589–90.

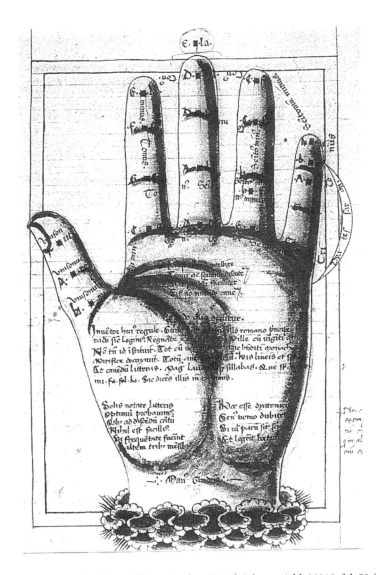

Fig. 6.4. Gallicus' Hand (from London, British Library, Add. 22315, fol. 50r).

[We read that one Guido Aretinus invented this rule in the year 1025, at the time of emperor Corradus, without, however, all the verbosities [of modern solmization]. This Benedictine monk brilliantly added his musical staff to the antiphonary, and praises the method of singing with the letters over that of the *ut-la* syllables, as proven in the following verses. We have demonstrated that it is best to sing with the letters only, [etc.]][37]

[37] Gallicus, *Ritus canendi*, vol. 2, p. 58.

Gallicus, in other words, pays lip service to the current fashion of the six syllables, yet he reminds budding singers of the marginal status of that method in Guido's own pedagogy.

Still, the presence of the syllables in Gallicus' Hand, and in the entire dialogue between the *magister* and the *discipulus*, points to a measure of latitude in Gallicus' argument that is perhaps surprising, considering his relentless condemnation of solmization throughout the treatise. But it is important to emphasize that Gallicus' modified solmization system was more distant from the earlier one than suggested by the surface similarities. With his '*fa* rule' Gallicus completely disbanded the notion that the six syllables formed a cohesive diatonic *set* that one could transpose over the entire gamut by transposition. If Guido and Hermannus might have hinted at ascribing some kind of normative significance to the major sixth that competed with that of the octave – but we have seen how difficult this conclusion is to sustain, upon close analysis – Gallicus cleared all doubts about it by showing that the "sixth-ness" of the *deductio/proprietas* could easily be dispensed with at no pedagogical or cognitive cost – indeed to the benefit of sight singing. There was no ingrained hexachordal perception of the gamut that had to be removed, no sense that this reform would require a reshaping of the diatonic system as understood in the 'post-Guidonian' musical era. It was simply a matter of swapping a method of sight singing with another that was preferable in spite of being older.

In the end, however, the *Ritus canendi* is a landmark contribution to humanist music theory not because of the specifics of the musical reforms it proposes, but for grounding its entire argument on a new interpretive strategy that placed traditional texts under unprecedented historical and philological scrutiny. Both rhetorically and methodologically, it stands out as a brilliant achievement of the first phase of musical humanism. Yet, significant as it is, this marriage of music and scholarship does not fully describe the breadth of the reformist agenda that informs this text.

Musical pedagogy as an instrument of spiritual *renovatio*

The excerpts quoted above show that Gallicus minced no words when it came to expressing his opinions on the method of the six syllables, particularly the technique of hexachordal mutation. The metaphors and verbal images he chooses to qualify the system – *ambages verborum, phylacteria, verbositas,* and *deliramenta* – convey all the vehemence of his attack. Two of these terms, *ambages* and *phylacteria*, are particularly interesting, because they seem to be extremely rare occurrences in the language of medieval music theory. More importantly, in late-medieval literary culture they carried connotations that further corroborate the reformist agenda of Gallicus' treatise.

The first idiom, *ambages*, means "circumlocution," "obscurity," or more precisely a crooked or roundabout way of doing or expressing things. Not surprisingly, it is a term with a rich philosophical background. The study of ambiguous locutions had been an important part of dialectics, so we encounter the term with St. Augustine and Peter Abelard. In these authors, ambiguity is an obstacle to the discernment of truth that needs to be removed through the dialectical method. In the fourteenth century, *ambages* was used to refer to the deceptive language of pagan oracles. For instance, in the seventeenth canto of the *Paradiso* (vv. 31–5) Dante calls the age before the coming of Christ the age of *ambages* in which mankind, having lost its way, was ensnared in ambiguity and falsehood until the love of God revealed the saving truth "in clear words and precise Latin."[38] Dante, however, was not read in Vittorino's school, where students were discouraged from speaking in the vernacular even during private conversations.[39] A more likely source for Gallicus was Virgil's *Aeneid*, which was a required text at the Ca' Giocosa along with all other works by Virgil.[40] The first mention of *ambages* occurs in book 1, lines 341–2, in which Venus, speaking to Aeneas, gives a short account of the "long list of wrongdoings and intrigues" ("Longa est iniuria, longae ambages") that afflict the land of Tyria (Carthage) ruled by Dido. The second occurrence of the term is more interesting because it occurs in a passage describing the "awful singing" of the Cumaean Sybil ("Cumaea Sybilla horrendas canit ambages," book VI, lines 98–9).[41]

The image of the six syllables as *phylacteria* is also carefully chosen: in Jewish religious practice, a *phylaterium* was a leather box containing Scriptural scrolls that was carried on the forehead or over the chest. It could

---

[38] "Né per ambage, in che la gente folle / già s'invischiava pria che fosse anciso / l'Agnel di Dio che le peccata tolle, / ma per chiare parole e con preciso / latin rispuose quello amor paterno" ("In no dark sayings, such as those in which the foolish folk of old once ensnared themselves, before the Lamb of God who takes away sins was slain, but in clear words and with precise discourse that paternal love replied"), D. Alighieri, *The Divine Comedy: Paradiso*, ed. and trans. C. S. Singleton, 2 parts (Princeton University Press, 1975), part I: Italian Text and Translation, p. 188.

[39] Woodward, *Vittorino da Feltre*, pp. 40 and 42.

[40] *Ibid.*, pp. 45–6.

[41] I have used the edition of the *Aeneid* by J. B. Greenough, available online at the *Perseus Digital Library*, URL: www.perseus.tufts.edu/hopper/; the English translation is by A. Mandelbaum, ed. and trans., *The Aeneid of Virgil* (Berkeley: University of California Press, 1971), pp. 13 and 136.

also be a trophy, an ornament, or a small reliquary hanging from a person's neck. Gallicus' possible source here is St. Jerome, who had used the label *phylacteria* to indicate the little scrolls containing the Torah that the Pharisees of Jesus' time carried around to flaunt their piety.[42]

By labeling Guidonian solmization as nothing but *ambages* and *phylacteria*, Gallicus qualifies it as a pedagogical method gone awry, reminiscent of pagan religious practices that deviated from the truthful and pristine habits of mind of the early church. Conversely, the abolition of hexachordal solmization will pave the way for a return to the purity and simplicity of the music of the early church, which will touch the ears and the hearts of the listeners and will make them experience all the nurture and beauty of the Christian message. Thus the two ideals of the *ritus canendi vetustissimus* and of *ecclesia primitiva* were for Gallicus two sides of the same coin and helped each other's cause: each represented a golden age in their own terms, a special historical circumstance that was perceived to be the answer to the evils of the present. Indeed, Gallicus' narration of his own "conversion" from the method of solmization that he had once used (*ut prius*) to Guido's letter-based system is reminiscent of a religious conversion: his encounter with the musical methods of the early church provided him with true and reliable answers, at the same time that the writings of the church fathers promoted a *renovatio* in the lives of many late-medieval souls, as well as in the policies of Christian institutions across Europe.

Gallicus' frequent reference to plainchant as "cantus divinus" or "cantus angelicus" – for instance in *Ritus canendi*, vol. 2, 13, 22, 41, 55, and 63 – confirms his view of music as an instrument of devotion and spirituality.[43] See also the excerpt cited above on the devastating effects of solmization (pp. 154–5), where Gallicus speaks of "that most sweet music ... bequeathed to us by the saints" (*cantum suavissimum ... quem nobis traddere Sancti*; *Ritus canendi*, vol. 2, p. 49).

The rhetorical tone of Gallicus' *Ritus canendi* evokes in several distinct ways the ideal of the *ecclesia primitiva* inspired by the truth of the Gospel. The second part of the treatise, which is dedicated to providing directions for sight singing, opens with a salutation that is directly modeled on the epistolary greetings of the Apostle Paul in the New Testament:

---

[42] The reference is found in St. Jerome's *Commentum in Evangelium Matthaei Libri Quattuor*, lib. IV, c. 23, verse 6; in J.-P. Migne, *Patrologia Latina* (Paris: J.-P. Migne, 1844–55; 1862–5), vol. 26, col. 168A. See D. C. Skemer, *Binding Words: Textual Amulets in the Middle Ages* (University Park, PA: Pennsylvania State University Press, 2006), pp. 35–7.

[43] Such labels appear to be quite rare in Latin music theory. Similar expressions, however, are found in Augustine's *Confessions* and, in the generation after Gallicus, in Herbenus Traiectensis' *De natura cantus ac miraculis vocis*.

Pauperibus Ecclesiae Dei clericis ac religiosis Deo laudes concinere dulciter optantibus, Frater Johanninus, indignus Cartusiae monachus, salutem ac illam, quam mundus dare non potest, pacem.

[Your brother John, an unworthy Carthusian monk, sends his greetings and that peace that the world cannot give to those poor clerics and religious men of the church of God who have chosen to sing sweetly the praise of God.][44]

Compare this passage with the so-called *praescriptio* of Paul's letter to the Ephesians:

Paulus apostolus Christi Iesu per voluntatem Dei sanctis omnibus qui sunt Ephesi et fidelibus in Christo Iesu gratia vobis et pax a Deo Patre nostro et Domino Iesu Christo.

[Paul, an apostle of Jesus Christ, by the will of God, to all the saints who are at Ephesus and to the faithful in Christ Jesus. Grace be to you, and peace from God the Father, and from the Lord Jesus Christ.][45]

Gallicus echoes Paul's epistolary greetings not only by wishing "peace" to his readers, but also by humbly characterizing himself as "unworthy" and by emphasizing the spiritual mission that binds him to the community of the faithful. Notice also the key reference to poverty (*pauperibus clericis ac religiosis*), as well as Gallicus' posture of *contemptus mundi* in his mention of "that peace that the world out there," marred by demonic polyphonies and Guidonian *phylacteria*, cannot give. Further confirmation of the Pauline overtones in this part of the treatise is Gallicus' custom of addressing his readers as *carissimi* ("my beloved"), which is also Paul's favorite form of address.[46]

To be sure, Gallicus' salutation follows epistolary conventions that had been in place for centuries. To remain in the domain of music theory, a similar kind of greeting appears in the *Cantuagium* that another Carthusian, Heinrich Eger von Kalkar, wrote in Cologne in 1380.[47] Eger, who died an old man in 1408, was himself a mystic who may have inspired to conversion Geerte de Groote, the later founder of the spiritual movement of the *devotio moderna*. In the *Cantuagium*, Eger also characterizes polyphonic

[44] Gallicus, *Ritus canendi*, vol. 2, p. 1.
[45] Eph. 1:1–2, Latin vulgate; I have used the Douay-Rheims Version and English translation, both available respectively at www.drbo.org/.
[46] Calvin Bower has detected echoes of Pauline letters in *Musica enchiriadis*, which he believes to have been written by a monk for a monastic community. See his "'Adhuc ex parte et in enigmate cernimus …' Reflections on the Closing Chapters of *Musica enchiriadis*," in A. Giger and T. J. Mathiesen, eds., *Music in the Mirror. Reflections on the History of Music Theory and Literature for the 21st Century* (Lincoln: University of Nebraska Press, 2002), pp. 21–44.
[47] For a modern edition, see H. Hüschen, ed., *Das Cantuagium des Heinrich Eger von Kalkar* Beiträge zur rheinischen Musikgeschichte 2 (Köln: Staufen, 1952).

music as *lascivia* and addresses his brother monks as "carissimi" and "Dilecti in Christo." Yet Eger admires the achievements of the mensural theory of Franco of Cologne, and in the end his condemnation of polyphony and instrumental music is lukewarm compared to Gallicus', explaining at the end of the treatise that he does not dare to recommend these types of music simply because he is a religious man. But more importantly, Eger's *Cantuagium* does not pursue at all the opposition between old and new musical practices that is so pervasive in Gallicus' treatise. Eger has no problems, for instance, with the hexachordal system.

What distinguishes Gallicus' *Ritus canendi* from similar manuals is not its strong moralistic tone, or its vivid and vaguely Pauline rhetoric, but rather its constant pursuit of a basic temporal opposition, its proposal of a historical narrative of "ancient-virtue-followed-by-modern-corruption" that is central to *renovatio* programs in general, including the program of intellectual and moral renewal embraced by humanism. It is that temporal opposition that colors so strongly Gallicus' treatise, just as it had been a hallmark of Ciconia's half a century earlier. In the end, it is not surprising that these sources may reflect momentous trends in contemporaneous religious life. What *is* cause for reflection, rather, is the determination and the passion for *renovatio* that exudes from these treatises, and the specific musical means by which they sought to achieve that goal.

In the backwash of Gallicus' reform: Nicolaus Burtius' *Opusculum*

As the foregoing discussion has demonstrated, Ramos de Pareja was perfectly justified in claiming Gallicus on his side of the dispute on solmization, even though the Carthusian probably would not have approved of his proposed eight-syllable solmization system (*psal-li-tur-per-vo-ces-is-tas*) any more than the *ut-la* syllables. Ramos hit the proverbial nail on its head when he wrote:

Bene quidem dixit de his mutationibus ipse frater Johannes Carthusinus: non dico vocis in vocem mutationem, sed ab ambage in ambagem variationem. Solum refert tonos et semitonia annotare et per litteras Gregorii canere.

[John the Carthusian spoke well about these mutations when he said: "I do not speak of the mutation of syllable after syllable, but of verbosity after verbosity. It only matters to designate whole tones and semitones and to sing with the letters of Gregory".][48]

---

[48] B. Ramos de Pareja, *Musica practica*, ed. J. Wolf, Publikationen der Internationalen Musikgesellschaft, Beihefte, 2 (Leipzig: Breitkopf und Härtel, 1901), p. 44. The translation

Unfortunately, Ramos possessed none of Gallicus' philological sophistication and eloquence. Whereas the Carthusian had stunningly demonstrated, *Micrologus* and *Regule* in hand, that Guido's pedagogical priorities had been by far centered on the seven letters, Ramos could only launch insulting sound bites ("Guido was a better monk than a theorist") that quickly discredited him. Nevertheless, Ramos' critique of the technique of hexachordal mutation as cumbersome, superfluous, and counterproductive was certainly mediated from Gallicus.[49]

For his part Nicolaus Burtius of Parma (ca. 1450–1528), having studied Gallicus' treatise carefully, must have known that Ramos' citation offered a fair representation of the Carthusian's views on the hexachordal system. He also must have realized that Gallicus' lengthy and articulate criticism of Guido and the existing modal system went in the direction of calling into question key aspects of the music curriculum of his time that he felt committed to defend. Thus Burtius knew that he could appeal to Gallicus' authority against Ramos only at the cost of misrepresenting Gallicus' views – a fairly safe plan to implement, so Burtius may have reasoned, given the limited circulation of the Carthusian's treatise.

The only piece of evidence documenting an actual relationship between Burtius and Gallicus is provided by the *explicit* to the copy of Gallicus' that Burtius allegedly completed in 1473, that is to say, right after the time of the Carthusian's death.[50] The inscription reads:

Explicit liber notabilis musicae venerandi viri Domini Johannis Gallici, multi inter musicos nominis: cujus ego Nicolaus Burtius parmensis discipulus tunc in ea delectans, totum hunc propria manu ex eo quem ediderat, transcripsi ac notavi. Obiit autem vir iste anno Domini MCCCCLXXIIJ. Cujus animam paradisus possidet, corpus vero Parma terra nobilis.

[Thus ends the notable book on music by Johannes Gallicus, a venerable man of God, who is widely known among the *musici*. I, Nicolaus Burtius of Parma, a disciple of his who delighted in his teaching, have transcribed and annotated this treatise from the exemplar that he edited. This man died in 1474. Heaven possesses his soul, the noble city of Parma his body.][51]

is from C. A. Miller, ed. and trans., *Bartolomeo Ramis de Pareia: Musica practica*, MSD 44 (Neuhausen-Stuttgart: American Institute of Musicology, 1993), p. 94.

[49] I will discuss Ramos' account of solmization in more detail in Chapter 7.

[50] The manuscript is London, BL, Add. 22315, fol. 1–60. For a discussion of this source, and for a reassessment of Burtius' career, see R. E. Murray, "New Documentation Concerning the Biography of Nicolò Burzio," *Studi musicali* 24 (1995): 263–82.

[51] "London, BL, Add. 22315, fol. 60r. The circumstances of this alleged sojourn by Gallicus in Parma are unclear. See Burtius, *Florum libellus*, p. 13; 18–9.

Because of this autograph note, it has seemed plausible to regard Burtius' *Florum libellus* as generally reflective of Gallicus' views.[52] Rightly so, for Burtius goes out of his way to emphasize the accuracy of the transmission from the source to the copy, while also presenting him as Gallicus' faithful student.

In addition, the *Opusculum* skillfully projects the impression of complete agreement between its author and Gallicus. Burtius culls passages from *Ritus canendi* on relatively unimportant or uncontroversial points – such as on the origin of the term "music," on the inventor of proportions, and on the range of the modes, but he carefully avoids direct citations on the key issue of the merit and shortcomings of hexachordal solmization that were central to his dispute with Ramos. In yet other parts of the treatise, Burtius borrowed extensively from Gallicus, without, however, acknowledging his source and often adding quite a different spin to the original excerpt. In the following section I will attempt to show that in the first book of *Florum libellus* Burtius pursued this strategy quite subtly and systematically.

In his chapter on mutation (book 1, ch. 18), for instance, Burtius portrays the Carthusian as the "eloquent follower" (*disertum imitatorem*) of the "pious monk Guido." The passage, however, distorts Ramos' position more than it does Gallicus', in that it seems to imply that Ramos was somehow a defender of the practice:

Et si a nunnullis et maxime sensatis: hec: quae mutationes nuncupatur: frivola et parvi momenti iudicentur: tamen ut varijs satisfaciam animis: meme super hoc brevitati constringam: ne longius procedens fatuitati prevaricatoris videar similis: qui scilicet se profitetur musicum: cum hercle a via veritatis seiunctus deliret. Hic enim immitatus marchetum: consumpsit quatuor et amplius carthas circa huiusmodi rationes insulsas: et omnino explodendas. Nam queso ubi invenerit [mutationem]? An apud scholam philosophorum a quibus omnis ordo consonantiarum emanavit? An apud Boetium: qui et auriga musicorum: et monarcha? Inuenit ne apud illum pium monachum Guidonem et eius disertum immitatorem Ioannem cartusiensem? Mutatio igitur vt dicunt: est variatio nominis: sive note in odem spatio: linea: ac sono. Dicunt ulterius quod mutatio potest fieri in quolibet loco manus: ubi due vel tres voces nomine sunt diverse: quae quidem sub una sola littera includuntur … Hec enim cum similibus recitantur ab insensatis illis viris: que proculdubio nullius firmitatis existunt.

---

[52] So, for instance G. Massera, "Burzio, Nicola," in *Dizionario enciclopedico universale della musica e dei musicisti* (Torino: U.T.E.T., 1985), "Le biografie," vol. III, pp. 756–7; C. A. Miller and B. Blackburn, "Burzio Nicolò," *NG 2*, vol. 4, pp. 649–50; A. Moyer, *Musica scientia* (Ithaca, NY: Cornell University Press, 1992), pp. 39–52; Strohm, *The Rise of European Music, 1380–1500*, pp. 595–6.

[Although mutations are considered frivolous and having little meaning by some very intelligent men, in order to satisfy various minds I will treat the subject with brevity, lest in proceeding at greater length I may seem similar to the foolish prevaricator who professes himself to be a musician, when by heavens he is deranged and cut off from the way of truth. For I ask, where did he encounter [mutation]? Is it in the school of philosophers, from whom every order of consonances emanate? Or is it in Boethius, the leader and monarch of musicians? Did he find it in the pious monk Guido or in Johannes the Carthusian, his eloquent follower? … Mutation is called the change of a name or note if it belongs to the same sound and line and line and space. It is said further that mutation can occur in any place on the Hand where two or three tones have different names, if they are contained in one single letter … These and similar cases are treated by those unintelligent men; such cases undoubtedly have no validity.][53]

It seems that Burtius wishes to align himself with those "very intelligent men" who are critical of hexachordal mutations. Such a stand, however, would place him in the same camp not only with Gallicus, but also with Ramos (even though those two authors were against solmization *tout court*, not just against mutation). Therefore he takes only a cursory look at the subject "in order to satisfy various minds," ending the chapter by observing that mutation is "without foundation", a strategy that ultimately seems designed to please both the defenders and the detractors of solmization. Along the way, Burtius harshly criticizes Ramos for following Marchetto of Padua on the subject of mutation: Ramos, however, had himself criticized Marchetto on this subject– he quipped that he regarded Marchetto to be worth less than four *marchetos* – and had attacked the practice of mutation head-on.[54] The entire section on mutation is replete with cryptic citations from the first satire of Aulus Persius Flaccus (known as Persius), a choice that adds to the overall ambiguity of the passage.[55]

The first twelve chapters of Burtius' treatise, dealing with such venerable topics as the *laus musices*, the genera, and the Boethian tripartite division of music (*mundana*, *humana*, and *instrumentalis*) are an extended homage to a long-standing theoretical tradition. The erudite tone of these sections may serve the purpose of convincing his readers of his readiness to tackle the topic at hand. It is only in the key chapters 13–15 that Burtius lays out his reply to Ramos. Predictably, in this section he does not cite Gallicus' precise words. However, he still bases his response on the Carthusian's

---

[53] Burtius, *Florum Libellus*, pp. 88–9; Miller, trans. *Nicolaus Burtius*, pp. 54–5.
[54] In fifteenth-century Venice a *marcheto* was a small silver coin of little value.
[55] Massera has traced these textual concordances in Burtius, *Florum libellus*, p. 54.

argument, which he modifies slightly, but substantially enough to alter its overall meaning.[56]

Consider, for instance, chapter 14 of Burtius' treatise ('Why Guido selected only six syllables'), which has been taken as a sign of Burtius' close relying on Gallicus.[57] The two chapters are reproduced side by side in Table 6.1 below. In addition to preserving the beginning of Gallicus' title, Burtius has borrowed material from the first and last paragraphs of his model, and used it in the first half of his own chapter. A comparison of the opening lines in the two treatises, however, soon reveals that Burtius is borrowing with a clear purpose in mind.

Although Burtius has modeled his chapter on Gallicus', and even borrowed entire passages from it, in the end he completely subverts Gallicus' text. The opening sentence is revealing: whereas Gallicus, in a typical fashion, begins this chapter by stating his desire to investigate Guido's rationale for introducing the method of the six syllables thoroughly and openly, Burtius begins with a most emphatic rhetorical figure ("It's no wonder that Guido did *that!*"), suggesting from the start that no such inquiry is desirable, and implying that Guido's method of solmization is beyond criticism. Presumably, Burtius knows that his audience has great admiration for Guido and that it accepts the method of solmization as a matter of course. A comparison of the next few lines reveals that Burtius has left out Gallicus' reference both to the Guidonian syllables as a *nova forma canendi*, which highlights the arbitrariness and the contingent character of the system, and to the pitch letters A, B, C, D, etc., an implicit recognition of a seven-fold diatonic layer that is alternative to Guidonian solmization.

On the other hand, Burtius does transfer into his own text Gallicus' technical explanation of the origin of the solmization system, i.e., the (spurious) argument that the major sixth subsumes the three species of tetrachord. It is essential to realize, however, that this explanation has very different connotations in the context of the *Florum libellus*: while Gallicus is trying

---

[56] It is quite possible that Burtius, who never held a musical position in his life, conceived the *Florum libellus* as a "Habilitationsschrift" of sorts that would earn him the professorship in music at the University of Bologna, the same one that may have been denied to Ramos in the fallout from the publication of his *Musica practica* five years earlier. The vast scope and erudite tone of *Florum libellus* would certainly have been appropriate for this purpose. Throughout the 1480s and 1490s Burtius lived in Bologna, quite possibly in search of a musical position at a civic or religious institution (Murray, "New Documentation," 267–9). He made at least one unsuccessful attempt to enter Ramos' restricted circle of students and musicians (see Burtius, *Florum libellus,* p. 19).

[57] Miller writes that this section of *Florum libellus* "is based" on Gallicus (Miller, trans. *Nicolaus Burtius*, p. 48, footnote 39); Massera simply relates this chapter to the corresponding passage in *Ritus canendi* (Burtius, *Florum libellus*, p. 82).

Table 6.1. Gallicus and Burtius on the origin of the six syllables (emphases mine)

Gallicus:	Burtius:
Primum ergo quaerendum est cur Guido novam illam introducere volens canendi formam sex solas syllabas elegerit, et non potius quindecim iuxta numerum ordinis philosophorum, aut tot quot voces communis sui temporis usus habebat, seu quatuor duntaxat aut plus aut minus. Ad quod respondendum breviter, quoniam musicus erat et non cantor purus, non nesciens omne quod canitur, quatuor tantum concludi vocibus ac duobus cum semitonio minori tonis, quod totum aut prima consonantia diatessaron ab antiquis philosophis appellatur aut tetrachordum, hoc est, quotuor cordarum. Quid enim ultra primam diatessaron agis quod non sit unum et idem. Nam cum a Γ gamma graeco sint quatuor voces in C grave duoque toni cum semitonio, quod diatessaron reddit aut primum tetracordum, ultra procedens hoc habebis ab ipso gravi C in F gravi, vel ab F gravi in b rotundum, et sic usque in infinitum.	**Non admirandum quippe est cur Guido** tantum sex voluerit voces eligere ad cantandum et non potius quindecim iuxta numerum philosophorum, aut tot quot communis usus sui temporis haberet seu quattuor dumtaxat aut plus aut minus.
	Nam cum musicus adaequatus fuisset, non immemor omne quod canitur quattuor tantum concludi vocibus ac duobus com semitonio minori tonis, quod totum diatessaron prima ab antiquis philosophis appellatur sive tetrachordum, idest quattuor chordarum compositio.
	Quid ultra primam diatessaron agis quod non sit unum et idem? Nam cum a gamma graeco in c grave sint quattuor voces duoque toni cum semitonio minori quod est diatessaron una de tribus, similiter si ultra paululum processeris a c in f grave hoc idem habebis. Idem etiam ab f grave in b rotundum et sic usque in infinitum.
Attamen quia diatessaron illa prima consonantiarum modo post duos tonos minus habet semitonium, ut est Γ gamma vel G, quod est unum, et A B♮ C, vel etiam C D E F, tam grave quam acutum aut superacutum modo inter duos tonos, ut est A B♮ C D vel D E F G, tam sursum quam deorsum, modo ante duos tonos quodquidem B♮ C D E monstrat et E F G A comprobat. Nimirum necesse fuit Guidonem, cuius propositum erat, quam breviter totum exprimere cantum has sex nec plus nec minus aut alias huiusmodi totidem fabricare syllabas. Quis enim nesciat per ba, be, bi, bo, bu, bam, id fieri potuisse, vel per aliud quippiam simile? Quicquid etenim canendo proferre velis, observa tonum et semitonium et optimum erit? Volens autem ille ritum, quem tunc modulando voces communis usus habebat, in manu sinistra tamquam in portatili tabula sicuti sunt ordinare,	Hoc igitur exachordum Guidonis nedum speciem unam diatessaron complectitur, sed etiam duas alias eiusdem primae constitutionis differentias, quamquam tertia in primo sit collocata termino.
	Nam ab a si inchoasset, tres nunquam sub sex litteris sequentibus diatessaron species, nisi maxima confusione vocum interveniente, exprimere valuisset. Exemplum: [see Fig. 6.5b].
	Vidistis apertissime quam facilis et vera quam et iucunda huiusmodi instructio quae omnem sex Guidonis melodiam vocum comprehendit. Frustra ergo fit per plura quod potest fieri per pauciora. Haec etenim sex vocum acervatio nedum tres diatessaron species, ut dictum est, complectitur sed etiam diapente primam ac quartam speciem ex quibus diapason conficitur harmonia.

nec ignorans quam etsi quatuor primae sibi succedentes litterae, sicut ibi mostratum est, unam de tribus diatessaron speciebus generent, quinta nihilominus et sexta subsequens littera duas alias eiusdem primae consonantiae gignunt differentias, ultra quod nihil habes, si rem aequa lance penses in vocibus dissimile, sex et ipse syllabas illas instituit ad placitum, quas in illa symphonia superius habes.

[To begin, we have to discuss the issue of why Guido, wishing to introduce a new method for singing, chose only six vocables and not rather fifteen of them, following the order of the philosophers, or as many as the then customary types of diatonic sounds, that is to say, no fewer and no more than four. The short answer is that Guido was a *musicus*, not a pure *cantor*, and did not ignore the fact that all that is sung is contained within four sounds spanning through a range two whole tones and one minor semitone, which the early philosophers had labeled first species of diatessaron or tetrachord (i.e., four notes). For whatever you sing beyond the first tetrachord reproduces the same pattern. In fact, there are four notes from Γ to low C, and two whole tones and a semitone generating the first species of diatessaron or tetrachord, and proceeding further you

Haec praeterea latinorum quinque continet vocales, quibus rejectis quidquam recte ac congrue haud exprimi potest. In prima enim syllaba est u: ut queant lexis etc. In secunda e; in tertia i; in quarta vero a; in quinta autem o; in sexta vero a, quod est replicatio ad quartam. Erunt ergo quinque, videlicet: a, e, i, o, u. Ecce doctrinae perfectio.

Non omittam similiter senarii numeri perfectionem tali exachordo comprehensam. is etenim primus est inter denarium numerum perfectus cum omnes partes suas praecise contineat aliquotas. Partes aliquotae sunt quae quotiens sumptae reddunt praecise totum suum integrum.

[Surely one should not wonder why Guido wished to choose only six vocables for singing and not the fifteen of many philosophers, or as many as were commonly used in their time, or only four, or more or less. Since Guido was a true musician he knew that everything sung was contained in four tones or two tones and one small semitone; the first fourth was called a complete tetrachord by ancient philosophers, that is, a composition of four strings.
What do you sing beyond the first fourth that is not one and the same thing? Since there are four tones from the Greek gamma to low c, or two whole tones and one small semitone, which form one of the three kinds of fourths, you will have the same thing if you go a little farther from c to f, also from low f to round b, and so forth ad infinitum.

Table 6.1. (cont.)

will obtain the same sequence from low C to low F, from F to B♭, and so on without end. Since the first species of diatessaron has a minor semitone after the two whole tones, such as Γ or G A B C, or also C D E F, both in the high and in the low register, but also between the two tones, such as A B C D or D E F G, or before the two whole tones, such as B C D E or E F G A, and since Guido's purpose was to find a concise formula for articulating all songs he had to concoct no more and no fewer than those six syllables, or other similar ones. Indeed, who does not know that he could have achieved the same goal by using ba, be, bi, bo, bu, bam, or some other labels? In fact, you will sing perfectly whatever you wish to by simply observing the correct distances between tones and semitones. In sum, seeking to visualize on the left hand or on a portable table that method which was common in his time for modulating musical sounds, and not ignoring that all letters after the first four can only result in additional tetrachords, as we saw above, and that the fifth and sixth letters generate two more species of fourth (beyond which no more species are possible), if you examine this entire matter impartially, he instituted for convenience those six syllables that you saw in the melody above [Ut queant laxis], so that he yoked the first syllable, ut, to the first letter of the hand, Γ, and likewise the second syllable re to A and the third syllable mi to B ...][58]

Thus this hexachord of Guido includes not only one fourth-species, but also two other species of the same consonance, although the third fourth-species is placed in the first [i.e., the lowest] position. If one begins the three fourth-species in a he will not be able to sing them in a sequence of six letters without incurring a very great confusion of tones. An example [Fig. 6.5b] follows. You see very clearly how easy, accurate and pleasant such instruction is which includes all six notes of the Guidonian scale [*omnem sex Guidonis melodiam vocum comprehendit*]. It is useless to do by more what can be done by less. For this series of six tones not only includes the three fourth-species as already mentioned, but also the first fifth- and fourth-species from which an octave harmony is formed. It also contains the five Latin vowels, without which nothing can be expressed correctly and suitably ... This is perfection in teaching. I may not omit here the perfection of number six in relation to such a hexachord. For this is the first perfect number within ten, since six contains all its aliquot parts exactly. Aliquot parts are those which as often as they are taken produce their complete total.]

[58] Gallicus, *Ritus canendi*, vol. 2, pp. 51–2, translation mine; Burtius, *Florum libellus*, p. 14; Miller, trans., *Nicolaus Burtius*, pp. 48–9 (slightly modified).

to show what made solmization *possible*, and why the system has those specific characters, Burtius presents the same argument as a way of demonstrating that solmization is not only *necessary*, but "perfect, easy and true"
– the very same terms that Gallicus had used repeatedly in reference not to
Guidonian solmization, but to the pre-Guidonian *ritus vetustissimus* based
on tones and semitones that he wishes to resurrect.

But the differences between Gallicus and Burtius go as far as to invest
their basic understanding of the foundations of musical space. The two
authors, in fact, belong to opposite music-semiotic worlds: whereas for
Gallicus the six syllables are an expression of the tetrachordal articulation of the gamut, in Burtius the hexachord has become the underlying
structure that is responsible for shaping the gamut into tetrachords – an
idea that will become the centerpiece of Franchino Gafori's defense of
Guido in the printed version of *Practica musicae* (see the next chapter).
The decisive factor, here, is Burtius' collapsing Gallicus' crucial distinction
between the seven-fold letters and the six-fold syllables, a point which
emerges rather clearly through a comparison between the two musical
examples of the corresponding sections in Gallicus and Burtius (see Figs.
6.5a and 6.5b).

With his musical example (Fig. 6.5a), Gallicus aims to show that the six
syllables *ut-la* embrace a segment of the gamut which is long enough to
contain all three kinds of diatessaron, G-C, A-D, and B [bequadro]-E, and
their transpositions (C-F, D-G-, and E-a). As we saw in Chapter 4, Jacques
de Liège had argued along this line to justify the number of six syllables
for solmization.[59] Notice that in Gallicus' example the letters precede the
syllables, in line with the author's argument that the seven letters are the
principal agent (the *dominae*) of the gamut. As the caption says, the six
syllables *ut, re, mi, fa, sol, la* are "extracted" from the letters and grouped
into the three species of tetrachords ("Hic est ut, re, mi, fa, sol, la, Tractum
ex sex illis litteris, Varietate triplici, Constans ex diatessaron"). In addition,
the use of the alphabetic letters in the example reveals that the three tetrachords (*ergo* the six syllables as well) do not exhaust the entire diatonic
menu: letter F is missing in columns 1–3 of Gallicus' graph (from left to
right), and letter B in columns 7–9. Thus the graph reflects the fact that,
while the six syllables form a paradigmatic unit, the six letters underlining
them do not. Gallicus' own commentary on his example leaves no doubt
about its intended meaning:

---

[59] See above, p. 100.

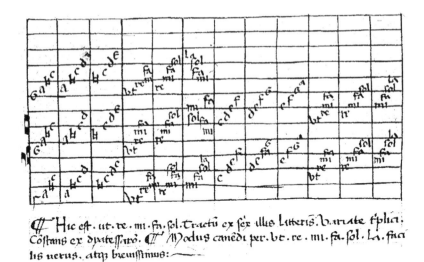

Fig. 6.5a. The six Guidonian syllables articulated into the three species of fourth (from J. Gallicus, *Ritus canendi*, London, British Library, Add. 22315, fol. 48r).

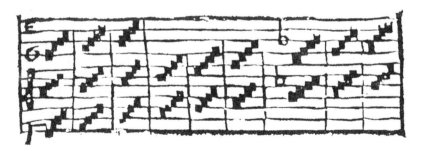

Fig. 6.5b. The Guidonian hexachord articulated into the three species of fourth (from N. Burtius, *Florum libellus* (Bologna, 1487), fol. cijr).

Videbis etiam ibi sex illas syllabas adeo litteris obligatas, ut quicquid ut, re, mi, fa, sol, la nobis insinuat, id totum Γ A ♮ C D E, vel etiam C D E F G A, vel F G A ♮ C D, tam sursum quam deorsum et ubique locorum exprimat. *Igitur neque sex litterae necque sex syllabae totum, ut dicitur, cantum in se continens, sed magis sex voces ita sub illis dispositae, quatenus et tres illas, quas ostendi diatessaron species enuntient et cum uno solo minori semitonio quatuor tonos integros habeant.*

[In the example you will notice that those six syllables are subject to the letters, so that whatever the six syllables force upon us [i.e., 'convey to us'], the letters Γ A ♮ C D E, C D E F G A, or F G A ♭ C D and their transpositions (ascending and descending) will express just as much. *Therefore, neither the six letters, nor the six syllables "contain all notes," as it is often said, but rather the six syllables, arranged in this particular order under the letters, spell out those three species of diatessaron that*

Fig. 6.6. Burtius' gamut articulated into hexachords (*Florum libellus* (Bologna, 1487), fol. cir).

I have shown in the example, so that they span through one minor semitone and four whole tones.][60]

Burtius' example (Fig. 6.5b) is modeled on Gallicus', but it erases the key difference between letters and syllables by showing undifferentiated strings of square notes on the staff. Thus Burtius needs only nine columns, not Gallicus' twelve. (Gallicus, unlike Burtius, does not show the three tetrachards with B^b, which would have required an additional six columns.) More importantly, however, Burtius shows that the three species of tetrachords may be built on the three *proprietates* (*durus* in columns 1–3, *naturalis* in columns 4–6, and *mollis* in columns 7–9). Whereas Gallicus had pointed out that the six syllables "spell out" the three tetrachords, Burtius' example suggests that three *proprietates* actually generate the tetrachordal species. In an earlier passage, Burtius had inserted a musical example suggesting that the gamut itself is organized by default into strings of six notes (see Fig. 6.6), an arrangement that a decade later Gafori will adopt in his *Practica musicae*. Significantly, Gallicus does not show this hexachordal arrangement of the gamut in his treatise.

The caption to this example completes Burtius' conflation of letters and syllables, as it implicitly ascribes the six-fold articulation of the latter onto the former. It reads: "These are the syllables of Guido [*Voces Guidonis*] taken from the hymn of St. John, which could be replicated endlessly if the human voice were not limited."[61]

In his chapter Burtius has also omitted other portions of Gallicus' chapter that are essential to the latter's argument, such as the view of the letters

---

[60] Gallicus, *Ritus canendi*, vol. 2, p. 52.

[61] "Voces Guidonis sub hymno Sancti Johannis deductae quae sic usque in infinitum possent replicari dummodo vox humana non deficeret," Burtius, *Florum libellus*, p. 81; Miller, trans. *Nicolaus Burtius*, p. 47.

and the syllables respectively as *dominae* and *subditae*, the suggestion that Guido could well have used other syllables, such as *ba, be, bi, bo, bu, bam*, and in general the whole idea that solmization was invented out of convenience, and not out of necessity.[62] In all the colorful vocabulary that Gallicus has in stock for the solmization system (*ambages, phylacteria, fabulae, garrulitas verborum*), does not appear in *Florum libellus*; nor does – not surprisingly – Guido's triplet "Solis notare litteris …" that occurs multiple times in Gallicus' treatise (see p. 152 above). In place of these arguments, Burtius lays out his theory about the perfection of number six, modeled after several classical sources.

As this discussion has shown, the misappropriation of Gallicus' views perpetrated by his alleged student was easily executed because it managed to preserve the very core of Gallicus' original positions. Gallicus' *Ritus canendi* is centered around the thesis of a unified musical system that transcends both historical and geographical boundaries and relies on God-given principles that can be studied mathematically, Boethius in hand. In line with this premise, Gallicus' goal was one of providing a pedagogical tool that reflects and takes advantage of the simplicity of music as "given by nature" a requirement that Guidonian solmization, in his view, could not meet. To him, the music curriculum of the church could make no *a priori* claim of adhering to the natural laws of music. No doubt, the *domina ratio* of his system, which defines tones and semitones, the gamut, the modes, and the consonances, had been given by God. However, such a *ratio* was intrinsically neither secular, nor sacred, and was not an exclusive property of the church by virtue of that *ratio*'s divine origin. On the contrary, Gallicus believed that the musical teaching proposed by the *moderni* had moved further and further away from the clarity and the simplicity of the method of the *antiquii*, whose musical practice was more attuned to the unchanging *ratio* of the system.

Therefore, far from being by definition attuned to the foundations of music, the church should now make an effort to adjust to it. Thus, in spite of its religious fervor and of its strong concern for the well-being of the church, the *Ritus* adopts an epistemology of open inquiry into natural phenomena according to which all authoritative statements, including those sanctioned by the church, are subject to criticism and revision. One may notice that Vittorino da Feltre was revered as a teacher because he fostered precisely this attitude of creative and unconstrained inquiry in his pupils.[63]

---

[62] See Gallicus' discussion of those points respectively in Gallicus, *Ritus canendi*, vol. 2, pp. 52, 51, and 49.

[63] David Robey has observed that the model of scholarship and the educational philosophy pursued by Vittorino and his teacher Pier Paolo Vergerio were not centered on religion and the

Quietly subverting this epistemological stance, Burtius substituted Guido's *ratio* – or, rather, his construction thereof, with the syllables at its center – to Gallicus' *domina ratio*. This strategy is lucidly implemented at the opening of ch. I, 15 of *Florum libellus*, which is borrowed from the very beginning of Gallicus' treatise (see above, pp. 145–6), yet with some key alterations:

Cum tot inventiones sint ad docendum, una dumtaxat et non plures ad cantandum sunt musicae. Tametsi omnium artium varia aliquando sit introductio, tamen omnes ad unum et idem reducunt mentis indaginem, non secus quam si per varias semitas in eundem plures convenirent locum. Tamen doctrina illius aptior clariorque habebitur quae omnibus communiter facilitate et brevitate approbatur, ut illa luculenta fuit Guidonis quae tamquam specimen iam diu celebrata altos per universum extensit ramos. ... Quam ob rem, amantissimi, etsi ritus modulandi varii sint, ut dictum est, atque varius ad docendum usus, non poterit tamen quisqua, quoquomodo cantet, vocem sursum intendere aut flectere deorsum quin iuxta genus dyatonicum proferat tonum aut minus semitonim [lists all the intervals] ... Oportet igitur primum ac discentibus ostendere quam multifarie possit ad huius artis notitiam perveniri, deinde quis sit introducendi modus facilior atque praestantior. His itaque peractis, omne genus hominum per sex Guidonis syllabas laudare deum posse probabit.

[Although there are many inventions in teaching music there is only one in singing it. Even though the beginning of all arts may be different, yet all of them bring intellectual investigation to one and the same thing, just as many come to the same place through different paths. The teaching of Guido is considered more fitting and clear, and is generally approved for its easiness and brevity. It has been the brilliant teaching of Guido which as a long celebrated example has extended its highest branches throughout the world ... Dearest friends, even if the practices of singing are varied, as has been said, and the manner of teaching varied, yet however anyone may sing, he cannot raise or lower a tone unless following the diatonic genus he sings a whole tone or a small semitone ...

So it was necessary to show first by instruction how knowledge of this art can have started in many ways, and then which manner of introducing it is easier and better. Now that this has been discussed every kind of man acknowledges that God can be praised by the six Guidonian vocables.][64]

Burtius here has deliberately corrupted the intended meaning of Gallicus' original passage. Gallicus' *modus facilior atque praestantior* for teaching and learning music was simply based on the recognition of the *litterae* and of the notes on the staff, not on Guidonian solmization; Burtius, however,

---

church, in spite of their strict enforcement of a rule of conduct inspired by Christian morals (see his "Vittorino e Vergerio" in Giannetto, ed., *Vittorino da Feltre e la sua scuola*, pp. 251–2).

[64] Brutius, *Florum Libellus*, ch. 15, pp. 84–5; Miller, trans., *Nicolaus Burtius*, pp. 50–1.

refers that sentence precisely to Guido's method of solmization, which he also portrays as a *doctrina facilis et brevis, atque luculenta*. For Gallicus, knowledge of the tones and the semitones was both necessary and sufficient; Burtius suggests that even the diatonic intervals are generated by the Guidonian syllables, since he systematically obscures the distinction between letters and syllables. Thus, it is not difficult for him to portray the syllables as an indispensable tool for learning music and for praising God, and Ramos as an arrogant "prevaricator" for daring to criticize them.[65]

At stake in the battle over Guidonian solmization, then, is the very *auctoritas* of the church, which both Ramos and Gallicus had threatened by proposing their radical reforms of long-standing chapters of the music curriculum and by taking the learning of the *antiqui* as a model for the present time. Burtius' *Florum libellus* ultimately shows how uncomfortable the theses of the Carthusian remained among the learned musical circles of Northern Italy decades after their original formulation. As we will now see, the radical views on solmization expressed by Gallicus and Ramos were also a cause for concern to Franchino Gafori, to judge from the changing accounts of the hexachordal system that he included in the different versions of both his *Theorica musicae* (1492), and his *Practica musicae* (1496).

Gafori's portrait of Gallicus in the *Theorica musicae*

During his 1478 sojourn in Mantua at the court of the Marquis Ludovico III Gonzaga – the son of Vittorino da Feltre's patron Gianfrancesco – Gafori had an opportunity to acquire a first-hand knowledge of Gallicus' music writings. Recent studies have shown that Gafori studied Gallicus' *Ritus canendi* carefully, as the discussion of the diatonic species and of the modes that he included in his own *Theorica musicae* (Milan, 1492) followed closely that by the Carthusian. However, an analysis of the two published versions of the *Theorica* also reveals that Gafori, like Burtius, was evidently unsettled

---

[65] This is perhaps the most blatant case of apparent similarity between the two texts that successfully hides the most glaring differences in meaning. Commenting on this very passage, Massera has written that "Burtius' central argument against Ramos is identical to Gallicus' … namely, that there is one truth and many different ways to access it. The challenge is choosing the best path to the truth, which in music was identified by Guido as the most elegant and easy. Pareja, on the other hand, had expressed a diametrically opposed view that emphasized the validity of what could be intuitively confirmed," Massera, "Burzio, Nicola," in *Dizionario enciclopedico universale della musica e dei musicisti,* "Le biografie," vol. III, p. 757. Elsewhere Massera asserts confidently that "Burzio did not betray his task of faithfully transmitting [Gallicus'] carefully conceived doctrine" (Brutius, *Florum libellus,* p. 19, translation mine).

by the critical remarks on solmization presented in the *Ritus*, and strived to offer a less threatening public portrait of his predecessor.[66]

The first edition of the *Theorica* appeared under the title *Theoricum opus* in Naples in 1480, during the period of Gafori's acquaintance with Johannes Tinctoris at the Aragonese court. Although the texts of the two editions are for the most part identical, there are at times significant differences between the two; indeed, the chapter of *Theoricum opus* that deals specifically with Guidonian theory (book V, chapter 6, hereafter V.6) was substantially revised in the later *Theorica*. The title change itself is revealing: the original header of the 1480 edition, "De ordinatione sonorum *per litteras et cordas latinas*" ("Of the order of sounds through the Latin letters and strings") has become "De applicatione *litterarum et sillabarum ad cordas* secundum Latinos" ("Of the application *of letters and syllables to the strings* according to the Latins," emphasis mine) – the new title clearly assigning more structural weight to the Guidonian syllables than the old one.

It is true that the abridgments and rewordings of the 1480 text of this chapter do not significantly alter the substance of Gafori's presentation.[67] The 1492 version, however, prominently displays the name of "Guido" four times in the margins, and the main text of the chapter refers to him more frequently. Readers, for instance, are told that the adoption of the seven letters took place "around the time of Guido of Arezzo" – a claim immediately followed by the famous verses beginning "Solis notare litteris," which had already appeared in the 1480 version.[68]

Gafori adjusts his remarks on the contribution of the Carthusian in a way that is no less subtle. Although Gallicus' name shows up only once in each of the two edition of the *Theorica*, the two citations appear in different contexts within the two texts and carry different connotations. In the *Theoricum*, Gallicus is quoted in the opening section of chapter V.6 as lamenting the singers' difficulties at reading musical notation before the introduction of the seven letters.

Et quidem ante litterarum huiusmodi constitutionem inventam sonorum primordia ac proprietates gravitatesque et acumina quibusdam difficilimis ciphris

---

[66] Both versions of the treatise are now available in modern editions: see C. Ruini, ed., *F. Gaffurio: Theoricum opus* (Lucca: Libreria Musicale Italiana, 1996); and F. Gafori, *Theorica musice* (Milan, 1492; reprint Bologna: Forni, 1969), eds. and Italian trans. I. Illuminati and C. Ruini (Florence: Edizioni del Galluzzo, 2005). On the spelling of Gafori's last name, see p. 14, n. 21.

[67] For a close comparison of the two texts, see G. Cesari, ed., *Franchini Gafuri Theorica musicae* (Rome: Reale Accademia d'Italia, 1934), pp. 79–83.

[68] W. Kreyszig, ed. and trans., *Franchino Gaffurio: The Theory of Music* (New Haven: Yale University Press, 1993), p. 172.

seu caracteribus proferrebant qui quippe pronuntiationis modus ob laboriosam sue prolationis difficultatem a musicis ipsis abiectus est atque relictus hinc idcirco recessit ab usu de quo quidem difficilimo canendi ritu latius tractavimus in quinto floris musices quem ad Illustrem marchionem directivum conscripsimus ac de ipso Johanninus cartusiensis in opre suo diffuse multa patefecit. Facilimum itaque septem pronuntiandarum litterarum modum ac ritum provida musicorum solertia constituit observandum quippe et greci nec non et hebrei alphabeti sui primas septem hoc ordine consitas litteras haud difficilime modulis dictantibus proferri consenserunt quas evidenter in primo quinti prealegati floris musices recta modulatione probavimus.

[Originally, before the introduction of the seven letters, musicians articulated low and high musical sounds by means of very difficult signs. The same musicians eventually rejected them, because of their extreme difficulty of pronunciation, and for that reason they fell out of use. We have written of this most difficult method of singing in our *Flos musices* [now lost], chapter 5, which we dedicated to the illustrious Marquis of Mantua. John the Carthusian has much to say about this topic in his work. Thus, the foreseeing ingenuity of the musici instituted the very easy method of the seven letters, observing that both the Greeks and the Hebrews had used the first letters of their alphabet without those most difficult signs. We have explained all this in the first chapter of the fifth book of *Flos musices*.][69]

In the 1492 edition of *Theorica*, Gafori deleted this entire passage, along with its emphasis on the introduction of the seven letters as a momentous development in the history of musical notation. Gallicus' name, however, is now featured much earlier, toward the end of the extensively revised *laus musicae* that constitutes the first chapter of the treatise. As Gafori – after his long survey of the musical authorities of classical antiquity – moves on to celebrate the Guidonian tradition of the present and the recent past, he tags in Gallicus' name as one of the illustrious heirs of Guido and Odo:

Guido autem Aretinus queque obscura viderentur et ignota faciliori perceptione apperuit hunc comunem vulgatumque modulationis ritum instituens quem ut ipse in epistola ad Michaelem pomposinum attestatur Ioannes papa apostolica auctoritate approbavit. Eo quoque tempore Odonem abbatem ferunt suum musices dialogum edidisse. Huiusquidem atque Guidonis traditionem immitatus Ioannes cartusinus musice facultatis libellum clericis perutilem descripsit.

[Guido of Arezzo made accessible whatever was regarded as obscure and unknown in a simpler form and instituted a common method of singing that received the approval of the Pope, as Guido himself attested in his *Epistola ad Michahelem*. It

---

[69] Gafori, *Theoricum opus*, ch. V.6, lines 39–57.

is also reported that at that time Abbot Odo published his *Dialogus de Musica*. Following Odo's and Guido's tradition, Johannes Cartusinus wrote a very useful small book on the art of music for clergymen.][70]

Two issues need to be carefully examined in order to understand this passage correctly. What does Gafori mean by "Odo's and Guido's tradition", and which particular image of John the Carthusian does he wish to propose to his readers when he portrays him as being in line with that tradition? The expression "method of singing" (*modulationis ritum*) at the beginning of the citation is crucial to addressing the first issue. In his English edition of *Theorica*, Kreyszig has translated it as "method of making melodies" – no doubt a justifiable choice, if one reads "making melodies" in the sense of "notating" them. As Kreyszig explains, Gafori likely refers here to the now lost antiphonary with the two colored lines indicating F and C, which Guido had described at length in the *Prologus in antiphonarium* and presented to Pope John XIX perhaps in the summer of 1032.[71] But Renaissance readers in the know – i.e., Gafori's main audience – may also have interpreted this passage as ambiguously conflating Guido's two main pedagogical contributions, i.e., the staffed antiphonary and the method of six-syllable solmization.[72] In particular, the expression "ignota apperuit faciliori perceptione" may recall Guido's solmization system, as many copies of the treatise that first introduced it, the *Epistola ad Michahelem*, announce it with the header *Ad inveniendum ignotum cantum*.[73] Moreover, Gafori unquestionably mediates here the term *ritus* from Gallicus, who had used it regularly with the meaning of "singing method" (*ritus canendi*). In short, the passage may be trying to establish a deliberately vague relationship between the Carthusian and the "Guidonian tradition" as a way of hiding the fact that the former had been indeed harshly critical of key aspects of the latter.

In short, it may be that the ambiguous sentence on Gallicus that Gafori inserted in the *Theorica* is ultimately not about Gallicus, but about taking the wind out of Ramos' sails – even though Gafori, unlike Burtius, carefully

[70] Gafori, *Theorica musice*, pp. 38–40; translation adapted from Kreyszig, ed. and trans., *Franchino Gaffurio*, pp. 28–9.
[71] Kreyszig, ed. and trans., *Franchino Gaffurio*, p. 28, footnote to line 285.
[72] Burtius' account of the same episode is also worded in such a way as to suggest that Guido submitted to the Pope John both the antiphonary and the method of the six syllables for approval; see Burtius, *Florum libellus*, ed. G. Massera, p. 80; Miller, trans., *Nicolaus Burtius*, p. 46.
[73] See *Pesce GA*, pp. 458–9.

avoided mentioning Ramos in his treatise, perhaps in an attempt not to give free publicity to his views. Gafori certainly read Ramos' *Musica practica* in the period between the two editions of the *Theorica*, probably in 1489.[74] He also read it as he was reworking his *Practica musicae,* to which the next chapter is dedicated.

[74] See J. Haar, "The Frontispiece of Gafori's *Practica musicae* (1496)," *Renaissance Quarterly* 27 (1974), 20; the article now appears also in J. Haar, *The Science and Art of Renaissance Music* (Princeton University Press, 1998), ch. 4, p. 79–92. It was Spataro who sent Gafori a copy of Ramos' treatise, now preserved in the Civico Museo Bibliografico Musicale of Bologna (A 80). Gafori's numerous comments on Ramos' text, which angered Spataro, are transcribed in Clement Miller's English translation of the treatise.

7 | Gafori's Hand: forging a new Guido for a new humanist culture

As we saw in Chapter 4, the theory of solmization in its mature stage was a product of the new rationalism that came to dominate the university curriculum in the second half of the thirteenth century. From the sketchy presentation of the six syllables in Guido's *Epistola ad Michahelem* to the impressive combinatorial edifice that emerged from the writings of Johannes de Garlandia, Magister Lambertus, and Amerus was no doubt a big step. Yet one of the main arguments of this monograph is that late-medieval theorists up until the generation of Ramos and Burtius still understood the six syllables as a virtual set of pitch labels superimposed onto the seven letters of pre-Guidonian times. Although the language of late-thirteenth-century music theory at times confers a foundational significance to the syllables, it never goes as far as to willingly present the complex machinery of solmization as embedded in musical sound; rather, on the whole that language conveys a basic distinction between the mental act of converting notated sounds into hexachordal labels and the heptachordal nature of diatonic space.

Until the end of the fifteenth century, for instance, theorists continued to refer to the six syllables as a *deductio*, not a *hexachordum* – that is to say, as a "virtual segment" devised as an aid to musical memory, rather than as a portion of the scale made of concrete sounds. It is significant that the two concepts lived separate existences throughout the Middle Ages even when hexachordal theory began to be couched in foundational terms at the end of the thirteenth century. The paradigmatic significance of the *virtual* segment (*deductio*) never trickled over to the *real* sixth of sounding intervals and pitches. Vice versa, in those rare cases in which the term *hexachordum* does occur in medieval surveys of the diatonic intervals, it always indicates the interval of a major or minor sixth that was more frequently called *diapente cum tono* (or *cum semitono*) and was invariably conceived as a portion of the octave.[1]

---

[1] I have discussed this point in much detail in my "Virtual Segments," pp. 440–6, and in the Interlude above, pp. 110–11.

Given such rigidly fixed conceptual boundaries, the introduction and rapid acceptance of the term *hexachordum* in discussions of Guidonian theory after 1480 surely appears as a momentous transition that profoundly affected the understanding of that theory until the present day. This chapter is dedicated to tracing the historical circumstances that led to such a transition, which signaled the advent of the hexachordal system as it has been known throughout the modern era. As I hope to demonstrate, the new structural view of Guidonian theory was not simply the outcome of the prolonged debate over the technical merits and shortcomings of the hexachordal system that kept busy theorists such as Ramos, Burtius, and Gafori in the 1480s and 1490s. Rather, the creation of a new strand of Guidonian theory was bound up with humanist historiography, the politics of patronage, and the redefinition of the power and the image of the author in the era of burgeoning print culture. My investigation will concentrate on Franchino Gafori's *Practica musicae*, a treatise that bears witness to the weight of such cultural transformations to a remarkable degree.

Toward a new meaning of "hexachordum"

The main catalyst for change in the long reception history of solmization theory was Ramos de Pareja's *Musica practica*, printed in Bologna in 1482. The work caused much scandal among the Italian readers of the time, perhaps more for the arrogant tone of its prose than for its actual content. In it, the Spanish-born Ramos dared to attack two veritable staples of medieval music theory: the Guidonian system and Pythagorean tuning. The second argument does not concern me here. I will limit my remarks to the argument that Ramos formulated as a critique of the method of six-syllable solmization.

In the first part of his treatise, Ramos introduces the subject of Guidonian solmization head-on. His account reads as follows:

Omnes quidem has litteras viginti Guido monachus melior quod musicus tetrachordo utens dum exachordum componit amplexus est. Et ad huiusmodi exachordum hac ratione compulsus est, quoniam senarius numerus a mathematicis perfectus dicitur, quia partes eius aliquotae simul sumptae ipsum senarium simul constituunt, scilicet 1. 2. 3., quae simul sex componunt, et qualibet huius hexachordi chorda a sex primis syllabis sex dictionum hymni sancti Johannis Baptistae nomen accepit, scilicet: *Ut queant laxis.*

[Guido, perhaps a better monk than a musician, encircled all twenty letters of the gamut when he developed the hexachord while practicing the tetrachordal subdivision of the gamut. And he was moved to create such a hexachord in this way because number six is called perfect by mathematicians, for its aliquot parts, namely 1, 2, 3, when added together make six, and each string of the hexachord receives a name from the first six syllables of six lines of the hymn of St. John the Baptist, namely: *Ut queant laxis.*][2]

And a page later, describing the superimposition of syllables onto the gamut, he states:

Et ut Boeti doctrina imitaretur que per tetrachorda totam dividit harmoniam, cum ad quartum locum pervenit videlicet C fa. Si autem cum c fa ut syllaba ponatur totum compositum c fa ut appellatur et continuatur cum d sol re et cum e la mi ubi primum finitur exachordum. Sed cum ex litteris f sequatur cum fa tetrachordi secundi syllaba ut iterum collocatur, que secundi tetrachordi Quarta vox est. Itaque cum sit f fa ut sibi iuncta tale nomen accipiet et sequitur cum g sol re et cum a la mi e ne se ignorasse similitudinem extremarum diapason includentium videretur rursum exachordum collocare incipit et cum ex preteritis tetrachordis duobus secundo videlicet et tertio duas voces habeamus ibi locatas, scilicet cum littera g sol re ut sibi addita ... Sicut prius et possent exachorda in infinitum multiplicari iuxta instrumenti sufficientiam. Se cum in omni scientia quandoque ad finem perveniendum sit iterari exachorda iam desinunt et propterea in c sol fa non ponitur amplius ut. Sed procedimus ad d la sol ubi sextum exachordum reliquum ... itaque posuit septem exachorda propter 7 voces dicentes ut sibi usum fuit quod substantia patefaciet figura. Vides ne rectam guidonis figuram. Ipse vero non sic sed per iunturas ponit digitorum hoc modo.

[In order to follow the Boethian doctrine, which divides the entire tonal series by tetrachords, when [Guido] comes to the fourth place namely *c fa*, he again creates another hexachord, another offspring as it were [*iterum exachordum quasi propagine facta aliud emittit*]. But if the syllable *ut* is joined to *c fa* the entire arrangement is called *c fa ut*, and it continues with *d sol re* and *e la mi*, where the first hexachord ends. Since *fa*, however, follows in the order of letters, the syllable *ut* is also joined to the second tetrachord's *fa*, which is the fourth tone of the second tetrachord ... Hexachords can be multiplied indefinitely according to the extent of the instrument, but since an end must be reached somewhere in all knowledge, the hexachords now stop repeating and therefore another *ut* is not placed with *c sol fa*, but we move to *d la sol*, where we leave the sixth hexachord, while the seventh ends on the syllable *e la*. And so [Guido] set down seven hexachords because of seven different tones, as it

___

[2] Ramos de Pareja, *Musica practica*, p. 11; Miller, trans., *Bartolomeo Ramis de Pareia: Musica practica*, p. 55.

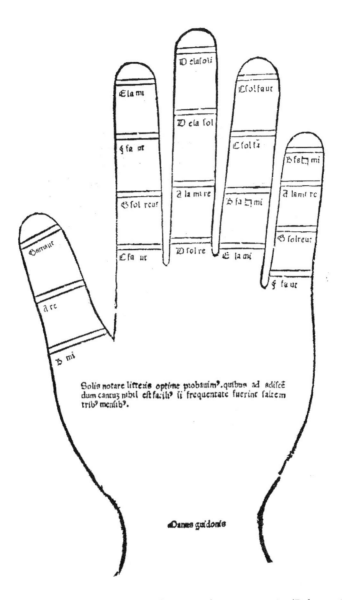

Fig. 7.1. The Guidonian Hand in Ramos' *Musica practica* (Bologna, 1482), p. 12.

had seemed to him, just as the following figure will show. Do you see the true figure of Guido? Indeed he himself does not, but he shows it through joints of the fingers in this way [a figure of the Guidonian Hand follows; reproduced here as Fig. 7.1].[3]

---

[3]   Ramos de Pareja, *Musica practica*, p. 10; Miller, trans., *Bartolomeo Ramis de Pareia: Musica practica*, p. 56. It is interesting that in the palm of the musical hand shown in Figure 1, Ramos inserts the excerpt from Guido's *Regule rithmicae* that Gallicus had used as a *leitmotif* in his

These two excerpts are of extraordinary significance in the history of Western music theory: for the first time ever in Latin music theory the term *hexachordum* designates the six syllables *ut, re, mi, fa, sol, la*. The terminological switch has more than a cosmetic significance, as the new term – so directly reminiscent of the classical *tetrachordum* – ascribes a structural weight to the Guidonian syllables that was foreign to the medieval mind. In Ramos' account, Guido *first* regrouped the notes of the gamut hexachordally, and *then* attached the famous syllables to each string of the newly derived "hexachords." Here the reader no longer encounters the oft-repeated story of how a pedagogical system of pitch names became superimposed onto the good old gamut, but rather a new exposition of how a radically new gamut resulted in a new pedagogical system.

The main casualties of Ramos' account are the long-standing conceptual dyad *deductio/proprietas* and the two-tier structure of syllables superimposed onto letters that went with it – as a matter of fact, the term *deductio*, which used to designate the syllabic set *ut-la*, is missing altogether in *Musica practica*. It was one thing to explain, with Johannes de Garlandia, that "three properties were necessary to all songs," and quite another to argue, as Ramos appears to have done for the first time in his treatise, that Guido instituted the "hexachord" as the primary operative segment of diatonic space by building over the classical tetrachords. Garlandia would still have understood the hexachordal *proprietas* as an ad hoc segmentation of the gamut that did not challenge the primacy of the octave in and of itself. Even his claim that "three properties are necessary for all song" can be read in a non-foundational sense. Presented as *hexachords*, however, those "properties" acquire the status of a *sine qua non* of the diatonic space, objectively *there* as an all-around structural device, and it is suddenly a short step to considering the segment of the major sixth as the cognitive and structural basis of early music.[4]

It is indeed no coincidence that all of Ramos' opponents – Burtius, Hothby, and Gafori – quickly embraced the new meaning of *hexachordum*, which greatly enhanced the status of Guido from pedagogue to creator of a new musical law.[5] Burtius and Hothby, however, made only limited steps

---

    Ritus canendi ("Solis notare litteris…," etc., see p. 152 above). This detail confirms that Ramos studied Gallicus' treatise closely, even though he is not concerned in his treatise with promoting a letters-only method of pitch recognition.

[4] I discuss this point in more detail in my "Virtual Segments," 463–7.

[5] See J. Hothby, *Tres tractatuli contra Bartholomeum Ramum*, ed. A. Seay, *CSM* 10 (Rome: American Institute of Musicology, 1964), pp. 41–2; Burtius, *Florum libellus*, p. 83; Miller, trans., *Nicolaus Burtius*, p. 49.

in that direction. Gafori, for his part, eventually placed this revised and classicizing image of Guido of Arezzo at the very center of his solmization theory, as the remainder of this chapter will now show.

Solmization theory in Gafori's *Practica musicae*

Proprietas and *deductio*

If Ramos, Hothby, and Burtius were the first theorists to refer to the Guidonian *deductio* as a *hexachordum* in their writings, it was Gafori who gave the final stamp of approval to that crucial terminological switch and handed it over to future generations. As I have shown in the previous chapter, Gafori's handling of solmization theory in the 1492 version of *Theorica* differed from the earlier version in important respects. Yet these changes must not have fully satisfied the author, because the description of the Guidonian system that he included in his next major publication, the *Practica musicae* of 1496, marks a radical departure from all his previous treatments of this topic, including the one he had offered in the very recent *Theorica*. As I hope to demonstrate in this section, Gafori's presentation of Guidonian solmization is meant to accomplish several goals, including that of formulating an effective, if covert, rebuttal of the opponents of the method of solmization, *in primis* Ramos de Pareja.[6]

Gafori began drafting *Practica musicae* in the early 1480s. Right before settling permanently in Milan as *maestro di cappella* of the Cathedral, he held the same position at S. Maria Maggiore in Bergamo for a few months. During this time he worked on the initial chapters of *Practica musicae*, which a Benedictine monk by the name of Alessandro Assolari later entered in a miscellaneous manuscript now housed at the Bergamo Civic Library.[7] Because the Bergamo draft of book 1 of *Practica musica* predates the printed version by about twelve years, it offers precious insights into the development of Gafori's thought. For ease of comparison, I have arranged the relevant portions of this initial version and the corresponding passages from the printed version of *Practica musica* in Tables 7.1 (on *proprietas*), 7.2 (on *deductio*), and 7.3 (on *mutatio*).

---

[6] The 1496 edition of *Practica musicae* is available in facsimile by Forni (Bologna,1972), UK, 1967); for the English translation I have generally referred to C. A. Miller, ed. and trans., *Franchinus Gaffurius: Practica musicae*, (N.p.: American Institute of Musicology, 1968).

[7] The source, dating to 1487, is Bergamo, Biblioteca Civica "Angelo Mai," MS MAB 21, fols. 1r–19r.

Table 7.1. Textual changes between the Bergamo draft and *Practica musicae* (bk. 1, ch. 4: "Proprietas")

Bergamo draft, ca. 1483	Gafori, *Practica musicae* (Milan, 1496) Trans. C. Miller, 1969.
[A.1]. [Fol. 5r] DE PROPRIETATIBUS ET MUTATIONIBUS VOCUM. CAP. QUARTUM.	**[B.1]** CAP. QUARTUM: DE PROPR-IETATIBUS ET MUTATIONIBUS VOCALIUM SYLLABARUM.
Proprietas in vocibus secundum Marchetum est derivatio plurium vocum ab uno et eodem principio. C. Johannes autem Tinctoris in sua musica plana proprietatem dicit quondam vocum deducendarum singularem esse qualitatem.	*Proprietas in notulis vocalibus secundum Marchetum est derivatio plurium vocum ab uno et eodem principio. C. Tinctoris autem in sua musica plana proprietatem dicit quondam vocum deducendarum singularem esse qualitatem.*
[According to Marchetto of Padua, a property is a derivation of several Guidonian syllables from one principle. Johannes Tinctoris, on the other hand, defines "property" as the special quality of arranging syllables in a particular order.]	[According to Marchetto of Padua, *proprietas* in vocal music is the derivation of several syllables from one and the same principle. Johannes Tinctoris, on the other hand, defines *proprietas* as the special quality of arranging syllables in a particular order.]
	[B.2] *Non enim proprium et proprietas idem sunt. Nam proprium est concretum, proprietas vero abstractum veluti Album et Albedo. Est enim proprium quaedam res et substantia coniuncta cum qualitate sive mavis dicere cum accidente, et hoc est concretum. Proprietas vero est quaedam passio sive qualitas seu accidens quod dum abstrahitur ab ipsa substantia cui inhaeret dicitur abstractum veluti est proprietas aut albedo.*
	[Property and propriety are not identical, for property is concrete while propriety is abstract, just as white is to whiteness. Property is a kind of matter and substance joined together with a quality, or if you prefer to say so, with an "accident," and this is concrete. Propriety, however, is a certain feeling or quality or accidence which is called abstract, since it is withdrawn from the substance to which it inheres, just as, moreover, the propriety of whiteness is.]

Table 7.1. (*cont.*)

[**A.3**] *Nos autem proprietatem huiusmodi sic diffinire solemus: Proprietas est **singularis processus uniuscuiusque deductionis**. Est autem deductio sex diversas [recte: diversarum] vocum gradatim ascendentium vel descendentium ordinatio que sunt scilicet ut re mi fa sol la septies in introductorio constitute.*

[**We wish to define "property" as the particular process by which any deduction is inferred.** A deduction is a set of six different syllables, that is to say, ut re mi fa sol la, in ascending or descending order, that is constituted seven times in the introductory gamut.]

[**A.4**] *Verum cum septem sint soni differentes omnem musicam facultatem nutrientes, teste Virgilio in sexton Eneidos, obloquitur numeris septem discrimina vocum, queri solet: cur non septem vocum nomina diversa a Guidone Aretino constituta sint?* Sicuti et septem diverse littere voces ipsas septem diversas representates [sic] conservate sunt: ad instar musice mundane, que septem planetarum volubilis armonia concipitur potiusque sex tantum: que nullius armonie comparatione firmantur. Ex quo notandum est quod cum armonica facultas naturaliter in singulis tetracordis dyatessaron consonantiam custodiat, cumque dyatessaron tres diversas species ducat ipsis sex vocum nominibus comprehensas, ipsas tunc sex voces ad omnem armoniam necessarias esse et satisfacere consideravit.*

[**B.3**] *Verum proprietatem huiusmodi modulationis dicimus esse <u>**singularem uniuscuiusque**</u> **exachordi** in introductorio dispositi deductionem. Deductio est sex ipsarum syllabarum diatonica ac naturalis progressio: vt ascendendo: hoc ordine: vt re mi fa sol la.*
descendendo vero: la sol fa mi re vt.

[**We call proprietas the step by step deductio of a hexachord as it is seen in the gamut.** A *deductio* is a natural and diatonic progression of six syllables in ascending or descending order, *ut, re, mi, fa, sol, la* [or] *la, sol, fa, mi, re, ut.*]

Table 7.1. (*cont.*)

[In truth, since the entire science of music is based on seven different sounds – witness Vergil's verse: "[the Thracian bard] strikes seven different notes" – the question is often raised, **Why did Guido of Arezzo not institute seven different names for the notes?** After all, seven different letters have traditionally represented those seven different notes in analogy with the music of the spheres, which originates from the harmonic rotations of seven planets, rather than six only (a set which in comparison would produce no harmony). On this point, we must observe that since […] the diatessaron yields three different species that are all encompassed by those six note names, Guido considered six syllables as necessary and sufficient to all harmony.]

The early draft of the treatise (column A) highlights Gafori's general indebtedness to the *Expositio manus* of his contemporary Johannes Tinctoris (ca. 1473), which had essentially restated the medieval tradition on the subject. Not surprisingly, then, the term *hexachordum* does not appear anywhere in this version (see Tables 7.1 and 7.2). Rather, Gafori points to the seven letters as the primary engine of the diatonic space. In Table 7.1, section A.4, for instance, Gafori wonders about the reason for introducing six solmization syllables against a pre-existing unit of seven letters, the logical primacy of which is here supported even by the idea of *musica mundana* and confirmed by Virgil. Significantly, the key question: "Why did Guido of Arezzo not institute seven syllables?" – one often raised by medieval theorists, and potentially endorsing an octave-based solmization system such as Ramos' – was not retained in the final version of the treatise. Its deletion, I suggest, is indicative of Gafori's intentions.

Table 7.2. Textual changes between the Bergamo draft and *Practica musicae* (bk. 1, ch. 4: "Deductio")

Bergamo draft, ca. 1483	*Practica musica* (1496)
[A.5] Septem igitur sunt **deductiones** diversis proprietatibus deputate. Proprietates autem sunt tres, scilicet ♮ duralis, naturalis et b mollis.	[B.5] *Haec enim septem* **exachorda** *vocant proprietates seu qualitates quarum tres ♮ quadrae vel ♮ durae: duas naturae: ac duas b rotundae vel molli ascribunt. Quae autem ♮ quadrales dicuntur sub littera G exordium sortiuntur. Naturales autem in littera C Sed B mollares in littera F principium possidere noscuntur: quod ex ordine introductorij liquido percipitur.* **Primam igitur exachordi figuram grauissima chorda scilicet Γ graeca littera producit:** *quam linea ♮ duralis qualitatis noscitur sustinere.*
Proprietas ♮ duralis est que oritur a G littera id est cum ut in g reperitur et tunc relique voces illius deductionis gradatim sucessiveque ascendentes licet diversis sub litteris comprehendantur proprietatis ♮. [Fol. 5v] **Proprietas autem naturalis est que originem trahit a littera C in introductorio, id est cum ut in C constituitur** …	***Secundam exachordi figuram: tertia literarij nota quartam chordam in spatio disponens producere cognoscitur:*** *hanc naturalem proprietatem seu qualitatem vocant.* **Tertiam autem exachordi figuram sextus litterarij character septimam chordam attingens recto ordine produ[c]it:** *hanc b mollarem qualitatem nominant.*
Proprietas autem b mollis est que ab F littera surgit, id est quando ut in F repperitur, et tunc omnes illius deductionis voces sunt proprietatis b mollaris.	
[**Thus there are seven deductions corresponding with the different properties, but the types of properties are three, that is to say, hard, natural, and soft.**	[**The seven hexachords are called** *proprietates* **or** *qualities,* [of which three are square or hard ♮, two are natural and two are round or soft b. Those called square ♮ begin on G, the natural begin on C, and soft b on F, as can be easily seen from their order in the [gamut].
The hard property originates from the letter G when ut is found on G and the remaining syllables of the same *deductio* ascend stepwise over the letters of the hard property.	Thus **the lowest pitch,** Greek letter Γ, **yields the first hexachord** placing hard ♮ on a line.

Table 7.2. (*cont.*)

Bergamo draft, ca. 1483	*Practica musica* (1496)
The natural property takes its origin from C, that is to say, it is constituted with *ut* on C and the remaining syllables of the same *deductio*, although matched to different letters, are said to be sung by nature; there are two *deductiones* of this property.	**Letter C is known to produce the second hexachord,** placing the fourth note from Γ in a space: this is called the natural *proprietas* or quality.
The soft property is the one that originates from the letter F, that is to say, when *ut* is found on F, and all the syllables of that deductio belong to the soft propriety.]	**In diatonic order the letter F produces the third form of hexachord,** which begins on the seventh note; this is called soft ♭ quality.]

Section A.5 (Table 7.2) also corroborates the impression that the Bergamo draft still resonates with the medieval understanding of the Guidonian system. Gafori's wording presents the *deductio* as a "soft" set of pitch labels superimposed onto the "hard" layer of the seven letters of the gamut. When he writes that the *proprietates take their beginning* from the letters ("oritur a G littera," "ut in G reperitur," "originem trahit a lettera C," "ut in C constituitur," "ab F littera surgit," "ut in F repperitur"), he is not at the same time implying that the letters lose their default heptachordal ordering because of it, just as the default seven-day week cycle is not disrupted by superimposing ad hoc strings of six days upon it. The letters G, C, and F do mark the beginning points of the *proprietates* that serve as the "walking paths" for the *deductiones*, but the basic "two-tier" structure of syllables superimposed onto letters is not ipso facto compromised.

The corresponding passages of the 1496 version of *Practica musicae*, however, tell quite a different story (see column B5 in Table 7.1). Here Gafori writes that the pitches of the gamut corresponding to the syllable *ut* actually "generate" hexachordal sets of letters/syllables called *hexachordi*. In other words, the six-fold sets of syllables are merely the by-product of the (alleged) hexachordal grouping of the letters. We see this idea at work at the beginning of chapter 4 of the printed version. At first, the text matches the Bergamo draft exactly (compare excerpts A.1 and B.1 in Table 7.1). Immediately after the first sentence, however, Gafori embarks on the philosophical excursus of

B.2, dedicated to teasing out the distinction between concrete and abstract properties, or between *proprium* and *proprietas*.

The very presence of such a discussion is especially intriguing when considered in the context of Gafori's "foundational" reinterpretation of the traditional concept of *deductio*. It would seem that the notion of *exachordum*, traditionally anchored to an audible musical object (i.e., the major sixth) should be kept separate from *proprietas*, if *proprietas* – by Gafori's own definition, based on Aristotle – is to reflect abstract qualities detached from their concrete and "accidental" realities. It is the "sixth-ness" of *hexachordum*, not *hexachordum* itself, which could be more easily related to *proprietas*, as medieval theorists arguably had in mind when they intuitively kept *exachordum* separate from both *deductio* and *proprietas*. More important is the question of what might have induced Gafori to interpolate this learned commentary on *proprietas* in a manual ostensibly dedicated to musical practice. I will address this point later at length. It is by now clear, however, that Gafori's *Practica* is addressing not only, or even primarily, an audience of practical musicians (who at best might have had only a tangential interest in such matters), but especially the educated elite.

Resuming his task of discussing the rudiments of Guidonian theory, in the 1496 version Gafori elaborates on the musical concept of *proprietas*, in the process eliminating also the references to Virgil's *septem discrimina vocum* and to the seven planets of the Bergamo draft:

Verum proprietatem huiusmodi modulationis dicimus esse singularem uniuscuiusque exachordi in introductorio dispositi deductionem. Deductio est sex ipsarum syllabarum diatonica ac naturalis progressio … Haec enim septem exachorda vocant proprietates seu qualitates: quarum tres [bequadro] quadrae vel [bequadro] durae, duas naturae, ac duas b rotundae vel molli ascribunt. Quae autem [bequadro] quadrales dicuntur sub littera G exordium sortiuntur. Naturales autem in littera C. Sed B mollares in littera F principium possidere noscuntur: quod ex ordine introductorii liquido percipitur. Primam igitur exachordi figuram gravissima chorda scilicet G graeca littera producit: quam linea [bequadro] duralis qualitatis noscitur sustinere. Secundam exachordi figuram tertia litterarii nota quartam chordam in spatio disponens producere cognoscitur: hanc naturalem proprietatem seu qualitatem vocant. Tertiam autem exachordi figuram sextus litterarii character septimam chordam attingens recto ordine produxit [sic]: hanc b mollarem qualitatem nominant …. At quibus proprietatibus qualitatibusve syllabes omnes vocales ascribuntur: his tribus figures facile percipitur [a table follows].

[We call *proprietas* the step by step *deductio* of a hexachord as it is seen in the [gamut]. *Deductio* is a natural and diatonic progression of six vocables, *ut, re, mi, fa, sol, la* or *la, sol, fa, mi, re, ut.* The seven hexachords are called *proprietates* or qualities of which three are by bequadro, two are natural and two are by b molle. Those called by [bequadro] begin on G, the natural ones begin on C, and those by b molle on F, as can be easily seen from their order in the [gamut].

Thus the lowest pitch, Greek letter [gamma], yields the first hexachord, placing a bequadro sign on a line.

Letter C is known to produce the second hexachord, placing the fourth note (from gamma) in a space: this is called the natural *proprietas* or quality.

In diatonic order letter F produces the third form of hexachord, which begins on the seventh note; this is called the quality by b molle ... All syllables of the gamut are allotted to these proprieties and qualities, and shown in the following figure.][8]

Most importantly, the excerpts marked B.3 and B.5 from the 1496 *Practica* obliterate the subtle "two-tier" construct between *proprietas* and *hexachordum* and between *voces* and *litterae*. Witness the opening sentence of B.3, where *proprietas* is defined as "the particular deduction of each hexachord, as placed in the introductory table (*proprietatem ... dicimus esse singularem uniuscuiusque exachordi in introductorio dispositi deductionem*), followed in B.5 by the misleading specification "those hexa-chords are named proprietates (*haec hexachorda vocant proprietates*). The survey of the *proprietates* on the following section does not even men-tion a single Guidonian syllable: Gafori tells his readers that the letter G, "produces the first hexachord" via bequadro (*primam exachordi figuram ... gravissima chorda ... producit*), that the third letter C "is known to produce the second one," and so on. Not only does Gafori use repeatedly the verb *producere* in this context, which points to the letters as the structural roots of the "hexachords;" he also makes no mention of the six syllables for a good portion of his account of the *proprietates*, as if those syllables were a mere afterthought.

Significantly, Gafori's description of the *proprietas naturalis* uses the expression *producere cognoscitur* ("is known to yield") by which Gafori may wish to suggest that he is simply reporting the common view on this topic. Gafori wishes to present himself as a reliable witness of the Guidonian tradition, perhaps as a way of implying that the "foundational spin" he is attributing to the system had been rooted in musical consciousness since Guido's time. Indeed, the entire account of *proprietas* found in the final ver-sion of the *Practica* appears to be fully in line with traditional wisdom on the subject, introduced as it is by self-protective and reassuring references to Marchetto and Tinctoris (B.1). In reality, Gafori is making mincemeat of medieval solmization theory.

---

[8] Gafori, *Practica musicae*, fols. avjr – avjv); Miller, ed. and trans., *Franchinus Gaffurius*, p. 34.

Mutation

The theory of hexachordal mutations that occupies the remainder of book 1, chapter 4 is also significantly different from the one found in the Bergamo draft. Gafori knew that both Johannes Gallicus and Ramos had harshly criticized this particular aspect of Guidonian theory as confusing and counterproductive for singers. As a matter of fact, Ramos had quoted Gallicus' unflattering words on this subject, and had pointed out that his proposed eight-syllable solmization system had the advantage of considerably reducing the number of syllabic mutations.[9] Perhaps as a veiled response to these charges, Gafori opens his section on mutations by offering a broad historical account of the etymology and applications of the term *mutatio* from late antiquity to Scholastic philosophy, from Bacchius Senior (fl. fourth century AD), to Peter of Abano (ca. 1250–1315) (see Table 7.3, sections B.6 and B.7). Such a learned overview of the subject is also visually emphasized by the prominent display of those venerable *auctoritates* on the margins of the page (see a reproduction of the book opening in Fig. 7.2, shown in the next two pages). In contrast to this section, the earlier draft had mentioned only the short digressions by Marchetto and Gregory into the general meaning of *mutatio* (see Fig. 7.3 and Table 7.3, A.6).[10]

Gafori's strategy is as clear as it is artfully implemented. With his erudite lecturing on the philosophic concepts of *proprietas* and *mutatio* he aims at artificially enhancing the pedigree of their Guidonian counterparts, and of catering to the most educated portion of his readership. Most importantly, his display of knowledge is not an end unto itself, but rather a veiled response to the opponents of solmization: Ramos' criticism of Guido's method would appear unjustified, if it could be shown that the governing principles of that same method were rooted in the highest philosophical tradition. Gafori no doubt sympathized with Burtius' argument against the Spaniard, but he evidently did not approve of his strategy of attacking Ramos head-on. His response to Ramos in *Practica musicae* takes a radically different path, that of a detached and highfalutin philosophic tone that quietly takes position in the controversy without becoming embroiled in it.

---

[9] "Friar John the Carthusian has indeed spoken truly about these mutations: 'I do not speak of the mutation of syllable into syllable, but of ambiguity into ambiguity. It only matters to designate whole tones and semitones with the letters of Gregory'. I say this about my syllables, for those who will have wished to sing with our syllables will be obliged to make only a single mutation in one octave." (Miller, trans., *Bartolomeo Ramis de Pareja: Musica practica*, pp. 94–5).

[10] On the significance of Gafori's *Practica* in the burgeoning print culture of the Renaissance, see C. Collins Judd, *Reading Renaissance Music Theory: Hearing with the Eyes* (Cambridge University Press, 2000), pp. 17–30.

Table 7.3. Textual changes between the Bergamo draft and *Practica musicae* (bk. 1, ch. 4: "Mutatio")

Bergamo draft, ca. 1483	*Practica musicae* (1496)
[ON MUTATION]	[ON MUTATION]
[**A.6**] *Sed de mutacionibus nominum vocum et proprietatibus que propter digressum unius proprietatis in alter am invente sunt quedam videntur necessarie describenda.*	[**B.6**] *Multimodas insuper sonorum mutationes clerici protestantur.* **Est enim Mutatio apud Baccheum Alteratio subiectorum seu Alicuius similis in dissimilem locum transpositio.**
Est enim mutacio secundum Marchetum variatio nominis vocis in eadem tono. *Nam mutari apud Gregorius in moralibus est ex alio in aliud ire et in semetipsum stabilem non esse. Unaqueque enim res quasi tot passibus ad aliam tendit: quot mutabilitatis sue motibus subiacet.*	*Hinc in moralibus Mutari Gregorius inquit est ex alio in aliud ire et in semetipsum stabilem non esse: unaquaeque enim res quasi tot passibus ad aliam tendit: quot mutabilitatis suae motibus subiacet.*
[Now it is necessary to discuss a few things about mutations of the names of the notes and of the properties that have been invented through a digression of one property into another. According to Marchetto, a mutation is the change of one vocable into another on the same pitch. Hence in his *Morals* Gregory says that to change is to go from one thing into another and not to be stable in respect to one's essential self, for each thing tends to move toward another, by as many steps, so to speak, as its distance requires.]	[Furthermore, churchmen acknowledge many kinds of pitch mutations. According to Bacchius, mutation is the exchange of substitutes, or the transposition of something similar into a dissimilar place. Hence in his *Morals* Gregory says that to change is to go from one thing into another and not to be stable in respect to one's essential self, for each thing tends to move toward another, by as many steps, so to speak, as its distance requires.]
	[**B.7**] *Verum huiusmodi mutationem Martianus transitum appellat: quem vocis variationem in alteram soni figuram interpretatur. Briennius autem mutationem dixit esse subiecti systematis ac vocis characteris alienationem. Fit autem Mutatio secundum genus quum scilicet in tetrachordo diatonico lychanos vel etiam paranetes chorda remittitur semitonio in graue: transeundo in chromaticam figuram: vel tono transeundo in enarmonicam: quae nusquam accidit ex grauitate in acumen variari ut Boetius noster in quarto explicuit.* [Boetius. Aristoteles. in marg.] *Id quoque et*

Table 7.3. (*cont.*)

Bergamo draft, ca. 1483	*Practica musicae* (1496)
	Aristoteles ipse in musicis problematibus [-f.aviįr-] intelligi voluit quum diceret Quod sapit naturam acuti plerumque pertransit in gravem: quod autem sapit naturam gravis non permutatur in acutum. Est et alia mutationis consyderatio in voce ac sono: nam quum sunt in motu et fiunt tantum voces et soni ipsi de genere creduntur entium successivorum ut vigessimo septimo problemate interpres exposuit: [Petrus apponensis. Marchetus. in marg.] *qua re vocis ipsius ac soni generatio consistit in quodam fieri et transmutari. Verum huiusmodi introductio defnitam a Marcheto consequitur mutationem. Is enim inquit: Mutatio est variatio nominis vocis in alterum in eodem sono. Syllabae enim ipsae vocibus et chordis suis scilicet notulis ascriptae si in una eademque linea vel eodem spatio consistunt: dicuntur quantitate pares sed qualitate seu proprietate diversae. Inde quum mutatio sit qualitas unius exachordi in alterius qualitatem transfertur stante eadem vocis quantitate: ut testatur Anselmus tertio suae musicae.* [Anselmus. in marg.] [Martianus [Capella] calls such mutation transposition, and he explains this as the variation of a pitch into another form of the pitch. Briennius, however, said that mutation was the transference of a substitute system and a vocable. Mutation occurs according to genus, that is, when the lichanos or else the paranete pitch in a diatonic tetrachord is lowered by a semitone, converting into the chromatic species, or by a whole tone transformation into the enharmonic. Such an alternative never occurs in ascending motion, as our Boethius has explained in book IV [of his *De musica*]. Aristotle himself in the *Musical Problems* also wished this to be understood when he said, "That which partakes of the nature of the acute generally moves to the grave, but that which knows the nature of the grave is not changed into the acute." There is another aspect of mutation in pitch and sound: for when these vocables are in motion and are only coming into existence, they are believed to be of the genus of successive entities. The Interpreter [Peter of Abano] explained this in the Twenty-seven *Problem*. According to him, the generation of pitch and sound itself consists of a certain

coming, into being and changing. Such a system, according to the writing of Marchettus, results in definite mutation. He says: 'Mutation is the change of one vocable into another on the same pitch'. For if these syllables which are assigned to sounds and pitches – to their notes, that is – stand on one and the same line or space, they are called equal in quantity but different in quality or propriety. Hence, when mutation occurs, the quality of one hexachord is transferred into the quality of another hexachord, the quantity of the sound remaining the same, as Anselm testifies in book III of *his Musica.*]

[see B.11 for a similar passage]

[A.8] *Quando igitur aliquam cum suis proprietatis deductionem modulando ingressi sumus ante finalem eius vocem mutare numquam debemus hinc rarius et tardius ut fieri potest mutandum est. Ex quo mutatio non est vocis nec soni, sed nominis tantum unde quando solfizamus tunc mutamus quia vocum nomina in prolatione exprimimus.*

[When we choose a particular deduction with its properties while singing, we must never leave it before its final note – hence one has to mutate as rarely and as late as possible. This shows that a mutation does not affect the actual notes or sounds, but only their names, so that when we solmize we mutate because we call out the names of the sounds as an extension.]

Table 7.3. (cont.)

Bergamo draft, ca. 1483	Practica musicae (1496)
[A.9] *Igitur cum mutatio fiat de una voce in alter am in uno sono permanente, ubicumque fuerunt unica vox sive in linea sive in spatio non potest fieri mutatio quia vox non transmutatur in alter am alter a deficiente.*	[B.9] *Voces autem ipsas exachordorum syllabas intelligo. Non igitur vox mutatur in vocem per intensionem aut remissionem sed syllaba in sillabam etproprietas seu qualitas in qualitatem. Quo fit vt quum syllabas tantum modulato transitu exprimimus ipsa quadret mutatio. Litterarii autem characteres in introductorio obseruati neque proferuntur neque mutantur. Syllaba item quae vel lineam vel spacium sola occupat mutationi non congruit.*
Therefore, since a mutation is a change of one syllable into another on the same sound, it cannot be performed on those pitches that correspond to only one syllable, regardless of whether they are placed on a line or in a space, because no transmutation of syllables is possible on that pitch.	From this I call mutation the changing of one tone into another tone of the same kind. But by tones I mean the syllables of hexachords. Therefore a tone is not changed into another tone by rising or falling, but by syllable into syllable, and *proprietas* or quality into another quality. Mutation is accomplished properly when only syllables of a melody are changed, for the letter names of notes in the *Introductorium* do not change. Similarly, a syllable which alone occupies a line or space is not suitable for mutation
	[B.10] *Constat enim tribus de causis mutationem fieri oportere. Primo ut supra et infra unumquodque exachordum voces ipsae modulato transitu possint in acutum intendi atque remitti in gravitatem. Secundo: ad concipiendum suavioris modulationis transitum. [f.aviĳv-] plerumque enim non minus melitum et suavem cantum reddit variata vocum qualitas: quam permutata quantitas modulati soni. Solet quandoque b mollis qualitas in locum ♮ quadrae deducta (quod Ambrosiani saepius observant) modulationem reddere suaviorem. Tertio ad faciliorem consonantium figurarum scilicet diatessaron ac diapentes transitum in tonorum permixtione dispositum.*
	It is agreed that a mutation should be made for three reasons: first, that notes in a melody can move up or down beyond one hexachord. Second, to aid a smoother melodic transition when the soft ♭ quality is sung in place of square ♮ (a practice frequent among Ambrosians), for a changed quality of sound generally produces a no less pleasant and

smooth melody than a quantitative change through permutation. Third, to facilitate a leap of consonant intervals, namely, fourths and fifths which occur in different hexachords.

[A.11] *In reliquis autem ijsdem motibus procedunt mutationes quibus et in predictis suis similibus monstratum est: quas cantis cantoribus examinandas perquirendasque relinquimus. C. Fit in super disiunctive mutacio unius proprietatis in alteram quando ascendimus vel descendimus in octavam vocem vel in alteram disiunctam per eam transgressionem qua nulla vox in alteram unisonam potest recte transmutari et dicitur disiunctio vel transgressio quod se plus evenit in cantibus figuratis.*

[The mutations on the remaining pitches follow the same methods shown above, and I leave it to the singers to analyze them in the songs. Finally I wish to mention the disjunct mutation from one propriety to another when we ascend or descend by an octave or to another similarly disjunct syllable by transference, because no syllable may be mutated into another on a unison. This technique is called disjunction or transference and is more frequently used in mensural music.]

[B.11] *Nec non et in caeteris consimiles mutationum motus concernentibus: singula scilicet singulis consimilibus referendo. Mutationum Insuper pluralitatem afferunt fugiendam: quum modulationis progressum unica mutatione constiterit esse congrue dispositum. Ac tardius longiusque quo ad fieri possit mutationem prosequendam esse ferunt. Evenit quandoque disiunctus mutationis transgressus: quum modulando fit transitus ultra ordinem exachordi: puta ascendendo vel descendendo per septem aut octo voces vel etiam per plures: quod in mensuratis cantilenis frequentius obseruatur. Possent item et per coniunctas complures fieri mutationes si tonorum interuallis disponerentur syllabae exachordorum tonos ipsos in duo inaequalia partientes semitonia. At cum vel chromatico vel permixto generi id sane competat: praesens haec cura refellit: diatonicam tantum Guidonis referens Institutionem.*

[Similar mutational movements apply to the other pitches. To discerning musicians they can be understood by comparing individual mutations to the ones to which they are similar. Further, they say that a plurality of mutations has to be avoided when one comes to the conclusion that the melodic progression has been suitably arranged in a single mutation. It is said too that mutation ought to be as rarely and as late as possible. Occasionally a disjunct mutation occurs in singing when a progression takes place beyond the range of a hexachord, ascending or descending – for example, through seven, eight, or even more pitches. This is more frequently encountered in mensural composition. Many mutations could be executed through conjunctions if the syllables of the hexachords were arranged in whole-tone intervals and these intervals were divided into unequal semitones. But since this coincides very closely with the chromatic or mixed genus, the present discussion, concerned only with the Guidonian diatonic system, rejects it.]

seu melius dixero inter ♮ durã & b mollem mediã collocauit quasi ipsa naturæ pro‑
prietas suauior secundum scilicet chromaticum genus sit disposita : Asperior autẽ ♮
quadræ in diatonico : Longeœ̃ suauior b mollis in Enarmonico deductę sint. Nam
vnũquodœ̃ exachordũ siue ♮ duræ qualitatis : siue naturalis : siue etiam b mollaris :
secundum diatonicum genus noscitur esse dimensum : hinc potius mihi ipsi persua‑
deo ipsam naturæ qualitatem quartæ chordæ inscriptam esse q̃ prioris ac grauioris
hypaton tetrachordi diatonici scilicet ac naturalis generis : potissimũ diastema cõ‑
tineret . b mollem vero q̃ primum sui ipsius tetrachordum ad coniunctam videli‑
cet tritessinemenon chordam perficiens : tritoniæam b fa positione mollificet as‑
peritatem . Ac ♮ durain e conuerso per disiunctam tonum ipsum inter Mesen &
Paramesen per ♮ mi reddat asperiorem Quod si hanc chordam medium chordo‑
toni terminum instituero : primus varistrorsum ductus circinus : grauiori sibi ipsi
consimili atœ̃ æquisonæ scilicet ♮ mi per diapason dupla mutuabit habitudi‑
ne : qua re : cum mi ipsa sit tertia exachordi ipsius chorda ac tertium obtineat In‑
troductorij locum : in prima & grauissima chorda scilicet Γ vt exordium propriæ
qualitatis suscipiat necesse est . At quibus proprietatibus qualitatibus ue syllabę
omnes vocales ascribuntur : his tribus figuris facile percipitur .

La in e	La in a	La in d
sol in d	sol in g	sol in c
Ois fa in c cantatur	.Ois fa in f cantatur	.Ois fa in b cantatur.
mi in ♮ p ♮ q̃drã.	mi in e p naturã.	mi in a p b mollé.
re in a	re in d	re in g
vt in g	vt in c	vt in f

Mutatio qd.
Baccheus .
Gregorius .

Multimodas insuper sonorum mutationes clerici protestantur . Est enim Mu‑
tatio apud Bacchcum Alteratio subiectorum seu Alicuius similis in dissimilem lo‑
cum trãspositio .   Hinc in moralibus Mutari Gregorius inquit est ex alio in aliud
ire & in semetipsum stabilem non esse : vnaquæœ̃ enim res quasi tot passibus ad
aliam tendit : quot mutabilitatis suæ motibus subiacet . Verum huiusmodi muta‑

Martianus .
Briennius .

tionem Martianus transitum appellat : quem vocis variationem in alteram soni fi‑
guram interpretatur .   Briennius autem mutationem dixit esse subiecti systema‑
tis ac vocis characteris aliena ionem . Fit autem Mutatio secundum genus quũ
scilicet in tetrachordo diatonico lychanos vel etiam parantes chorda remittitur
semitonio in graue : transeundo in chromaticam figuram : vel tono transeundo

Boetius .
Aristoteles .

in enarmonicam : quæ nusœ̃ accidit ex grauitate in acumen variari vt Boetius no‑
ster in quarto explicuit . Id quoœ̃ & Aristoteles ipse in musicis problematibus

Fig. 7.2. Gafori's *auctoritates* on the subject of *mutatio* (Gafori, *Practica musicae*,
fol. aviv‑avijr).

The scholarly *excursus* at the beginning of the section on mutation is a fit‑
ting introduction to the discussion that follows, in which Gafori reconcep‑
tualizes hexachordal mutations from a merely technical or operative shift
into a meaningful musical event, in the process turning a systemic liability
into a compositional asset. This strategy becomes apparent in another inter‑
polated *excursus* dedicated to explaining the *raison d'être* of hexachordal
mutations (B.10):

Constat enim tribus de causis mutationem fieri oportere. Primo ut supra et infra
unumquodque exachordum voces ipsae modulato transitu possint in acutum

intelligi voluit quū diceret Quod ſapit naturam acuti plerūꝗ pertrāſit in grauem:
quod autem ſapit naturam grauis non permutatur in acutum.   Eſt & alia muta‑
tionis conſyderatio in voce ac ſono: nam quum ſunt in motu & fiunt tantum voces
et ſoni ipſi de genere credūt entium ſucceſſiuorum vt vigeſſimo ſeptimo problema‑   Petrus appo‑
te interpres expoſuit: qua re vocis ipſius ac ſoni generatio conſiſtit in quodā fieri   nenſis.
& tranſmutari.   Verum huiuſmodi introductio definitā a Marcheto conſequitur   Marchetus.
mutationem. Is enim inquit: Mutatio eſt variatio nominis vocis in alterū in eodem
ſono. Syllabæ enim ipſæ vocibus & chordis ſuis.ſ.notulis aſcriptæ ſi in vna eadéꝗ
linea vel eodem ſpatio conſiſtunt: dicuntur quantitate pares ſed qualitate ſeu pro‑
prietate diuerſæ. Inde quum mutatio fit qualitas vnius exachordi in alterius qua‑
litatem tranſfertur ſtante eadem vocis quantitate: vt teſtatur Anſelmus tertio ſuæ   Anſelmus.
muſicæ. hinc mutationem voco alternam vocis in vocem delationem vniformi ex‑
tenſione depræhenſam. Voces autem ipſas exachordorum ſyllabas intelligo. Nō
igitur vox mutatur in vocem per intenſionem aut remiſſionem ſed ſyllaba in ſilabā
& proprietas ſeu qualitas in qualitatem. Quo fit vt quum ſyllabas tantum modu‑
lato tranſitu exprimimus ipſa quadret mutatio. Litterarij autem charactercs in in‑
troductorio obſeruati neꝗ proferunt neꝗ mutantur. Syllaba item quæ vel linea
vel ſpacium ſola occupat mutationi non congruit. Qua re in Γvt: In Are: In
♮ mi: & In Ela: nuſquam fit mutatio: ꝗ quum fieri neceſſitate contingeret: exa‑
chordorum conglutinatorum priſtinum ordinem iterabis.   In C faut duæ al‑
ternatim eueniunt mutationes: prima mutando præ‑
cedentem ſyllabam in ſequentem ſcilicet fa in vt di‑
citurꝗ aſcendens mutatio ex ♮ quadra in naturam. vt
harum exponit natularum deſcriptio.

Secunda mutatio ſit quum modulando mu‑
tamus ſequentem ſyllabam in præcedétem ſci‑
licet vt in fa: quæ quidem dicitur deſcendens
ex natura in ♮ quadram vt hic patet.

Conſtat.n. tribus de cauſis mutationem fieri oportere.   Primo vt ſupra & infra
vnūquodꝗ exachordum voces ipſæ modulato tranſitu poſſint in acutum intēdi atꝗ
remitti in grauitatem.   Secundo: ad cōcipiendum ſuauioris modulationis tran‑

Fig. 7.2. (*cont.*)

intendi atque remitti in gravitatem. Secundo ad concipiendum suavioris modulationis transitum. Plerumque enim non minus melitum et suavem cantum reddit
variata vocum qualitas quam permutata quantitas modulati soni solet quandoque
b mollis qualitas in locum [bequadro] quadrae deducta (quod Ambrosiani saepius
observant) modulationem reddere suaviorem. Tertio ad faciliorem consonantium
figurarum scilicet diatessaron ac diapentes transitum in tonorum permixtione
dispositum.

[It is agreed that a mutation should be made for three reasons: first, that notes in
a melody can move up or down beyond one hexachord. Second, to aid a smoother
melodic transition when the soft [round b] quality is sung in place of square
[bequadro] (a practice frequent among Ambrosians), for a changed quality of
sound generally produces a no less pleasant and smooth melody than a quantitative

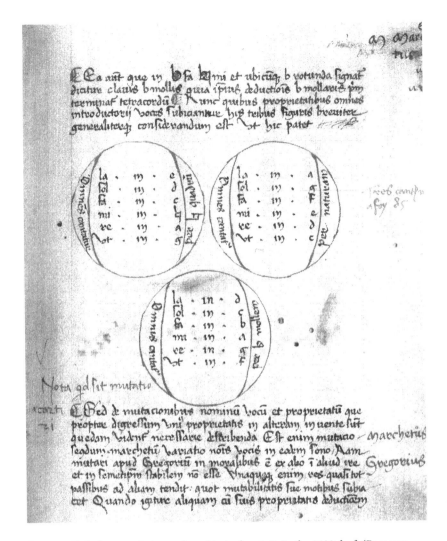

Fig. 7.3. Gafori's *auctoritates* on the subject of *mutatio* in the 1483 draft (Bergamo, Biblioteca Civica "Angelo Mai", MS MAB 21, fol. 6r).

change through permutation. Third, to facilitate a leap of consonant intervals, namely, fourths and fifths which occur in different hexachords.][11]

In this passage, which is significantly absent from the Bergamo draft, Gafori portrays hexachordal mutations as the carrier of structural and aesthetic

---

[11] Gafori, *Practica musicae*, fol. avijr-avijv; Miller, trans., *Franchinus Gaffurius*, p. 37. In the last sentence, Gafori points to fourths and fifths in relation to the modes (*permixtione tonorum*) rather than to hexachords, as suggested by Miller's translation. See Irving Young's rendition of this passage in I. Young, ed. and trans., *The* Practica musicae *of Franchino Gafurius*, (Madison, WI: University of Wisconsin Press, 1969) p. 31.

implications, that is to say, as musically meaningful events that somehow contribute to the *varietas* and *suavitas* of a composition. In a subtle way, Gafori is proposing the thesis that mutations, far from being a cumbersome aspect of Guidonian solmization, belong to the fundamentals of musical composition as much as to those of singing.[12]

The final paragraph of the chapter completes the subtle transformation of mutation from a merely operative shift performed by the singer to a meaningful event objectively present in the musical part. In the Bergamo draft Gafori – almost quoting Tinctoris word by word – had stated that mutations should be kept to a minimum (A.11).[13] The point of this wide-spread recommendation was to avoid unnecessary complications while sight singing: as the Guidonian system of solmization is the more useful, the more singers are able to mentally group as many notated intervals as possible within the same *deductio*. The unstated conclusion here seems to be that to perform unnecessary mutations would complicate the task of sight singing, but it would not necessarily result in an inaccurate perform-ance of a part.

However, in the printed version of the *Practica*, shown at B.11, Gafori introduces a substantial variant to this passage by claiming that "a plural-ity of mutations has to be avoided when one comes to the conclusion that the melodic progression has been suitably arranged in a single mutation" (*Mutationum insuper pluralitatem afferunt fugiendam: quum modulationis progressum unica mutatione constiterit esse congrue dispositum*). Such reason-ing begs the question of why would a singer choose to perform more muta-tions than necessary anyway, if the only mutation(s) that he ought to consider were easily identified and objectively present in the notation? *Pace* Gafori, the language of medieval and Renaissance music theory overwhelmingly

---

[12] Gafori's brief (and completely irrelevant) foray into the classical and philosophic uses of the term "mutatio" also serves the purpose of raising the intellectual profile of Guido's method. See also Moyer, *Musica scientia*, p. 75.

[13] "Unde postquam aliquam proprietatem ingressi sumus, ante finalem eius vocem mutare numquam debemus; et sic intelligitur quod rarius ac tardius ut fieri potest mutandum est.Denique mutatio cuiuslibet vocis non est soni sed nominis ipsius. Unde quando solfisamus, tantum mutamus quia tunc voces nominatim exprimimus, namque solfisatio est canendo vocum per sua nomina expressio," ("Hence, after we have entered one particular property, we must never mutate before its last available pitch name; and so we understand by this that mutation should occur as rarely and as late as possible. Again, mutation on any note does not alter its sound, but only its name. Hence, when we solmize, we mutate only because at that particular time we are performing the notes by name, for solmization is indeed the sung performance of notes by means of their names"), from J. Tinctoris, *Expositio manus*, in *The Theoretical Works of Johannes Tinctoris: a new online edition*, ed. R. Woodley (URL: www.stoa. org/tinctoris/tinctoris.html), lines 443–8.

presents mutation as something *made by* the singers, not *fitted in* by composers, as we saw in Chapter 4.[14] The juxtaposition of the six syllables over the seven letters was to some extent arbitrary, even though it could be performed more or less effectively.

In sum: it would not be an exaggeration to claim that Gafori's revisions of the chapter on *proprietas* and *mutatio* quietly revolutionized the medieval understanding of those concepts. But Gafori's strategic defense of Guidonian theory relies on additional rhetorical weapons, as we will now see.

Guido and the Greeks

Modern scholars have pointed out that the opening chapter of *Theorica musicae*, "De musicis et effectibus atque comendatione musice discipline," is a much expanded version of the first chapter of *Theoricum opus*. As Leofranc Holford-Strevens has recently pointed out, many of the numerous new references to classical authors that populate Gafori's *Laus musice* of 1492 were most likely taken from Francesco Filelfo's *Convivia mediolanensia* (Milan, 1483–1484).[15] The inclusion of Christian authors at the end of this classicizing chapter, however, appears neither in Filelfo's *Convivia*, nor in *Theoricum opus*, and may be regarded as an attempt to establish a firm line of continuity between the *antiqui* and the *moderni*. Gafori's account of the elements of musical pitch and rhythmic notation in his *Practica musicae* (book 1, chapters 1–15) points to Guido as the decisive figure in the history of the evolution of musical thought from classical antiquity to the present, a father figure whose hexachordal restructuring of the gamut was the culmination of centuries of speculations on musical pitch. Book 1, chapter 1 opens with a reminder of the many merits of musical practice. Orpheus, Amphion, Linus of Thebes, and Timotheus achieved ever-lasting fame not only by mastering the theory of music, but also through their extraordinary performing skills, by which they charmed stones, forests, monsters, and rustic spirits.[16] On the subject of the educational benefits of the practice of music for the youth had waxed eloquent scores of Greek philosophers,

[14] I also discuss this point in my "Virtual Segments," 456–7.
[15] L. Holford-Strevens, "The *Laudes musicae* in Renaissance Music Treatises," paper presented at the 2005 Annual Meeting of the American Musicological Society in Washington, D.C (forthcoming).
[16] Most likely, this section of Gafori's treatise is also mediated from Ramos de Pareja, who mentions the same mythological figures and the miraculous effects of their performances in the "Prologue" to his *Musica practica* (Ramis de Pareja, *Musica practica*, p. 2). Such references, however, were relatively common in the humanist era.

as well as Cicero himself. Furthermore, theoretical precepts are generally worthless unless they are experienced and appreciated through practical applications.

Gafori then lists four loosely defined categories of "sounding voices": the speeches of the rhetoricians, who modulate their voices yet do not sing (this category include the singers of plainchant, which Gafori conceives as a "sonorous reading"); the declamation of poetry according to its metrical organization; polyphony sung by professional singers; plays and pantomimes, that is, music produced by bodily gestures. After describing these four categories, Gafori writes:

Constat itaque Guidonem Aretinum ipsius frugiferae musicae introductorium descripsisse septem litteris: atque sex syllabis chordas omnes denominantibus ad instar quindecim chordarum naturalis et perfecti diatonici systematis perornatum. Confert quidem plurimum humanae vocis actioni lyrae aut cytharae vel monochordi percussas concordes chordulas immitari: quarum alias graues: alias acutas: reliquas Graeci medias dicebant. [Graeci in marg.] Verum ecclesiastici nostri Guidonis huiusmodi traditionem quam manum vocant: in graue: acutum [-f.aijr-] et superacutum distingunt: ut viginti ac duarum chordularum lineis et interuallis seu spacijs alternatim inscriptarum: connumeratis scilicet ipsius sinemenon tetrachordi causa et immitatione duabus coniunctis.

[And so it is well known that Guido of Arezzo inscribed the *Introductorium* of his productive book on music with seven letters, and by assigning six syllables to the strings he applied them consistently to the natural and perfect diatonic system of fifteen strings … The Greeks called the strings high, low, and median. But our ecclesiastics teach the tradition of Guido through the Guidonian Hand. They distinguish between low, high, and highest, so that twenty-two pitches are placed on alternate lines and spaces; two of the pitches are considered as connected for the sake of the *synemmenon* tetrachord.][17]

The very idea of a *hexachordum synemmenon* is illogical: in Greek music theory, each tetrachord from *meson* to *hyperbolaion* was truly conjunct to the immediately lower one within the Greater Perfect System. Guido's adjacent hexachords, on the other hand, were neither conjunct nor disjunct, but rather overlapping with each other to a variable degree.

Gafori's adoption of the notion of *hexachordum synemmenon*, then, calls for an explanation. We may observe, as a start, that Gafori's account of the hexachordal system in the 1496 *Practica* posits Guido as a key link between the music of antiquity and Gafori's age. The momentous transfer of the baton from *tetrachordum* to *hexachordum* as the organizing range of the diatonic space implicitly ascribes a distinct aura to the engineer of that transfer:

[17] Gafori, *Practica musicae*, fol. aiv-aijr; Miller, trans. *Franchinus Gaffurius*, p. 23.

Atque icciro singula in systemate perfecto diatonice ac naturaliter disposita semitonia duabus ipsis syllabis mi et fa intercidere pernoscuntur: tanta fuit ad com-
mixtotum septem exachordorum dispositionem ipsius Guidonis animadversio.
Namque uniuscuiusque exachordi principium vel primo praecedentis exachordi
tetrachordo coniunxit: vel ipsum ab eo toni disiunctum instituit interuallo. Qua
ex re in eptachordo: duorum exachordorum prima comprobantur tetrachorda. At
ubi primum secundi exachordi tetrachordum terminatur: tertium exachordum b
molle dictum: quod et coniunctum dici potest: summit exordium superductum
quidem: ut et trittoni asperitas fiat in modulatione suavior: et nonnullorum tonorum compositio possit per variatas consonantiarum species commixte atque item
acquisite procedere. Quartum vero exachordum a primo secundi exachordi tetrachordo toni interuallo disiungitur in acutum. Quintum autem exachordum primo
quarti exachordi coniungitur tetrachordo. Verum primo quinti huius exachordi
tetrachordo sextum connexum est exachordum. Quod sinemenon seu coniunctum
potest appellari. Septimum exachordum a primo quinti exachordi tetrachordo toni
distantia disiungitur in acutum.

[Thus each semitone arranged diatonically and naturally in the perfect system is
correctly understood to fall between the two syllables *mi* and *fa*. This was Guido's
observation in his arrangement of seven overlapping hexachords. Thus the first
note of a hexachord is either conjunct with the first note of the tetrachord within
a preceding hexachord or it is disjunct by a whole tone. Therefore the first two tetrachords of the first two hexachords make a heptachord. But the first tetrachord of
the second hexachord ends where the soft and conjunct third hexachord begins, so
that the sharpness of the tritone in a melody may be softened and its tonal succes-
sion may proceed through acquired consonances. The fourth hexachord begins a
whole tone above the first tetrachord of the second hexachord. The fifth hexachord
is conjunct with the first tetrachord of the fourth hexachord. The sixth hexachord,
which can be called *synemmenon* or conjoined, is conjunct with the first tetrachord
of the fifth hexachord. The seventh hexachord is a whole tone higher than the first
tetrachord of the fifth hexachord.][18]

Such an account of the gamut is unquestionably based on the excerpt from
Ramos' treatise cited above (see p. 184), as neither Burtius, nor Hothby
explored the notion of *hexachordum* to this level. There is no way of telling
whether Gafori saw this passage as a legitimate interpretation of Guido's
theories or not. But the fact that for the printed version of the treatise
he chose this wording over the traditional one suggests that he found it
preferable – regardless of considerations of accuracy – perhaps because
it provided an attractive narrative for defending hexachordal solmization
against its critics. For if *hexachordum* could be convincingly portrayed as

---

[18] Gafori, *Practica musicae*, fol. aiijr-aiijv; Miller, trans., *Franchinus Gaffurius*, pp. 25–6.

the natural outgrowth of the venerable *tetrachordum* of the Greeks, then who was to deny the basic soundness and even historical necessity of hexachordal solmization? If this was indeed Gafori's reasoning, then the fact that he modeled his printed account of solmization theory after Ramos highlights not only Gafori's impressive rhetorical subtlety, but (most of all) the extent to which Ramos shot himself in the foot with his new-fangled theory of *hexachordum*.[19]

Herein lies the key to appreciating the peculiar mode of presentation of Guido's system permeating Gafori's exposition of the Guidonian system and the modes of the printed version of *Practica musicae*. By developing Ramos' idea of the six syllables as a *hexachordum*, Gafori was able to portray the method of solmization not only as the expression of a fundamental mode of articulation of the gamut, but also as naturally linked to classical music theory. Guido's *hexachordum*, in the end, would emerge from the pages of the *Practica* as nothing less than the inspired contribution of the Christian era to the discipline of music, the symbol of a modern ecclesiastical musical culture that was both directly connected with the classical tradition and superior to it. This thesis emerges with remarkable consistency throughout book 1 of the *Practica*, if only between its beautifully printed lines.

In chapter 2, for example, the Greeks are again invoked to provide a prestigious historical background to Guido's contribution:

Septem tantum essentiales chordas septenis litteris a Gregorio descriptas sexto eneidos hoc carmine Maronis auctoritas celebravit. Necnon thraytius longa cum veste sacerdos Obloquitur numeris septem discrimina vocum. Inde et introductorium ipsum Guido septem commixtis perfecit exachordis. [E]xachordum enim est compraehensio sex chordarum diatonica dimensione dispositarum. Quarum nomina sunt: ut re mi fa sol la. Sunt enim ut re graves dum graecis assentior sol la acutae: et mi fa mediae. Ecclesiasticorum vero mos est: ut re graves vocare: mi fa acutas: et sol la superacutas. Has quidem Guido ipse ita disposuit: ut singula perfecti ac diatonici systematis intervalla duabus tantum huiusmodi syllabis deffiniret. Namque inter ut et re sesquioctava dimensione toni clauditur intervallum.

[Seven essential pitches with their seven letters described by Gregory have been celebrated in verse by the authoritative Maro in book 6 of the Aeneid: "There, too, the long-robed Thracian priest [Orpheus] matches their measures with the seven clear notes." Thus Guido completed his *Introductorium* with seven overlapping

---

[19] Of course, that Gafori would borrow ideas from Ramos is not at all surprising: as James Haar showed thirty years ago, the famous frontispiece of *Practica musicae*, showing the correspondences between the diatonic modes, the planets, and the Muses, was also modeled after a similar table in Ramos' *Musica practica* (Haar, "The frontispiece of Gafori's *Practica musicae*," 14).

hexachords, for a hexachord is an aggregation of six pitches arranged in a diatonic order, whose names are *ut, re, mi, fa, sol, la*. *Ut, re* are low sounds, and I agree with the Greeks that *sol, la* are high and *mi, fa* are median. But it is the custom of ecclesiastics to call *ut, re* low, *mi, fa* high, and *sol, la* the highest. Guido has arranged these syllables so that each interval of the diatonic perfect system is defined by only two such syllables. So between *ut* and *re* in a nine to eight ratio, the interval of a whole tone is enclosed.[20]

Gafori's bizarre suggestion that the Greeks had used four of Guido's six syllables comes from a passage in Ugolino of Orvieto's *Declaratio* that Ramos himself had already criticized as "laughable and ridiculous."[21] The argument sounded far-fetched to at least another prominent reader, the Bolognese composer, theorist, and *maestro di canto* Johannes Spataro, who had once studied with Ramos. In his famous *Errori di Franchino Gafori da Lodi*, published in 1521, Spataro exposed the argument as one of the many "dreams" that populate Gafori's treatises.[22]

Along the same line, Gafori now refers to Virgil's *septem discrimina vocum* no longer to question the rationale behind the six-syllables solmization system (as he had done in the earlier draft; see Table 7.1, section A.4), but rather as a way of justifying Guido's articulation of the gamut into seven hexachords. There is of course no direct connection between

[20] Gafori, *Practica musicae*, fol. aiijr; Miller, trans., *Franchinus Gaffurius*, p. 25.

[21] See Ugolino of Orvieto, *Declaratio musicae disciplinae*, ed. A. Seay, *CSM* 7 (N.p.: American Institute of Musicology, 1959), vol. I, chapter 6 ("De Graecae manus vocibus ordinatis"), p. 26. The passage concludes with the sentence: "Ex his apparet musicos Graecos philosophos has tantum quinque voces invenisse, scilicet, re, mi, fa, sol, la et eas quater in manu sua replicasse, quae secundum supradictam rationem XX numero esse dicuntur" ("it is apparent that the Greek musical philosophers knew only these five syllables, namely re, mi, fa, sol, la, which they replicated four times on the hand for a total of twenty notes, as we have shown above"). Gafori copied this passage in his early treatise *Extractus parvus musice* (Parma, Biblioteca Palatina, MS 1158, fol. 6v; ed. F. Alberto Gallo [Bologna, 1969], p. 43). For Ramos' comment on Ugolino's excerpt, see Miller, ed. and trans., *Bartolomeo Ramis de Pareia: Musica practica*, p. 95.

[22] In his *Errori di Franchino Gaffurio da Lodi* (1521), Spataro quotes Gafori's "*Sunt enim*" sentence word by word, then adds the following comment: "Io te ho scripto the hai pleni li tractati toi de sogni, perchè se le predicte sei chorde [ut re mi fa sol la] son state invente da Guido monacho, el quale fu multi anni dopo la greca introductione, el non potrà essere vero che da li greci tale sei predicte chorde siano state considerate et exercitate per tale modo come tu dici" ("I have told you in writing that your treatises are full of dreams, because if the six strings were invented by Guido of Arezzo, who lived many years after the Greek gamut, it cannot be true that the Greeks knew and used those six strings in the way that you are suggesting," p. 4). Spataro, a former student of Ramos de Pareja who had previously been involved in a controversy with Nicolaus Burtius, also dealt with solmization in a series of letters that he exchanged with his friends Pietro Aaron and Giovanni del Lago. They are edited and translated in Blackburn, Lowinsky, and Miller, eds. and trans., *A Correspondence of Renaissance Musicians*.

the seven primary letters of *musica recta* and the number of hexachords that can be superimposed onto them, a number that indeed allowed some flexibility.[23] Only four years earlier, Gafori in his *Theorica* (book 5, chapter 1) had cited not only the *Aeneid*, but also a similar verse from Virgil's *Eclogue* to make the case for the primacy of the seven letters.[24] The *Theorica* is also reminiscent of the Bergamo draft in that immediately after the references to Vergil it cites the harmony of the seven planets as a significant numerical correspondence with the series of notes in the scale.[25] The subtle recontextualization of the *Aeneid* citation in the *Practica* is an index of Gafori's methodical and highly sophisticated recasting of solmization theory.

Gafori's argument that the Guidonian syllables define the individual intervals (*Has [syllabas] quidem Guido ipse ita disposuit: ut singula perfecti ac diatonici systematis intervalla duabus tantum huiusmodi syllabis deffiniret*) is also questionable, although it can also be found on occasion, in a rather oblique form, in medieval music theory.[26] Guido – and later Guidonian theory – did not lay out the syllables in such a way as to obtain the intervals (if so, no musical interval could have existed before the eleventh century!). To the contrary, the Guidonian system found its *raison d'être* and acquired its particular shape in the pre-existing scaffolding of the octave-based Greater Perfect System, as modified by medieval chant theory.

Once again, Giovanni Spataro objected to Gafori's strong characterization of the syllables by unequivocally emphasizing their dependency on the seven letters:

Pare a te che lo introductorio del mio preceptore sia tanto obscuro essendo el semitonio in esso introductorio pronunziato per dissimile denominatione. Certamente nui abbiamo che Sancto Gregorio constituì e ordinò lo Antiphonario e altri libri musici tutti exemplati per septe littere, nel processo de le quale alcuna volta el semitonio cadeva tra B e C e tra E e F aliquando tra a e b per la quale cosa appare che el pronuntiare del semitonio (per dissimile denominatione in Musica) è de nulla

---

[23] Some medieval sources, such as book 1 by the Berkeley Anonymous, allow an additional hexachord to begin on F below gamma-ut for the sake of including a B-fa among the *graves*. See Ellsworth, ed. and trans., *The Berkeley Manuscript*, pp. 34–5.

[24] Gafori, *Theorica musice*, eds. and trans. I. Illuminati and C. Ruini, fol. hir; Kreuszia, ed. and trans. *Franchino Gaffurio*, pp. 144–51. In Kreyszig's translation, the citation from the *Aeneid* occurs in clauses 14–15, pp. 144–5; the verse from *Eclogues*, 2: vv. 36–37, in clauses 40–2, which translate as: "Therefore, only these seven tones are different and dissimilar, as elsewhere Virgil expresses it, 'a pipe, fitted together from seven stalks of hemlock'" (p. 146).

[25] Gafori, *Theorica musice*, eds. and trans. I. Illuminati and C. Ruini, fol. hir; Kreuszia, ed. and trans. *Franchino Gaffurio*, clauses 16–17, p. 145.

[26] I discuss this point in my "Virtual Segments," 459–60.

importantia. La quale varia denominatione più è stata laudata da Guido monaco che non fa la inventione de la simile denominatione constituta tra Mi e Fa e Fa e Mi da lui inventa, come esso Guido demonstra in quilli versi li quali dicono in questo modo scilicet: 'Solis notare litteris optimus probavimus'.

[You are of the opinion that the diatonic system proposed by my teacher [Ramos de Pareja] is very complicated because it labels each semitone with different syllables [in Ramos' solmization system, the semitones correspond to the syllabic pairs *tur per* and *is tas*]. But surely we know that Saint Gregory commissioned and compiled his antiphonary and other music books using the system of seven letters, so that the semitone at times fell between B and C, at times between E and F, and other times yet between a and b flat. This shows that the actual pronunciation of the semitone by means of different names is completely irrelevant. In fact, even Guido favored the different labeling of the semitone over his own suggestion of using identical labels throughout (either Mi Fa or Fa Mi), as he indicated in the following verse: 'We have proved that music is best notated with the letters only'.][27]

By the same token, Gafori's subdivision of the notes of the hexachord into *graves*, *acutae*, and *superacutae* – *pace* the spurious recalling of Greek theory – is nonsensical: a simple look at Gafori's gamut, as well as a rudimentary knowledge of the practice of hexachordal solmization, demonstrates that in the Guidonian system the syllables *ut* and *re* will often correspond with pitches that are *higher*, not *lower*, than other pitches corresponding with *sol* and *la*, as Conrad of Zabern pointed out (see pp. 138–9). As a matter of fact, there is no evidence that musicians and theorists up to Gafori's time ever mentioned, let alone accepted, this classification of the syllables.

In the 1496 *Practica*, the citation linking the seven hexachords to the seven letters and to the ancient Greeks appears on the recto of fol. aiij. On the verso of the previous folio, Gafori inserts a gamut showing not only the series of diatonic *claves* and seven *deductiones*, but also the Greek pitch terminology on the right and the numerical values associated with each "string," showing the proportions regulating the musical intervals, mediated from Boethius (see Fig. 7.4). This particular representation of the gamut is a conflation of speculative and practical layers that were traditionally kept distinct. Gafori's own *Theorica musicae* shows the Boethian/Pythagorean scale, with the Greek names and the numerical values, and in a separate place the "Guidonian" gamut showing only the letters from gamma to high e' and the

---

[27] Spataro, *Errori di Franchino Gaffurio da Lodi*, Quinta Pars, Error 20, f. 31v-32, translation mine. Spataro also discussed the role of the Guidonian syllables in imitative counterpoint in an epistolary exchange with Venetian theorist Giovanni del Lago. See my "*Si quis manus non habeat*," 210–6.

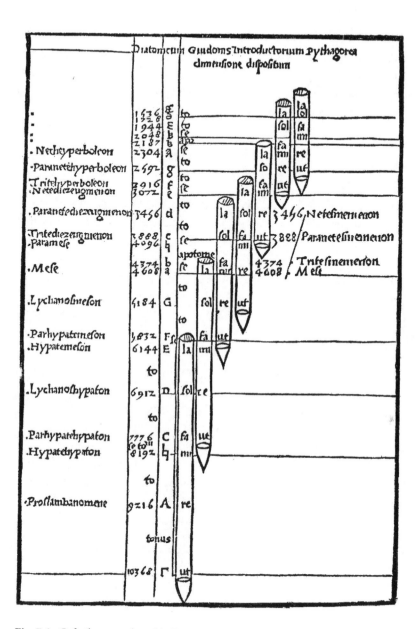

Fig. 7.4. Gafori's gamut from his *Practica musicae*, fol. aijv.

seven *deductiones*.[28] The table of the diatonic system of the *Practica* carries the title "Diatonicum Guidonis Introductorium Pythagorea dimensione dispositum"). Given the particular context in which it appears, this caption may

---

[28] In the *Theorica*, a figure showing the series of Greek pitch names and their intervallic distances is in book 5, chapter 3; the Guidonian *scala* is in book 5, chapter 6. See Gafori, *Theorica*

be intended as yet another attempt on Gafori's side to dress the ecclesiastical musical curriculum of his time in classical garb. But the graph seems also designed to add musical weight to the seven *deductiones* by depicting them, quite ingeniously, as organ pipes – yet another sign of the treatise's contribution to the subtle metamorphosis of the six syllables into a six-note scale.

Modal theory

The classicizing rhetoric adopted by Gafori in the early pages of *Practica musicae* also pervades the discussion of modal theory that occupies the second half of book 1. Although previous studies have offered an extensive treatment of this portion of the *Practica*, it is important to revisit it here in the context of both the unusual account of solmization of the earlier chapters of the treatise and the modal theory of the Bergamo draft. My intention is to demonstrate that the modal theory of the *Practica* further develops the historiographic theme that he meticulously sets up in his treatment of solmization.

Prior to the 1496 *Practica*, Gafori's account of the modes conformed to what Bernhard Meier called the "Western ecclesiastical" tradition of modal theory in its late-medieval stage – that is to say, as reshaped by Marchetto of Padua in his widely influential *Lucidarium* (ca. 1317). According to this theory, the main modal markers of the eight modes were the diatonic species and the four finals. The practical destination of the theory explains the fact that it made only rare references to Boethius and Greek modal terminology. The following excerpt, from Gafori's Bergamo draft, illustrates these points:

Has et enim dyapason species philosophi modos dixerunt a modulatione tractos, quorum nomina et proprietates ultimo prime partis capitulo octavo congrue apperuimus. Posteri insuper has septem dyapason species quattuor maneriebus [recte: maneries] subiugarunt, quarum primam prothus appellabant. Secundam deuterum, Tertiam tritum, Quartam Tetrardus. Hec et enim maneries terminos cantibus constituebant ultra quos nulla intensione uel remissione possent extendi. Hin[c] constituciones dicte sunt quare dyapason ac dyatexaron unaqueque comprehendebat. Est namque huiusmodi constitutio apud Boetium plenum modulationis corpus ex consonantiarum coniunctione consistens. C. Prima enim maneries ab

musicae, fols. hvir and kiv; Kreuszia, ed. and trans., *Franchino Gaffurio*, pp. 158–9 and 178.
Nowhere in the *Theorica* does Gafori discuss the Boethian numerical values that appear in the gamut of the *Practica*.

Are ad Dlasolre procedebat, scilicet per dyatessaron et dyapason et terminabitur in dsolre ubi dyatexaron et dyapason giunguntur. C. Secunda maneries extendebatur a [sqb] mi gravi ad Elami acutam et terminabatur in Elami gravem. C. Tertia maneries residebat inter C fa ut et F fa ut acutam et terminabatur in F fa ut gravem. C. Quarta constitutio seu maneries procedebat a d sol re ad G sol re ut acutam et terminabatur in G sol re ut gravem. Omnis namque planus cantus his quattuor regulis seu maner-iebus regebatur et terminabatur ut dictum est ad quartam vocem gravitati deputatam ubi Sinaphe dyatessaron et dyapason coniungebat ita ut unusquisque cantus planus per dyapason a fine suo elevaretur et per dyatexaron sub fine deprimetur […] Has preterea octo maneries posteri tonos nuncuparunt, quia ex tonis et tonorum parti-bus videlicet semitonis componuntur. Eorum namque impares dicti sunt autentici quasi superiores nam ascendunt dyatexaron supra dyapenten. Pares vero dicti sunt plagales quasi inferiors: nam descendunt dyatexaron sub dyapente. C. Tonus igitur huiusmodi secundum Guidonem est regula que per ascensum et descensum omnes cantus in fine diudicat. Sed e singulis seriatim procedendum est.

[The philosophers called "modes" these species of the diapason, from the term "modulation." Their names and structural properties I have elucidated in the eighth chapter of the first part. Later authors established four different *manerie* over the seven octave species, the first of which they called *protus*, the second *deuterus*, the third *tritus*, and the fourth *tetrardus*. And these *maneries* provided the boundaries beyond which no chant could be extended either in the upper or in the lower range. They are labeled "constitutions" because each one of them comprised an octave and a fourth. Indeed, Boethius defines a "constitutio" as the full range of modulation, consisting of a conjunction of consonances. The first *maneria* extends from A re to D la sol re, that is to say through a diatessaron and a diapason, and terminates on d sol re, where the diatessaron and the diapason are joined together. The second *maneria* goes from low B mi to high E la mi and ends on low E la mi. The third *maneria* is confined between C fa ut and high F fa ut and ends on low F fa ut. The fourth *maneria* or constitution stretches from d sol re to high G sol re ut and ends on low G sol re ut. All plainchant melodies are governed by these four rules or *manerie*, and end on the fourth note of the low range, as I have said, in which the diatessaron is joined with the diapason, so that each and every chant melody can either reach up an octave from its final, or descend a fourth below it […] Moreover, later authors called these *manerie* "tones," because they consist of whole tones and their parts of them, that is to say, semitones. The odd-numbered ones are called authentic, or superior ones, for they ascend by a diatessaron over the diapente. The even-numbered ones are called plagal, or inferior, for they descend by a diatessaron below the diapente. According to Guido, a tone is a rule for judging all melodies from its end, according to their ascent and descent. The modes must now be treated one by one.][29]

---

[29] Bergamo, Biblioteca Civica "Angelo Mai," MS MAB 21, fol. 12v.

The default use of the term *maneria* is comparatively rare in fifteenth-century Italian modal theory. However, it may indicate a measure of exposure to Cistercian modal theory, which routinely described the modes as *maneriae* following eleventh- and twelfth-century practices. A more important peculiarity is the consistent presence of solmization syllables in Gafori's pitch designations. This follows Tinctoris' practice in both the *Expositio manus* and the *Liber de natura tonorum*, but is positively at odds with much of fourteenth- and fifteenth-century modal theory (including Marchetto's *Lucidarium*), which more frequently indicated pitch by means of letters only.[30] In the late 1470s, Gafori had studied the musical writings of Johannes Gallicus, who had strongly advocated a way of singing that relied exclusively on the seven letters, as we saw in Chapter 6. The Bergamo draft indicates that already by the early 1480s, after his Neapolitan sojourn, Gafori had decided to reject Gallicus' view in favor of Tinctoris' – what might perhaps be seen as the beginning of his elaborate strategy in defense of the Guidonian system.

The corresponding passage from the 1496 *Practica* is on the whole similar to the earlier version. Its tone of presentation, however, is more scholarly, as suggested by the numerous references to both the Greek *tonoi* and the notions of harmonic and arithmetical means. In addition, as one perhaps might expect, Gafori is careful to highlight the tradition of Ambrosian chant as distinct from the larger "Gregorian" family. The entire excerpt goes as follows:

Has autem diapason formulas Antiqui constitutiones dixerunt quasi plenum quodammodo modulationis corpus ex consonantiarum coniunctione consistens unaquaeque species conduceret. Ptholomeus autem quod ipsas et modos appellarent proprijs nominibus distinctos, ut totum perfectissimi quindecim chordarum systematis hijsce modulationibus adimpleret, octavum modum superduxit in acutum, a prima diapason non specie sed integro primae ipsius intervallo distantem quam hypermixolydium quasi supra mixolydium nuncupavit … Primam enim diapason speciem quam duximus ab Are graui ad Alamire acutam, in Dsolre mediatam, Hypodorium vocabant, quasi subiectum Dorio seu placalem vel subiugalem dorij propter eius tetrachordum in graue reflexum a media chorda quam clerici finalem vocant. Secunda Hypophrigius vocitata est, quasi sub Phrygio, quae deducta est a [sqb]mi graui ad [sqb]mi acutam mediata in propriam finalem, scilicet Elami grauem. Tertiam speciem diapason Hypolydium dixerunt quasi sub lydio quoniam varistrosum subvertit acutum lydij tetrachordum … Plerumque enim alterna lydiae et mixolidiae modulationis commutatione redditur concentus suavior, quod

30 I discuss this issue at length in my *"Si quis manus non habeat,"* 195–210.

potissime Ambrosiani nostri in ecclesiasticis observant modis quum quintum ipsum et septimum commutatione [sqb] durae qualitatis in b mollem tanquam dia-pentes vel diatessaron specie commixtos modulari solent.

[Ancient musicians called these forms constitutions, as if each species would bring together in a certain way the entire melodic structure consisting of the connection of consonants. Since they were also called modes and were given special names, Ptolemy formed an eighth mode on the highest string in order to complete the Greater Perfect System of fifteen strings. This mode, which he named Hypermixolydian, as being above the Mixolydian, does not differ from the first octave-species in its diatonic interval relationship … The first octave-species, extending as we said, from low *A re* to high *a la mi re* and divided on *D sol re*, is called Hypodorian, subject to the Dorian as it were, or plagal and subjugate because its tetrachord descends below the median tone of division which ecclesiastics call the final. The second octave-species is called Hypophrygian, as if under the Phrygian, and extends from low [sqb] *mi* to high [sqb] *mi*, with its division and final on low *E la mi*. The third octave-species is called Hypolydian, as if under the Lydian, because it inverts the high Lydian tetrachord … Frequently the alternate exchange of a Lydian and Mixolydian melody creates a more pleasant harmony, a change which our Ambrosians in particular observe in eccle-siastical songs when hard [sqb] is changed into soft [rob] in the fifth and seventh modes, just as in the respective species of fourth and fifth.[31]

The most prominent change from the earlier draft is obviously the addi-tion of the Greek modal labels. More subtly, the historical agents credited with contributing to modal theory differ in the two versions: the "philoso-phers" and "Boethius" in the Bergamo draft have become "the ancients" in the final version, and the "later authors" are relabeled as "the clergy."[32] Later, Gafori suggests that the historical links between the "ancients" and the "clergy" is more than the result of happenstance. When he states that "later generations [of ecclesiastical musicians] divided the *maneriae* in such a way as not to diverge from the order of ancient authority," he presents historical continuity as the result of a self-conscious design on the part of the modern.

Gafori had good reasons for taking a defensive stance on the issue of the modes, as Johannes Gallicus had hinted at the logical possibility of a fourteen-mode system in his *Ritus canendi vetustissimus et novus*,[33] thus rekindling a debate on the composition and configuration of the ecclesiastical modal system that had been simmering since the Carolingian era. In the early

[31] Gafori, *Practica musicae*, fol. biiijr; Miller, trans., *Franchinus Gaffurius*, pp. 47–8 (slightly adjusted).
[32] The omission of Boethius' name in the 1496 reference to the *constitutiones* is puzzling, considering the prominence of that concept in Boethius' *De institutione musica*.
[33] See B. Meier, "Heinrich Loriti Glareanus als Musiktheoretiker," 89–90.

quattrocento, composer and theorist Johannes Ciconia still appealed to the eight-fold subdivision of grammar as a decisive element in favor of the argument that the system ought to include only eight modal categories. Nicolaus Burtius was also disturbed enough by Gallicus' suggestion of an expanded system to write a strong paragraph on this matter that recalled Gallicus' prose even as it altered it.[34]

For his part, Gafori developed an original line of argument for the same purpose, as he deftly played the classical card to shore up from criticism both the Guidonian and the modal systems. As a result, the modes of presentation of two topics, though technically unrelated, support each other in his text and converge under a coherent master plan that is effective not only because of its plausibility, but also because of its comprehensive character.

Music scholars have long been suspicious of the subtle historiographic plot pervading the *Practica*. Bernhard Meier, for one, saw the classicizing modal theory of *Practica musicae* as a conflation of two distinct and ultimately irreconcilable theoretical traditions, a practical oriented and a speculative one. Meier's comments are especially relevant here. His perceptive conclusion is that "Gafori [in the *Practica*] appears to make an attempt … at interpreting the [music-theoretical] textual tradition as a series of documents of a historical process, and to bring them in relation with one another without opposition."[35] I would argue that Gafori's recasting of solmization in *Practica musica* was meant to pursue exactly such a historiographic plan, by which Guido's hexachordal system ceased to be a mere music-pedagogical tool and became the cherished musical symbol of a particular musical tradition.

More importantly, viewed in the context of each other, Gafori's accounts of the hexachordal system and the modes in the 1496 *Practica* appear to be the result of a planned rhetorical strategy, itself a kind of propagandistic response to the disciplinary crisis of the 1480s that was magnified by the new responsibilities placed on the author (suddenly more visible on the public arena than ever before) by the emerging medium of the press. In other words, Gafori may have believed only half-heartedly in the historical lineage he himself constructed. He knew, however, that his Milanese readers were likely to be attracted by the veneer of timelessness that he conferred to

---

[34] Compare Gallicus, *Ritus canendi*, vol. II, pp. 23–6 ("On plainchant melodies ending on A, ♮, and C"), with N. Burtius, *Florum libellus* fol. dvv-dvjr ("On A-ending antiphons, called irregulars by the moderns").

[35] "Gafurius scheint also… den Versuch zu machen… die überlieferten Aussagen als Documente eines historischen Prozesses zu fassen und so miteinander in widerspruchslosen Zusammenhang zu bringen," Meier, "Heinrich Loriti Glareanus als Musiktheoretiker," 75.

the musical system of his time. I will discuss this point more in detail in the next and last section of this chapter.

Gafori's *Practica* and Sforza politics in late fifteenth-century Milan

In his assessment of Gafori's confrontation with Greek music theory Claude Palisca observed that the Milanese theorist had an altogether shallow and second-hand knowledge of it, due primarily to his unfamiliarity with classical Greek.[36] Palisca has shown that Gafori's references to classical authors are frequently marred by ambiguities and misinterpretations, and that his level of familiarity with the Greek musical authors did not deepen with time: a comparison of the printed version of Gafori's last treatise, the *De harmonia musicorum instrumentorum* of 1518, with the manuscript drafts of ca. 1500–7 reveals that the textual changes introduced by Gafori had to do with present issues, rather than with aspects of classical music theory. Palisca concluded that Gafori "may have lost interest in the classical authors after 1500." [37]

As earlier portions of this chapter have shown, references more or less precise to the classical authorities figure rather prominently in the *Practica*. But why did he appeal to the ancient sources at all in a treatise ostensibly dedicated to issues of *musica practica*? More specifically, what convinced Gafori that the ambitious historical narrative he set up in book 1 of *Practica musicae* would encounter his readers' approval, and which types of considerations led him to alter the early version of the *Practica* so methodically and dramatically? What follows is an attempt to address these questions by placing *Practica musice* within the context of the dominant cultural currents of late *quattrocento* Milan.

By the time Gafori published *Practica musice*, the ruler of the city, Ludovico Sforza, called il Moro, had received the much-coveted title of Duke from the Holy Roman Emperor Maximilian I, albeit in exchange for the hand of his niece Bianca Maria and the fabulous dowry of 400,000 ducats. The granting of the title was a major political victory for Ludovico.

---

[36] See C. Palisca, "Gaffurio as an Humanist," in *Humanism in Italian Renaissance Musica Thought* (New Haven: Yale University Press, 1985), pp. 191–225. The texts he most frequently cited were those very few that were available to him in Latin, thanks to the translations that he himself commissioned from some of his colleagues. On this topic, see F. A. Gallo, "Le traduzioni dal Greco per Franchino Gaffurio," *AcM* 35 (1963): 172–4.

[37] Palisca, "Gaffurio as an Humanist," p. 203.

Having seized power from the rightful heir to the duchy – his young nephew Gian Galeazzo Sforza – after the murder of Gian Galeazzo's father Galeazzo Maria in 1476, he faced the constant challenge of justifying his position as the legitimate ruler of Milan, both to his own citizens and to the many European powers who had laid claims on the duchy since the death of Filippo Maria Visconti in 1447. Even more troublesome was the fact that the Sforza family was not of aristocratic origins. The first Sforza ruler, Ludovico's father Francesco, was related to the Visconti only by virtue of having married Filippo Maria's illegitimate daughter Bianca Maria. Ironically, he had even campaigned against Milan during the turbulent years of the Ambrosian Republic (1447–1450).

In his ongoing effort to legitimize his political rule, Ludovico il Moro continued the cultural politics of his predecessors by privileging those artistic and intellectual endeavors that directly or indirectly supported the Sforza rule. In addition, he promoted lavish forms of spectacles and entertainment at court, as a way of cementing his relationship with the local nobility and of creating a general atmosphere of optimism. Already Francesco Sforza, soon after becoming the *de facto* governor of Milan in 1450, had actively sponsored a meticulous historiographic campaign that was to bolster the Sforza claim to the duchy – a propagandistic strategy that was being pursued also by other Italian states, increasingly eager to employ scholars for the sole purpose of compiling coherent and persuasive accounts of the historical background of the ruling dynasty and of the specific events by which the present government had become established.[38] Ludovico was well aware that the more he could present himself as the heir of a unified Visconti-Sforza lineage, the more he could justify the Sforza claim to the dukedom of Milan.

Given this general scenario, it is not surprising that Ludovico's cultural policy was instrumental to his campaign of self-legitimization. Particularly during the early years of his governorship of Milan, Ludovico pursued the ambitious project of producing a compelling historiographic narrative that would portray the history of the Sforza family as one particular chapter in the long history of the city of Milan.[39] To this purpose, soon after seizing

---

[38] Historian Gary Ianziti speaks of "a context of rivalry" in which the same historical events often took on a different spin when told by different historians, in an obvious attempt to cast a positive light on their patrons' rise to power. See G. Ianziti, *Humanistic Historiography under the Sforzas: Politics and Propaganda in Fifteenth-Century Milan* (Oxford: Clarendon Press, 1988), pp. 201–9.

[39] *Ibid.*, p. 234. See also G. Resta, "La cultura umanistica a Milano alla fine del Quattrocento," in *Milano nell'età di Ludovico il Moro. Atti del convegno internazionale, 28 febbraio-4 marzo 1983,*

power Ludovico commissioned the compilation of a history of the Visconti family to a prominent humanist, Giorgio Merula.[40]

In a city where the patronage of the arts and sciences by the nobility was relatively weak, the marked cultural and political interests of the court inevitably had a direct impact on the orientations of the local intellectual elite. Predictably, Milanese humanists looked at the medieval world less as a long period of cultural decadence separating classical antiquity from their age, and more as the period in their city's history when the civic, religious, and political roots of present society were laid. Gianvito Resta has singled out this particular attitude as a peculiarity of late fifteenth-century Milanese cultural trends that also informed contemporaneous publishing initiatives, as reflected for instance in the issuing of numerous editions of the works of St. Ambrose, Thomas Aquinas, and medieval hagiographic literature.[41] Even a scholar as seasoned as Giorgio Merula gave his public endorsement to the myth of the Visconti origins from the ancient Longobards, who were thus rehabilitated as the distant founders of the modern duchy and as the defendants of order and peace, in short as the venerable ancestors of modern Lombards.[42]

Gafori honors the Longobards-Visconti-Sforza genealogy by addressing Ludovico with the attribute of "Anglus" in the dedicatory letter of the *Practica*. The term evokes the mythical Longobard founder of the town of Angleria (now Angera, located on the eastern shore of Lago Maggiore, north of Milan), whom fourteenth-century chronicles indicated as the fountainhead of the Visconti family. Some court historians of the Visconti and Sforza went as far as to present Anglus as the grandson of Aeneas, the mythical founder of Rome.[43]

The prominent reference to Ludovico as "Anglus" at the beginning of the *Practica* may indicate that Gafori was striving to situate himself squarely within Milanese cultural politics, obviously as a way of ingratiating himself to his powerful patron. There should be no doubt about Gafori's alertness to Ludovico's expectations and about his sensitivity to Milanese cultural politics, if only because the size of his salary and entitlements depended largely

2 vols. (Milan: Comune di Milano, Archivio Storico Civico e Biblioteca Trivulziana, 1983), vol. 1, p. 207.

[40] Ianziti, *Humanistic Historiography*, p. 226.

[41] "A hallmark of Milanese humanist culture was a peculiar interest in the medieval past, which resulted also in a number of philological projects," in Resta, "La cultura umanistica a Milano," p. 207 (translation mine).

[42] *Ibid.*

[43] See Young, *The* Practica musicae *of Franchino Gafurius*, p. 3. Clement Miller omits the term in his translation.

on ducal disbursements. In his double position as *maestro di cappella* of the Cathedral of Milan and *lector* in music at the local academy (the *Gymnasium Mediolanense*, founded by Ludovico), Gafori was relatively close to Ludovico's court and to the cultural circles that gravitated around it. His friendship with court poet Lancinus Curtius and Ludovico's secretary Jacopus Antiquarius is well documented, and one may assume that Gafori was also well acquainted with the authors of the panegyric poems that punctuate his three main treatises.[44] Yet throughout the 1490s Gafori strove to attract Ludovico's attention, mostly – it seems – to improve his economic condition. His salary at the *Gymnasium* was barely higher than that of a *bidello* (janitor), and his overall income too small to allow for the acquisition of expensive manuscripts and translations that were needed by a humanist of his caliber. Thus the long list of supplications for benefices that Gafori submitted to the ducal chancery in the period from 1494 to 1497.[45]

Gafori's dedicatory letter displays other notable fingerprints of Milanese courtly humanism and Ludovician politics. The document reads as a clever *captatio benevolentiae* that celebrates music as a positive social force and as a mirror of princely power, while singing the high praises of il Moro as a most enlightened ruler. While such topics are the stuff of Renaissance dedicatory letters, the *realpolitik* tone of Gafori's prose reveals an author who is well aware of his patron's instrumental view of humanist learning and of music in particular. Consider for instance the *exordium* of the letter, in which Gafori invites Ludovico to follow the example of the "strictest governments" of the past, who treated music as the "mother and nurse of morals":

Quantae musicae artis professio Illustrissime Princeps apud Priscos non authoritatis modo sed etiam venerationis extiterit facile edocemur et summorum

[44] For instance, Lucinus Conagus, Johannes Jacobus Lomatio, and one Maurus Ugerius of Mantua, all of whom wrote panegyric poems included in the *Practica* and in the *De harmonia* (the *Theorica* features a poem by Curtius). On these figures, see W. Kreyszig, "Beyond the Music-Theoretical Discourse in Franchino Gaffurio's Trilogy: The Significance of the Paratexts in Contemplating the Magic Triangle Between Author, Opus, and Audience," in I. Bossuyt, N. Gabriëls, D. Sacré, and D. Verbeke, eds., *'Cui dono lepidum novum libellum?': Dedicating Latin Works and Motets in the Sixteenth Century*, Proceedings of the International Conference held at the Academia Belgica, Rome, August 18–20, 2005, Supplementa Humanistica Lovaniensia 23 (Leuven University Press, 2008), esp. pp. 176–87. On Lancinus Curtius' Neo-Platonic leanings, see G. F. Piccaluga, "Gli affreschi di casa Panigarola e la cultura Milanese tra Quattro e Cinquecento," *Arte lombarda* 86–7 (1988), 14–25.

[45] See L. Cremascoli, "Note storiche sulla vita di Franchino Gafurio," in A. Caretta *et al.*, *Franchino Gaffurio* (Lodi: Edizioni dell'Archivio Storico Lodigiano, 1951), pp. 91–101. Cremascoli observes that the cost of a printed book amounted to half of Gafori's monthly salary from the Duomo, while the sum equivalent to three months' pay was required for a new manuscript (p. 82).

Philosophorum exemplo qui se admodum senes ad hanc disciplinam velut in ea summam studiorum suorum manum imposituri contulerunt: et seuerissimarum rerum publicarum instituto: quae cum summa diligentia quicquid moribus publice officeret: circuncidi curassent: hanc tamen artem non modo non eiecerint: sed etiam velut morum parentem Altricemque summo studio excoluerunt: et vt claudam semel omnium gentium omniumque nationum consentienti stabilique confirmatur iudicio apud quas nihil vnquam fuit cura maiore celebratum. Quae enim alia disciplina tanto mortalium assensu: tantaque omnis vel aetatis vel sexus conspiratione recepta es.

[Illustrious sovereign, we are easily apprised of how greatly both in reputation and veneration the profession of the art of music was held among the ancients. The most distinguished philosophers applied themselves to this discipline as if to impose on it the imprint of their most profound concepts, and through the institution of very severe regulations for society, they took the greatest care to remove anything that would be detrimental to social mores. Yet they did not discard the art of music but cultivated it zealously as parent and guardian of public morals. Moreover, the art is supported by the unanimous and immutable judgment of all peoples and nations, among whom no other discipline was celebrated with greater solicitude.][46]

In this passage, Gafori is not pointing to an abstract ideal of morality, or to the practice of virtue for its own sake. Rather, he is suggesting that because music works its wonders on the *collectivity* of listeners, it can be used as an effective means of attaining social order, and perhaps even political consensus.

Shortly thereafter Gafori reminds his patron that the *gravissimi viri* of antiquity regarded the "professors of music" (*professores*, probably an implicit reference to Gafori's own academic status) as seers and philosophers. A few sentences later the author emphasizes the practical orientation of his new work and his intention to serve the "public good" (*profectui publico*), again reminding Ludovico that, "as was said previously, music is connected with morality" (*moralitati ut predictum est coniungitur*). The third mention of music's positive effects on morals leaves no doubts as to Gafori's intentions:

Caeterum cum de Musica loquor, non hanc Theatralem atque effoeminatam intelligo que mores publicos corrumpit potius quam informet, sed illam modestam atque virilem antiquis heroibus celebratam, que Mensis Regum Convivialibusque epulis admota, recubantium concertatione circumlata inter eos cythara clarissimorum virorum egregia facinora decantabat, quod maximum profecto ad virtutis studia incitamentum fuit.

[But when I speak about music I do not mean the theatrical and effeminate music that corrupts public morals, rather than molding them, but the former moderate and virile music in praise of ancient heroes. In those times, at royal feasts and

---

[46] Gafori, *Practica musicae*, fol. Γiiijv; Miller, trans., *Franchinus Gaffurius*, p. 14.

banquets a cithara was circulated among the reclining guests for their emulation, and to its strains illustrious deeds of the most distinguished men were sung – truly a great incentive to the practice of virtue.][47]

The mention of the practice of singing *ad citharam* for ancient kings and heroes seems to evoke Serafino Aquilano's performances for Ludovico and his court of the 1490s, and thus has the obvious function of warming up the dedicatee's interest in the pages that follow. Of course Ludovico was far more interested in fostering *musica practica* as an attribute of regality, than as the subject of dry academic disquisitions.[48] Still, Gafori is leaving no stone unturned in pursuing his goal of building consensus around himself among the members of the political elites of his time. For instance, the noticeable emphasis that he places in the *Practica* on Ambrosian music and liturgical practice would have played favorably among the Milanese clergy, traditionally proud of their measure of autonomy from Rome.

In short, Gafori's personal interest and concerns militated against proposing a reform of the solmization system of the kind proposed by Gallicus and Ramos, even if Gafori – and it is a big "if" – had felt so inclined. Indeed, the negative reception of Ramos' treatise in the early 1480s, vastly amplified by the new medium of the press, had left no doubts about the riskiness of such an endeavor. Gafori was so concerned with the reception of his views among Milanese musicians that in June 1492 he published a treatise on mensural notation – the *Tractato vulgare di canto figurato* – under the name of his student Francesco Caza in order not to face the potential criticism of Northern musicians in the city. The treatise, however, was well received, and a few months later Gafori published the revised text of the *Theoricum opus* with the name of *Theorica musicae*.[49]

Gafori's quiet homage to the venerable theme of *musica mundana* in the famous frontispiece of the *Practica* may be understood along the same line of argument.[50] This much discussed page establishes analogical correspondences between the Muses, the planets, the modes, and the individual notes of the Greater Perfect System, and is an index of the resurgence of Neo-Platonism in late-fifteenth-century Italy.[51] Claude Palisca aptly draws

[47]   Gafori, *Practica musicae*, fol. Γiiijr; Miller, trans., *Franchinus Gaffurius*, p. 16.

[48]   See F. Degrada, "Musica e musicisti nell'età di Ludovico il Moro," in *Milano nell'età di Ludovico il Moro* (Milan: Comune di Milano, 1983), vol. II, pp. 409–14.

[49]   Cremascoli, "Note storiche sulla vita di Franchino Gafurio," p. 86.

[50]   See a reproduction in Haar, "The Frontispiece of Gafori's *Practica musice* (1496)," 9.

[51]   In addition to the article by James Haar just cited, see the analyses of this image by J. Seznec, *The Survival of the Pagan Gods; The Mythological Tradition and Its Place in Renaissance Humanism and Art* (New York: Pantheon Books, 1953), pp. 140–3.

attention to the civic, or political, implications of the theme of celestial harmony, as he observes that Gafori's idea of cosmic harmony "mediates between public bodies and between individual people to make possible civic peace and well-being and friendship."[52] Indeed, it is telling that Gafori mentions this venerable topic even in his dedicatory letter to Ludovico in the *Practica*, where the reader is reminded that the soul of every living being "is affected and rejoices in harmonies congruent with its own nature"[53] – surely another nod to Ludovico about the instrumental value of music toward the ideal society.

Renaissance scholars have emphasized the role of Florentine Neo-Platonism behind the popularity of the theme of celestial harmony in late *quattrocento* Italy. Florence was the city of Marsilio Ficino, who had translated all of Plato's dialogues and had published a commentary on the *Timaeus*.[54] Ramos himself, who discusses the topic of *musica mundana* in his treatise, may have befriended Ficino during his Florentine years. Gafori also had owned a copy of Ficino's *Compendium in Timaeum* since 1489, although he likely had an opportunity to become acquainted with the topic through other medieval and classical sources. References to celestial harmony appear in all major works by Gafori, beginning with the *Theoricum opus* of 1480 and culminating with book 4 of the *De harmonia* of 1518, dedicated primarily to this topic.[55]

The vision of all-harmonious and all-pervasive correspondences between microcosm and macrocosm, or between gods and humans, was a *leitmotif* of Milanese culture during Ludovico's tenure at the head of the duchy. In particular, the extravagant music-theatrical entertainments that were staged at court in that period – in clear imitation of Florentine models – were often based on mythological themes drawn primarily from the *Metamorphoses*

---

[52] Palisca, *Humanism in Italian Renaissance Musical Thought*, pp. 174–5.

[53] "Et enim si Platoni credimus qui Mundi animam Musica modulatione constare dixit: non video profecto cur dubitari possit caetera quoque qualicunque anima degentia: quam eis coelitus datam liquet: non affici laetarique nature suae congruentia: cum similitudinem sibi amicam esse iam palam constet" ("If we believe Plato, who said that the world soul consists of musical melody, surely we do not see why it should be doubted that any other living thing possessing a soul, which, it is clear, is a gift of heaven, is also affected by and rejoices in harmonies congruent with its own nature, since it is well known that one is inclined toward something like oneself"), Gafori, *Practica musicae*, fol. Γiijv; I have used the translation by Palisca, *Humanism in Italian Renaissance Musical Thought*, p. 177.

[54] G. Tomlinson, *Music in Renaissance Magic: Toward a Historiography of Others* (University of Chicago Press, 1992) p. 90. The author also suggests that Ramos may have been familiar with Arabic tracts dedicated to this theme that circulated in his native Spain.

[55] For a comprehensive view of this topic, see again Palisca, *Humanism in Italian Renaissance Musical Thought*, pp. 166–78.

by Ovid and Apuleius, both of which had appeared in new editions around 1470. Cynthia Pyle has observed that the staging of Neo-Platonic themes became more common in the increasingly unstable Italian political scene (that is, after the assassination of Galeazzo Maria Sforza in 1476 and of the Congiura de' Pazzi in Florence in 1478), and culminated more and more with a "lieto fine."[56] Such Neo-Platonic trends have predictably been portrayed as a regress from earlier brands of humanism, more sensitive to their civic mission and committed to fostering moral virtue and disciplinary renewal.[57] More recently, Cynthia Pyle has noticed both a direct connection and a strident contrast between the optimistic story lines of late-fifteenth-century Italian theatrical productions and the anxieties of contemporary socio-political life. The actions of benevolent gods in the human world, and the inevitable final ending of Good and Virtue, were to instill reassuring feelings in the spectators. Neo-Platonism, then, provided a salutary escape from reality with a not-so-covert propagandistic purpose. As a retreat from reality, its immediate social function (call it propagandistic purpose) was one of defending the political and religious *status quo* under the benevolent umbrella of universal harmony.

The present remarks are not to imply that Gafori's unflinching defense of the medieval music curriculum was merely expedient to promote the Ludovician politics of continuity. Like many of his contemporaries, Gafori was no doubt genuinely convinced of the fundamental soundness of the Guidonian system, in spite of the writings by Gallicus and Ramos, well known to him, that had exposed its limitations. Rather, I wish to suggest that Gafori's portrayal of Guido as a sort of "modern Boethius" or "modern Pythagoras," far from mere rhetorical hyperbole, characterizes a new generation of humanists that was becoming more and more self-conscious about the public dimensions of their scholarly activities and more responsive to the political strategies and needs of the local courts. Thus, by firmly defending Guido's hexachordal system against the increasingly vocal argument of its detractors, Gafori not only protected the church music curriculum, but he also contributed to shoring up a bridge to a medieval past that was both vital to Ludovician politics and key to the self-image of the Milanese-Ambrosian church. In other words, at the root of the phenomenal success of the *Practica* during Gafori's time may have been a perfectly executed marriage between

---

[56] C. M. Pyle, *Milan and Lombardy in the Renaissance. Essays in Cultural History* (Rome: La fenice, Roma, 1997), pp. 163–82.

[57] A. Rabil, Jr., "The Significance of 'Civic Humanism' in the Interpretation of the Italian Renaissance," in A. Rabil Jr., ed., *Renaissance Humanism: Foundations, Forms, and Legacy* (Philadelphia: University of Pennsylvania Press, 1988), vol. II, "Humanism in Italy," p. 159.

the old music curriculum and the fashionable humanist erudition of ca. 1500, with an attentive eye to courtly politics – a rather exemplary case of "old wine in new bottles." Gafori's idyllic picture of a unified Greco-Guidonian tradition is perhaps the surest sign of the conservative character of his intellectual project. His was a brand of humanism that aimed at defending, rather than at challenging, the political and educational *status quo*.

Eugenio Garin offered a lucid analysis of this transformation decades ago, when he argued that the late fifteenth century witnessed "the formation and the establishment of a new kind of secular cultural operators, increasingly aware of their role and status, and of the indestructible tie between civic life and their knowledge and expertise." The new brand of humanist culture, according to Garin, was more public-oriented, international, and encyclopedic in scope than the earlier brand of civic humanism practiced by Leonardo Bruni, Coluccio Salutati and Pier Candido Decembrio.[58] Skilled political leaders such as Ludovico Sforza were savvy enough to clearly appreciate the need to channel the robust humanist ideals of the previous age as an effective public medium for the creation of political consensus.

Gafori's *Practica musicae* is fully embedded in the "new humanist culture" of Ludovico's age, indeed more deeply and self-consciously than its subject matter might perhaps suggest. To appreciate this aspect of Gafori's treatise is to begin to make sense of its marked scholarly tone, which remains somewhat at odds with its stated purpose of describing the rudiments of "practical music." The truly original aspect of that treatise lies not in its historicist or antiquarian posture *per se*, or even in its positing a line of historical development from the Greek to the Christian era. Rather, it has to do with the author's keen perception and methodical implementation of the idea that a historical narrative may be read as a statement about the present. Gafori seems to have realized that the new medium of the press had conferred authors an unprecedented power of influence and persuasion over their readers (now suddenly turned into an "audience"), yet a great responsibility as well, because of their position of public mediators of traditions of knowledge and scholarship that inevitably carries political connotations.

Garin's point about the encyclopedic character of the new Milanese culture also finds corroboration in Gafori's writings on music. Gafori was no musical reformer; he did not seize on individual aspects of contemporary music theory or practice in order to offer new critical perspectives on them. (Indeed, even his tacit acceptance of Ramos' new presentation of the Guidonian system aimed at perpetuating the old, hexachord-based model of musical pedagogy, as we have seen.) The very fact that Gafori's three mature treatises (the 1492 *Theorica*, the 1496 *Practica*, and the 1518 *De harmonia*) are often described as a "trilogy" aptly reflects Gafori's goal of producing a *summa* of the standard musical knowledge of his age.

Neither should we overlook the distinct secular tone of Gafori's scholarship, one that surfaces through the pages of the *Practica* – beginning with the frontispiece – in spite not only of the author's intellectual formation and clerical status, but also of the general subject matter of the treatise (sacred polyphonic music) and of the (church-rooted) tradition of music education to which it belongs. The letter to Ludovico, for instance, mentions the evocative tableau of singing poets entertaining kings at banquets, but makes not a single reference to religious musical practices. Thus, when at the end of the letter Gafori writes "we wish that anything we might have accomplished through our study and industry be dedicated and forever consecrated to your name,"[59] his words are more than conventional rhetoric. Rather, they reflect his full awareness of the new deal between patronage and print culture that was being forged in the city culture of his time.

The *Practica* is a fully courtly treatise, even though its internal content and references are dedicated to the rudiments of ecclesiastical music. It no doubt stands out from the large number of contemporaneous treatises for its highly sophisticated defense of the medieval curriculum. Possibly even more remarkable was its author's keen realization that more than just the fate of Guidonian pedagogy was at stake in the success of that defense.

---

[59] Gafori, *Practica musicae*, fol. l̄iiijv ("sic quicquid studio industriaque effecerimus nomini tuo tempus in omne dicatum consecratumque esse volumus"); Miller, trans., *Franchinus Gaffurius*, p. 17.

8 | Hexachordal theory and deductive method
in Gioseffo Zarlino's *Dimostrationi*
harmoniche (1571)

Old and new notions of "hexachordum" in Zarlino's music theory

Many German and Italian treatises of the first half of the sixteenth century bear witness to Franchino Gafori's reinterpretation of medieval solmization theory. Manuals such as the *Tetrachordum musices* by Johannes Cochlaeus (1514), the *Enchiridion utriusque musicae practice* by Georg Rhau (1520), *Libri tres de istitutione harmonica* by Pietro Aaron (1516), and the *Recanetum de musica aurea* by Stephanus Vanneus (1533) – to name only a few – appear to endorse the "strong" view of *hexachordum* as a diatonic yardstick that had figured prominently in Gafori's *Practica musicae*. Such doctrinal links are of course not surprising in the least, considering the enormous impact of the *Practica* on subsequent generations of theorists.[1]

It was Gioseffo Zarlino, however, who developed new theoretical applications of the Gaforian notion of *hexachordum*, even though the older, pre-humanistic concept of *hexachordum* as a diatonic interval never disappears completely from the scene. For instance, in the various editions of Zarlino's *magnum opus*, the *Istitutioni harmoniche* (first published in 1558), the term *hexachordo* indicates first and foremost the interval or consonance of the major or minor sixth (*essachordo maggiore* or *minore*) – that is to say, exactly as earlier authors from Theinred of Dover to Johannes Ciconia (and beyond) had understood it. Zarlino has a lengthy presentation of the major sixth in Part III, chapter 20 (p. 165), reproduced here as Fig. 8.1. It translates as follows:

[…] [The large hexachord is formed by the proportions of the superbipartiente tertia, which is the first proportion of this class, between the root terms 5 and 3. This interval cannot be called absolutely simple, for the terms of its proportion can be divided by the number four in this manner: 3:4:5, and we might say that it is

---

[1] A detailed investigation of these sources cannot be carried out here. The topic of the reception of Gafori's modal theory in Germany is briefly addressed in W. Werbeck, *Studien zur deutschen Tonartenlehre in der ersten Hälfte des 16. Jahrhunderts* (Kassel: Bärenreiter, 1989), pp. 60–1.

composed of a combination of the ratios of the diatessaron and ditone. Nonetheless it is simple in a certain sense. Although it is composed of two intervals, one of them is not the diapason, so it is not composed of a whole to which is added one of its parts. Therefore when we consider only the extremes of this interval, with no intermediate sound, we find that it has one species only, whether the pitch is low or high. But divided diatonically, it will have as many species as there are ways of placing the semitone it contains, according to the manner in which its intermediate steps are arranged. Three species result as shown below [see the central portion of Fig. 8.1]. Musicians call this interval a hexachord because it contains six steps. The Greek word was *hex*, meaning "six," and *chordon*, meaning "string." Thus it is the interval containing six strings, or the consonance of six steps, for it is made up of that many steps. Practical musicians call it the major sixth to distinguish it from the minor sixth, which is of smaller proportion.][2]

Such an account does not differ in any significant way from the standard, and generally more concise *Intervallehre* of the late Middle Ages. Zarlino diverges somewhat from the theoretical tradition in his consideration of the hexachord as the sum of a diatessaron and a ditone, whereas earlier authors would have typically defined it as the combination of a fifth and a whole tone. The difference is significant in one important respect (see p. 248).

Earlier in the *Istitutioni*, however, Zarlino had used the term *hexachordo* in the new sense proposed by Ramos and Gafori, i.e., as a new "diatonic yardstick" by which Guido of Arezzo had allegedly restructured the gamut:

Et benché gli antichi Greci nella fabrica, o divisione del Monochordo, considerassero solamente Sedici chorde, divise in cinque Tetrachordi, ne tentassero di passar più oltra, per la ragione detta di sopra; nondimeno li Moderni non contenti di tal numero, lo accrebbero passando più oltra hora nel grave, & hora nell'acuto: Imperoche Guidone Aretino nel suo *Introduttorio*, oltra le nominate chorde, ve ne aggiunse delle altre alla somma di Ventidue, & le ordinò in sette Essachordi; & tale ordinatione fu, & e più che mai accettata, & abbracciata dalla maggior parte de i Musici prattici: essendo che in essa sono collocate, & ordinate le chorde al modo delle mostrate Pithagorice. Et perche ciascuno Essachordo si compone di Sei chorde, però è denominato da tal numero: che vuol dire Di sei chorde. E ben vero, che a ciascuno di essi, aggiunse per commodità de i cantanti alcune di queste sei sillabe, cioè Ut, Re, Mi, Fa, Sol, La: cavate dall'Hinno di Santo Giouanni Battista, il quale incomincia in tal modo; *Ut queant laxis* [etc.] & li concatennò con tale artificio, & in tal maniera; che ciascuno contiene tutte le specie della Diatessaron, le quali sono tre, come vederemo nella Terza parte; accommodando il Semituono, circoscritto da queste due sillabe mezane Mi, & Fa nel mezo di ciascuno.

[2] G. Zarlino, *The Art of Counterpoint: Part Three of the Istitutioni harmoniche, 1558*, ed. G. Marco and C. Palisca (New York: W. W. Norton, 1968), pp. 39–40.

Dello Eſſachordo maggiore, ouero Seſta maggiore.   Cap. 20.

 ENENDO *Hora a quelli, che hanno le forme loro tra le proportioni del genere Su-*
perpartiente, dico, che lo Eſſachordo mag giore hà la ſua forma dalla proportione Super-
perbipartiente terza, la quale è la prima proportione di queſto genere, tra queſti termi-
ni radicali 5 & 3. Et benche queſto interuallo non ſi poſſa chiamare aſſolutaměte Sem-
plice, ſe non ad vn certo modo: percioche gli eſtremi della ſua proportione poſſono eſſer
trameʒati dal numero Quaternario, in cotal maniera 3. 4. 5; & lo potemo dire compoſto della forma della
Diateſſaron, & della forma del Ditono; tuttauia lo chiamaremo Semplice in vn certo modo; non gia per
che ſia compoſto di due interualli: ma ſi bene, per che non è compoſto dello interuallo della Diapaſon, che è il
Tutto, & di alcuna ſua parte. Quando adunque conſideraremo queſto interuallo ne i ſuoi eſtremi ſolamente,
& ſenʒa alcun meʒo, ritrouaremo, che è di vna ſola ſpecie; ancora che fuſſe poſta nel graue, o nello acuto.
Ma quando lo conſideraremo diuiſo diatonicamente; tante ſaranno le ſue Specie, quanto ſaranno le varia-
tioni de i luoghi del Semituono, compreſo in eſſo, ſecondo i modi delle diuiſioni, che fanno le ſue chorde meʒa-
ne, le quali ſaranno tre; come qui ſi vede.

Prima ſpecie.   *Seconda ſpecie.*

Terʒa ſpecie.

Li Muſici chiamano queſto interuallo Eſſachordo, per il numero delle chorde, che contiene, che ſono Sei: Per-
cioche appreſſo de i Greci tanto vuol dire E'ξ, quanto ſignifica Sei appreſſo di noi; & ſimilmente tanto vuol
dire Χoρδὴ appreſſo di loro, quanto Chorda appreſſo di noi. Onde è detto Interuallo, che contiene Sei chorde;
ouero Conſonanza di ſei voci: percioche è compreſo da tal numero di chorde. La onde li Prattici lo chiamano

 *Seſta mag giore, a differenza della minore, la quale è compreſa da minor pro-*
portione; & dicono, che la Seſta mag giore, ouero il mag giore Eſſachordo è
vna compoſitione di ſei voci, ouer ſuoni, che contiene quattro Tuoni, & vn
Semituono mag giore. Quando adunque ſaranno due parti nelli noſtri contra-
punti, diſtanti l'vna dall'altra per il graue, & per l'acuto, ſecondo la ragio-
ne de gli eſtremi di alcuno delli ſoprapoſti eſſempi; allora diremo, che tal par-
ti ſeranno diſtanti l'vna dall'altra per vno Eſſachordo, ouer Seſta mag gio-
re; come qui in eſſempio ſi vede.

Fig. 8.1. Zarlino's species of the major and minor hexachords (from *Le istitutioni harmoniche,* 1558, repr. 1965, part III, ch. 20, p. 165).

[Although the ancient Greeks considered only sixteen strings divided into five tetrachords when they divided the monochord, and did not attempt to go beyond that range for the reasons explained above, the Moderns, not satisfied with that small range of notes, went beyond it both in the low and in the high range. Thus, in his *introductorium* Guido of Arezzo added several additional notes to the pre-existing ones [from *Proslambanomenos* to *Nete hyperboleon*], reaching the sum of twenty-two notes that he disposed in seven hexachords. This arrangement was and still is widely accepted by the majority of practical musicians, because it reflects the order of the above-mentioned Pythagorean strings. And each hexachord is called that way because it consists of six strings. For the convenience of singers, Guido added to each hexachord the six syllables Ut, Re, Mi, Fa, Sol, La taken from the Hymn of St. John *Ut queant laxis* [etc.], and disposed them in such a way that each one of them contains the three species of Diatessaron (as I will explain in Part III), with the semitone in the middle corresponding with the central syllables *Mi-Fa*.][3]

This characterization of the hexachord in foundational terms gains increasing visibility in later editions of the *Istitutioni* and, even more, in the new arrangements of the twelve modes that Zarlino proposed in his *Dimostrationi harmoniche* of 1571. The present chapter takes a close look at Zarlino's expansion of the Gaforian notion of *hexachordum* in the final phase of his career. My ultimate goal is to emphasize this aspect of Zarlinian musical thought as the product of a new and ambitious vision for the discipline of music theory. The spark for Zarlino's new musical science was a concern with the methods chosen for ascertaining the truth: any statement on musical phenomena was to be derived deductively from a set of a priori and unquestionable principles. As we will see, the rationalistic ideal pervading the self-conscious method of Zarlino's *Dimostrationi* conferred a stronger foundational role to *hexachordo* than envisioned even by Gafori.

Zarlino's case for modal reform

In the 1558 edition of the *Istitutioni* Zarlino had endorsed Heinrich Glarean's twelve-mode systems (*Dodecachordon*, 1547), which recognized the two modal pairs on A and C in addition to the traditional eight modal categories with finals on D, E, F, and G. Because he wished to present his modal theory as a continuation of ecclesiastical music theory, Glarean did not alter the order of the traditional eight modes: he still labeled the two modes on D as modes 1 and 2, those on E as modes 3 and 4, and so forth, down to the 'new' modes on A (numbered as mode 9 and 10), and C (11 and 12). Thus, the diatonic sequence projected by the modal finals of Glarean's system, as well as of the 1558 *Istitutioni*, ends with a leap of a minor third (D E F G a c). Although the note B is unsuitable as a modal final because of its tritone

[3] G. Zarlino, *Le Istitutioni Harmoniche* (Venice, 1558; facsimile New York: Broude Brothers, 1965), Part II, ch. 30, p. 103, trans. mine. Most likely, the term 'introductorium' in this citation stems from Gafori's *Practica*. As a matter of fact, the header of the gamut that follows is an almost literal Italian translation of the header used by Gafori in his treatise. It reads: "Introductorio di Guidone Aretino ordinato secondo le divisioni Pitagoriche nel genere Diatono Diatonico" (see p. 211 above, and Fig. 7.4).

Fig. 8.2. Zarlino's new arrangement of the twelve modes, with C as the first modal final (G. Zarlino, *Le Institutioni harmoniche* (Venice, 1573; repr. Ridgewood, N.J.: Gregg Press, 1966), p. 404).

relationship with F, both Glarean and Zarlino recognized it as the 'confinal' of the two E modes (Phrygian and Hypophrygian).

In his 1571 treatise called *Dimostrationi harmoniche*, however, Zarlino expressed his discomfort with Glarean's arrangement and renumbered the twelve modes beginning from C, rather than D, thus generating the sequence of notes C D E F G a. In his subsequent revisions of the *Istitutioni* in 1573 and 1589, Zarlino continued to adopt this new modal order (see Fig. 8.2).

The similarity between this tone sequence and Guido's "hexachord" was not lost on Zarlino, who indeed explicitly referred to it as his primary justification for adopting the new modal order. But more noteworthy than the numerical reform *per se* is the way in which Zarlino puts forward the hexachordal argument to support it – namely, from the mouth of one of the most authoritative musicians of his age, Adrian Willaert, and in the context of a treatise that has the overarching goal of instilling a new methodological rigor into the discipline of music theory.

As Zarlino explains in the introduction to the treatise, the text of the *Dimostrationi* is the written record of a series of conversations on music that had taken place in April 1562 in the house of an ailing Willaert and in the company of the organist Claudio Merulo, the Ferrarese musician Francesco della Viola, and a fictitious character also in his old age, called Desiderio. The not insignificant differences in the text of the two editions of the treatise (published in 1571 and 1589) suggest that the author edited those conversations quite freely – assuming, of course, that they ever happened. Whatever the case may be, the *Dimostrationi*, for all its pedantic verbosity, offers to its readers a quintessentially Venetian and highly entertaining mix of science and theater, polite manners and intellectual sophistication, casual remarks and causal modes of explanation. The dialogue form enlivens the rather dry quality of the subject matter and highlights the historical and practical sides of the various topics, often complementing the Apollonian pretension of the entire enterprise with a "real life" touch. But more subtly, the rhetorical fiction of the dialogue creates an all-important impression of neutrality and objectivity, as it creates the impression that Zarlino has really nothing to do with the frequent corroborating remarks, additional proofs, and constructive criticisms voiced by the *dramatis personae* of this musical "play." At the very least, the reader is led to believe that each and every sentence of the *Dimostrationi* is invariably supported by the expert judgment of some of the most knowledgeable musicians of the time. Perhaps Zarlino felt that even the ambitious scope of his *Dimostrationi* would have attracted little attention, if he had not enlisted the authority of Venice's most famous musicians to make the case for it.[4]

The conversation on the modes begins in the *Dimostrationi* with a survey of the seven octave species and their individual intervallic structure.[5] Zarlino distances himself from earlier theorists by labeling the C-c octave as the "prima specie della diapason," the D-d octave as the second, and so on. Pressed by Merulo to justify this new order, Zarlino replies that the C-c octave features the most natural series of major whole tones, minor whole tones, and semitones.[6]

At this point Adrian Willaert, invited to join the discussion, points out a crucial relationship between Zarlino's new order of the finals and the pitches of the hexachord:

Voltosi allora M. Claudio verso M. Adriano, & disse; Che ne dite voi Messere? parmi ch'à questo non si possa contradire per alcun modo. In verità, rispose il buon Vecchio; che non si puote; & parmi che M. Gioseffo habbia una gran ragione. Et per dirvi il ero; non vi era cosa nella Musica, che mi paresse più strana di questa. Percioche havendo noi quest'ordine de uoci Ut. Re. Mi. Fa. Sol. La. era pur contra 'l douere, che la Prima specie de tutte le Prime consonanze havesse ad incominciar nella Seconda voce, & non nella prima di tale ordine; però sommamente hò in piacere, che M. Gioseffo voglia ragionar di questa cosa; & che sia entrato in questa buona opinione di ordinar questo disordinato ordine. Messere; gli dissi allora; mi allegro molto, che à voi piaccia questo mio pensiero. Onde havendoui sempre conosciuto per Huomo d'intelletto & di giudicio; non mi poteva capire nell'animo, che

---

[4] Thus, Cristle Collins Judd points to the *Dimostrationi* as a mature example of Zarlino's "self-fashioning" via a careful "manipulation of the dialog format" and of the medium of the press. See her *Reading Renaissance Music Theory*, pp. 181–4 and 251.

[5] Ragionamento Quinto, Definizione VIII: "La Prima specie della Diapason è quella, che tra la terza & la quarta chorda graue, & tra la settima & la ottaua acuta, contiene il Semituono maggiore. La Seconda è quella, che lo contiene tra la seconda & la terza; & tra la sesta & la settima. La Terza… [and so on until all seven octave species have been accounted for as particular configurations of whole tones and semitones]" (G. Zarlino, *Dimostrationi harmoniche* (Venice, 1571; facsimile Ridgewood, NJ: Gregg Press, 1966), p. 270).

[6] *Ibid.*, Rag. Quinto, Def. VIII, p. 246.

le cose fatte con ragione vi hauessero à dispiacere. Però voglio seguitare allegra-
mente la Seconda cagione, la quale è quell'istessa, c'hà mosso voi. Perche havendo i
nostri Maggiori ridotto l'ordine delle Chorde musicali in Hexachordi; & hauendoli
attribuito quell'ordine de Voci, che nominato havete; più tosto bisognava dar principio à queste Specie nella prima voce Ut; che nella Re, che è la Seconda; accioche
quando si perviene alla Quarta specie, al modo loro; non si havesse à ritornare in
dietro, & incominciar nel Quarto luogo di tale ordine dalla voce Ut, la quale, per
ogni dovere, dovrebbe tenere il primo, & non l'ultimo luogo; come vedete fatto nella
loro Quarta specie de tutte le prime Consonanze. Questa adunque fù la Seconda
cagione. Questa è cagione ragioneuole, disse il Viola.

[M. Claudio then asked M. Adriano: "What is your opinion about all this, sir?
It seems to me Zarlino's argument cannot be contradicted in any way". "Indeed
it cannot," the old master replied. "I think M. Gioseffo is absolutely right. To tell
you the truth, I always found that there is no greater contradiction in the theory
of music: that since we recognize the order of the syllables *ut, re, mi, fa, sol, la*, it
is against logic that the first species of all first consonances has to begin on the second syllable, rather than on the first, and it pleases me greatly that M. Gioseffo
is studying the problem and is determined to bring order in this ordered chaos."
"Sir – I replied – I am delighted that you agree with me on this. Since I have always
known you as an intelligent and judicious man, I could not entertain the idea that
you would dislike a sensible proposal such as this one. But I wish to elaborate on the
second argument, the one that you found most convincing. Since earlier musicians
organized all the tones of the diatonic space in hexachords, and attributed to them
the six syllables that you just mentioned, it was necessary that the diatonic species
began on the first syllable *ut*, rather than on the second, *re*. So that when you reach
the fourth step [in that octave] it is not necessary to go back and begin again from
ut, which should be the first, not the last syllable, as it is apparent from the fourth
species of all first consonances. This, then, is the second argument." "It is a reasonable one," replied Mr. Viola.][7]

In his comments on this passage from the *Dimostrationi*, Richard Crocker
emphasized the historical significance of Zarlino's hexachordal argument
in support of his modal reform.[8] To Crocker, Zarlino's derivation of the
C-c octave from the "sonorous number" belonged to speculative theory,
rather than to the world of musical practice, and thus carried little historical weight. Zarlino's hexachordal argument, on the other hand, was more
worthy of consideration in that it directly connected the new modal order
to the world of musical performance – indeed, Zarlino cleverly invites this
conclusion by having none other than the "buon Vecchio" Adrian Willaert
point to that connection in his answer to Claudio Merulo's solicitation. By

[7] *Ibid.*, Rag. Quinto, Defin. VIII, p. 271.
[8] Crocker, "Perchè Zarlino," 48–58.

invoking the Guidonian syllables at that point, Crocker explains, "Willaert speaks from the perspective of contemporary practice and of the conventions of pitch designation. It is for this reason that Willaert's answer becomes so important."[9]

Zarlino's reordering, according to Crocker, subordinated the entire modal system to the hexachord – what amounts to a quasi-Copernican inversion of hierarchies that is ripe with implications and consequences for our understanding of medieval and Renaissance music:

> At least to Zarlino, the modes were far less important, less fundamental than the hexachord. For he mapped the modes against the hexachord, not vice-versa. In order to put order in the existing disorder, it is the modes that are changed and adapted to the hexachord, not vice-versa … The order of pitches within the hexachord constituted a solidly rooted tonal structure, one that 16th-century musicians took for granted. Modern scholars should also consider the hexachord, rather than the modes, as the starting point for our understanding of tonal identity, tonal relationships, and tonal function in the music of the *cinquecento*.[10]

Crocker, however, does not wish to present Zarlino's modal reordering as a theoretical revolution, but rather as a late recognition in writing of a state of affairs that had long dominated musical practice. Indeed, as we have seen in Chapter 2, Crocker has elsewhere argued that the hexachord had functioned as the *de facto* ruler of the diatonic space throughout the Middle Ages. In his view, even the modal system eventually had to be adjusted to the "reality of the hexachord".[11]

However, the theory that the hexachord shaped, or contributed to shaping, the inner organization of the modal system faces a number of contradictory elements and opposing factors. As I have demonstrated in Chapters 3 and 4, Guido's six syllables had no more than a marginal presence in the music-theoretical literature until the thirteenth century. By that time, the ecclesiastical modal system had already been in place for centuries as a classificatory tool for liturgical chant; nor did it change significantly (if at all) when the Guidonian syllables became a standard pedagogical tool. In later times, it remained common for theorists to indicate the musical pitches via the seven letters only in their presentations of modal theory, often after relying heavily on the Guidonian syllables in other portions of their treatises.

---

[9] *Ibid.*, 53.

[10] *Ibid.*, 54.

[11] *Ibid.*, 54–7. Dolores Pesce argued along similar lines by describing the hexachord as the "seats of the modes" in her *Affinities and Medieval Transpositions* (Bloomington, IN: Indiana University Press, 1987).

Italian modal theory of the fourteenth and fifteenth centuries, for instance, was modeled after book 11 of Marchetto of Padua's *Lucidarium* (ca. 1318), which avoids mentioning the syllables almost completely in its survey of the modes. Even when the syllables do appear in late-medieval treatises, they do so more frequently in particular contexts (such as the rules for modal recognition), than in others (such as the discussion of the constituent diatonic species).[12]

But perhaps the main weakness of Zarlino's argument about the logical necessity of a hexachordal reordering of the modes has to do with the very timing of his proposal. If Zarlino's reasoning had merit, then it is not clear why so many centuries had to pass before a twelve-mode system – not to speak of a twelve-mode system beginning with the C mode – was formulated and accepted. Surely, if post-Guidonian theorists and musicians had understood the Guidonian hexachord along the lines suggested by Crocker and other modern scholars, it seems likely that they would have accepted the possibility of a twelve-mode system much earlier, and with fewer qualms, than in the mid-sixteenth century. Instead, the evolution of modal theory tells a very different story: Glarean never put forward the hexachordal argument in support of his revised modal system, and at any rate he did not propose a hexachordal line-up of his six finals. Furthermore, he was open to the possibility of integrating even the B mode into the system, if new trends in musical practice called for such an addition.[13]

Ironically, the few medieval theorists before Zarlino who advocated an expansion of the modal system either did not have much use for the solmization syllables, or were downright opposed to them. It is surely significant, for instance, that the twelfth-century Cistercian reform of liturgical chant, which emphasized the connection between mode and octave species and accepted all seven pitch letters as legitimate modal finals (albeit still in the context of the four *maneriae*), bypassed Guidonian solmization altogether, as we saw in Chapter 3. The same could be said for those authors, such as Wilhelm of Hirsau and Johannes Gallicus, who advocated a modal system organized around the principle of the double division of each modal octave – an idea that would eventually inspire Glarean's theory.[14] In short: both the general opposition to the twelve-mode system in the Middle Ages, and the

---

[12] I explore this topic in greater detail in my "*Si quis manus non habeat*," 181–218.

[13] The reference is to a passage in *Dodecachordon* in which Glarean invites future theorists – musical "gatekeepers" of sorts – to make the necessary adjustments to the modal system in accordance with trends in musical practice. See Glarean, *Dodecachordon*, ed. and trans. C. A. Miller, vol. I, p. 140.

[14] See H. Powers and F. Wiering, "Mode," § I-III, in *NG 2*, vol. 16, pp. 807–8 and B. Meier, "Heinrich Loriti: Glareanus als Musiktheoretiker," pp. 89–90.

lack of any reference to the hexachordal argument by those few authors who did advocate such a system, place into perspective the entire issue of the role of the hexachord in medieval and Renaissance music theory.

None other than Zarlino himself points to the "accidental" relationship between modes and hexachord at the end of the same chapter in which he presents his new modal order. Immediately after receiving the praise of his companions for his new order, Zarlino feels the need to forestall an important criticism:

Non voglio pero che crediate, che io voglia esser destruttore delle cose de gli Antichi: percioche non hebbi mai tanto tristo pensero: ma uoglio ben, che pensate: che lasciando le cose loro nel loro essere: le verrò à mutare solamente secondo certi accidenti [...] Ne vi pensate ancora, ch'io possa fare altramente: essendo che qual si voglia Specie di consonanza: quanto alla sua forma è sempre immutabile & invariabile: ma quanto poi à gli accidenti, i quali anco sono estrinsechi: come di prima, ò seconda: ò di graue, ò di acuto: si può senza alcuna alteratione quanto al nome variare. Et volete vedere, che cosi sia: pigliate qual si voglia Diapason, & datele nome di Prima, ò di Seconda: come meglio vi piace: tale accidente non havrà forza di farle variar forma. Percioche se voi le attribuisti mille & poi mille nomi: & la riportaste, overo le deste mille luoghi variati: mai ella si cambierà di forma & sostanza: ma resterà sempre quella: essendo che 'l nome di Primo, ò di Secondo nasce da pura Relatione: la quale tra gli altri accidenti è debolissimo: & estrinseco delle cose ridotte in un ordine. Onde tale Relatione si può ad ogni nostro piacere mutare: senza varietà alcuna della Forma, ò della Sostanza delle cose. Ma se in lei si rimoverà alcun Tuono ò Semituono: trasportandolo verso l'acuto, ò verso 'l grave: non è dubio, che tale Diapason non sarà com' ella era prima: ma cambierà la prima forma in un'altra [...] Et se gli Antichi ["I nostri Antichi" in the 1589 edition] attribuirono alla Diapason posta tra Proslambanomenos & Mese la prima specie di essa Diapason: lo fecero, perche la Proslambanomenos era la Prima chorda dell'ordine de i loro Suoni: la onde era 'l douere che in cotal chorda, come prima d'ogni altra, dessero principio alle loro Specie.

[However, I do not wish you to conclude that my goal is to destroy the achievement of the ancients, for such an appalling thought has never crossed my mind. On the contrary, my proposal leaves the substance of things intact, and changes only their surface (*certi accidenti*) ... And it could not be otherwise, since the species of the consonances are immutable in their form; as far the accidents go, they are external to their object, such as their cardinality (first, second), or their range (low, high). Even their label may be changed without introducing any substantial alteration. For instance, you can take any species of the diapason and label it first or second as you see fit, without thereby introducing any change in the form of the consonance. Indeed, you could attach to it thousands of different names, or transpose it to thousands of different places, without changing its form and substance in the least; on the contrary, it would remain the same. This is so because the names "first," "second," and so on express a relationship that is the weakest of all other accidents, and external to any set of objects arranged in a particular order. But if you alter the sequence of tones and semitones [in a species of consonance], you will obtain a new species of the Diapason, with a new form ... And if the ancients labeled the diapason between Proslambanomenos and Mese as the first one, they did so because Proslambanomenos was the lowest pitch of their gamut, thus the natural starting point of the species of consonances.][15]

Zarlino was legitimately concerned that his modal reform could be interpreted as an implicit criticism of the cultural heritage of antiquity, which to his humanistically inclined readers, and to himself, had provided the intellectual foundation for scholarly inquiries. In defending that heritage, Zarlino proposes what we might call a historicist argument: the modal system of the *Antichi* and their numbering of the species were appropriate, given the structure of *their* gamut.[16] This argument still does not imply, however, that there is only one possible rational order of the modes for any particular gamut. On the contrary, the option of renaming and renumbering the modes in different ways *ad beneplacitum* is always available, and at any rate will only affect the exterior, "extrinsic" aspects of the modes, at the same time leaving unaltered their "intrinsic form and substance" determined by a characteristic sequence of tones and semitones. Such a thesis, persuasive as it may be, threatens to compromise the scope and the significance of Zarlino reform, inasmuch as it suggests that there is no compelling need to order the modal finals in one way or another. At the very least, the passage reads like a frank acknowledgement of the ultimately "cosmetic" nature of the author's modal reform: by Zarlino's own reasoning, the relationship between the hexachord and the six modal finals is nothing but a *debolissimo accidente*.

Zarlino's admission may explain the reason why his proposed reform appears to have attracted little interest among future generations of musicians, including those active in or around Venice. The modally ordered collections published by prominent organists of S. Marco, such as Claudio Merulo and the Gabrielis, for instance, do not reflect Zarlino's new modal order. Most intriguing is Merulo's *Ricercari d'intavolatura d'organo* of 1567, which contains eight compositions (see Table 8.1).

It is interesting that Merulo (or his publisher) labels the two pieces in F as belonging to the eleventh and twelfth mode, rather to the fifth and sixth,

---

[15] VII Rag. quinto, Def. Zarlino, *Dimostrationi harmoniche*, 1571, p. 248, translation mine.
[16] Zarlino's '*Antichi*' are the authors of classical antiquity, as clearly stated in chapters 3 and 4 of book 4 of the *Istitutioni*.

Table 8.1. Modal designations and modal
finals of Merulo's *Ricercari* of 1567

1. Ricercar del primo tuono	[D]
2. Ricercar del secondo tuono	[D]
3. Ricercar del terzo tuono	[E]
4. Ricercar del quarto tuono	[E]
5. Ricercar dell'undecimo tuono	[F]
6. Ricercar del duodecimo tuono	[F]
7. Ricercar del settimo tuono	[G]
8. Ricercar dell'ottavo tuono	[G]

as the numerical progression of the modes would demand. Thus, Merulo's
anthology reads like an indirect endorsement of Glarean's modal theory
(and likewise of Zarlino's 1558 *Istitutioni*), which had argued that the traditional F mode with B flat should in fact be considered a transposition of
the C mode up a fourth.[17] Likewise, the modal labeling used by Andrea and
Giovanni Gabrieli and Girolamo Diruta for their instrumental adopts the
twelve-mode system beginning with D.[18] Rare instances of music anthologies ordered according to Zarlino's new numbering are those by Claude Le
Jeune (*Dodecacorde*, 1598; *Printemps*, 1603; *Octonaires*, 1606).[19] One may
speculate that the ostensible benefit of the reform (a better and more "natural" sequence of the twelve modal categories) did not outweigh its main
liability, namely, its going against a deep-rooted musical practice, relent-
lessly committed to memory, that from time immemorial had associated D
with *protus*, E with *deuterus*, and so on, with no difficulties whatsoever in
spite of the parallel practice of hexachordal solmization.

Given the centuries-old convention of considering D as the first modal
final, it is not surprising that the suggestion to reorder the modal finals
against an underlying hexachord fell on deaf ears. *Pace* Zarlino's claim that
his new order was more "natural" than the old one, his proposal reads like a
solution in search of a problem. But Zarlino's attempt to blend together the
theories of the hexachord and the modes was not limited to the issue of the
diatonic order of the modal finals, as we will now see.

---

[17] For a description of this collection, see H. M. Brown, *Instrumental Music Printed Before 1600*
(Boston: Harvard University Press, 1965), catalogue number [1567]$_2$. A second edition of
the *Ricercari* was published in 1605. The eight compositions, which mark a stylistic turning
point in the history of the genre, have recently been edited by J. Morehen (Madison, WI: A-R
Editions, 2000).

[18] See Brown, *Instrumental Music*, catalogue numbers 1589$_3$ 1593$_3$, 1593$_4$, 1595$_3$, and others.

[19] See F. Dobbins and I. His, "Claude Le Jeune," *NG 2*, vol. 14, pp. 531–4.

Modal transposition via the hexachord

After proposing his new numbering of the modes in the 1571 *Dimostrationi*, Zarlino incorporated it in the 1573 edition of the *Istitutioni*. Towards the end of his life, in 1589, he also published a collected edition of both his musical and non-musical works. Although the 1589 edition of the *Istitutioni* was largely a reproduction of the 1573 text, it also introduced occasional textual variants that confirm the author's marked interest in hexachordal theory in the last years of his life.[20]

One of these variants pertains to the issue of modal transposition, which Zarlino discusses first as a general property of the modes in *Istitutioni*, book 4, chapters 16 and 17, then also in the following twelve chapters dedicated to each individual modal category. In these pages Zarlino gives full endorsement to an argument that Glarean had invoked a decade earlier to justify the formal recognition of the A and C modes in addition to the traditional eight. Glarean had contended that a composition ending on D with B natural as a regular pitch should not be assigned to the same modal category as another D piece emphasizing B-flat instead.[21] According to this view, any diatonic mode featuring a default B-flat is in fact a transposition down a fifth (or up a fourth) of a "white-key-only" modal type. Thus, A-Aeolian transposes down to D with B-flat, C-Ionian to F with B-flat, and D-Dorian to G with B-flat (and E-natural). Traditional octenary theory accepted this argument in the case of G pieces with B-flat, which it understood as transposed D "Dorian" pieces. It did not accept it, however, in the case of D pieces, which theorists before Glarean ascribed to the *protus* mode irrespective of whether they featured B-flat or B-natural as a default pitch.

In line with Glarean, Zarlino maintains that to alter the status of the B key is to alter the position of the semitone within the diatonic species that are constitutive of the mode, thus those species themselves. Because the Greater Perfect System assigned B natural and B flat to two different

---

[20] A facsimile of the 1573 edition of *Istitutioni* is available from Gregg Press (Ridgewood, NJ, 1966); for the 1589 edition I have relied on the online edition by F. Wiering available in the *TMI*), and on G. Zarlino, *Le istitutioni harmoniche, Venezia, 1561*, ed. I. Fenlon and P. Da Col (Bologna, BO: Forni, 1999), which also provides the variants of the 1589 edition (Appendix I, pp. 56–95).

[21] 'So the Aeolian and Hypoaeolian conclude their songs on *D*, but with *fa* on the *b* key ... The Ionian and Hypoionian end on *F*, the Dorian and Hypodorian on *G*, but likewise with *fa* on the *b* key, for the *synemmenon* tetrachord has been invented so that the lowest systems could have a place in the upper keys [i.e. so that the modes could be transposed a fourth higher]', in Miller, trans., *Henricus Glareanus: Dodecachordon*, Vol. I, p. 140.

Tetrachords – respectively "disjunct" (*diezeugmenon*) and "conjunct" (*synemmenon*) – Renaissance theorists such as Zarlino and Glarean also tended to explain modal change and transposition as involving a modification of the structural species of fourth, often described as *Diatessaron* or *Tetrachordo*. In Chapter 16, for instance, Zarlino writes:

> Quando per tutta la cantilena, cioè in ciascuna parte, in luogo del Tetrachordo Diezeugmenon usiamo il Synemmenon, e in luogo di cantar la detta cantilena per la proprietà del ♮ quadrato, la cantiamo per quella del b molle ... questo Tetrachordo non è posto accidentalmente nella cantilena, ma è naturale, e il Modo si chiama Trasportato ... e cotale Tetrachordo ha possanza di trasmutare un Modo nell'altro.

> [When the tetrachord Synemmenon [i.e., a-b flat-c-d] is used in place of the Diezeugmenon [i.e., b-c-d-e] throughout the whole composition, that is, in every voice, and instead of singing the composition according to the property of b-natural, it is sung according to that of b-flat ... [that] tetrachord is not placed in the composition accidentally, but rather is natural, and the mode is said to be transposed ... When used in this manner, the tetrachord Synemmenon has the power to transform one mode into another.[22]

In the following chapter, Zarlino explains that the most common transposition level of any mode is up a fourth, with the exchange of B-natural for B-flat ("every composition using ♮ may be transposed a fourth higher with the help of B-flat, and vice versa").[23] Although in this particular context Zarlino does not explicitly connect the two alternative B keys with the underlying tetrachords (as he had just done in chapter 16), there is no reason to doubt that such implicit tetrachordal grouping is still in place. Indeed, at least since the twelfth century theorists had referred to the B flat "string" either in isolation, or as part of the *synemmenon tetrachord*.[24]

Zarlino left unaltered those two chapters of book 4 on modal change and modal transposition in all subsequent editions of the *Istitutioni*.[25] This is not the case, however, for the references to transposition in the chapters dedicated to each of the twelve modes that constitute the bulk of book 4.

---

[22] Zarlino, *Le istitutioni harmoniche*, 1558, repr. 1965, book 4, ch. 16, p. 318; Zarlino, *Le istitutioni harmoniche*, 1573, repr. 1966, p. 389; Zarlino, *Le istitutioni harmoniche*, 1589, online ed. book 4, ch. 16, p. 409; G. Zarlino, *On the Modes: Part Four of Le istitutioni harmoniche*, ed. V. Cohen (New Haven: Yale University Press, 1983, p. 50.

[23] " ... ogni cantilena che procede per la Chorda [sqb] si [può] trasportare per una Diatessaron in acuto, con l'aiuto della Chorda b; overo il contrario ... " (Zarlino, *Le istitutioni harmoniche*, 1558, repr. 1965, p. 319).

[24] Theogerus of Metz (d. 1120), for instance, points out that "Quidam (autem) musici non ponunt tetrachordum synemmeni, sed tantum unam chordam, et vocant eam mollem" ("Some musicians ... do not apply the tetrachord synēmmenōn, but only one degree, and call it soft," (*GS* II, p. 187).

[25] These are chapters 16 and 17, respectively.

Usually in the last sentence of these chapters, Zarlino reminds the reader of the possibility of transposing that mode from its regular "seat" (with white keys) a fifth lower or a fourth higher, with the addition of B♭. His account of what exactly gets transposed, however, differs slightly in the three editions (see Table 8.2).

The 1558 text mentions almost exclusively the "B♭ string" – referred to as *trite synemmenon* in only one case – as the means by which transposition takes place. The exception is Mode 11, which to Zarlino may be transposed "passando per le chorde del Tetrachordo Synemmenon" (Section 5, left column). In 1573 this reference to *synemmenon tetrachord* appears in two additional excerpts, i.e., in the chapters on the plagal C mode (now renumbered as Mode 2), and on the authentic D mode (now renumbered as Mode 3) (Sections 1 and 6, central column). Presumably, this reference to the tetrachord as the material agent of transposition applies also to the remaining nine modes. Two years earlier, however, Zarlino had also briefly referred to the *hexachord* as the agent of modal transposition in the last chapter of his 1571 *Dimostrationi*:

Ma perchè tali trasportationi si possono fare commodamente per tutti li Modi, col favore dell'Hexacordo Synemennon [*sic*], però dico, che la Modulatione di ciascheduno delli Dodici modi si può trasportare in acuto per una Diatessaron .... Et ... verso il grave per una Diapente.

[But because all modes can be easily transposed with the help of the *synemmenon* hexachord, I conclude that the modulation of each of those twelve modes can be transposed either a fourth higher ... or a fifth lower.][26]

Yet Zarlino himself may have been only half-convinced of this explanation, since he did not pursue it at all in the 1573 *Istitutioni*. Or did he retain the old wording from the 1558 *Istitutioni* through oversight?

The real surprise comes in the 1589 edition of the *Istitutioni* (see the right column of Table 8.2), which for the first time features the term "Hexachordo" not only in those three places that had read "Tetrachordo" in the 1573 edition (Sections 1, 5 and 6, right column), but also in the surveys of Modes 8, 9, and 10 (Sections 2, 3 and 4, right column). In the remaining six cases (Modes 4, 5, 6, 7, 11, and 12, not shown in Table 8.2), Zarlino still observes that transposition occurs "with the help of the Bb string." It seems as if Zarlino had a dramatic change of mind on the nuts and bolts of transposition right before committing his final edition of the *Istitutioni* to the press. But to invoke the hexachord as the means by which modal transposition is

[26] Zarlino, *Dimostrationi harmoniche,* Rag. Quinto, prop. xxv, p. 310.

Table 8.2. Zarlino's changing account of modal transposition (comparing *Istitutioni harmoniche* 1558, 1573, and 1589)

ISTITUTIONI HARMONICHE, 1558	ISTITUTIONI HARMONICHE, 1573	ISTITUTIONI HARMONICHE, 1589
1. on Mode 1 (D authentic): "Questo Modo col Nono hà strettissima parentella: percioche li Musici compongono nel suo luogo propio le loro cantilene del Nono modo, fuori delle sue chorde naturali, trasportandolo **nell'acuto per vna Diatessaron, ouero nel graue per vna Diapente; lassando la chorda ♮, & ponendoui la ♭**" (p. 321).	**1. on Mode 3 (D authentic):** "Questo Modo hà strettissima parentela... con l'Undecimo... percioche li Musici compongono nelle sue Chorde le loro Canzoni del Modo Undecimo, trasportandole nell'acuto per una Diatessaron; **lasciando da un canto la chorda ♮; e ponendovi la ♭; la qual serve al Tetrachordo synemennon**" (p. 397).	**1. on Mode 3 (D authentic):** "Questo Modo hà strettissima parentella... con l'Undecimo... percioche i Musici compongono nelle sue Chorde le lor Canzoni del Modo Vndecimo, trasportandolo nell'acuto per una Diatessaron; **lasciando da un canto la chorda ♮, & ponendoui la ♭, la qual serue all'Hexachordo synemennon**" (p. 417).
2. on Mode 6 (F plagal): "Questo Modo si può trasportare come gli altri fuori delle sue chorde naturali, ponendolo in acuto per vna Diatessaron, **con l'aiuto della chorda ♭**" (p. 329).	**2. on Mode 8 (F plagal):** "Questo [Modo] etiandio si puo trasportare nell'acuto per una Quarta, **con l'aiuto della Chorda b;** come si trasportano gli altri" (p. 407).	**2. on Mode 8 (F plagal):** "Questo etiandio si può trasportare nell'acuto per una Quarta, **con l'aiuto dell'Hexachordo synemennon; cioè con la Chorda b. che contiene;** come si trasportano gli altri" (p. 425).
3. on Mode 7 (G authentic): "Ma questo Modo si può trasportare per vna Diapente nel graue, **con l'aiuto della chorda ♭,** come si trasporta etiandio gli altri" (p. 332).	**3. on Mode 9 (G authentic):** "Questo modo è molto in uso appresso gli Ecclesiastici, e nelle cantilene de gli altri Musici si trova il più delle volte nelle sue Chorde naturali; ma molte volte **con l'aiuto della Chorda b** è trasportato nel grave per una Diapente, senza alcuno incommodo." (p. 407).	**3. on Mode 9 (G authentic):** "Questo modo... nelle cantilene de gli altri Musici si trova il più delle uolte nelle sue Chorde naturali; ma molte uolte **con l'aiuto della Chorda b, cioè, col mezo dell'Hexachordo synemennon,** è trasportato nel graue per una Diapente, senz'alcun'incommodo" (p. 428).

4. on Mode 8 (G plagal):
"Trasportasi questo Modo **per vna Diapente nel graue con l'aiuto della chorda** ♭" (p. 332).

5. on Mode 11 (C authentic):
"Questo Modo si trasporta fuori delle sue chorde naturali per vna Diatessaron nell'acuto; ouero per vna Diapente nel graue, con l'aiuto della chorda ♭; **passando per le chorde del Tetrachordo synemennon**" (p. 333).

6. on Mode 12 (C plagal):
"… li Musici, **con l'aiuto della chorda ♭, lo trasportano per vna Diatessaron nel graue**" (p. 335).

4. on Mode 10 (G plagal):
"Questo Modo si può trasportare come gli altri, fuori delle sue chorde naturali, ponendolo in acuto **per vna Diatessaron, con l'aiuto della chorda ♭ …**" (p. 409).

5. on Mode 1 (C authentic):
"Questo Modo si trasporta fuori delle sue Chorde naturali per vna Diatessaron verso l'acuto, tra la Diapason F & f; **passando per le Chorde del Tetrachordo Synemmenon, nelle quali si ritrova la Chorda ♭ …** " (p. 394).

6. on Mode 2 (C plagal):
"… li Musici con l'aiuto della chorda **♭ del Tetrachordo synemennon** lo trasportano nell'acuto per vna Diatessaron, tra le chorde della Diapason c & C" (p. 396).
And p. 394 reads: "ma li Moderni, **con l'aiuto del Tetrachordo synemmenon, nel quale si trova la Chorda ♭,** hanno fatto la maggior parte delle loro cantilene, che erano dell'Ottavo modo, del modo Secondo."

4. on Mode 10 (G plagal):
"Questo modo si può trasportar come gli altri, fuori delle sue chorde naturali; ponendolo in acuto **per una Diatessaron, con l'aiuto della chorda ♭, ò dell'Hexachordo synemennon**" (p. 428).

5. on Mode 1 (C authentic):
"Questo Modo si trasporta fuori delle sue Chorde naturali per vna Diatessaron uerso l'acuto, tra la Diapason F. & f, **passando per le Chorde del Hexachordo Synemennon, nelle quali si troua la Chorda ♭**" (p. 413).

6. on Mode 2 (C plagal):
"Et se ben le chorde naturali di questo Modo sono le mostrate di sopra, tuttavia i Musici con l'aiuto della chorda ♭, **dell'Hexachordo synemennon lo trasportano nell'acuto per una Diatessaron, tra le chorde della Diapason c. & C**" (p. 415).

achieved is in flagrant contradiction with other sections of the treatise, not to speak of medieval and Renaissance theory. Nowhere else in the *Istitutioni* does Zarlino recognize the hexachord as a structural component of individual modes, and the general discussion of modal change and modal transposition in the 1589 edition (again, in book 4, chapters 16 and 17) is a virtual duplication of the text from the 1558 edition.[27] In short: if the *diapason* and the species of fourth and fifth regulate the notion of individual mode, as Zarlino still firmly maintains, then why should modal transposition require a different operative segment, the "hexachord," for it to be performed?

For an explanation of these contradictory signals, we may go back to the "Ragionamento Quinto" in the 1571 *Dimostrationi harmoniche*. During the series of conversations held in Willaert's house shortly before the master's passing, Zarlino had defended his new "hexachordal" order of the octave species with the argument that "our main musicians have organized the musical strings into hexachords," and that consequently the first species of diapason should begin on C-*ut* rather than on D-*re*. In later sections of the Ragionamento he elaborates on the nature and the origin of such pitch ordering. Definition 20, for instance, reads as follows:

Hexachordo è un ordine di sei chorde che contiene quattro tuoni e uno semituono maggiore nel terzo luogo e contiene tra le sue quattro chorde più acute l'uno delli tetrachordi de gli antichi, quale ello piglia il suo nome.

[The hexachord is an arrangement of six strings that spans four tones with one semitone in the middle. It subsumes in its four upper notes one of the tetrachords of the ancient Greeks [i.e., E-F-G-a], from which it derives its name.][28]

The following five *definitioni* (XXI–XXV, pp. 280–1) describe each *hexachordo* from the lowest to the highest. Here Zarlino transfers the tetrachordal terminology of the Greater Perfect System (*hypaton, meson, diezeugmenon, synnemmenon,* and *hyperboleon*) directly onto his new hexachordal partitioning, so that the old *tetrachordo hypaton* is included in the new *hexachordo hypaton* from Γ to E, the *tetrachordo meson* in the *hexachordo meson* from C to a, and so on for all the others. Several pages later, in the "Proposta Quarta," Zarlino inserts one graph showing how the sixteen notes of the gamut from Γ to *aa* are grouped into the four overlapping *hexachordi*.[29] But such an explanation does not quite satisfy Willaert, who prompts Zarlino to add the *hexachordo synemmenon* as well:

[27] Compare Zarlino, *Le istitutioni harmoniche,* 1558, repr. 1965, pp. 317–20, with Zarlino, *Le istitutioni harmoniche,*1589, online ed. F. Wiering (*TMI*) pp. 408–11.
[28] Zarlino, *Dimostrationi harmoniche,* 1571, repr. 1966, p. 279.
[29] The graph is accessible online in the site of the *Thesaurus musicarum italicarum,* http://euromusicology.cs.uu.nl/. It is virtually identical to the upper half of Fig. 8.3.

Se li nostri hexachordi hanno a corrispondere, come fanno in effetto, alli tetrachordi de gli antichi, bisogno è che ve ne sia un altro che corrispondi allo synemennon. Però se'l vi è in piacere, dimostratecelo, acciò abbiamo la cosa perfetta.

[If our hexachords are to correspond to the tetrachords of the ancients, as they
do, then it is necessary to institute another one of them to match the synemmenon
tetrachord. Please demonstrate to us how this can be achieved if you wish, so that
we can fully understand this subject.][30]

Zarlino obliges to Willaert's request by presenting a new version of the
gamut that includes the *hexachordo synemmenon* (Fig. 8.3).

One may venture that a clearer statement of the alleged takeover of the
hexachord as the main diatonic segment from the old tetrachord is likely
not found anywhere else in the history of Western music theory, whether in
Latin or in the vernacular. But what are the practical implications of Zarlino's
hexachordal subdivision of the gamut? What factors led to this kind of partitioning, and what is its regulative power? Is it intended to represent the
default organization of the diatonic system ever since the "hexachord" was
introduced in music pedagogy in the eleventh century? Which of the three
diatonic units (tetrachords, octaves, and hexachords) has logical priority
over the others, and for which purposes? Zarlino comes nowhere close to
addressing such issues in his writings. He limits himself to the claim that
the hexachord provides a "more reasonable" articulation by virtue of two
main factors: firstly, the hexachord is preferable to the tetrachord as diatonic yardstick because it encompasses all three species of *diatessaron*; and
secondly, its internal series of tones and semitones is in line with a natural
order that calls for the more consonant intervals (such as the whole tone
and the major third) to be lower than the less consonant ones (such as the
semitone).[31]

Unquestionably, Zarlino mediated the idea of the hexachordal articulation of the gamut, as well as its terminology, from Gafori's *Practica musicae* of 1496. But Zarlino borrowed from Gafori more than the mere idea
of the hexachord as a yardstick; rather, his entire goal of providing the
"institutions of harmony," *pace* the openly Boethian reference in the title of
Zarlino's magnum opus, situates itself in the footsteps of Gafori. Boethius'
De institutione musica, after all, had dealt with musical mathematics to
the virtual exclusion of *musica practica* – with the possible exception of
the chapter on modal theory in book 5. On the other hand Zarlino, like

---

[30] Zarlino, *Dimostrationi harmoniche*, Rag. Quinto prop. IV, p. 290.
[31] See *Ibid.*, Rag. Quinto prop. VI, p. 293; Zarlino, *Le istitutioni harmoniche*, 1558, repr. 1965,
   book 2, ch. 48, p. 142, and the corresponding passage in Zarlino, *Le istitutioni harmoniche*,
   1589, online ed. F. Wiering (*TMI*) book 2, ch. 48, pp. 173–4.

Quinto.   291

PROPOSTA. V.

Si può aggiungere alli quattro primi il quinto Hexachordo detto Synemennon.

*Iano, come nella Penultima, accommodate le chorde Γ. ᴄA. ♮. C. D. E. F. G.
a. ♮. c. d. e. f. g. & aa: sopra la notata chorda ♮ & ♮: le quali, come nella Pre-
cedente : contengono i quattro primi Hexachordi : Hypaton : Meson : Diezeug
menon : & Hyperboleon. alli quali sia dibisogno aggiungere il quinto detto Synemennon.
Accomodo prima sopra la chorda a K, per la Decimanona del Terzo giorno : il Semituo*

Hexachordo hypaton.		Hexachordo diezeugmenon.	
Γ. A. ♮. C. D. E. F. G. a.		♮. c. d. e. f. g. aa.	
Tuono. Tuono. Se.mag. Tuono. Tuono. Se.mag. Tuono. Tuo-	no. Se.mag. Tuono. Tuono. Se.mag. Tuono.		
	Hexachordo meson.		Hexachordo hyperboleo

♮.	F. G. a.	b.	c. d.	K.
	Tuono. Tuono. Se.mag.	Tuono.	Tuono.	
	Hexachordo Synemennon.			

*no maggiore alla sua uera & naturale proportione : onde ne uiene a K,& l K. Ma pche a
K & l K è Semituono maggiore : & è contenuto nella sua forma naturale : però bisogna,
secondo la sua Definitione : che ello sia maggiore di una quarta parte di uno Comma. Onde accommodo prima esso Comma, per la Trentesima del Terzo ragionamento, alla sua
proportione : di modo che la chorda l K sia l'estremo graue di questo interuallo : & m K
l'acuto : dipoi lo diuido, per la Vndecima simigliantemente del Terzo nominato, in quattro parti equali : & aggiungendo l b con a l: tra a K & b K haueremo, per la sua Definitio
ne,il Semituono maggiore : accresciuto però: per la Ventesima sesta definitione di hoggi:
di una quarta parte del Comma l K & m K: & come al senso è manifesto. Hora dico, che
ritrouandosi tra F.G. a. b. c. & d. quattro Tuoni & uno maggior Semituono : si come tra
F G : G a : b c : & c d il Tuono : & tra a b.il nominato Semituono : dico per la Ventesima
definitione F. G. a. b. c. & d, essere Hexachordo. Et perche F corrisponde, per la Decima
ottaua Definitione, alla Parhypatemeson : G alla Lychanos : a alla Mese : b alla Tritesy
nemennon : c alla Paranetesynemennon : & d alla Netesynemennon : & l'ordine di queste Sei chorde ha principio nella Parhypate meson : & contiene anco nelle quattro più
acute chorde il tetrachordo Synemennon : però F. G. a. b. c. & d, per la Ventesima quinta
Defini-*

Fig. 8.3. Zarlino's hexachordal division of the gamut (Zarlino,
Dimostrationi harmoniche, Rag. Quinto prop. V, p. 291).

Gafori in his *Practica*, aimed at offering to his readers not just the basic precepts for music making, but rather a systematic and even an aesthetic/ philosophic perspective on *musica practica* – a view of the discipline that raised music to the level of a science worthy of being known and admired by cultivated readers. Most importantly, Zarlino followed Gafori and other contemporaries, such as Vicentino and Glarean, in proposing a view of music as a historical discipline that has been thoroughly molded by cultural change. Once again, then, the hexachord functions in Zarlino more as a historical than a strictly music-theoretical category: it operates as a symbol of the contribution of the musical knowledge of the *moderni* over that of the *antichi*. But from *contributing* to *surpassing* is an easy step: in a veiled fashion, Zarlino describes the newly minted hexachord as the bearer of progress over the old and worn-out tetrachord, a new musical paradigm that is destined to open up new vistas to both music *and* music theory.

Zarlino's intellectual background and orientations go a long way toward explaining the speculative approach to hexachordal theory at work in both the *Istitutioni* and the *Dimostrationi*. The range of the major sixth for him was not a pedagogical or pragmatic tool, as it had been to Guido and Hermannus some five centuries earlier, but rather an abstract analytic tool able to provide new and "more natural" alignments between the various components of the musical system, such as the modal finals. Thus, in spite of Zarlino's claim that his hexachordal division of the octave was rooted in medieval practice (see his frequent references to "i nostri musici"), his hexachord, like Gafori's, was only a distant relative of either Guido's or Hermannus': firstly, whereas Hermannus derived his major sixth by expanding the tetrachord of Hucbald by one step in both directions (C+DEFG+a), Gafori and Zarlino obtained their hexachord by extending the Greek tetrachord down a major third (CD+EFGa). Secondly, whereas Guido and Hermannus came to ascribe a particular (and limited) significance to the hexachord after a close study of the *modi vocum* and chant melodies, Gafori and Zarlino clearly had lost sight of the very reasons why the hexachord had a particular role to play within the 'heptachordally conceived' gamut.

But Zarlino also differed from Gafori in one crucial respect, namely, his complete lack of familiarity with medieval music pedagogy, particularly with the medieval understanding of hexachordal solmization. Gafori's interest in the music theory of classical antiquity had been no weaker than Zarlino's. At the same time, however, in his early years he had received at least some exposure to chant theory, having read Marchetto, Muris, and Ugolino in addition to the works by his contemporaries, such as Gallicus, Burtius, Tinctoris, and Ramos. For his part Zarlino appears to have had, astoundingly, no direct exposure to any "Latin" author between Boethius and Gafori. Thus, not only was his knowledge of the medieval hexachordal system thoroughly second-hand; it also relied exclusively on the distorting filter of Gafori's *Practica*.[32]

The hexachord as a rational object: the Neo-Scholasticism of the *Dimostrationi*

In the eyes of its author, the *Dimostrationi harmoniche* were to overhaul the disciplinary foundations of musical knowledge by placing them on a new, scientific basis. Zarlino's overarching goal is to present the traditional subject matter of music theory – i.e., the organization of the gamut, the location of pitches and their distances on the monochord, modes, consonances, etc. – as the result of logical necessity, that is to say, of a rigorous method of demonstration by which particular premises lead indisputably to particular results. As Zarlino explains in the long dialogue introducing the *Ragionamento Primo*, his new model of musical science will lead to a knowledge of "things in themselves" that are necessarily true.

In his recent dissertation on this treatise, John Emil Kelleher has shown that Zarlino had at his disposal two complementary methods for the realization of his dream of a scientific music theory.[33] The first one was the inductive method of argumentation that had constituted the basis of natural philosophy at least since Aristotle's *Posterior Analytics*. The principle challenge faced by any form of inductive knowledge is how to convincingly turn the knowledge of sensible objects, obtained through the channels of perception, into knowledge of *classes* of objects acquired through reason. The instrument of the demonstrative syllogism provides this logical "bridge" from the particular to the general, and it does so by reducing the material elements of objects to formal ones that are susceptible to being

---

[32] The composition of Zarlino's private book collection confirms his complete lack of exposure to medieval music theory. It is striking that of the more than 1,100 volumes listed at the time of his death, only one was in manuscript format and may have contained medieval texts (on Zarlino's library, see Collins Judd, *Reading Renaissance Music Theory*, pp. 181–4). Frans Wiering has demonstrated that the only medieval treatises mentioned by Zarlino in his writings are Guido of Arezzo's *Micrologus* and John Cotto's *De musica*. All other references are either to recent authors (i.e., no older than Gafori), or to the classics. See his "The Language of the Modes: Studies in the History of Polyphonic Modality (Ph.D. diss., University of Amsterdam, 1995), pp. 199.

[33] J. E. Kelleher, "Zarlino's 'Dimostrationi harmoniche' and Demonstrative Methodologies in the Sixteenth Century," (Ph.D. diss., Columbia University, 1993).

comprehended and defined by reason.[34] The method of syllogism, however, plays a comparatively minor role in the *Dimostrationi* and has no bearings on Zarlino's handling of the hexachord.

The second, "axiomatic" method is complementary to the first one. Whereas syllogism proceeds from the particular to the general, the axiomatic method is based on the assumption of *a priori* principles accounting for universal characteristics or behaviors, and proceeds to derive from them the knowledge of particular instances.[35] This method is central to Euclidian geometry, to which Zarlino refers extensively in the *Dimostrationi*. Furthermore, Zarlino's treatise borrows frequently from the *Elementa musicalia* by Jacques Lefèvre d'Étaples (Faber Stapulensis), itself based on Euclid's *Elementa*, the anonymous *Sectio canonis*, and Boethius' *De institutione musica*.[36]

As Fend and Kelleher have shown, the overall structure of the *Dimostrationi* reflects the treatise's adherence to the axiomatic method of argumentation. Each *ragionamento* (corresponding to one day of musical conversations in Willaert's house) begins with several "definitions" that introduce the main subject for that section of the treatise (for instance, the notion of "sonorous body" or the link between numerical ratios and diatonic intervals). The *Ragionamento Primo* opens with an especially long list of first principles of different kinds, to which Zarlino will refer in the rest of the treatise to lay out his harmonic science; these first principles are grouped into "definitions" (*definitioni*), "postulates" (*dimande*), and "axioms" properly said (*dignità*). The main function of the postulates is to create the condition for the final derivation of particular cases from the general definitions; as Kelleher aptly puts it, they establish the "sphere of action" within which certain operations may take place. For example, the postulate of *Ragionamento Terzo* asserting that space is divisible in an infinite number of ways allows for the

---

[34] *Ibid.*, pp. 1–10.

[35] "… tale Dimostratione i nostri addimandano *a priori*: et dimostratione *propter quid*. Et questa è differente dalla Dimostratione, che si chiama *a posteriori* et *quia*: che è quella, la quale si piglia da i segni e dale cagioni universali, si come del secondo modo di Sapere di sopra ho dichiarato [i.e., knowledge by accident, not subject to the laws of necessity]" (Zarlino, *Dimostrationi harmoniche*, Rag. primo p. 13).

[36] M. Fend, "Zarlinos Versuch einer Axiomatisierung der Musiktheorie in den *Dimostrationi harmoniche* (1571), *Musiktheorie* 4 (1989): 113–26. The treatise by Stapulensis was first published in 1496, but later editions came out with the title *Musica libris quatuor demonstrata*, which more closely recalls the title of Zarlino's treatise. In the opening pages of the *Dimostrationi* Fend finds traces of the Latin translation of Euclid's *Elementa*, published in 1560 by Francesco Barocchi (p. 115). For a modern edition of Lefèvre d'Etaples' treatise – under the name of *Musica libri quatuor demonstrata* (Paris, 1551) – see O. Trachier, ed., *Renaissance française: traités, methods, prefaces, ouvrages generaux*, 4 vols. (Courlay, France: Éditions Fuzeau classique, 2005), vol. II, pp. 141–228.

division of the gamut into various segments of different lengths, such as tetrachords, hexachords, and others. Finally, the "axioms" consist of general principles that are valid for all disciplines. Axioms correspond to general logical principles expressing relationships between the part and the whole, the transitive property of equality, and others.

After the exposition of the first principles, each *ragionamento* proceeds to demonstrate the particular consequences and applications of those principles. Zarlino calls each of these derivative statements a *proposta* (literally: "proposal," better translated as "proposition"). A common type of proposition in the *Dimostrationi* is operational in nature; Zarlino uses it, for instance, to demonstrate that certain intervals may be derived in reality (once they have been formally defined) by calculating the corresponding proportional lengths on a vibrating string. In Zarlino's axiomatic method, then, propositions bring to existence the subjects previously identified in the definition. The demonstration of the proposition takes place via a "construction," which Kelleher defines as:

The representation of the objects posited in the enunciation of the proposition's *proposta* … as a means of demonstrating the "existence" of the defined term. By this means the transition from the nominal definitions of "subjects" and their hypothetical cause to an "objective" definition in things occur. When the proposition shows that the object's characteristics agree with those illustrated in prior definitions, absolute knowledge of the objects is achieved."[37]

Zarlino's demonstration of the hexachordal division of the gamut follows precisely this logical chain. Before examining this section in detail, it is important to realize that this type of division is one of the main subjects of the *Ragionamento Quinto*, the only truly original section of the treatise, dedicated to introducing new contributions to musical science that were unknown to the ancients. In this final discussion of the treatise, along with the hexachordal division of the *nostri musici*, Zarlino also proposes several modified tuning systems for the instruments (i.e., temperaments), which do away with the venerable tradition of pure Pythagorean tuning that had reigned unchallenged for many centuries.

The hexachordal division of the gamut is the subject of six consecutive definitions in the opening pages of the *Ragionamento Quinto* (def. 20–5). The first definition describes the hexachord as an "order of six notes containing four tones and one semitone in the middle, as well as a full tetrachord of the ancients – from which its name 'hexachord' comes – in its upper

[37] Kelleher, "Zarlino's 'Dimostrationi harmoniche," pp. 167–8.

four notes."[38] The subsequent five definitions locate the five hexachords on the gamut. Their names (*hypaton, meson, diezeugmenon, hyperbolaion,* and *synemmenon*), add further weight to the claim that they originated from the old tetrachords of the Greek *systema teleion,* which eventually became the basis for the medieval gamut.[39]

By now readers are well aware, of course, that the definitions are only the first step of Zarlino's axiomatic method. In propositions 4 and 5, Zarlino proceeds to physically "construct" those hexachords on the gamut, and to show them with the help of *ad hoc* tables (290–1). His prose becomes once again quite detailed, as he demonstrates the exact location of the hexachordal sets on the gamut. The constant reference to Greek pitch names in this section (i.e., *hypate meson, paranete diezeugmenon,* etc.), rather than to the A-G letters implicitly confirms the basic narrative of ancient tetrachords giving way to modern hexachords. In turn, this demonstration legitimizes other key harmonic innovations by Zarlino, such as the new order of the modes and the new, hexachord-based notion of transposition discussed above.

But Zarlino's hexachords exist only as formal or rational entities outside of any clear referential context. Several times in the *Dimostrationi* Zarlino points out that the Latin musicians (called *i nostri musici* or *i musici Latini*) substituted a new hexachordal division of the gamut to the old, tetrachordal one. The exact effects and the scope of this division are not clear, however, not only because Zarlino discusses them nowhere in his treatise, but also because he continues to refer to the classical, tetrachordal division of the gamut to justify the three musical genera (diatonic, chromatic, and enharmonic), modal transposition, and modal ranges. Nor is it clear how Zarlino understands the new division proposed by the *musici Latini* in relation to the organizing principle of the octave, which he always considers as the theoretical first principle (*a primum*) of his musical science. Again, in which sense is it possible to argue that the *musici Latini* divided the gamut hexachordally, given Zarlino's contention that they also accepted octave duplication and octave-based modal categories articulated into fourths and fifths?

In short, by considering the hexachord as a formal category, Zarlino lost sight of its history, which in turn might have advised him against considering it as a formal category in the first place. His axiomatic method gave final legitimation to the recent notion of *hexachordum* as the diatonic yardstick of Christian music. More importantly, the a historical approach

---

[38] Zarlino, *Dimostrationi harmoniche,* Rag. Quinto Def. xx, pp. 279–80.
[39] *Ibid.,* Rag. Quinto Deff. xxi–xxv, pp. 280–1.

to musical science proposed by Zarlino has lost all connection with the ideals of humanist scholarship and education as expressed, for instance, by Johannes Gallicus a century earlier. Recall that Gallicus' scholarly method was primarily rooted in a dialogical interpretation of authoritative texts as much as in personal experience. It was his dissatisfaction with Guidonian solmization that led him to obtain a first-hand knowledge of Guidonian and pre-Guidonian sources, just as it was his concern with the poor state of musical life in the church that led him to explore alternatives to the six syllables. To Gallicus, the knowledge of music was instrumental to a spiritual practice. As such, it could not reside within the formal constraints of a system, but rather existed necessarily in history: the best musical science was the one that had once provided a satisfactory answer to pressing musical problems. Zarlino, on the other hand, had neither any awareness of the historical origins and functions of Guido's "hexachord," nor, as it seems, any interest in reconstructing it. Rather, he studied it as an abstract tool for segmenting the gamut, in a manner reminiscent of the formalism displayed by Garlandia and Lambertus and other late-thirteenth-century authors. For this reason alone, the reforms of hexachordal theory advocated by Gafori and Zarlino may be viewed as proposing a counter-reformation of sorts that emphasized the combinatorial and speculative sides of music theory over its practical orientation. More importantly, in the context of the long span of hexachordal theory, Gafori and Zarlino emerge as the authors who parted ways from the medieval tradition once and for all, whether intentionally or not.

Epilogue: Discarding the Guidonian image of early music

Without a doubt, the Guidonian *querelle* of the late fifteenth century marked a decisive major turning point in the long history of the hexachordal system. Not only did the understanding of hexachordal theory change substantially as a result of that dispute, but its original proponent, Guido of Arezzo, in the process came to acquire the status of a "founding father" who had single-mindedly provided a new "tonal" foundation for church music and *ipso facto* relegated the old Greek tetrachord to the status of a museum piece. As a music-historical consciousness gradually emerged in the second half of the Guidonian millennium, the classicizing, post-Renaissance image of Guido of Arezzo became indissolubly linked with the modern understanding of the medieval hexachordal system as the very backbone of "antient music."

In the post-Renaissance era, the confrontation between the reformist side of the Guidonian debate, initiated by Ciconia and Gallicus, and what we might label the "counter-reformation" wing of Burtius and Gafori never quite reached a final resolution. Rather, it simply morphed from a pedagogical debate pro or against solmization as a tool for sight singing to a historiographic and music-analytic one that ultimately had to do with the structural idiosyncrasies of early music and with the nature of its musical grammar vis-à-vis those of modern music. Guido's hexachord in the process became the symbol of a bygone musical era to be either championed or condemned, and the marker of historical, national, and cultural identities that in turn became the focus of political and ideological confrontations.

For instance, to the members of conservative eighteenth-century musical circles in London and Vienna, such as John Christoph Pepusch, Guido's hexachordal theory remained a pedagogical model to imitate, a symbol of the wisdom and moral soundness of the ancients (in this case identified with Renaissance and Baroque musicians) that was to be upheld against the corrupt (and corruptive) tendencies (musical and not) of the Moderns.[1] Indeed, it has been pointed out that his *Treatise* "represents a last-ditch attempt to restore solmization as a basis for the instruction of

---

[1] J. C. Pepusch, *A Treatise of Harmony*, London, 1730; facs. (New York: Broude, 1966).

harmonic theory."[2] As I have shown elsewhere, Pepusch fully endorsed the Gaforian theory of the hexachord's origin from the Greek tetrachord; not surprisingly so, as Gafori's foundational reading of hexachordal theory provided a tangible means to isolate and idealize a particular historical period.[3]

Decades later, Charles Burney and John Hawkins followed suit, as shown by the following excerpts:

That the fourth was a favourite and important interval in the music of the ancients, is plain from the great system of two octaves having been composed of five of these tetrachords, in the same manner as the scale of Guido is of different hexachords ... the fourth in the ancient music served as a boundary to a system of four sounds, in the same manner as a hexachord did in the Guido scale, and as an octave does for eight sounds in the more modern practice.[4]

[T]he scale, as it stood in the time of Guido, was not adapted for the reception of the six syllables, and therefore the application which he made of them does necessarily imply some previous improvements of the scale ... It is pretty certain that this improvement could be no other than the converting [of] the ancient tetrachords into hexachords.[5]

But more significant than the acceptance of the strong view of the hexachord in the writings of the earliest music historians of the modern era is their open acknowledgement that their views on the subject were shaped to a great extent by Renaissance authors. Hawkins, in particular, praises Gafori's *Practica* as a most authoritative witness of the musical theories and practices of the Middle Ages:

Many other manuscripts on this subject [the church modes] there are ... but as a comparison of the several definitions therein contained, might introduce a degree of confusion which no diligent enquirer would wish to encounter, it is safest to rely on those authors who have written since the invention of printing, and whose works have stood the test of ages. Of these Gaffurius, as he is of the greatest antiquity, so is he of unquestionable authority. In his book entitled *Practica Musicae utriusque Cantus*, printed in the year 1502, he has entered into a large discussion of the ecclesiastical tones.[6]

---

[2] M. Boyd and G. Beeks, "Pepusch, John Christoph," in *NG 2*, vol. 19, p. 326.

[3] Pepusch, *A Treatise on Harmony*, pp. 67–8. See my "Virtual Segments," 426–8.

[4] C. Burney, *A General History of Music, from the Earliest Ages to the Present Period* (London, 1789), vol. 1, p. 3 and 6.

[5] J. Hawkins, *A General History of the Science and Practice of Music* (London, 1776), vol. I, book 4, chapter 34, p. 156. See also chapter 35, pp. 158–61.

[6] *Ibid.*, vol. 1, book 3, chapter 28, p. 132.

One cringes at Hawkins' suggestion to those "diligent enquirers" forced to deal with barely legible and confusing medieval manuscripts; his "safest" path is of course a recipe for philological disaster. But the real significance of the passage lies in Hawkins' justification for selecting Gafori as a reliable historical witness: on the one hand, he was "ancient" enough to be able to speak as a "native observer" of medieval musical practice and theory; on the other hand, he was also modern or enlightened enough to adopt the medium of the press, which almost by definition brings clarity, order, and authority to the thorny problems of textual criticism posed by the manuscript era.

By the early 1800s, the critical assessments of the Guidonian contribution to music theory had acquired a more overtly political and nationalistic color. One of the most influential studies on this subject in the nineteenth century was the publication of Luigi Angeloni (1759–1842), an intellectual *émigré* and political activist who tirelessly fought for the cause of Italian unification and independence.[7] To Angeloni, Guido's adoption of the hexachord as the main yardstick of the diatonic scale was one of the many factors that pointed to the cultural primacy of Italy in Europe and in the world at large. It is perhaps indicative of the nationalistic overtones fast accruing on this topic in the early nineteenth century that non-Italian music scholars (such as Guillaume André Villoteau and Raphael Georg Kiesewetter) seem to have been less inclined to espouse the strong view of Guido as *inventor musicae* favored by the Italians throughout the *risorgimento*.[8]

The coming of age of musicology as a scholarly discipline at the end of the nineteenth century created the conditions for a more cautious assessment of Guido's contribution, exemplified by the works of Michele Falchi and Antonio Brandi, both published in 1882.[9] However, musicological endeavors of more recent generations have also found new layers of meaning in the post-Renaissance notion of *hexachordum* as a diatonic yardstick. In particular, the high call for historically informed reconstructions and interpretations of medieval and Renaissance musical cultures – together with the consolidation, after World War II, of the music-historical canon, conceived as a series of self-standing historical eras – has led to privileging

---

[7] L. Angeloni, *Sopra la vita, le opere, ed il sapere di Guido d'Arezzo, restauratore della scienza e dell' arte musica* (Paris, 1811).

[8] G. A. Villoteau, *Recherches sur l'analogie de la musique avec les arts* (Paris, 1807); R. G. Kiesewetter, *Guido von Arezzo. Sein leben und wirken* (Leipzig, 1840). Kiesewetter's study was conceived as a reply to Angeloni's, which was in turn a response to Villoteau's.

[9] M. Falchi, *Studi su Guido Monaco* (Florence: G. Barbera, 1882); A. Brandi, *Guido Aretino, monaco di S. Benedetto: della sua vita, del suo tempo e dei suoi scritti; studio storico-critico* (Florence: Arte della stampa, 1882).

the more conceptually distant and idiosyncratic aspects of early music that are documented in the music-theoretical sources. The theme of the opposition between hexachord- and octave-based notions of musical space that has informed numerous musicological studies of the last few decades – with a few notable antecedents, as we have seen – has to be read as partly the outcome of that scholarly orientation.[10]

In short, modernity has often had more reasons to embrace the foundational image of Guido that it received from the hands of prominent authors such as Gafori and Zarlino, than to reject it. Not only does that image carry the signs of authority and authenticity; it also provides an attractive alternative to notions of musical space that are perceived to be distinctly modern, such as those of octave equivalence and harmonic tonality, and by extension also phrasing, syntax, and ultimately form. Authenticity is the key term here: it is not a coincidence that the rapid ascendancy of hexachord-based analytical approaches to early music in the 1960s and 70s coincided with the embracing of the related ideals of authentic performance and authentic analysis of early music.

The Guidonian image of early music closely recalls the "cathedralist" approach to medieval art that Christopher Page discusses in his acute analysis of the enduring "generalizations" regulating the modern perception of the Middle Ages.[11] Just as "cathedralism" emphasizes the piecemeal character of medieval architectonic and pictorial spaces, so medieval melodic lines and harmonies, understood as the result of complex hexachordal operations, appear as the visible signs of an additive and often counterintuitive process that seems to contravene the very coherence and logic of musical phrases as they unfold in time. For better or for worse, to place the hexachord at the center of the medieval diatonic system is to underscore the primitive quality of that system and to portray the musical *mentalité* of the Middle Ages as a nebula that is light years away from its modern counterpart. If, as Daniel Leech-Wilkinson has recently observed, "shock and de-familiarization" have been a defining feature of early music analysis as it has been practised since the 1950s, then the hexachord-based approaches of the last few decades must surely be counted as one of the preferred means to that goal, whether deliberately or subliminally pursued.[12]

[10] On this point, see D. Leech-Wilkinson, *The Modern Invention of Medieval Music*, pp. 208–9, and my "Constructing Difference: The Guidonian Hand and the Musical Space of Historical Others," 108–16.

[11] C. Page, *Discarding Images: Reflections on Music and Culture in Medieval France* (Oxford University Press, 1993).

[12] Leech-Wilkinson, *The Modern Invention of Medieval Music*, p. 202.

Of course, early music should retain its power to surprise us and even to de-familiarize ourselves from musical habits and expectations that we may have come to take for granted. Calling into question the legitimacy of the Guidonian image that is customarily attached to early music is not to deny or to challenge the "alterity value" of that music – i.e., of its unique sound-scape, aesthetic qualities, cultural meanings and modes of performance and transmission. Rather, it is an invitation to rethink the precise nature of that alterity and of the effort required from us in order to come to terms with it.

Bibliography

Manuscripts cited

Augsburg, Archiv des Bistums Augsburg, K 81 (I)

Barcelona, Biblioteca de Catalunya, 883

Basel, Universitätsbibliothek, A IX 2

Basel, Universitätsbibliothek, F IX 54

Bergamo, Biblioteca Civica 'Angelo Mai', MAB 21

Berkeley (CA), University of California, Bancroft Library, 744 (Phillips 4450)

Berkeley (CA), University of California, Bancroft Library, 1087

Berlin, Staatsbibliothek Preussischer Kulturbesitz, MS lat. qu. 576

Berlin, Staatsbibliothek Preussischer Kulturbesitz, MS mus. theor. 1520

Berlin, Staatsbibliothek Preussischer Kulturbesitz, MS mus. theor. 1599

Berlin, Staatsbibliothek Preussischer Kulturbesitz, MS theol. lat. qu. 261

Bologna, Biblioteca Universitaria, 2573

Bologna, Biblioteca Universitaria, 2931

Bologna, Civico Museo Bibliografico Musicale, A 48

Bologna, Civico Museo Bibliografico Musicale, A 56

Bologna, Civico Museo Bibliografico Musicale, A 80

Brussels, Bibliothèque du Conservatoire Royal e Musique, M 16.857 (FA IV 66)

Brussels, Bibliothèque royale, 5266

Brussels, Bibliothèque royale, II 4147

Catania, Biblioteche Riunite Civica e Antonio Ursino Recupero, D 39

Cambridge, Trinity College, R.14.52

Ebstorf, Klosterarchiv, V 3

Eichstätt, Universitätsbibliothek, 685

El Escorial, Real Biblioteca del Monasterio de San Lorenzo, S.III.5

Erfurt, Collegium Amplonianum, 4° 375

Erfurt, Collegium Amplonianum, 8° 93

Erfurt, Collegium Amplonianum, 8° 94

Erlangen, Universitätsbibliothek, 613

Florence, Biblioteca Medicea Laurenziana, Ashburnham 1119

Florence, Biblioteca Nazionale, II I 406

Florence, Biblioteca Nazionale, II XI 18

Frankfurt a.M., Stadt- und Universitätsbibliothek, Frag. Lat. VII 92

Frankfurt a.M., Stadt- und Universitätsbibliothek, MS Barth. 170

Freiburg i.B., Universitätsbibliothek, 22
Freiburg i.B., Universitätsbibliothek, 77
Gent, Universiteitsbibliotheek, 70 (71)
Graz, Universitätsbibliothek, 873
Graz, Universitätsbibliothek, 1010
Graz, Universitätsbibliothek, 1584
Heiligenkreutz, Stiftsbibliothek, 20
Karlsruhe, Badische Landesbibliothek, St. Peter Pm 29ª
Kassel, Landesbibliothek und Murhardsche Bibliothek der Stadt Kassel, 4° Mss
    Math. 1
Leiden, Rijksuniversiteit, Bibliotheek, B. P. L. 194
Leipzig, Universitätsbibliothek, 1492
Leipzig, Universitätsbibliothek, 1493
London, British Library, add. 18347
London, British Library, add. 22315
London, British Library, add. 33519
London, British Library, add. 34296
London, British Library, Harley 281
London, British Library, Harley 6525
London, British Library, Lansdowne 763
London, British Library, Royal 12.C.VI
Lucca, Biblioteca Statale, 359
Mainz, Stadtbibliothek, Hs. II 223
Mainz, Stadtbibliothek, Hs. II 248
Melk, Benediktinerstift, 109
Melk, Benediktinerstift, 1099
Milan, Biblioteca Ambrosiana, D 75 inf.
Milan, Biblioteca Trivulziana e Archivio Storico, 2146
Montecassino, Biblioteca Abbaziale, 318
Montpellier, Bibliothèque de l'École de Médecine, H 384
Munich, Bayerische Staatsbibliothek, clm 950
Munich, Bayerische Staatsbibliothek, clm 4382
Munich, Bayerische Staatsbibliothek, clm 5539
Munich, Bayerische Staatsbibliothek, clm 6002
Munich, Bayerische Staatsbibliothek, clm 6037
Munich, Bayerische Staatsbibliothek, clm 7614
Munich, Bayerische Staatsbibliothek, clm 7907
Munich, Bayerische Staatsbibliothek, clm 8093
Munich, Bayerische Staatsbibliothek, clm 9599
Munich, Bayerische Staatsbibliothek, clm 9921
Munich, Bayerische Staatsbibliothek, clm 14965b
Munich, Bayerische Staatsbibliothek, clm 18932
Munich, Bayerische Staatsbibliothek, clm 18961

Munich, Bayerische Staatsbibliothek, clm 19693
Munich, Bayerische Staatsbibliothek, clm 19694
Munich, Bayerische Staatsbibliothek, clm 19818
Munich, Bayerische Staatsbibliothek, clm 26670
Munich, Bayerische Staatsbibliothek, clm 29770
Munich, Bayerische Staatsbibliothek, clm 30058
Munich, Bayerische Staatsbibliothek, clm 30060
Naples, Biblioteca Nazionale, VIII D 12
Ottobeuren, Benediktinerabtei, Bibliothek, O.54
Oxford, Bodleian Library, 77
Oxford, Bodleian Library, 842
Oxford, Bodleian Library, Can. lit. 216
Oxford, Bodleian Library, Rawlinson C 270
Paris, Bibliothèque nationale de France, lat. 7203
Paris, Bibliothèque nationale de France, lat. 7211
Paris, Bibliothèque nationale de France, lat. 7372
Paris, Bibliothèque nationale de France, lat. 11266
Paris, Bibliothèque nationale de France, lat. 16201
Paris, Bibliothèque nationale de France, lat. 16663
Paris, Bibliothèque nationale de France, lat. 17487
Paris, Bibliothèque nationale de France, lat. 18514
Paris, Bibliothèque nationale de France, nouv. acq. lat. 1411
Parma, Biblioteca Palatina, 1158
Perugia, Biblioteca Comunale Augusta, M 36 (1013)
Pesaro, Biblioteca Comunale Oliveriana, 83
Pesaro, Biblioteca Comunale Oliveriana, 1336
Regensburg, Turn- und Taxis'sche Hofbibliothek, 103/1
Rio de Janeiro, Biblioteca Nacional, Cofre 18
Rochester (NY), Sibley Music Library, 92 1200 (*olim* Admont 94)
Rome, Biblioteca Apostolica Vaticana, lat. 3101
Rome, Biblioteca Apostolica Vaticana, lat. 5129
Rome, Biblioteca Apostolica Vaticana, lat. 5320
Rome, Biblioteca Apostolica Vaticana, Reg. lat. 577
Rome, Biblioteca Apostolica Vaticana, Reg. lat. 1146
Rome, Biblioteca Apostolica Vaticana, Reg. lat. 1578
Rome, Biblioteca Corsiniana e dell'Accademia Nazionale dei Lincei, 2067
Rome, Biblioteca Vallicelliana, C 105
Sevilla, Biblioteca Capitular y Colombina, 5-1–43
Siena, Biblioteca Comunale, L. V. 36
St. Petersburg, National Library of Russia, Q. v. I. N° 62
St. Florian, Stiftsbibliothek, XI 649
St. Gallen, Stiftsbibliothek, 937
Strasbourg, *olim* Bibliothèque publique, B II 15

Stuttgart, Württembergische Landesbibliothek, Donaueschingen 250
Stuttgart, Württembergische Landesbibliothek, Donaueschingen 880
Trier, Seminar-Bibliothek, Hs. 44
Tübingen, Universitätsbibliothek, De 4
Uppsala, Universitetsbiblioteket, C 55
Utrecht, Universiteitsbibliotheek, 406
Valencia, Biblioteca General i Històrica de la Universitat, 835
Venice, Biblioteca Nazionale Marciana, Lat. VIII 24
Venice, Biblioteca Nazionale Marciana, Lat. VIII 35
Venice, Biblioteca Nazionale Marciana, Lat. VIII 64
Venice, Biblioteca Nazionale Marciana, Lat. VIII 85
Vienna, Österreichische Nationalbibliothek, 51
Vienna, Österreichische Nationalbibliothek, 55
Vienna, Österreichische Nationalbibliothek, 787
Vienna, Österreichische Nationalbibliothek, 2390
Vienna, Österreichische Nationalbibliothek, 3571
Vienna, Österreichische Nationalbibliothek, 3646
Vienna, Österreichische Nationalbibliothek, 3839
Vienna, Österreichische Nationalbibliothek, 4702
Vienna, Österreichische Nationalbibliothek, 5160
Vienna, Österreichische Nationalbibliothek, 12811
Vienna, Österreichische Nationalbibliothek, 15033
Vipiteno, Archivio Comunale, [no call number]
Washington (D.C.), Library of Congress, Music Division, ML171 J6
    Case
Wilhering, Stiftsbibliothek, Fragment in Chl 28
Wolfenbüttel, Herzog-August-Bibliothek, Gud. lat. 8°
Wolfenbüttel, Herzog-August-Bibliothek, 696 Helmst.
Wroclaw, Biblioteka Uniwersytecka, I.Q. 466
Würzburg, Franziskanerkloster, I 83

Primary sources

Aaron, P., *Libri tres de institutione harmonica* (Bologna, 1516). Facs., New
    York: Broude Brothers, 1976.
Adam von Fulda, *Musica. GS III*, pp. 329–81.
Alighieri, D., *The Divine Comedy: Paradiso,* ed. and trans. C. S. Singleton, 2 parts.
    Princeton University Press, 1975.
Amerus, *Practica artis musicae,* ed. C. Ruini, *CSM* 25. [N.p.]: American Institute of
    Musicology, 1977.
Angeloni, L., *Sopra la vita, le opere, ed il sapere di Guido d'Arezzo, restauratore della
    scienza e dell' arte musica,* Paris, 1811.

Anonymous, *Opusculum monacordale*. In F. Feldmann, *Musik und Musikpflege im mittelalterlichen Schlesien*. Darstellungen und Quellen zur schlesischen Geschichte, vol. 37. Breslau: Trewendt und Granier, 1938, pp. 157–88.

Anonymous XI, *Tractatus de musica plana et mensurabili*. Richard J. Wingell, "Anonymous XI (CS III): An Edition, Translation, and Commentary," 3 vols. Ph.D. diss., University of Southern California, 1973, vol. 1, p. 1–173.

Babb, W., trans., and C. Palisca, ed., *Hucbald, John, and Guido on Music: Three Medieval Treatises*. New Haven: Yale University Press, 1978.

Banchieri, A., *Cartella musicale nel canto figurato, fermo e contrappunto*. (Bologna, 1614). Facs. Bologna: Forni, 1968.

Blockland de Montfort, C., *Instruction méthodique fort facile pour apprendre la musique pratique* (1573). Minkoff Reprints [Genève: 1972] [together with Yssandon, see below].

Brandi, A., *Guido Aretino, monaco di S. Benedetto: della sua vita, del suo tempo e dei suoi scritti; studio storico-critico*. Florence: Arte della stampa, 1882.

Burney, C., *A General History of Music, from the Earliest Ages to the Present Period*. London, 1789.

Burtius, N., *Florum libellus* (Bologna 1487), ed. G. Massera. Florence: Olschki, 1975.

Cerone, P., *Le regole più necessarie per l'introduttione del canto fermo*, ed. B. Baroffio. Pisa: Libreria Musicale Italiana Editrice, 1989.

Chartier, Y., ed. and trans., *L'œuvre musicale d'Hucbald de Saint-Amand*. [Saint-Laurent, Québec]: Bellarmin, 1995.

Colk Santosuosso, A., *Paris, Bibliothèque nationale, Fonds latin 7211: analysis, inventory, and text*. Ottawa: Institute of Mediaeval Music, 1991.

Coussemaker, E. de, ed., *Scriptorum de musica medii aevi nova series a Gerbertina altera*, 4 vols. (Paris: Durand, 1864–76); repr. Hildesheim: Olms, 1963.

de la Fage, A., *Essais de diphthérographie musicale*. (Paris: Legouix, 1864); repr. Amsterdam: Frits A. M. Knuf, 1964.

Ellsworth, O. B. ed. and trans., *The Berkeley Manuscript*. Lincoln: University of Nebraska Press, 1984.

Johannes Ciconia: 'Nova musica' and 'De proportionibus' (Lincoln: University of Nebraska Press, 1993).

Engelbert of Admont, *De musica*. In *GS II*, pp. 287–369.

Erikson, R., ed. and trans., *Musica Enchiriadis and Scholica Enchiriadis*. New Haven: Yale University Press, 1995.

Falchi, M., *Studi su Guido Monaco*, Florence: G. Barbera, 1882.

Franco of Cologne, *Ars cantus mensurabilis*, ed. G. Reaney and A. Gilles. *CSM* 18. [Rome]: American Institute of Musicology, 1974.

Frutolfus of Michelsberg, *Breviarium de musica et Tonarius*, ed. Fr. C. Vivell, O.S.B. In *Akademie der Wissenschaften in Wien*, Philosophisch-historische-Klasse. Sitzungsberichte, vol. 188, fasc. 2, Vienna, 1919.

Fulgentius, F. P., *Opera*, ed. R. Helm. Leipzig: B. G. Teubner, 1898.

Gafori, [Gaffurius, Gafurius, Gaffurio] F., *Extractus parvus musice*, ed. F. A. Gallo. Bologna: [s.n.], 1969.

Practica musicae (Milan, 1496; repr. Bologna: Forni, 1972).

Theorica musice (Milan, 1492; repr. Bologna: Forni, 1969). Ed. G. Cesari. Rome: Reale Accademia d'Italia, 1934; eds. I. Illuminati and C. Ruini, Florence: Edizioni del Galluzzo, 2005.

Theoricum opus (Naples, 1480). Ed. C. Ruini, Lucca: Libreria Musicale Italiana, 1996.

Gallicus, J., *Ritus canendi*, 2 vols., ed. A. Seay. Colorado Springs: Colorado College Music Press, 1981.

Gerbert, M., ed., *Scriptores ecclesiastici de musica sacra potissimum*, 3 vols. St. Blasien, 1784; repr. Hildesheim: Olms, 1963.

Glarean, H. L., *Dodecachordon* (Basel, 1547). Facs. New York: Broude Brothers, 1967.

Guentner, F. J., ed., *Epistola S. Bernardi De revisione cantus Cisterciensis, et Tractatus Cantum quem Cisterciensis*, CSM 24. [N.p.]: American Institute of Musicology, 1974.

Guido of Arezzo, *Micrologus*, ed. J. Smits van Waesberghe, CSM 4 American Institute of Musicology, 1955.

Gümpel, K.-W., ed., "Die Musiktraktate Conrads von Zabern." *Akademie der Wissenschaften und der Literatur Mainz. Abhandlungen der Geistes- und Sozialwissenschaftlichen Klasse*, 1956/4. Wiesbaden: Steiner, 1956: "Novellus musicae artis tractatus," pp. 184–244; "Opusculum de monochordo," pp. 245–59; and "De modo bene cantandi," pp. 260–82.

Hawkins, J., *A General History of the Science and Practice of Music*. London, 1776.

Herbenus Traiectensis, *De natura cantus et miraculis vocis*, ed. J. Smits van Waesberghe, Beiträge zur rheinischen Musikgeschichte, vol. 22, Köln: Arno Volk, 1957, p. 16–78.

Herlinger, J. W., ed. and trans., *Prosdocimus de Beldemandis: 'Plana musica' and 'Musica speculativa.'* New critical texts, translations, annotations, and indices. Urbana, IL: University of Illinois Press, 2008.

Prosdocimus de Beldemandis: 'Brevis summula proportionum quantum ad musicam pertinet' and 'Parvus tractatulus de modo monacordum dividendi.' Lincoln: University of Nebraska Press, 1987.

The Lucidarium of Marchetto of Padua. A Critical Edition, Translation, and Commentary. University of Chicago Press, 1985.

Hermannus Contractus, *Musica*, ed. and trans. L. Ellinwood. Rochester, NY: Eastman School of Music, University of Rochester, 1936.

Hieronymus of Moravia, *Tractatus de musica*, ed. S. M. Cserba. Freiburger Studien zur Musikwissenschaft, 2. Regensburg: Pustet, 1935.

Hieronymus of Strido, *Commentum in Evangelium Matthaei Libri Quattuor*. In J.-P. Migne, *Patrologia Latina*. Paris: J.-P. Migne, 1844–55; 1862–5, vol. 26.

Hothby, J., *Tres tractatuli contra Bartholomeum Ramum*, ed. A. Seay. *CSM* 10. Rome: American Institute of Musicology, 1964.

Hüschen, H., *Das Cantuagium des Heinrich Eger von Kalkar*. Beiträge zur rheinischen Musikgeschichte, 2. Köln: Staufen, 1952.

Jacques de Liège, *Speculum musicae*, ed. Roger Bragard. *CSM* 3. [Rome]: American Institute of Musicology, 1955–73, 7 vols.

John Cotto (of Afflighem), *De musica cum tonario*, ed. J. Smits van Waesberghe. *CSM* 1. [Rome]: American Institute of Musicology, 1950.

John of Tewkesbury, *Quatuor principalia*. In *CS* IV, pp. 200–98.

Kiesewetter, R., *Guido von Arezzo. Sein leben und wirken*. Leipzig, 1840.

Kreuzig, W., trans., *Franchino Gaffurio: The Theory of Music*, ed. C. V. Palisca. New Haven: Yale University Press, 1993.

Latin Vulgate. Douay-Rheims Version, URL: www.drbo.org/.

Lefèvre d'Étaples, J. (Jacobus Faber Stapulensis), *Elementa musicalia* (Paris, 1496). Reprinted as *Musica libri quatuor demonstrata* (Paris, 1551). Facsimile of the 1551 edition: Trachier, O., ed., *Renaissance française: traités, methods, préfaces, ouvrages generaux*, 4 vols. Courlay, France: Éditions Fuzeau classique, 2005, vol. II, pp. 141–228.

Magister Lambertus [Ps.-Aristoteles], *Tractatus de musica*. In *GS 1*, pp. 251–81.

Maître, C., ed., *Un antiphonaire cistercien pour le temporal: XIIe siècle: Paris, Bibliothèque Nationale de France, Nouvelles acquisitions Latines 1411*. Poitiers: Maison des sciences de l'homme et de la société de Poitiers: Centre d'études supérieures de civilisation médiévale, 1998.

Merulo, C., *Ricercari d'intavolatura d'organo* (1567), ed. J. Morehen. Madison: AR Editions, 2000.

Meyer, C., ed., *Musica plana Johannis de Garlandia*, Collection d'études musicologiques 91. Baden-Baden & Bouxwiller: Koerner, 1998.

Miller, C. A. trans., *Bartolomeo Ramis de Pareja: Musica practica*, *MSD* 44. American Institute of Musicology, 1993.

Franchinus Gaffurius: Practica musicae, *MSD* 20. American Institute of Musicology, 1968.

Henricus Glareanus: Dodecachordon, with introduction and commentary. American Institute of Musicology, 1965, 2 vols.

Johannes Cochlaeus: Tetrachordum musices, *MSD* 23. American Institute of Musicology, 1970.

Nicolaus Burtius: Musices opusculum, *MSD* 37. American Institute of Musicology, 1983.

Odington, W., *De speculatione musice*, ed. F. Hammond, *CSM* 14. [Rome]: American Institute of Musicology, 1970.

Ornithoparchus, A., *Musice active micrologus*. G. Reese and S. Ledbetter, eds., *A Compendium of Musical Practice: Musice active micrologus, by Andreas Ornithoparchus; Andreas Ornithoparcus his Micrologus, or introduction, containing the art of singing by John Dowland*. New York: Dover, 1973.

Osbern of Canterbury, "'De vocum consonantiis' and 'De re musica." In *Codex Oxoniensis: Biblioteca Bodleiana, Rawlinson C 270, Pars A*, ed. J. Smits van Waesberghe, Divitiae Musicae Artis A. 10a. Buren: Frits Knuf, 1979.

Page, C., ed. and trans., *The Summa Musice: A Thirteenth-Century Manual for Singers*. Cambridge University Press, 1991.

Pepusch, J. C., *A Treatise of Harmony* (London, 1730). Facs. New York: Broude Brothers, 1966.

Pesce, D., ed. and trans., *Guido d'Arezzo's* Regule Rithmice, Prologus in Antiphonarium, *and* Epistola ad Michahelem: *A Critical Text and Translation with an Introduction, Annotations, Indices, and New Manuscript Inventories*, Ottawa: The Institute of Mediaeval Music, 1999.

Pseudo-Odo, *Dialogus de musica*. In *GS I*, pp. 251–64.

Ramos de Pareja, B., *Musica practica*, ed. J. Wolf. Publikationen der Internationalen Musikgesellschaft, Beihefte, 2. Leipzig: Breitkopf und Härtel, 1901; trans. C. A. Miller, *Bartolomeo Ramis de Pareja: Musica practica*, MSD 44. Neuhausen–Stuttgart: American Institute of Musicology, 1993.

Rausch, A., ed., *Opusculum de musica ex traditione Iohannis Hollandrini: A Commentary, Critical Edition, and Translation*. Ottawa: The Institute of Mediaeval Music, 1997.

Reisch, G., *Margarita Philosophica cum additionibus novis: ab auctore suo studiosissima revisione quarto super additis* (1517; originally published in Freiburg, 1503). Repr. Düsseldorf: Stern-Verlag Janssen & Co. [1973].

Rhau, G., *Enchiridion utriusque musice practice*. Leipzig, 1520.

Salomon, E., *Scientia artis musicae*. In *GS III*, pp. 16–64.

Schmid, H., ed., *Musica Enchiriadis et Scholica Enchiriadis una cum aliquibus tractatulis adiuncti*. Veröffentlichungen der Musikhistorischen Kommission, 3. Munich; Bayerische Akademie der Wissenschaften, 1981.

Seay, A., trans., "The Expositio Manus by Johannes Tinctoris." *JMT* 9 (1965), 194–232.

Smits van Waesberghe, J., ed., "XVII tractatuli a quodam studioso peregrino ad annum MC collecti." In *Codex Oxoniensis: Biblioteca Bodleiana, Rawlinson C 270, Pars B*, Divitiae Musicae Artis A.10b. Buren: Frits Knuf, 1979.

   Expositiones in Micrologum Guidonis Aretini. Amsterdam: North-Holland Publishing Company, 1957.

Spataro, G., *Errori di Franchino Gaffurio da Lodi da Maestro Ioanne Spatario, musico bolognese, in sua deffensione, et del suo preceptore maestro Bartolomeo Ramis hispano subtilemente demonstrate*. Bologna, 1521.

Steglich, R., ed., *Die* Quaestiones in musica: *Ein Choraltraktat des zentralen Mittelalters und ihr mutmasslicher Verfasser Rudolf von St. Trond (1070–1138)*. Leipzig: Breitkopf und Härtel, 1911, pp. 12–99.

Theinred of Dover, *De legitimis ordinibus pentachordorum et tetrachordorum*: A Critical Text and Translation, with an Introduction, Annotations, and Indices by J. L. Snyder. Ottawa: Institute of Mediaeval Music, 2006.

Tinctoris, J., *Expositio manus*. In A. Seay, ed., *Johannis Tinctoris Opera theoretica*, *CSM* 22. [Rome]: American Institute of Musicology, 1975–8, vol. I, pp. 27–57.

Proportionale musices, In A. Seay, ed., *Johannis Tinctoris Opera theoretica*, 3 vols., *CSM* 22. [Rome]: American Institute of Musicology, 1975–8, vol. IIa.

Terminorum musice diffinitorium. (ca. 1494) Facs. New York: Broude Brothers, 1966; ed. and Eng. trans. C. Parrish, *Dictionary of Musical Terms*. New York: Free Press of Glencoe, 1963; facs., with German trans. ed. H. Bellermann and P. Gülke, Kassel: Bärenreiter, 1983; ed. and Italian trans. C. Panti, *Diffinitorium musice. Un dizionario di musica per Beatrice d'Aragona*. Florence: Edizioni del Galluzzo, 2004.

Ugolino of Orvieto, *Declaratio musicae disciplinae*, (ca. 1435) ed. A. Seay, 3 vols. *CSM* 7. Rome: American Institute of Musicology, 1959–62.

Tractatus monochordi, In Ugolino of Orvieto, *Declaratio musicae disciplinae*, ed. A. Seay, vol. III. *CSM7*. Rome: American Institute of Musicology, 1959–62, pp. 227–53.

Valendrinus, J., *Musica magistri Szydlovite*. In Gieburowski, W., *Die 'Musica Magistri Szydlovite': ein polnischer Choraltraktat des XV. Jahrh. und seine Stellung in der Choraltheorie des Mittelalters, mit Berücksichtigung der Choraltheorie und -Praxis des XV. Jahrhundert in Polen, sowie der Nachtridentinischen Choralreform*. Posen: St. Adalbert, 1915, pp. 9–72.

Vanneus, S., *Recanetum de musica aurea* (Rome, 1533). Repr. Kassel: Bärenreiter, 1969.

Vergilius Maro, P., *Aeneis*, ed. J. B. Greenough. In *Perseus Digital Library*, Tufts University. URL: www.perseus.tufts.edu/hopper/; ed. and trans. A. Mandelbaum, *The Aeneid of Virgil*. Berkeley: University of California Press, 1971.

Villoteau, G. A., *Recherches sur l'analogie de la musique avec les arts*. Paris, 1807.

Woodley, R., ed. and trans., *The Theoretical Works of Johannes Tinctoris: A New Online Edition* (in progress). URL: www.stoa.org/tinctoris/.

Wylde, J., *Musica manualis cum tonale*, ed. C. Sweeney, *CSM* 28. Neuhausen-Stuttgart: American Institute of Musicology, 1982.

Young, I., trans., *The "Practica musicae" of Franchino Gafurius*. Madison, WI: University of Wisconsin Press, 1969.

Yssandon, J., *Traité de la musique pratique* (1582). Minkoff Reprints, 1972 [together with Blockland de Montfort's treatise, see above].

Zarlino, G., *Dimostrationi harmoniche* (Venice, 1571). Repr. Ridgewood, NJ: Gregg Press, 1966.

Le istitutioni harmoniche (Venice, 1558). Repr. New York: Broude Brothers, 1965.

Le istitutioni harmoniche, Venezia, 1561, ed. I. Fenlon and P. Da Col, with variants from the 1589 edition. Sala Bolognese, BO: Forni, 1999.

Le istitutioni harmoniche (Venice, 1573). Repr. Ridgewood, NJ; Gregg Press, 1966.

On the Modes: Part Four of Le Istitutioni harmoniche, ed. V. Cohen. New Haven: Yale University Press, 1983.

The Art of Counterpoint: Part Three of the Istitutioni harmoniche, 1558, ed. G. Marco and C. Palisca. New York: W. W. Norton, 1968.

Secondary works

Adkins, C., "Gallicus, Johannes." In *NG 2*, vol. 9, p. 474.

"The Theory and Practice of the Monochord." Ph.D. diss., University of Iowa, 1963.

Allaire, G. G., *The Theory of Hexachords, Solmization and the Modal System, MSD* 24. [N.p.]: American Institute of Musicology, 1972.

André, M., "L'œuvre théorique de Johannes Ciconia." *Revue de la société liégeoise de musicology* 4 (1996), 23–40.

Atlas, A., *Renaissance Music*. New York: W. W. Norton, 1999.

Baltzer, R., "Johannes de Garlandia." *NG 2*, vol. 13, pp. 139–42.

"Magister Lambertus." *NG 2*, vol. 14, pp. 169–70.

Becker, A., "Ein Erfurter Traktat über gregorianische Musik." *Archiv für Musikwissenschaft* 1 (1918–19), 145–65.

Beiche, M., "Der Begriff der Silbe im Kontext Musktheorie." In *Mittelalter und Mittelalterrezeption: Festschrift für Wolf Frobenius*, ed. H. Schneider. Hildesheim: Georg Olms, 2005, pp. 1–21.

"Dur-moll." In Eggebrecht, H. H., ed., *Handwörterbuch der musikalischen Terminologie*, vol. 2. Stuttgart: F. Steiner, 1995.

Bent, M., "Ciconia, Prosdocimus, and the Workings of Musical Grammar." In P. Vendrix, ed., *Johannes Ciconia: musicien de la transition*, pp. 65–106.

Counterpoint, Composition, and Musica Ficta. New York: Routledge, 2002.

"Diatonic *ficta*." *EMH* 4 (1984), 1–48.

"Diatonic *ficta* revisited, Josquin's *Ave Maria* in context." *Music Theory Online*, September 1996. URL: www.societymusictheory.org/mto/.

"Music and the Early Veneto Humanists." *Proceedings of the British Academy* 101 (1998), 101–30.

"Musica recta and musica ficta." *MD* 26 (1972), 73–100. Reprinted in *Counterpoint, Composition, and* Musica Ficta, pp. 199–218.

"The Grammar of Early Music: Preconditions for Analysis." In C. Collins Judd, ed., *Tonal Structures in Early Music*, pp. 15–59.

Berger, C., *Hexachord, Mensur, und Textstruktur: Studien zum französischen Lied des 14. Jahrhunderts*. Beihefte zum Archiv für Musikwissenschaft, 35. Stuttgart: Franz Steiner Verlag, 1992.

Berger, K., "The Hand and the Art of Memory." *MD* 35 (1981), 87–120.

"The Expanding Universe of *Musica Ficta* in Theory from 1300 to 1550." *JM* 4 (1986), 410–30.

Musica ficta. Theories of Accidental Inflections in Vocal Polyphony from Marchetto da Padova to Gioseffo Zarlino. Cambridge University Press, 1987.

Bernhard, M., *Die Thomas von Aquin zugeschriebenen Musiktraktate*. Munich: Bayerische Akademie der Wissenschaften, 2006.

"*La Summa musice* du Ps.-Jean de Murs: Son auteur et sa datation." *Revue de Musicologie* 84 (1998), 19–25.

"Zu Reception der Werke des Hermannus Contractus." In W. Pass and A. Rausch, eds., *Beiträge zur Musik, Musiktheorie und Liturgie der Abtei Reichenau.* Tutzing: H. Schneider, 2001, pp. 99–126.

Bernhard, M. ed., *Lexicon musicum Latinum medii aevi.* Munich: Bayerische Akademie der Wissenschaften, 1992- in progress. URL: www.lml.badw.de/.

Bielitz, M., *Hexachord und Semantik.* Neckargemünd: Männeles, 1998.

Musik und Grammatik. Munich: Katzbichler, 1977.

Blackburn, B. J., "Masses Based on Popular Songs and Solmization Syllables." In R. Sherr, ed., *The Josquin Companion*, pp. 51–87.

"Music Theory and Musical Thinking after 1450." In *Music as Concept and Practice in the Late Middle Ages*, ed. R. Strohm and B. J. Blackburn, *The New Oxford History of Music* III/1, Oxford University Press, 2001, pp. 301–45.

"Properchant: English Theory at Home and Abroad, with an Excursus on Amerus/Aluredus and his Tradition." In D. B. Cannata, G. Ilnitchi Currie, R. C. Mueller, and J. L. Nádas, eds., *Quomodo cantabimus canticum? Studies in Honor of Edward H. Roesner*, Miscellanea 7. Middleton, WI: American Institute of Musicology, 2008, pp. 81–98.

"The Lascivious Career of B flat" (forthcoming).

Blackburn, B. J., Lowinsky, E. E., and C. A. Miller, eds., *A Correspondence of Renaissance Musicians.* Oxford: Clarendon Press 1991.

Bower, C., "'Adhuc ex parte et in enigmate cernimus …' Reflections on the Closing Chapters of *Musica enchiriadis*." In *Music in the Mirror. Reflections on the History of Music Theory and Literature for the 21st Century*, ed. A. Giger and T. J. Mathiesen. Lincoln: University of Nebraska Press, 2002, pp. 21–44.

"The Transmission of Ancient Music Theory into the Middle Ages." In T. Christensen, ed., *The Cambridge History of Western Music Theory*, pp. 136–67.

Boyd, M., and Beeks, G., "Pepusch, John Christoph." *NG 2*, vol. 19, pp. 324–7.

Brothers, T., *Chromatic Beauty in the Late Medieval Chanson: An Interpretation of Manuscript Accidentals.* Cambridge University Press, 1997.

Brown, H. M., *Instrumental Music Printed Before 1600.* Boston: Harvard University Press, 1965.

Busse Berger, A. M., *Medieval Music and the Art of Memory.* Berkeley: University of California Press, 2005.

Caretta, A., Cremascoli, L., and Salamina, L., *Franchino Gaffurio.* Lodi: Edizioni dell'Archivio Storico Lodigiano, 1951.

Carpenter, N. C., *Music in the Medieval and Renaissance Universities.* Norman: University of Oklahoma Press, 1958; repr. New York: Da Capo Press, 1972.

Carvell, B., "Notes on *una nota super la*." In *Music from the Middle Ages through the Twentieth Century: Essays in Honor of Gwynn S. McPeck*, ed. C. Comberiati and M. C. Steele. New York: Gordon and Beech, 1988, pp. 94–111.

Cattin, G., "Ricerche sulla musica a S. Giustina in Padova all'inizio del primo quattrocento. Il copista Rolando da Casale. Nuovi frammenti musicali nell'archivio di stato." *AnnMusic* 7 (1964), 17–41.

"Tradizione e tendenze innovatrici nella normative e nella pratica liturgico-musicale della Congregazione di S. Giustina." *Benedictina. Fascicoli di studi benedettini*, 17 (1970), 254–99.

Chafe, E. T., *Monteverdi's Tonal Language*. New York: Schirmer, 1992.

Chailley, J., "*Ut queant laxis* et les Origines de la Gamme." *Act AcM* 56 (1984), 48–69.

Christensen, T., ed., *The Cambridge History of Western Music Theory*. Cambridge University Press, 2002.

Clercx, S., "Johannes Ciconia théoreticien." *AnnMusic* 3 (1955), 39–75.

Cohen, D., "Notes, scales, and modes in the earlier Middle Ages." In *The Cambridge History of Western Music Theory*, ed. T. Christensen, pp. 307–63.

Colk Santosuosso, A., *Letter Notations in the Middle Ages*. Ottawa: The Institute of Mediaeval Music, 1989.

Collins Judd, C., *Reading Renaissance Music Theory: Hearing with the Eyes*. Cambridge University Press, 2000.

"Renaissance modal theory: theoretical, compositional, and editorial perspectives." In T. Christiansen, ed., *The Cambridge History of Western Music Theory*, pp. 364–406.

Tonal Structures in Early Music. New York: Garland, 1998.

Courtenay, W., "Antiqui and Moderni in Late Medieval Thought." *Journal of the History of Ideas* 48 (1987), 3–10.

Cremascoli, L., "Note storiche sulla vita di Franchino Gafurio" In A. Caretta, L. Cremascoli, and L. Salamina, *Franchino Gaffurio*, pp. 27–135.

Crocker. R., "Perchè Zarlino diede una nuova numerazione ai modi." *Rivista italiana di musicologia* 3 (1968), 48–58.

"Hermann's Major Sixth." *JAMS* 25 (1972), 19–37.

Review of *Musica enchiriadis and Scolica enchiriadis*, trans., with introduction and notes by R. Erickson. *Notes* 53/1 (1996), 60–1.

Dahlhaus, C., "Die Termini Dur and Moll." *AFM* 12 (1955), 280–96.

Untersuchungen über die Entstehung der harmonische Tonalität. Kassel: Bärenreiter, 1968. Engl. trans. R. Gjerdingen, *Studies on the Origin of Harmonic Tonality*. Princeton University Press, 1990.

Day-O'Connell, J., *Pentatonicism from the Eighteenth Century to Debussy*. University of Rochester Press, 2007.

Degrada, F., "Musica e musicisti nell'età di Ludovico il Moro." In *Milano nell'età di Ludovico il Moro*, vol. II, pp. 409–14.

De La Fage, A., *Essais de diphthérographie musicale*. Paris, 1864; repr. Amsterdam: Frits A. M. Knuf, 1964.

Di Bacco, G., and Nádas, J., "Verso uno 'stile internazionale' della musica nelle cappelle papali e cardinalizie durante il Grande Scisma (1378–1417): il caso di Johannes Ciconia da Liège." In A. Roth, ed., *Collettanea I: Capellae Sixtinaeque*

Collectanea Acta Monumenta 3. Vatican City: Biblioteca Apostolica Vaticana, 1994, pp. 7–74.

Dobbins, F., and His, I., "Claude Le Jeune." *NG 2*, vol. 14, pp. 531–4.

Duffin, R. W., "Mi chiamano Mimi ... but my Name is Quarti toni: Solmization and Ockeghem's Famous Mass." *EM* 29 (2001), 164–85.

Dumitrescu, T., "The Solmization Status of Sharps in the 15th and 16th Centuries." *Studi musicali* 33 (2004), 253–83.

Dyer, J., Review of *The Summa Musice: A Thirteenth-Century Manual for Singers*, ed. C. Page. *EMH* 12 (1993), 203–23.

"Singing with Proper Refinement from De Modo Bene Cantandi (1474)." *EM* 6 (1978), 207–27.

"Speculative 'Musica' and the Medieval University of Paris." *Music and Letters* 90 (2009), 177–209.

'The clavis in thirteenth-century music theory'. *Cantus Planus* 1995, 195–212.

Ellsworth, O. B., "The Origin of the Coniuncta: A Reappraisal." *JMT* 17 (1973), 86–109.

Everist, M., "Music and Theory in Late Thirteenth-Century Paris: The Manuscript Paris, Bibliothèque Nationale, Fonds lat. 11266." *The Royal Musical Association Research Chronicle* 17 (1981), 52–64.

Fast, S., Review of *Ars cantus mensurabilis per modos iuris*, by M. Balensuela, ed., and *Johannes Ciconia: 'Nova musica' and 'De proportionibus'* by O. Ellsworth, ed. *Plainsong and Medieval Music* 4 (1995), 209–17.

Fend, M., "Zarlinos Versuch einer Axiomatisierung der Musiktheorie in den Dimostrationi harmoniche (1571)." *Musiktheorie* 4 (1989), 113–26.

Flotzinger, R., "Johannes de Garlandia und Anonymus IV: zu ihrem Umfeld ihren Persönlichkeiten und Traktaten." In *Gedenkschrift für Walter Pass*, ed. M. Czernin. Tutzing: Schneider, 2002, pp. 81–98.

Fuller, S., "An Anonymous Treatise dictus de Sancto Martiale: A New Source for Cistercian Music Theory." *MD* 31 (1977), 5–30.

"Defending the Dodecachordon: Ideological Currents in Glarean's Modal Theory." *JAMS* 49 (1996), 191–224.

"Modal Discourse and Fourteenth-Century French Song: A 'Medieval' Perspective Recovered?" *EMH* 17 (1998), 61–108.

Review of *The Affinities and Medieval Transposition* by D. Pesce. *JMT* 33 (1989), 439–48.

Galiano, C., "Gaffurio, il conte di Potenza e la prima dedicatoria inedita del *Theoricum opus musice discipline* (London, British Library, Hirsch IV. 1441)." In *Medioevo Mezzogiorno Mediterraneo: Studi in onore di Mario Del Treppo*, ed. G. Rossetti and G. Vitolo, 2 vols. (Naples: Liguori, 2000), vol. 2, pp. 271–302.

Gallico, C., "Musica nella Ca' Giocosa." In N. Giannetto, ed., *Vittorino da Feltre e la sua Scuola*, pp. 189–98.

Gallo, F. A., "Le traduzioni dal Greco per Franchino Gaffurio." *AcM* 35 (1963), 172–4.

Garin, E., "La cultura a Milano alla fine del Quattrocento." In *Milano nell'età di Ludovico il Moro*, vol. I, pp. 21–8.

Giannetto, N., ed., *Vittorino da Feltre e la sua scuola: umanesimo, pedagogia, arti.* Florence: Olschki, 1981.

Gieburowski, W., *Die 'Musica Magistri Szydlovite': ein polnischer Choraltraktat des XV. Jahr. und seine Stellung in der Choraltheorie des Mittelalters, mit Berücksichtigung der Choraltheorie und -Praxis des XV. Jahrhundert in Polen, sowie der nachtridentinischen Choralreform.* Posen: St. Adalbert, 1915.

Gilles, A., "De musica plana breve compendium (Un témoignage de l'enseignement de Lambertus)." *MD* 43 (1989), 39–51.

Gross, G., *Chanter en polyphonie à Notre-Dame de Paris aux 12e et 13e siècles.* Turnhout: Brepols, 2007.

Gümpel, K.-W., "A Didactic Musical Treatise from the Late Middle Ages: Ebstorf, Klosterarchiv, MS V,3." In S. Parisi, ed., *Music in the Theater, Church, and Villa: Essays in Honor of Robert Lamar Weaver and Norma Wright Weaver.* Warren, MI: Harmonie Park Press, 2000, pp. 50–64.

"Des Tastenmonochord Conrads von Zabern," *AfM* 12 (1955), 143–66.

Haar, J., "The frontispiece of Gafori's *Practica musicae* (1496)." *Renaissance Quarterly* 27 (1974), 7–22. Reprinted in J. Haar, *The Science and Art of Renaissance Music*, Princeton University Press, ch. 4, 1998. pp. 79–92.

Haggh, B., "Ciconia's *Nova musica*: A Work for Singers in Renaissance Padua." Paper presented at the Conference on Renaissance Music in Lisbon and Évora, May 2003. Text currently available online at URL: www.music.umd.edu/Faculty/haggh-huglo/barbeleven.html.

"Ciconia's Citations in *Nova musica*: New Sources as Biography." In S. Clark and E. E. Leach, eds., *Citation and Authority in Medieval and Renaissance Musical Culture: Learning from the Learned.* Woodbridge, UK: Boydell, 2005, pp. 45–56.

Haines, J., and DeWitt, P., "Johannes de Grocheio and Aristotelian Natural Philosophy." *EMH* 27 (2008), 47–98.

Hallmark, A., "Gratiosus, Ciconia, and Other Musicians at Padua Cathedral: Some Footnotes to Present Knowledge." In *L' Ars Nova italiana del Trecento, VI.* Centaldo, 1992, pp. 69–84.

"*Protector, imo verus pater*: Francesco Zabarella's Patronage of Johannes Ciconia." In J. A. Owens and A. M. Cummings, eds., *Music in Renaissance Cities and Courts: Studies in Honor of Lewis Lockwood.* Warren, MI: Harmonie Park Press, 1997, pp. 153–68.

Handschin, J., *Der Toncharakter: eine Einführung in die Tonpsychologie.* Zürich: Atlantis, 1948; repr. Darmstadt: Wissenschaftliche Buchgesellschaft, 1995.

Heath, T., "Logical Grammar, Grammatical Logic, and Humanism in Three German Universities." *Studies in the Renaissance* 18 (1971), 9–64.

Henderson, R. V., "Solmization Syllables in Music Theory, 1100–1600." Ph.D. diss., Columbia University, 1969.

Herlinger, J., "Music Theory of the Fourteenth and Early Fifteenth Centuries." In *Music as Concept and Practice in the Late Middle Ages*, ed. R. Strohm and B. J. Blackburn, *The New Oxford History of Music* III/1, Oxford University Press, 2001, pp. 244–300.

Hirshberg, J., "Hexachordal and Modal Structure in Machaut's Polyphonic Chansons." In J. W. Hill, ed., *Studies in Musicology in Honor of Otto Albrecht*. Kassel: Bärenreiter, 1980, pp. 19–42.

Holford-Strevens, L., "Fa mi la mi so la: The Erotic Implications of Solmization Syllables," (forthcoming).

"Humanism and the Language of Music Treatises." *Renaissance Studies* 15 (2001), 415–49.

"The *Laudes musicae* in Renaissance Music Treatises," (forthcoming).

Hughes, A., Review of *The Theory of Hexachords, Solmization and the Modal System: A Practical Application* by G. Allaire. *JAMS* 27 (1974), 132–9.

Huglo, M., "Der Prolog des Odo zugeschriebenen 'Dialogus de Musica.'" *AfM*, 28 (1971), 134–46.

"L'auteur du traité de musique dédié à Fulgence d'Affligem." *Revue belge de musicology* 31 (1977), 5–37.

"La place du *Tractatus de Musica* dans l'histoire de la théorie musicale du XIIIᵉ siècle: Etude codicologique." In C. Meyer, ed., *Jérôme de Moravie: un théoricien de la musique dans le milieu intellectuel parisien du XIIIe siècle*. Actes du Colloque de Royaumont, 1989, Paris: Créaphis, 1992, pp. 33–42.

Les Tonaires: inventaire, analyse, comparaison. Paris: Société Française de Musicologie, 1971.

Ianziti, G., *Humanistic Historiography under the Sforzas: Politics and Propaganda in Fifteenth-Century Milan*. Oxford: Clarendon Press, 1988.

Ilnitchi, G., *The Play of Meanings: Aribo's De musica and the Hermeneutics of Musical Thought*. Lanham, MD: Scarecrow, 2005.

Kelleher, J. E., "Zarlino's 'Dimostrationi harmoniche' and Demonstrative Methodologies in the Sixteenth Century." Ph.D. diss. Columbia University, 1993.

Kite-Powell, J., ed., *A Performer's Guide to Renaissance Music*, 2nd edn. Bloomington, IN: Indiana University Press, 2007.

Kohl, B., "Humanism and Education." In A. Rabil, Jr., ed., *Renaissance Humanism: Foundations, Forms, and Legacy*, 3 vols. Philadelphia: University of Pennsylvania Press, 1988, vol. III, "Humanism and the Disciplines." pp. 5–22.

Kretzmann, N., Kenny, A., and Pinborg, J., eds., *The Cambridge History of Later Medieval Philosophy*, Cambridge University Press, 1982.

Kreutziger-Herr, A., *Johannes Ciconia (ca. 1370–1412)*. Hamburg: Karl Diter Wagner, 1991.

Kreyszig, W. K., "Beyond the Music-Theoretical Discourse in Franchino Gaffurio's Trilogy: The Significance of the Paratexts in Contemplating the Magic Triangle Between Author, Opus, and Audience." In '*Cui dono lepidum novum libellum?*': *Dedicating Latin Works and Motets in the Sixteenth Century*, Proceedings of the International Conference held at the Academia Belgica, Rome, August 18–20, 2005, ed. I. Bossuyt, N. Gabriëls, D. Sacré, and D. Verbeke, Supplementa Humanistica Lovaniensia 23, Leuven University Press, 2008, pp. 161–93.

Lange, G., "Zur Geschichte der Solmisation." *Sammelbände der Internationalen Musikgesellschaft* 1 (1899–1900), 535–622.

Leclercq, J., O.S.B., "Monastic and Scholastic Theology in the Reformers of the Fourteenth to Sixteenth Century." In E. Rozanne Elder, ed., *From Cloister to Classroom: Monastic and Scholastic Approaches to Truth*. Kalamazoo, MI: Cistercian Publications, 1986, pp. 178–201.

Leech-Wilkinson, D., *The Modern Invention of Medieval Music*. Cambridge University Press, 2002.

Lefferts, P., "A Riddle and a Song: Playing with Signs in a Fourteenth-century Ballade, *EMH* 26 (2007), 121–79.

Lester, J., *Compositional Theory in the Eighteenth Century*. Cambridge, MA: Harvard University Press, 1992.

Lovato, A., "Dottrine musicali nel Trecento padovano." In O. Longo, ed., *Padova carrarese*. Padova: Il Poligrafo, 2005, pp. 215–25.

Maître, C., *La réforme cistercienne du plain-chant. Étude d'un traité théorique.* Beernem, Belgium: Brecht, 1995.

Malcolm, J., "Epistola Johannis Cottonis ad Fulgentium Episcopum." *MD* 47 (1993), 159–69.

Maloy, R., "The Role of Notation in Frutolf of Michelsberg's Tonary." *JM* 19 (2002), 641–93.

Markovits, M., *Das Tonsystem der abendländischen Musik im frühen Mittelalter.* Bern: Paul Haupt, 1977.

Martin, D., "The Via Moderna, Humanism, and the Hermeneutics of Late Medieval Monastic Life." *Journal of the History of Ideas* 51 (1990), 179–97.

Massera, G., "Burzio, Nicola." In *Dizionario enciclopedico universale della musica e dei musicisti*, "Le biografie." Torino: U.T.E.T., 1985, vol. III, pp. 756–7.

Mathiesen, T., ed. *Thesaurus musicarum latinarum*. Database of the Latin music theory written during the Middle Ages and Renaissance. URL: www.chmtl. indiana.edu/tml/.

Mauro, L., ed., *La musica nel pensiero medievale*. Ravenna: Longo, 1999.

McManamon, J., *Pierpaolo Vergerio the Elder: The Humanist as Orator*. Tempe, AZ: Medieval and Renaissance Texts and Studies, 1996.

Mead, S., "Renaissance Theory." In J. Kite-Powell, ed., *A Performer's Guide to Renaissance Music*, 2nd edn., pp. 343–51.

Meier, B., "Heinrich Loriti Glareanus als Musiktheoretiker." *Beiträge zur Freiburger Wissenschafts- und Universitätsgeschichte* 22 (1960), 65–112.

Mengozzi, S., "'Clefless' Notation, Counterpoint, and the Fa-degree." *EM* 36 (2008), 51–64.

"Constructing Difference: The Guidonian Hand and the Musical Space of Historical Others." *Studies in Medievalism* 16 (2008), 98–121.

"Josquinian Voices and Guidonian Listeners." In *Essays on Music and Culture in Honor of Herbert Kellman*, ed. B. Haggh. Paris: Minerve, 2001, pp. 253–79.

"Si quis manus non habeat: Charting Non-Hexachordal Musical Practices in the Age of Solmization." *EMH* 26 (2007), 181–218.

"The Ciconian Hexachord." In *Johannes Ciconia, musicien de la transition*, ed. P. Vendrix, Turnhout: Brepols, 2003, pp. 279–304.

"Virtual Segments: The Hexachordal Theory in the Late Middle Ages." *JM* 23 (2006), 426–67.

Mercer, R. G. G., *The Teaching of Gasparino Barzizza with Special Reference to his Place in Paduan Humanism*. London: The Modern Humanities Research Association, 1979.

Meyer, C., "Die Musiktheorie der Zisterzienser." In *Die Lehre von einstimmigen liturgischen Gesang, Geschichte der Musiktheorie* 4, ed. T. Ertelt and F. Zaminer. Darmstadt: Wissenschaftliche Buchgesellschaft, 2000, p. 183–96.

"Die Tonartenlehre im Mittelalter." In T. Ertelt and F. Zaminer, eds., *Die Lehre von einstimmigen liturgischen Gesang. Geschichte der Musiktheorie*, vol. 4. Darmstadt: Wissenschaftliche Buchgesellschaft, 2000, pp. 135–215.

"La tradition du Micrologus de Guy d'Arezzo: une contribution a l'histoire de la reception du texte." *Revue de Musicologie* 83 (1997), 5–31.

Mensura monochordi: la division du monocorde (IXe-XVe siècles). Publications de la Société Française de Musicologie. Paris: Klincksieck, 1996.

Milano nell'età di Ludovico il Moro. Atti del convegno internazionale, 28 febbraio-4 marzo 1983, 2 vols. Milan: Comune di Milano, Archivio Storico Civico e Biblioteca Trivulziana, 1983.

Miller, C. A., "Gaffurius' *Practica Musicae*: Origins and Contents." *MD* 22 (1968), 105–28.

Miller, C. A., and Blackburn, B. J., "Burzio Nicolò." In *NG 2*, vol. 4, pp. 649–50.

Moyer, A. E., *Musica Scientia. Musical Scholarship in the Italian Renaissance*. Ithaca, NY: Cornell University Press, 1992.

Murray, R. E., "New Documentation Concerning the Biography of Nicolò Burzio." *Studi musicali* 24 (1995), 263–82.

Niemöller, K., *Untersuchungen zu Musikpflege und Musikunterricht an den deutschen Lateinschulen vom ausgehenden Mittelalter bis um 1600*. Regensburg: Bosse, 1969.

"*Super voces musicales*: Deutsche Hexachordkompositionen im Lichte der Musiktheorie und in ihrem europäischen Kontext." In *Vom Isaac bis Bach. Studien zur älteren deutschen Musikgechichte. Festschrift Martin Just zum 60. Geburtstag*, ed. F. Heidelberger, W. Olsthoff, and R. Wiesend. Kassel: Bärenreiter, 1991, pp. 127–37.

Owens, J. A., "Waelrant and Bocedization. Reflections on Solmization Reform." *Yearbook of the Alamire Foundation*, 2 (1997), 377–94.

Pabel, H. M., "Reading Jerome in the Renaissance: Erasmus; Reception of the 'Adversus Jovinianum.'" *Renaissance Quarterly* 55 (2002), 470–97.

Page, C., *Discarding Images: Reflections on Music and Culture in Medieval France*. Oxford: University Press, 1993.

"Towards: Music in Medieval Europe." *The Musical Times*, vol. 136 (1995), 127–34.

Palisca, C., *Humanism in Italian Renaissance Musical Thought*. New Haven: Yale University Press, 1985.

Panti, C., "Una fonte della 'Declaratio musicae disciplinae' di Ugolino da Orvieto: Quattro Anonime 'Questiones' della Tarda Scolastica." *Rivista Italiana di Musicologia* 24 (1989), 3–47.

Pascoe, L. B., S. J., "Jean Gerson: the 'Ecclesia primitiva' and Reform." *Traditio* 30 (1974), 379–409.

Perkins, L., *Music in the Age of the Renaissance*. New York: W. W. Norton, 1999.

Pesce, D., *The Affinities and Medieval Transposition*. Bloomington, IN: Indiana University Press, 1987.

Picasso, G. M., "Gli studi nella riforma di Ludovico Barbo." In *Los monjes y los estudios. IV semana de estudios monasticos*. Poblet 1961. Abadia de Poblet, 1963, p. 295–324.

Piccaluga, G. F., "Gli affreschi di casa Panigarola e la cultura Milanese tra Quattro e Cinquecento." *Arte lombarda* 86–7 (1988), 14–25.

Pike, L., *Hexachords in Late-Renaissance Music*. Aldershot: Ashgate, 1998.

Pitigliani, R., *Il Ven. Ludovico Barbo e la diffusione dell' Imitazione di Cristo per opera della Congregazione di S. Giustina*. Padova: Badia S. Giustina, 1943.

Planchart, A., Review of *The Theory of Hexachords, Solmization and the Modal System: A Practical Application* by G. Allaire. *JMT* 18 (1973), 213–23.

Powers, H. S., "From Psalmody to Tonality." In C. Collins Judd, ed., *Tonal Structures in Early Music*. New York: Garland, 1998, pp. 275–340.

"Monteverdi's Model for a Multimodal Madrigal." In F. della Seta and F. Piperno, eds., *In Cantu et in Sermone: for Nino Pirrotta on His 80th Birthday*. Firenze: Olschki and [s.l.]: University of Western Australia Press, 1989, pp. 185–219.

"Tonal Types and Modal Categories in Renaissance Polyphony." *JAMS* 34 (1981), 428–70.

Powers, H. S., and Wiering, F., "Mode." § I-III. In *NG 2*, vol. 16, pp. 775–823.

Preußner, E., "Solmisations-Methoden im Schulunterricht des 16. und 17. Jahrhunderts." In *Festschrift Fritz Stein zum 60. Geburtstag*, ed. H. Hoffman and F. Rühlmann. Braunschweig: H. Litolff, 1939, pp. 112–28.

Pyle, C. M., *Milan and Lombardy in the Renaissance. Essays in Cultural History*. Rome: La fenice, Roma, 1997.

Rabil, A., Jr., "The Significance of 'Civic Humanism' in the Interpretation of the Italian Renaissance." In *Renaissance Humanism: Foundations, Forms, and Legacy*, ed. A. Rabil, Jr, 3 vols. Philadelphia: University of Pennsylvania Press, 1988, vol. II: "Humanism in Italy." pp. 141–74.

Rainbow, B., "Fasola." In *NG 2*, vol. 8, pp. 589–90.

Rausch, A., "Zur Musiklehre der Kartäuser im Mittelalter." In *Gedenkschrift für Walter Pass*, ed. M. Czernin. Tutzing: Schneider, 2002, pp. 201–16.

Reckow, ed., "Clavis." In Eggebrecht, H. H., ed., *Handwörterbuch der musikalischen Terminologie*. Stuttgart: F. Steiner, 1971.

Répertoire International des Sources Musicales / International Catalogue of Musical Sources (RISM). Series B/III, "The Theory of Music. Manuscripts from the Carolingian Era up to *c.* 1500. Descriptive Catalogue," 6 vols. Munich: G. Henle, 1961–2003. Vol. 1: Austria, ed. J. Smits van Waesberghe, in collaboration with P. Fischer and C. Mass (1961); vol. 2: Italy, ed. P. Fischer (1968); vol. 3: Federal Republic of Germany, ed. M. Huglo and C. Meyer (1986); vol. 4: Great Britain and the United States of America, ed. M. Huglo and N. Phillips (1992); vol. 5, Czech Republic, Poland, Portugal, and Spain, ed. C. Meyer, E. Witkowska-Zaremba, K-W Gümpel (1997); vol. 6, Addenda, Corrigenda, ed. C. Meyer, G. Di Bacco, P. Ernstbrunner, A. Rausch, C. Ruini (2003).

Resta, G., "La cultura umanistica a Milano alla fine del Quattrocento." In *Milano nell'età di Ludovico il Moro*, vol. I, pp. 201–14.

Riemann, H., *Handbuch der Musikgeschichte*, Leipzig: Breitkopf & Härtel, 1920–3; repr. New York: Johnson Reprints, 1972.

Ripin, E. M., Barnes, J., Huber, A., Kenyon de Pasqual, B., Kernfeld, B., "Clavichord." *NG 2*, vol. 6, pp. 4–18.

Robey, D., "Vittorino e Vergerio." In N. Giannetto, ed., *Vittorino da Feltre e la sua scuola: umanesimo, pedagogia, arti*. Florence: Olschki, 1981, pp. 241–53.

Rosa Barezzani, M. T., "Guido d'Arezzo fra tradizione e innovazione" In A. Rusconi, ed., *Guido d'Arezzo monaco pomposiano. Atti dei Convegni di studio, Codigoro (Ferrara), Abbazia di Pomposa 3 ottobre 1997; Arezzo, Biblioteca Città di Arezzo, 29–30 maggio 1998*. Florence: Olschki, 2000.

Ruini, C., "Eredità di Guido nei teorici dei secoli XIII e XIV." In A. Rusconi, ed., *Guido d'Arezzo monaco pomposiano*, ed., *Guido d'Arezzo monaco pomposiano. Atti dei Convegni di studio, Codigoro (Ferrara), Abbazia di Pomposa 3 ottobre 1997; Arezzo, Biblioteca Città di Arezzo, 29–30 maggio 1998*. Florence: Olschki, 2000, pp. 171–7.

Russell, T. A., "A Poetic Key to a pre-Guidonian Palm and the Echemata." *JAMS* 34 (1981), 109–18.

Russell Williams, D., and Balensuela, C. M., *Music Theory from Boethius to Zarlino: A Bibliography and Guide*. Hillsdale, NY: Pendragon Press, 2007.

Russo, M., "Hexachordal Theory in the Late Thirteenth-Century." Ph.D. diss., Michigan State University, 1997.

Santoro, C., *Gli Sforza*. Milano: Corbaccio, 1994.

Schünemann, G., "Ursprung und Bedeutung der Solmisation." In *Schulmusikalische Zeitdokumente. Vorträge der VII. Reichs-Schulmusikwoche in München.* Leipzig: Quelle & Meyer, 1929, pp. 41–52.

Seay, A., "An Anonymous Treatise from St. Martial." *AnnMusic* 5 (1957), 13–42.

"Guglielmo Roffredi's Summa musicae artis." *MD* 24 (1970), 69–77.

Seznec, J., *The Survival of the Pagan Gods; The Mythological Tradition and Its Place in Renaissance Humanism and Art.* New York: Pantheon Books, 1953.

Sherr, R., *The Josquin Companion.* Oxford University Press, 2000.

Sisko, J., "Space, Time, and Phantasms in Aristotle, De Memoria 2, 452B-7–25." *The Classical Quarterly* 47 (1997), 167–75.

Skemer, D. D., *Binding Words: Textual Amulets in the Middle Ages.* University Park: Pennsylvania State University Press, 2006.

Smits van Waesberghe, J., *De musico-pedagogico et theoretico Guidone Aretino eiusque vita et moribus.* Florence: Olschki, 1953.

Musikerziehung. Lehre und Theorie der Musik im Mittelalter, Musikgeschichte in Bildern, ed. H. Besseler and W. Bachmann, vol. III/3. Leipzig: VEB Deutscher Verlag für Musik, 1969.

Snyder, J., "A Road Not Taken: Theinred of Dover's Theory of Species." *Journal of the Royal Musical Association* 115 (1990), 145–81.

"Theinred of Dover on Consonance: A Chapter in the History of Harmony." *Music Theory Spectrum* 5 (1983), 110–20.

Sorabji, R., *Aristotle on Memory*, 2nd edn. London: Duckworth, 2004.

Stinger, C., *Humanism and the Church Fathers: Ambrogio Traversari (1386–1439) and Christian Antiquity in the Italian Renaissance.* Albany: State University of New York Press, 1977.

Storia di Milano, vol. VIII. "L' età sforzessa dal 1450–1500." Milan: Treccani, 1956.

Strohm, R., *The Rise of European Music, 1380–1500.* Cambridge University Press, 1993.

Strohm, R., and Blackburn, B. J., eds., *Music as Concept and Practice in the Late Middle Ages. The New Oxford History of Music* III/1. Oxford University Press, 2001.

Sweeney, C., "John Wylde and the Musica Guidonis." *MD* 29 (1975), 43–59.

Tanay, D., *Noting Music, Making Culture: The Intellectual Context of Rhythmic Notation, 1250–1400.* Holzgerlingen: American Institute of Musicology, 1999.

Thibaut, J.-B., *Monuments de la Notation Ekphonétique et Neumatique de l'Eglise Latine.* St. Petersburg, 1912; repr. Hildesheim: Georg Olms, 1984.

Toft, R., *Aural Images of Lost Traditions: Sharps and Flats in the Sixteenth Century.* University of Toronto Press, 1992.

Tomlinson, G., *Music in Renaissance Magic. Toward an Historiography of Others.* University of Chicago Press, 1992.

Treitler, L., "The Early History of Music Writing in the West." *JAMS* 35 (1982), 237–79.

Urquhart, P., "Cross-Relations by Franco-Flemish Composers after Josquin." *Tijdschrift van de Vereniging voor Nederlandse Muziekgeschiedenis* 43 (1993), 3–41.

Vasoli, C., "Vittorino da Feltre e la formazione umanistica dell'uomo." In N. Giannetto, ed., *Vittorino da Feltre e la sua scuola: umanesimo, pedagogia, arti.* Florence: Olschki, 1981, pp. 13–33.

Vendrix, P., ed., *Johannes Ciconia: musicien de la transition.* Turnhout: Brepols, 2003.

Wegman, R. C., "*Musica ficta.*" In T. Knighton and D. Fallows, eds., *A Companion to Medieval and Renaissance Music.* Berkeley: University of California Press, 1992; repr. 1997.

   The Crisis of Music in Early Modern Europe: 1470–1530. New York: Routledge, 2005.

Weijer, O., "La place de la musique à la Faculté des arts de Paris." In L. Mauro, ed., *La musica nel pensiero medievale*, pp. 171–2.

Weiss, S., "The Singing Hand." In C. Richter Sherman and P. M. Lukehart, eds., *Writing on Hands: Memory and Knowledge in Early Modern Europe.* Carlisle, PA: Trout Gallery, Dickinson College, and Washington, D.C.: Folger Shakespeare Library, 2000, pp. 35–45.

Werbeck, W., *Studien zur deutschen Tonartenlehre in der ersten Häfte des 16. Jahrhunderts.* Kassel: Bärenreiter, 1989.

Whitcomb, P., "Teachers, Booksellers and Taxes: Reinvestigating the Life and Activities of Johannes de Garlandia." *Plainsong and Medieval Music* 8 (1999), 1–13.

Wiering, F., "The Language of the Modes: Studies in the History of Polyphonic Modality." Ph.D. diss., University of Amsterdam, 1995.

   ed., *Thesaurus musicarum italicarum.* Electronic corpus of Italian music treatises from the Renaissance and early Baroque. URL: http://euromusicology.cs.uu.nl/.

Wiora, W., "Zum Problem des Ursprung der mittelalterlichen Solmisation." *Die Musikforschung* 9 (1956), 263–74.

Woodward, W. H., *Vittorino da Feltre and Other Humanist Educators.* Cambridge University Press, 1897; repr. Toronto and Buffalo: The University of Toronto Press in association with the Renaissance Society of America, 1996.

Yardley, A. B., *Performing Piety: Musical Culture in Medieval English Nunneries*, New York: Palgrave MacMillan, 2006.

Yudkin, J., "The Anonymous Music Treatise of 1279: Why St. Emmeram?" *ML* 72 (1991), 177–96.

   "The *Copula* according to Johannes de Garlandia." *MD* 34 (1980), 7–31.

   "The Influence of Aristotle on French University Music Texts." In Barbera, A., ed. *Music Theory and Its Sources: Antiquity and the Middle Ages.* South Bend: University of Notre Dame Press, 1990, pp. 173–89.

Zaminer, F., ed., *Geschichte der Musiktheorie*, in progress. Darmstadt: Wissenschaftliche Buchgesellschaft, 1984– . Vol. 3: M. Bernhard, A. Borst, D. Illmer, A. Riethmüller, K.-J. Sachs, *Rezeption des antiken Fachs im Mittelalter*, ed. F. Zaminer (1990); vol. 4: M. Huglo, C. Atkinson, C. Meyer, K. Schlager, and N. Phillips, *Die mittelalterliche Lehre von Mehrstimmigkeit*, ed. T. Ertelt and F. Zaminer (1984).

Index

52959710R00170

Made in the USA
Lexington, KY
16 June 2016